BISON
BOOKS

Five Seasons A BASEBALL COMPANION BY ROGER ANGELL

University of Nebraska Press
Lincoln and London

Manufactured in the United States of America

♾

First Nebraska paperback printing: 2004

Except for Chapter 4, all of the material in this book first appeared in *The New Yorker*, some of it in different form.

Library of Congress Cataloging-in-Publication Data
Angell, Roger.
Five seasons: a baseball companion / by Roger Angell.
p. cm.
Originally published: New York: Simon and Schuster, © 1977.
ISBN 0-8032-5950-6 (pbk.: alk. paper)
1. Baseball—United States—History. I. Title.
GV863.A1A53 2004
796.357'0973—dc22
2003023117

Contents

Foreword

THE FIVE BASEBALL SEASONS just past are the most significant half-decade in the history of the game. On the field, they were notable for remarkable individual feats—by Hank Aaron, Lou Brock, and Nolan Ryan, among others—that eclipsed or threatened records previously considered entirely secure. The long pennant races and the famous doings of the playoffs and the World Series were dominated by two vivid and absolutely different champion clubs—the Oakland A's and the Cincinnati Reds; and in 1975 we were given a World Series—between the Reds and the Boston Red Sox—of unmatched intensity, brilliance, and pleasure. These sporting events, however, were almost obscured by the turmoil and bitter public wrangling that have accompanied the business side of the game in the past few years. The strikes and lockouts and other labor skirmishings of the players and owners, the bartering of franchises, the adulteration of the game by sudden gate-enhancing innovations, the deadening influence of network television, the arrival of player free-agency, the inflation of player salaries, and the purchased loyalties of most of the principals in the game have come as a shock to most of us, for we have begun to understand at last that baseball is most of all an enormous and cold-blooded corporate enterprise, and as such is probably a much more revelatory and disturbing part of our national psyche than we had supposed.

Like many fans, I suspect, I tried at first to ignore or make light of these distractions. I continued to write mostly about baseball as I saw it played—in spring training, during the summer campaigns, and in the noisy and cheerful Octoberfests—and also to pursue my private discoveries of the beauties and complications of this old sport. In the end, however, I had to think about the true meanings and ironies of contemporary big baseball, because they had begun to intrude on my feelings about the game. Most grown-ups, I believe, will find little pleasure now if they try to isolate the game—simply to sit in the stands as before and smile upon the familiar patterns and adventures on the bright lawns below. When I came to know some of the baseball people who appear in this book—three devoted fans, a long-time owner with a famous baseball name, a scout, a suddenly and mysteriously failed pitcher, and many others—I noticed that they were all affected, in different ways, by the contemporary business realities of baseball, and I saw the painful, almost excruciating effort with which each of them was attempting to sustain his lifelong attachment to the game in spite of its violent alterations. All of us who care about baseball are making this effort now.

The game, we may conclude, is worth the candle. We have no other choice if we wish to hold on to this unique attachment, this particular patch of green. Only by looking at baseball entire, I believe, will we be able to to fit it into our understanding of ourselves and our times, and only that clear view will allow us to go on watching the game and to take pleasure in its scarcely diminished splendors. As for me, I am still a fan—a companion to the game and a grateful recipient of its good company.

NOTE: Since this is a running account, attention should be given to the date-line at the beginning of each chapter; a number of players and other principals have changed clubs, of course, since these reports were written.

1 On the Ball

Summer 1976

It weighs just over five ounces and measures between 2.86 and 2.94 inches in diameter. It is made of a composition-cork nucleus encased in two thin layers of rubber, one black and one red, surrounded by 121 yards of tightly wrapped blue-gray wool yarn, 45 yards of white wool yarn, 53 more yards of blue-gray wool yarn, 150 yards of fine cotton yarn, a coat of rubber cement, and a cowhide (formerly horsehide) exterior, which is held together with 216 slightly raised red cotton stitches. Printed certifications, endorsements, and outdoor advertising spherically attest to its authenticity. Like most institutions, it is considered inferior in its present form to its ancient archetypes, and in this case the complaint is probably justified; on occasion in recent years it has actually been known to come apart under the demands of its brief but rigorous active career. Baseballs are assembled and hand-stitched in Taiwan (before this year the work was done in Haiti, and before 1973 in Chicopee, Massachusetts), and contemporary pitchers claim that there is a tangible variation in the size and feel of the balls that now come into play in a single game; a true peewee is treasured by hurlers, and its departure from the premises, by fair means or foul, is secretly mourned. But never mind: any baseball is beautiful. No other small package comes as close to the ideal in design and utility. It is a perfect object for a man's hand. Pick it up and it instantly suggests its purpose; it is meant to be thrown a considerable distance—thrown hard and with precision. Its feel and heft are the beginning of the sport's critical dimensions; if it were a fraction of an inch larger or smaller, a few centigrams heavier or lighter, the game of baseball would be utterly different. Hold a baseball in your hand. As it happens, this one is not brand-new. Here, just to one side of the curved surgical welt of stitches, there is a pale-green grass smudge, darkening on one edge almost to black—the mark of an old infield play, a tough grounder now lost in memory. Feel the ball, turn it over in your hand; hold it across the seam or the other way, with the seam just to the side of your middle finger. Speculation stirs. You want to get outdoors and throw this spare and sensual object to somebody or, at the very least, watch somebody else throw it. The game has begun.

Thinking about the ball and its attributes seems to refresh our appreciation of this game. A couple of years ago, I began to wonder why it was that pitchers, taken as a group, seemed to be so much livelier and more garrulous than hitters. I considered the possibility of some obscure physiological linkage (the discobologlottal syndrome) and the more obvious occupational discrepancies (pitchers have a lot more spare time than other players), but then it came to me that a pitcher is the only man in baseball who can properly look on the ball as being his instrument, his accomplice. He is the only player who is granted the privilege of making offensive plans, and once the game begins he is (in concert with his catcher) the only man on the field who knows what is meant to happen next. Everything in baseball begins with the pitch, and every other part of the game—hitting, fielding, and throwing—is reflexive and defensive. (The hitters on a ball team are referred to as the "offense," but almost three quarters of the time this is an absolute misnomer.) The batter tapping the dirt off his spikes and now stepping into the box looks sour and glum, and who can blame him, for the ball has somehow been granted in perpetuity to the wrong people. It is already an object of suspicion and hatred, and the reflex that allows him occasionally to deflect that tiny onrushing dot with his bat, and sometimes even to relaunch it violently in the opposite direction, is such a miraculous response of eye and body as to remain virtually inexplicable, even to him. There are a few dugout flannelmouths (Ted Williams, Harry Walker, Pete Rose) who can talk convincingly about the art of hitting, but, like most arts, it does not in the end seem communicable. Pitching is different. It is a craft ("the crafty portsider . . .") and is thus within reach.

The smiling pitcher begins not only with the advantage of holding his fate in his own hands, or hand, but with the knowledge that every advantage of physics and psychology seems to be on his side. A great number of surprising and unpleasant things can be done to the ball as it is delivered from the grasp of a two-hundred-pound optimist, and the first of these is simply to transform it into a projectile. Most pitchers seem hesitant to say so, but if you press them a little they will admit that the prime ingredient in their intense personal struggle with the batter is probably fear. A few pitchers in the majors have thrived without a real fastball—junk men like Eddie Lopat and Mike Cuellar, superior control artists like Bobby Shantz and Randy Jones, knuckleballers like Hoyt Wilhelm and Charlie Hough—but almost everyone else has had to hump up and throw at least an occasional no-nonsense hard one, which crosses the plate at eighty-five miles per hour, or better, and thus causes the hitter to—well, to *think* a little. The fastball sets up all the other pitches in the hurler's repertoire—the curve, the slider, the sinker, and so on—but its other purpose is to intimidate. Great fastballers like Bob

Gibson, Jim Bunning, Sandy Koufax, and Nolan Ryan have always run up high strikeout figures because their money pitch was almost untouchable, but their deeper measures of success—twenty-victory seasons and low earned-run averages—were due to the fact that none of the hitters they faced, not even the best of them, was immune to the thought of what a 90-mph missile could do to a man if it struck him. They had been ever so slightly distracted, and distraction is bad for hitting. The intention of the pitcher has almost nothing to do with this; very few pitches are delivered with intent to maim. The bad dream, however, will not go away. Walter Johnson, the greatest fireballer of them all, had almost absolute control, but he is said to have worried constantly about what might happen if one of his pitches got away from him. Good hitters know all this and resolutely don't think about it (a good hitter is a man who can keep his back foot firmly planted in the box even while the rest of him is pulling back or bailing out on an inside fastball), but even these icy customers are less settled in their minds than they would like to be, just because the man out there on the mound is hiding that cannon behind his hip. Hitters, of course, do not call this fear. The word is "respect."

It should not be inferred, of course, that major-league pitchers are wholly averse to hitting batters, or *almost* hitting batters. A fastball up around the Adam's apple not only is a first-class distracter, as noted, but also discourages a hitter from habitually leaning forward in order to put more of his bat on a dipping curve or a slider over the outer rim of the plate. The truth of the matter is that pitchers and batters are engaged in a permanent private duel over their property rights to the plate, and a tough, proud hurler who senses that the man now in the batter's box has recently had the better of things will often respond in the most direct manner possible, with a hummer to the ribs. Allie Reynolds, Sal Maglie, Don Drysdale, Early Wynn, and Bob Gibson were cold-eyed lawmen of this stripe, and the practice has by no means vanished, in spite of strictures and deplorings from the high chambers of baseball. Early this year, Lynn McGlothen, of the Cards, routinely plunked the Mets' Del Unser, who had lately been feasting on his pitches, and then violated the ancient protocol in these matters by admitting intent. Dock Ellis, now a Yankee but then a Pirate, decided early in the 1974 season that the Cincinnati Reds had somehow established dominance over his club, and he determined to set things right in his own way. (This incident is described at length in a lively new baseball book, *Dock Ellis in the Country of Baseball*, by Donald Hall.) The first Cincinnati batter of the game was Pete Rose, and the first pitch from Ellis was at his head—"not actually to *hit* him," Ellis said later, but as a "*message* to let him know that he was going to be hit." He then hit Rose in the side. The next pitch hit the next Red batter, Joe Morgan, in the kidney. The third batter was Dan Driessen, who took Ellis's second pitch in the back. With the bases loaded, Dock now threw four pitches at Tony Perez (one behind his back), but missed with all of them, walking in a run. He then missed Johnny Bench (and the plate) twice, whereupon Pirate manager Danny Murtaugh came out to the mound, stared at Ellis with silent surmise, and beckoned for a new pitcher.

Hitters can accept this sort of fugue, even if they don't exactly enjoy it, but what they do admittedly detest is a young and scatter-armed smoke-thrower, the true wild man. One famous aborigine was Steve Dalkowski, an Oriole farmhand of the late nineteen fifties and early sixties who set records for strikeouts and jumpy batters wherever he played. In one typical stay with a Class D league, he threw 121 strikeouts and gave up 129 walks and 39 wild pitches, all in the span of 62 innings. Dalkowski never made it to the majors, but, being a legend, he is secure for the ages. "Once I saw him work a game in the Appalachian League," a gravel-voiced retired coach said to me not long ago, "and nothing was hit *forward* for seven innings—not even a foul ball." An attempt was once made to clock Dalkowski on a recording device, but his eventual mark of 93.5 mph was discounted, since he threw for forty minutes before steering a pitch into the machine's recording zone.

Better-known names in these annals of anxiety are Rex Barney, a briefly flaring Brooklyn nova of the nineteen forties, who once threw a no-hit game but eventually walked and wild-pitched his way out of baseball; Ryne Duren, the extremely fast and extremely nearsighted reliever for the Yankees and other American League clubs in the fifties and sixties, whose traditional initial warm-up pitch on his being summoned to the mound was a twelve-foot-high fastball to the foul screen; and a pair of rookies named Sandy Koufax and Bob Feller. Koufax, to be sure, eventually became a superb control artist, but it took him seven years before he got his great stuff entirely together, and there were times when it seemed certain that he would be known only as another Rex Barney. Sandy recalls that when he first brought his boyish assortment of fiery sailers and bouncing rockets to spring-training camp he had difficulty getting in any mound work, because whenever he picked up his glove all the available catchers would suddenly remember pressing appointments in some distant part of the compound. Feller had almost a career-long struggle with *his* control, and four times managed to lead his league simultaneously in walks and in strikeouts. His first appearance against another major-league club came in an exhibition game against the Cardinals in the summer of 1936, when he was seventeen years old; he entered the game in the fourth inning, and eventually struck out eight batters in three innings, but when his searing fastball missed the plate it had the batters jumping around in the box like roasting popcorn. Frank Frisch, the St. Louis player-manager, carefully observed Feller's first three or four deliveries and then walked down to the end of the dugout, picked up a pencil, and removed himself from the Cardinal lineup.

•

The chronically depressed outlook of major-league batters was pushed to the edge of paranoia in the nineteen fifties by the sudden and utterly unexpected arrival of the slider, or the Pitcher's Friend. The slider is an easy pitch to throw and a hard one to hit. It is delivered with the same motion as the fastball, but with the pitcher's wrist rotated approximately ninety degrees (to the right for a right-hander, to the left for a southpaw), which has the effect of placing the delivering forefinger and middle finger slightly off center on the ball. The positions of hand, wrist, and arm are almost identical with those that produce a good spiral forward pass with a football. The result is an apparent three-quarter-speed fastball that suddenly changes its mind and direction. It doesn't break much—in its early days it was slightingly known as the "nickel curve"—but a couple of inches of lateral movement at the plateward end of the ball's brief sixty-foot-six-inch journey can make for an epidemic of pop-ups, foul balls, and harmless grounders. "Epidemic" is not an exaggeration. The slider was the prime agent responsible for the sickening and decline of major-league batting averages in the two decades after the Second World War, which culminated in a combined average of .237 for the two leagues in 1968. A subsequent crash program of immunization and prevention by the authorities produced from the laboratory a smaller strike zone and a lowering of the pitcher's mound by five inches, but the hitters, while saved from extermination, have never regained their state of rosy-cheeked, pre-slider good health.

For me, the true mystery of the slider is not its flight path but the circumstances of its discovery. Professional baseball got under way in the eighteen-seventies, and during all the ensuing summers uncounted thousands of young would-be Mathewsons and Seavers spent their afternoons flinging the ball in every conceivable fashion as they searched for magic fadeaways and flutter balls that would take them to Cooperstown. Why did eighty years pass before anybody noticed that a slight cocking of the wrist would be sufficient to usher in the pitchers' Golden Age? Where were Tom Swift and Frank Merriwell? What happened to American Know-How? This is almost a national disgrace. The mystery is deepened by the fact that—to my knowledge, at least—no particular pitcher or pitching coach is given credit for the discovery and propagation of the slider. Bob Lemon, who may be the first man to have pitched his way into the Hall of Fame with a slider, says he learned the pitch from Mel Harder, who was an elder mound statesman with the Indians when Lemon came up to that club, in 1946. I have also heard some old-timers say that George Blaeholder was throwing a pretty fair slider for the St. Louis Browns way back in the nineteen-twenties. But none of these worthies ever claimed to be the Johnny Appleseed of the pitch. The thing seemed to generate itself—a weed in the bullpen which overran the field.

The slider has made baseball more difficult for the fan as well as for the batter. Since its action is late and minimal, and since its delivery does not require the easily recognizable arm-snap by the pitcher that heralds the true curve, the slider can be spotted only by an attentive spectator seated very close to home plate. A curve thrown by famous old pretzel-benders like Tommy Bridges and Sal Maglie really used to *curve;* you could see the thing break even if you were way out in the top deck of Section 31. Most fans, however, do not admit the loss. The contemporary bleacher critic, having watched a doll-size distant slugger swing mightily and tap the ball down to second on four bounces, smiles and enters the out in his scorecard. "Slider," he announces, and everybody nods wisely in agreement.

•

THE MYSTERY of the knuckleball is ancient and honored. Its practitioners cheerfully admit that they do not understand why the pitch behaves the way it does; nor do they know, or care much, which particular lepidopteran path it will follow on its way past the batter's infuriated swipe. They merely prop the ball on their fingertips (not, in actual fact, on the knuckles) and launch it more or less in the fashion of a paper airplane, and then, most of the time, finish the delivery with a faceward motion of the glove, thus hiding a grin. Now science has confirmed the phenomenon. Writing in *The American Journal of Physics*, Eric Sawyer and Robert G. Watts, of Tulane University, recently reported that wind-tunnel tests showed that a slowly spinning baseball is subject to forces capable of making it swerve a foot or more between the pitcher's mound and the plate. The secret, they say, appears to be the raised seams of the ball, which cause a "roughness pattern" and an uneven flow of air, resulting in a "nonsymmetric lateral force distribution and . . . a net force in one direction or another."

Like many other backyard baseball stars, I have taught myself to throw a knuckleball that moves with so little rotation that one can almost pick out the signature of Charles S. Feeney in midair; the pitch, however, has shown disappointingly few symptoms of last-minute fluttering and has so far proved to be wonderfully catchable or hittable, mostly by my wife. Now, at last, I understand the problem. In their researches, Sawyer and Watts learned that an entirely spinless knuckler is *not* subject to varying forces, and thus does not dive or veer. The ideal knuckler, they say, completes about a quarter of a revolution on its way to the plate. The speed of the pitch, moreover, is not critical, because "the magnitude of the lateral force increases approximately as the square of the velocity," which means that the total lateral movement is "independent of the speed of the pitch."

All this has been perfectly understood (if less politely defined) by any catcher who has been the battery mate of a star knuckleballer, and has thus spent six or seven innings groveling in the dirt in imitation of a bulldog cornering a nest of field mice. Modern catchers have the assistance of outsized gloves (which lately have begun to approach the diameter of tea trays), and so enjoy a considerable advantage over some of their ancient predecessors in capturing the knuckler. In the middle nineteen-forties, the receivers for the Washington Senators had to deal with a pitching staff that included *four* knuckleball specialists—Dutch Leonard, Johnny Niggeling, Mickey Haefner, and Roger Wolff. Among the ill-equipped Washington catchers who tried to fend off almost daily mid-afternoon clouds of deranged butterflies were Rick Ferrell and Jake Early; Early eventually was called up to serve in the armed forces—perhaps the most willing inductee of his day.

•

THE SPITBALL was once again officially outlawed from baseball in 1974, and maybe this time the prohibition will work. This was the third, and by far the most severe, edict directed at the unsanitary and extremely effective delivery, for it permits an umpire to call an instantaneous ball on any pitch that even looks like a spitter as it crosses the plate. No evidence is required; no appeal by the pitcher to higher powers is permissible. A subsequent spitball or imitation thereof results in the expulsion of the pitcher from the premises, *instanter*, and an ensuing fine. Harsh measures indeed, but surely sufficient, we may suppose, to keep this repellent and unfair practice out of baseball's shining mansion forever. Surely, and yet . . . Professional pitchers have an abiding fondness for any down-breaking delivery, legal or illegal, that will get the job done, and nothing, they tell me, does the job more effectively or more entertainingly than a dollop of saliva or slippery-elm juice, or a little bitty dab of lubricating jelly, applied to the pitching fingers. The ball, which is sent off half wet and half dry, like a dilatory schoolboy, hurries innocently toward the gate and its grim-faced guardians, and at the last second darts under the turnstile. Pitchers, moreover, have before them the inspiring recent example of Gaylord Perry, whose rumored but unverified Faginesque machinations with K-Y Jelly won him a Cy Young Award in 1972 and led inevitably to the demand for harsher methods of law enforcement. Rumor has similarly indicted other highly successful performers, like Don Drysdale, Whitey Ford, and Bill Singer. Preacher Roe, upon retiring from the Dodgers, in 1954, after an extended useful tenure on the mound at Ebbets Field, published a splendidly unrepentant confession, in which he gave away a number of trade secrets. His favorite undryer, as I recall, was a full pack of Juicy Fruit gum, and he loaded up by straightening the bill of his cap between pitches and passing his fingers momentarily in front of his face—now also illegal, alas.

It may be perceived that my sympathies, which lately seemed to lie so rightly on the side of the poor overmatched hitters, have unaccountably swung the other way. I admit this indefensible lapse simply because I find the spitter so enjoyable for its deviousness and skulking disrespect. I don't suppose we should again make it a fully legal pitch (it was first placed outside the pale in 1920), but I would enjoy a return to the era when the spitter was treated simply as a misdemeanor and we could all laugh ourselves silly at the sight of a large, outraged umpire suddenly calling in a suspected wetback for inspection (and the pitcher, of course, *rolling* the ball to him across the grass) and then glaring impotently out at the innocent ("Who—*me?*") perpetrator on the mound. Baseball is a hard, rules-dominated game, and it should have more room in it for a little cheerful cheating.

•

ALL THESE speculations, and we have not yet taken the ball out of the hands of its first friend, the pitcher. And yet there is always something more. We might suddenly realize, for instance, that baseball is the only team sport in which the scoring is not done with the ball. In hockey, football, soccer, basketball, lacrosse, and the rest of them, the ball or its equivalent actually scores or is responsible for the points that determine the winner. In baseball, the score is made by the base runner—by the man down there, just crossing the plate—while the ball, in most cases, is a long way off, doing something quite different. It's a strange business, this unique double life going on in front of us, and it tells us a lot about this unique game. A few years ago, there was a suddenly popular thesis put forward in some sports columns and light-heavyweight editorial pages which proposed that the immense recent popularity of professional football could be explained by the fact that the computerlike complexity of its plays, the clotted and anonymous masses of its players, and the intense violence of its action constituted a perfect Sunday parable of contemporary urban society. It is a pretty argument, and perhaps even true, especially since it is hard not to notice that so many professional football games, in spite of their noise and chaos, are deadeningly repetitious, predictable, and banal. I prefer the emotions and suggestions to be found in the other sport. I don't think anyone can watch many baseball games without becoming aware of the fact that the ball, for all its immense energy and unpredictability, very rarely escapes the control of the players. It is released again and again—pitched and caught, struck along the ground or sent high in the air—but almost always, almost instantly, it is recaptured and returned to control and safety and harmlessness. Nothing is altered, nothing has been allowed to happen. This orderliness and constraint are among the prime attractions of the sport; a handful of men, we discover, can police a great green country, forestalling unimaginable disasters. A slovenly, error-filled game can sometimes be exciting, but it never seems serious, and is thus never truly satisfying, for the metaphor of safety—of danger subdued by skill and courage—has been lost. Too much civilization, however, is deadly—in this game, a deadly bore. A deeper need is stifled. The ball looks impetuous and dangerous, but we perceive that in fact it lives in a slow, guarded world of order, vigilance, and rules. Nothing can ever happen here. And then once again the ball is pitched—

sent on its quick, planned errand. The bat flashes, there is a new, louder sound, and suddenly we see the ball streaking wild through the air and then bounding along distant and untouched in the sweet green grass. We leap up, thousands of us, and shout for its joyful flight—free, set free, free at last.

2 Starting to Belong

June 1972

June is when baseball really begins. Now partisanship deepens, and we come to the time when the good weather and the sights and sounds of the game are no longer quite enough. In June, even casual semi-fans begin to watch the standings, and true believers—adherents of free silver and the Expos and similar causes—secretly put aside some of their wild April hopes as they see that this season, like the others, will be mostly pain and misadventure, and that part of their attention must now be given to the leaders and the other principals in the long pennant drama. For me, at least, all this has been slow to happen this year. Part of that is attributable to the bitter, unprecedented strike called by the Players Association at the end of March, which wiped out the first two weeks of the season and did away with most of the anticipation and good cheer of baseball's spring. But I have begun to notice I am more hesitant than I once was to give my full attention to the games and adventures of the early season, and more inclined to linger on the one that is just past. This year, April and May seemed to deepen my recollection of last October, when the Pirates and Orioles played that brilliant and breathless turnabout seven-game World Series, which was won in the end by the hitting and throwing and the burning will of Pittsburgh's Roberto Clemente. It was a Series especially worth thinking about and putting to memory, but I suspect that many fans may suffer from a similar nostalgia every spring. We are afraid to commit ourselves too quickly or eagerly to the time at hand. We hold back a bit, remembering the passions and rewards of the season just past, remembering how we cared, and wondering if this new season can matter as much to us. It's almost like being in school—being back in college again. Can this term be as good as the last one? Who will my friends be? Will I fall in love again? Will these new courses be any good? Waiting, we watch and take notes.

•

SCORECARD: EARLY June. July and midseason creeping up, yet baseball year still at loose ends. Distracting sort of campaign, suggesting no-score ball game in which 15 base runners stranded in first 4 innings; eventful yet forgettable. To date: Hank Aaron wafts 1 doz. homers, passing W. Mays and running maybe 1½ seasons short of the Babe's 714. Willie probably relieved. Willie also rejuvenated & rejoicing as new Met, out from under heavy 20-yr. burden as Giants' deity & leader, plays occasional 1B or OF for Metsies, signs autogs., runs bases like a 10-speed bike, wins games. Maysless Giants (also McCoveyless, thanks to broken McC. wing) plummet to NL West cellar. Similar early fatuity for a while afflicts Baltimore, perennial AL Ozymandias (now down to 1 Robinson, after winter trade of F. Robby to Dodgers), whose grizzled vets rarely hit ball beyond infield, let alone into stands. Total early Oriole departure from race prevented only by lack of consist. or zing among other AL East clubs. Cleveland like a mayfly—takes early wing, expires on same afternoon. Tigers like bullfrog escaping a well—jumps up three feet, slips back two.

Yankees . . . Yankees like nothing in nature. Most sedative BB team in memory, so uninspired as to suggest bestowal of new sobriquet: Bronx Sashweights? CBS Plastercasts? Red Sox, diminished by tradeoff of dissidents & gripers, lose injured Yastrzemski for early going; Yaz previously heavily booed at Fenway, has not hit much for almost 1 yr. Mystery.

Unhappy celebs also include Giants' Juan Marichal, in bed with aching back after early 1 win–8 loss record, and Cards' Bob Gibson, now back on track after early zip–5 mark. But prime addition this yr. to annals' human fatuity is to be seen in utter inability to retire major-league hitters (and later, in and around bushes of Birmingham, Ala., *minor*-league hitters) displ. by once colorful, now pathetic Denny McLain. Denny's extinguishment nearly accompanied by similar disapp. of Vida Blue, last year's Lochinvar & this year's toilet-fixture exec., who took new employment during long salary holdout vs. Oakland boss Charles O. Finley (chance here to use word "ineffable")—the *ineffable* Charles O. Finley, whose difficulties with help are legend. *All* BB owners' difficulties with help now legend. Owners mostly, almost wholly, respons. for players' strike. (Chance here to use other descript. adjectives. Resist impulse.) Strike wipes out 1st 2 weeks of play, gets season off to unstart that prob. still casts aforesaid sense of distraction & foolishness over entire BB scene.

(Historical note, proving game no longer hobbled by hoary traditions, superstitions: Phillies, in midst of terrible losing streak, refuse to fire manager. Fire *general* manager instead. Go on losing.)

•

THE STRIKE: There will be no attempt here to recapitulate all the issues in that painful and tedious dispute, but it does seem essential to recall that the Players Association from the beginning offered to compromise or submit to arbitration its ultimate point of difference with the owners—the use of accumulated funds in the players' pension plan to increase the benefits currently being paid out. The owners declared any accommodation to be an absolute impossibility until a total of eighty-six games and several million dollars in revenue had drained away, whereupon they compromised, exactly as they could have done before the deadlock set in. A last-minute modicum of patience on both sides might have averted the whole thing, but not everyone wanted peace. It is clear that some of the more dedicated Cro-Magnons among the owners (including the Cardinals' Gussie Busch, the Reds' Frank Dale, the Mets' Donald Grant, and the Royals' Ewing Kauffman) saw the strike as a precious opportunity to strain, and perhaps crack, the labor union of their upstart, ungrateful young employees and, above all, to discredit its executive director, Marvin Miller. Most of the owners, to be sure, would deny such an intention, but the unchanging and apparently unchangeable characteristic of their fraternity is its total distaste for self-discipline—a flaw that anarchizes the entire body and repeatedly renders it victim to its loudest and least responsible minority. Commissioner Bowie Kuhn, who has been criticized for not playing a stronger hand in settling the strike, does not in fact have any power over the owners in such a crucial situation; these businessmen, in contrast to the players, chose to remain undirected and largely unadvised throughout the crisis.

The corporate masochism of baseball scarcely ranks as news, and neither labor relations nor the size of players' pensions is the end of the game's problems. Among the other hovering anxieties is the deepening disparity in quality and attendance between the two major leagues. Last year's record total attendance did not conceal the fact that the National League outdrew the American by nearly five and a half million customers—17,324,857 to 11,858,560. The gap is widening this year, with the NL running ahead of last season's comparable attendance figures, and the AL behind. The difference between the leagues in quality and attractiveness of play is harder to prove, but it can be suggested: so far this spring,

National League batters have hit over one hundred more home runs than their American League counterparts. New ball parks attract new customers: the American League has four modern parks (counting the stadium to be opened next year in Kansas City), but with the exception of Wrigley Field, every park in the National League is less than fifteen years old. I am not attracted to this means of rebalancing, however, because I detest the appearance and flavor of most modern ball parks, which seem to have sprung from the same architectural tradition that brought us the shopping mall. I also believe that fans would respond with pleasure and alacrity to a more challenging but far less expensive solution to the American League's problems—better ball teams.*

One lively, long-range proposal to increase attendance is a suggested future realignment of all twenty-four major-league clubs into new leagues—possibly a regional lineup of three eight-team leagues: Eastern, Central, and Southern-Western. A further, accompanying alteration would be the introduction of a limited number of interleague games during the regular season, arranged so that every big-league ballplayer could be seen by fans in every big-league city within the span of two seasons. The plan is startling and perhaps imperfect, but it is surely worth hopeful scrutiny at the top levels of baseball. I am convinced, however, that traditionalists need have no fear that it will be adopted. Any amalgamation would require all the owners to subdue their differences, to delegate real authority, to accept change, and to admit that they share an equal responsibility for everything that happens to their game. And that, to judge by their past record and by their performance in the strike, is exactly what they will never do.

Most recently, the Supreme Court's refusal to consider the

* The qualitative difference between the two leagues has diminished since this gloomy report was written. The AL continues to trail the NL in attendance, but the disparity is now down to about two million, and since 1973, when the American League invented the designated hitter, it has usually slightly surpassed the National League in homers and batting average.

antitrust implications of baseball's reserve clause, which was challenged in Curt Flood's suit, means without a doubt that this difficult and inflammatory issue will now be thrown down between the owners and the Players Association. It will form a central area of contention when the overall players' agreement, governing every aspect of their profession, comes up for renegotiation this winter. Congress is holding a number of hearings on the monopolistic aspects of professional sports, but few congressmen in an election year are anxious to shiver the foundations of a national institution like baseball. Next winter could be another long one, and coming seasons are already clouded with foreboding.

•

HOME STAND: Shea Stadium was instant compensation for the emptiness of early April. I first got there for an afternoon game with the Cubs that matched up Tom Seaver and a junior right-hander named Burt Hooton, who in his previous start had startled the nation's news-famished fans by pitching an opening-day no-hitter against the Phillies. Any statistical anxiety he may have brought with him because of this feat was dispersed by Bud Harrelson, who hit his third pitch of the game to left field for a double. Hooton throws an anomaly called the knuckle curve—a unique private invention that causes the pitched ball to drop into the catcher's glove like a coin into a pay telephone—and he now began retiring Mets in clusters. Seaver responded with plain but honest All-American fastballs, and in one stretch twenty-one successive Mets and Cubs (both clubs, admittedly, devout practitioners of nonviolence at the plate) between them managed two outfield flies before Eddie Kranepool finally singled in the fifth and came around to score the first run in Seaver's 2–0, four-hit win. There were some new faces in the Mets' lineup, and one painfully missed figure in the dugout: Manager Gil Hodges, who had collapsed and died two days after the end of spring training. There must be very few of us who exulted through the

Mets' triumphant campaign of 1969 who do not retain some common permanent portrait of Gil Hodges—enormous hands thrust inside the pockets of his blue windbreaker; his heavy, determinedly expressionless face under the long-billed cap; and his pale, intelligent gaze that presided over that turbulent summer and somehow made it come right for his young team and for us all.

Two stimulating comeback wins over the Dodgers and the Giants in the same week in May began to suggest to me the resourcefulness of this particular Met team, already surprisingly settled into first place in its division. On a frigid leftover-winter night, the Los Angelenos surprised the Mets' rookie starter, Jon Matlack, with eight hits and four runs in the first four innings, one score coming on a home run by Frank Robinson, the famous ex-Oriole. It was a Robby Special—a first-pitch line drive jerked to left with the loud and terminal "*whock!*" that causes sensitive pitchers instantly to avert their gaze, as if from a grade-crossing accident. In the fourth, however, the Mets executed a dandy outfield peg and relay—Agee to Martinez to Grote—that wiped out a Dodger runner at the plate, and Matlack, thus heartened, pitched obdurately while his teammates caught up. The tying run came on Rusty Staub's homer in the eighth inning, and the winning run—deep in the stilly night, hours after the last hot coffee had run out at Shea—came in the fourteenth, on a tiny two-out infield poke by Teddy Martinez, who outran the peg to first while Harrelson scored from third.

Two nights later, with the Giants at Shea, everyone in the park took out his pencil and put a circle around Willie Mays' name on the left-hand, San Francisco side of the scorecard and then drew a long line and an arrow that moved it over to the right-hand roster. Willie had been signed up by the Mets the day before, and was on the field as a non-Giant for the first time in his life. It was a strange feeling; something fixed in our baseball universe had been taken down. He did not play that night, but the subtraction of Mays and the injured Mc-

Covey from the Giants' lineup gave that team an entirely new aspect; they were suddenly a young, fast, largely unknown club, far from contention now but full of new promise. The Mays deal, one sensed, had been right for them, too. Their next star was well in evidence. He is Dave Kingman, an angular, six-foot-six, uppercutting power hitter with a reputation for frequent bad strikeouts and occasional moon-shot home runs; showing us some speed on the bases as well, he rapped out a double and two singles.

The Mets, I could see, had been considerably altered by the *addition* of two names this season—Staub and Jim Fregosi, the latter a useful and experienced All-Star infielder acquired from the Angels.* For the first time in recent memory, the Mets' batting order seemed to have both a top and a bottom. Its middle—the No. 4 man—is Staub, late of the Montreal Expos, a large, marmalade-colored right fielder, who invariably plays bare-armed, catches fly balls one-handed, and hits against left- and right-handed pitchers in the same fashion—that is, with consistency, adequate power, and a burning, almost exultant concentration. He should be a sporting deity in New York for years to come.

In that Giant game, the Mets were shy a run in the bottom of the eighth when the pitcher was due to bat, and enormous cries of "We want Willie!" now rose in the night air. Manager Yogi Berra, however, resisted the invitation and sent up a left-handed hitter, John Milner, who walked and was duly moved up and neatly scored. In the ninth, the bottom of the order finished it off—walk to Jones, single by Fregosi, and the game-

* Met fans should be forgiven if they are overtaken here by groans or a sudden wish to lie down. Fregosi, who was in fact well past the best summers of his playing career, lasted for a season and a half with the Mets. To acquire him, the club had sent California a young, hopelessly wild right-handed pitcher whose lifetime record stood at 29–38. Once on the side of the Angels, the pitcher (it was Nolan Ryan) became a certified twenty-game winner, led his league in strikeouts for three years running, and set other notable records, thus establishing himself as one of the greatest fastball pitchers in the annals of the game.

winning hit up the middle by Grote. The Mets, winning by 2–1, were on their way to what eventually became an eleven-game victory streak. Two days later, Willie Mays made his debut as a Met, playing against his old team. Displaying his customary sense of occasion, always as close to perfect as that of Mme. Perle Mesta, he smashed a fifth-inning home run that won the game.

(Miniquiz: Willie Mays had always worn No. 24 on his uniform. The same number was worn this spring by a reserve outfielder for the Mets named Jim Beauchamp. Q: When Willie became a Met, which of them was asked to change his uniform number? *Answer next week.*)

•

On the road: I began my first road trip one day too late. The night before I arrived in Los Angeles, the Houston Astros had beaten the Dodgers with a three-run catch-up homer struck with two out in the ninth by Astro third baseman Doug Rader, and then a bases-loaded squeeze bunt by Tommy Helms in the eleventh. I saw the same teams in three taut, edgy pitchers' duels—the Dodgers winning the first two by 2–1 and 3–0, to recapture a fractional lead in their division, which they then lost right back to the visitors in the last game, 2–1. Excellent baseball, I had to admit, if a bit austere. And not all *that* austere, either, since Dodger manager Walt Alston was trying out an infield—third baseman Steve Garvey, shortstop Bill Russell, second baseman Bobby Valentine, and first baseman Bill Buckner—that averages twenty-two and a half years old and plays electrifying, in more than one sense of the word, ball. Buckner won the first game with a two-run double, making up for a run flung away by Garvey; Valentine and Garvey drove in two of the three runs the next day, atoning for an egregious bobble and an embarrassing wild heave by Russell. The Dodger pitchers in those games, Claude Osteen and Al Downing, threw a lot of sinker balls, which the Astro batters helpfully hammered into the dirt, thus giving the home-team kiddies plenty of infield practice.

That second game, on Saturday, was actually settled on Houston hurler Dave Roberts' first pitch of the evening, which Bobby Valentine hit over the center-field fence. Everybody was swinging at first pitches, it turned out, and the game went by so quickly that there was scarcely time for a visiting Easterner to appreciate the soft, late sunshine gilding the nearby San Gabriel Mountains, or for the Dodger promotion corps to get all its messages up on the scoreboard: "HAPPY ANNIVERSARY NO. 1 TO THE KEITH GUSTAVSONS." . . . "HAPPY BIRTHDAY TO BRUCE GERSON, SPENDING HIS 8TH STRAIGHT BIRTHDAY AT A DODGER GAME." . . . "WELCOME TO DORITH ZACHAIM, SEEING THE DODGERS SHE READ ABOUT IN HAIFA, ISRAEL." Downing whizzed through the Astro lineup, giving up but two singles, and the game was over in exactly ninety minutes, a new Dodger Stadium record ("I don't think we ought to get paid for that one," Wes Parker said) and probably the quickest game of baseball that Bruce Gerson or any of the rest of us there will see in our lifetimes.

The Houston infield, though less winsome than the Los Angeles youth movement, is splendidly accomplished. It is half home-grown—Doug Rader and a redoubtable shortstop named Roger Metzger—and half imported—Tommy Helms at second and the dangerous Lee May at first, the latter two having arrived from Cincinnati last winter in a trade that has vivified the lackadaisical Houstons. Whatever the adventures of the Astros this summer, none of them will immediately forget the ending of the final Dodger game. Walter Alston, with his club down by a run in the bottom of the ninth, now began to make use of his varsity. Wes Parker (who had played the entire game at first) led off with a single—only the fifth hit off Astro starter Jerry Reuss. Maury Wills, pinch-hitting, sacrificed Parker to second. Jim Lefebvre, pinch-hitting, ripped a scorching grounder past Doug Rader at third base.

It *was* past, between Rader and the bag, but Rader dived full-length to his right, flinging out his glove cross-handed as he skidded in the dirt, and came up with the ball. He sprang up, losing his cap, and managed a colliding tag of the astonished Wes Parker, who was on his way in from second with the sure tying run. The game ended a minute later, and afterward Walt Alston, now in his ninteenth year at the Dodger helm, said, "That may be the greatest infield play I've ever seen." Doug Rader, a sharp-faced young man, burnished with freckles, said, "Ah, I made one just as good back with Durham in '65." Joke. Rader had also hit that two-out homer in the first game of the series, and now he said, "Everything is so damned *different* when you're with a club up on top. It's great, isn't it? Isn't it great? Oh, I hope it's like this all year." * I hung up the Rader catch in my gallery—in the small inner room, between an early Clete Boyer and a couple of Brooks Robinsons.

•

MOTOWN: YOU never can tell. Approaching Detroit, my next stop, I told myself that a couple of upcoming mismatches between the Tigers and the cellar-dwelling Milwaukee Brewers, a club then batting .184, would at least offer a chance to watch such celebrated veteran Detroit sluggers as Al Kaline, Norm Cash, and Jim Northrup strut their stuff. The only stuff on view the first night, it turned out, was some marvelous pitching by the Brewers' Jim Lonborg, the erstwhile Boston ace, who entirely dominated the evening. It was a warm late-May night, summer having finally caught up with baseball, and the smallish crowd, having nothing much to cheer about, fell into a soft, languid murmuration. Tiger Stadium is an old-style city ball park, an ancient green chamber, and the sounds of baseball enclosed there seemed to come out of the past—the click of the news ticker in the rooftop press box, an infielder's whistle, a brief little burst of clapping from somewhere down

* It wasn't. The Astros and the Dodgers finished the season in a tie for second place, ten and a half games behind the Cincinnati Reds.

the third-base line, and then some laughter in the stands following a mighty strike call ("*Streuahh!*") by the home-plate ump. The baseball writers were eating ice cream. In time, a cool evening breeze sprang up, and the Brewers scored a pair of runs in the seventh, and Lonborg, with his sinking fastball reminding us of his great summer of 1967, wrapped up his four-hit shutout. Just another baseball evening, but in Detroit there is a dreadful hovering possibility that evenings like this may not continue. I heard much talk there that within three or four years the Tigers will give up their park (formerly known as Briggs Stadium, Navin Field, and—way back—Bennett Park), where they have always played ball, and move into a new enclosed stadium on Detroit's waterfront. A domed palace, however, may be almost beyond the city's economic reach, and we may hope, with the utmost selfishness and good sense, that a continuation of the current business recession and dollar inflation may ensure another decade or two of life for the Tigers' grassy old boathouse.

The Tigers won the next night, but not in style. In the sixth, their starter, Les Cain, was sailing along, still untouched, when he suddenly lost all poise and control, walked the bases full, and was yanked, shockingly, while still working on a no-hitter. There were other causes for dismay—errors by the Brewer infield and unfervent play by the Tiger outfield—before Detroit came from behind for a 5–3 win.

The quiet I observed in the stands during this two-game set was not wholly attributable to the torpid play. Now and then, an evening zephyr brought me unmistakable emanations of Acapulco and other sunny climes, and when I inquired about it, a Tiger front-office man smiled and said yes, the bleacher crowds did now include large numbers of young fans from Wayne State and other nearby centers of learning who seemed to be heightening their worship of the god Kaline with certain holy substances. "We leave 'em alone," he told me. "To tell you the truth, we have a lot more trouble with the beer-drinkers from the auto plants."

•

BAL'MORE: ONE possible cure for the American League's attendance problems might be some form of massive group therapy for baseball fans in Baltimore. Although the Orioles are the class of the league, having attained the World Series four times in the past six years, their townspeople have responded with gingerly enthusiasm. The Orioles invariably draw more on the road than at home, where attendance barely reaches the million mark each year, and there are always a few seats in Memorial Stadium that go begging at World Series time. This year, Baltimore may be the only city to evidence any continuing public disaffection as a result of the players' strike, and when I got to town early in June a number of cabdrivers (famous, even in this capital of low confidence, for their grousing) told me with relish how quickly Bal'more folks had turned against Brooks Robinson for saying during the strike that the players' cause was a just one. The Orioles' attendance, I learned, was already ninety thousand lower than last year's comparable figures, but some of this was attributable to rainouts and to the fact that the team, though still only a half game out of first place, was bumping along barely above the .500 mark. Most of the Birds' old regulars had been suffering frightful difficulties at the plate. Don Buford was batting .217, Mark Belanger .170, Andy Etchebarren .164, and Boog Powell .157, and Brooks Robinson had not hit a homer all year. (When I asked Earl Weaver, the Baltimore manager, if he missed Frank Robinson, he said, "Hell, we've missed Boog a lot more.") Only the ardent play of some young strangers named Terry Crowley, Don Baylor, and Bobby Grich—all up from Rochester, in the Orioles' richly stocked farm system—had kept the team alive while it waited for the seniors' inevitable untracking.

Losing is hard on champions. That first evening, before another minuscule audience, the estimable Dave McNally, a twenty-game winner for the past four years, fell behind the visiting Red Sox in the very first inning, two runs coming in on a single by Rico Petrocelli that barely wormed its way through the left side of the infield. An inning later, McNally was groaning and glaring at home-plate ump Art Frantz, who was not giving him the corners. Now, in quick succession, the Sox' Doug Griffin nubbed a little infield single and Carlton Fisk hit a fly ball that barely slipped over the left-field fence for a homer. Boston pitcher Sonny Siebert smashed the next pitch on a line right at McNally, who just managed to get his glove up in time to avoid dismemberment. With steam now pouring from his ears, McNally nailed the next batter, Tommy Harper, on the elbow and, his day and game ruined, departed the mound almost before Manager Weaver could come out and get him. Later in the evening, with the Red Sox ahead by 7–1 after an unchallenging single had gone right past Brooks Robinson at third, Boog Powell took a Siebert strike thrown just as he started to back out of the box, took a called change-up, took a fast ball up and in, and fanned badly on still another junky curve to end the inning; he spun his batting helmet away and, finding the ball on the ground, kicked it all the way into center field.

A somewhat larger company turned up the next evening to see Vida Blue and the Oakland A's, the best of the West. Weaver benched both Powell and Brooks Robinson, and Don Baylor and Bobby Grich each hit a single and stole a base in the second inning, giving the home team the lead in its eventual and reassuring 5–1 win. Blue, making only his second start since the end of his long holdout, worked with his customary and delightful coiled-python delivery and looked as quick as ever, if not yet quite fine. He departed after five innings, down by four runs but having thrown only one bad pitch—a high curve that Paul Blair hit way up and way out for a homer. The A's looked formidable even while losing, and now bear the mysterious but essential demeanor of total confidence that always marks a superior ball team. The Oakland players also bore some other new distinguishing marks—mustaches that the entire team (with the brave exception of infielder Mike Hegan) had sprouted at the behest of owner Finley for a coming Mustache Day promotion at his home park. Bribe, not behest: Finley paid three hundred dollars for each mustache.

In the clubhouse, Vida Blue (his own mustache is a barely visible first effort) said that he was unsatisfied with his performance but not entirely surprised. Pitching form is not instantly attainable. Since his holdout and, before that, his sudden celebrity of last summer, Blue has become a guarded, somber, and apparently unhappy young man. His salary dispute did not win much support from his teammates (who also proved that they can win without him), and the famous holdout seems in retrospect an unfortunate affair in which both sides took defensible but conceivably mistaken stands. Yes, Vida brought out many thousands of fans last year, and yes, he was badly underpaid. On the other hand, yes, he had shown only a bare half-season of brilliance in his career so far. What was lost, in the end, was a spring-training season in which Blue could have worked on his curve and otherwise directed his shining talents toward the time when he becomes a truly great pitcher—which is a position far more secure than that of a great gate attraction. He has, however, already improved in one respect over last year, for he is visibly larger and even more impressively muscled. I mentioned this to him, and he managed a smile. "I'm just a growin' boy," he said.

•

SCORECARD, CHI.: Quick trip Windy City to ck. out ex-doormat White Sox. Attend. up 338 thou. last yr., already up another 120 thou. this yr. Pale Hose BO smash, also in 2nd place AL West. More bad planning: Arrive 1 day after Sox sweep Yanks in Sunday doubleheader, before 51,904 ecstat. fans. Popular Mgr. Chuck Tanner drew raspberry when he benched new Chi. godling Dick Allen for much-needed rest in nightcap. Tanner then drew heavy mitting when he called on Allen to pinch-hit in bottom ninth with Sox down by 4–2.

Allen hit 3-run homer, won game. All Chi. transported, mad with old-fash. BB fever. Typical perform. by Allen. Typical perform. by Tanner. Dick Allen is ex-Richie Allen, erstwhile unhappy itinerant NL big bopper traded off by 3 clubs in 3 yrs., includ. last winter from LA Dodgers. Richie now Dick by own request. See Dick hit. See Dick run. Dick happy in new home.

Out to White Sox Park, still known everywhere by old handle, Comiskey Park. Old, white, steep-sided park, looks like docked paddle-wheel steamer. (Rumors used to hold environs of Park—Southside Chi.—a dangerous place for fans after night games; Sox began winning, rumors heard no more.) Chisox uniforms feature red pinstripes & red hose with *picture* of white sock on each calf. Decadence?

Night game vs. Boston (again). Wilbur Wood, portly portside knuckleballer, winner 22 games last season, starts vs. Siebert (again). Bosox win, natch: 2–0. No foundation all down the line. No matter. Stay happy watching Richie—oops, Dick—doing his thing. Enormous man. Head nearly hidden under dishlike batting helmet. Glittery eyeglasses, droopy mustachios, odd eyebrows. Somehow suggests Levantine prince. Platformlike shoulders & long, lean legs also suggest Allen poured into uniform upside down. Nifty glove in field around 1B, has all the moves. *Enjoys* self. In bat. box, shifts minutely back & forth on long, floppy feet, awaiting pitch. Waves tremendous 40-oz. bat, swings through, holds back wrists. *Strong.* In v. first inning, whips bat like flyswatter—*whap!*—& ball leaps to deep LF, caroms off wall on 1 bounce. Dick instant. into 2B with double. V. fast runner. Allen currently tied for 2nd place AL homers (11), tied 3rd place BA (.315), 1st place RBI (40). Whew.

Next day. Mgr. Tanner soft-spoken yet volub. skipper. Young, bronzed face, snowy sideburns. Credits many for Chisox rise, incl. famed pitching coach J. Sain, known for unorth. methods. Much-traveled Sain the grand guru of 20-game winners. Tanner emphs. defense, shows tactical charts kept of every opp. AL hitter. Charts color-coded accord. to Chi. pitchers, show site of every fair ball hit in season, suggest defens. shifts. No wonder modern bat. aves. so low! Tanner on Allen: Finest BB player anywhere. Will go from Chisox straight into Hall of Fame, etc. Does not comment on Allen's distaste for reg. hours, public appearances, batting pract., spring training, etc. Tanner knows right thing to know about Allen: Superstar.

Chisox take on Bosox again in afternoon. Chisox now play all home Wed. games in sunshine, for night workers, children, etc. Commendable. V. pop. Chisox broadcaster Harry Caray also works Wed. games from seat in CF bleachers, delighting kids. Kids further delighted now when Dick Allen rips 1st inn. pitch to CF for triple & RBI. Whew. Game then runs down, stops, dies, thanks to Luis Tiant, Bost. pitcher. Tiant, noted for odd pitching mannerisms, is also a famous mound dawdler. Stands on hill like sunstruck archeologist at Knossos. Regards ruins. Studies sun. Studies landscape. Looks at artifact in hand. Wonders: Keep this potsherd or throw it away? Does Smithsonian want it? Hmm. Prepares to throw it away. Pauses. Sudd. discovers *writing* on object. Hmm. Possible Linear B inscript.? Sighs. Decides. Throws. Wipes face. Repeats whole thing. Innings & hours creep by. Spectators clap, yawn, droop, expire. In stands, 57 disloc. jaws set new modern AL record, single game. Somebody wins game in end, can't remember who.*

•

BELONGING: Arriving late for an afternoon game against the Reds, I found the Shea parking lot filled and was forced to explore some of the distant Queens outback before finding an

* What Tiant was probably thinking about out there was his control, which he was in the process of recovering after a succession of injuries and poor performances, which had at one time driven him down to the minors. Once he got back his poise, he became a livelier pitcher to watch—the most entertaining, in fact, in baseball.

empty space in front of a lumberyard. The game was already under way when I came hurrying across the lot past acres of metal heating in the sun. Looking up around the big scoreboard, I could see crowds packing the steep, curving stands against the sky. Tom Seaver was starting for the Mets, so I wasn't worried about missing much, but then, as I came closer, I heard the voice of the public-address announcer from inside the stadium: "Batting for Cincinnati in the fourth poh-sition . . ." Bad. The Reds had a man on, at least. There were confused cries, and I heard "Batting in the fifth poh-sition . . ." I had never before realized that a public-address man omits all the essential information about a game. I began to run. More noises, more cries. "Batting in the sixth poh-sition . . ." What was going *on*? Maybe there had been a last-minute switch in the Mets' pitching rotation. Maybe— There was a long ascending roar, suddenly cut off. Now I was almost next to the stands in left. Sweating, I stopped and tried to peer back at the face of the scoreboard, but the angle was still wrong. "Batting in the seventh poh-sition . . ."

It was all true. In time, I got to my seat and saw the big "4" up on the board for the Reds' first. I picked up the details of the disaster from my neighbors: three singles, a sacrifice, and then a two-run homer, *just* fair, by Joe Hague. All this off Tom Seaver. It looked like a ruined day, but things picked up a little when the Mets scratched out a run in the first, and when Seaver fanned Bench and Perez, both on big, swinging strikes, in the third. Then Willie Mays, leading off in the fifth, banged a single off Cincinnati pitcher Ross Grimsley's leg. Bud Harrelson, going with an outside pitch, doubled off the left-field wall, and then Rusty Staub lined a low shot that Joe Morgan leaped for and missed, and the score was suddenly up to 4–3, and the noise at Shea insupportable.

So much and then no more. A double play ended that part of things, and in the sixth John Milner's bid for a pinch-hit home run was pulled down a few feet short. He had batted for Seaver, necessarily, and a few minutes later Tony Perez hit a

1-1 pitch by Danny Frisella over the 371-foot mark in right center, and the game was gone, this time for good. All that for nothing, and later, as I walked back to the lumberyard and then fought my way slowly home through the traffic, there were other troubles to think about. This was the eighth straight game that Seaver had failed to finish, and his earned-run average, the best in the league last year, was way up. Jerry Koosman's arm was still untested, and the rest of the Mets' starting corps was unsteady at best. The team had now lost its last two series and most of its lead; the Pirates were only a couple of games back. In contrast to the familiar and often frail-looking home hitters (flash of Bud Harrelson leaning across the plate and flicking that double over third base), the Reds had looked frightening—Rose and then those two cool, quick batsmen Morgan and Tolan, and then the sluggers Bench and Perez. And yet the Pirates looked even better. Stargell and Clemente and Sanguillen . . . *Seven* of their regulars were batting over .300. And the Cubs were coming on fast, too. . . .

Cares abound among other teams, of course, and also some hopes. Just lately, the Orioles won nine straight games, but still trail the Tigers by one. The White Sox are still second to Oakland, but slipping back. The Dodgers have fallen behind Houston; Houston has fallen behind Cincinnati. The Giants are seventeen games down. Yaz is back, and hitting a little. Three, maybe four, real pennant races are under way. Somehow, after that ridiculous and painful afternoon against the Reds, it all mattered to me again. Anxiety and difficulties afflict me, a fortunate fan, and this baseball season has begun to happen after all.

3 Buttercups Rampant

October 1972

IT WAS A splendid year for losers. The Oakland A's, the first (and possibly the last) big-league team to wear green-and-gold uniforms and white shoes, and also (if one thinks of them by their old and infinitely better sobriquet and thus considers them a continuance of the erstwhile Kansas City, and previously erstwhile Philadelphia, Athletics) a team unrewarded by a pennant over the past forty-one consecutive summers, and also (if one has watched them play important but truly lonely games at home at all times of the season) a team almost entirely without a following, and also (if one has been there even briefly) a team spiritually representing the losers' capital of the West *and* the East—the A's stand undisputed as Champions of the World. Elsewhere, Steve Carlton, a pitcher with the last-place (in the National League East) Phillies, won 27 games while losing 10, thereby accounting for nearly half of his team's total victories for the year (59), and also led his league in complete games (30), innings pitched (346), strikeouts (310), and earned-run average (1.98). The White Sox' unpredictable Dick Allen, a capricious slugger hastily traded away by three different teams in the last three years, led *his* league in home runs (37) and runs batted in (113), and will presumably be permitted to wear the same uniform again next year. Among the top pitchers in the American League was Luis Tiant, of the Red Sox, who last year was dropped by the Minnesota Twins, toiled for two minor-league clubs, and finally ran up a 1–7 record with Boston; this year he won 15 games (including 6 shutouts) while losing 6, and led all the pitchers in the majors with an earned-run average of 1.91. Then, too, there was the totally mysterious season-long batting slump that afflicted the Baltimore Orioles, heretofore considered the best team in baseball, whose falling-off in all offensive categories not only unseated them as the perpetual American League Series defenders but also permitted an unexpected and wonderfully welcome down-to-the-wire pennant race in their division. Finally, and most splendidly of all, this baseball year concluded in two violently contested five-game playoffs and then in an absolutely first-class World Series, which went the full seven games and produced baseball of such prolonged and grating intensity that, perhaps for the first time, the pain of losing became as vivid and memorable to us, the fans, as the more familiar, leaping joys of victory in October.

The Yankees, surely the most conspicuous losers of the past half-decade, lost again, but this time with distinction, remaining in real contention in that AL East scramble until the last few days, and finishing a bare six and a half games behind the Tigers. Their true defeat, to be sure, was at the hands of the Mets, in the box-office standings; the Mets, although a far less stimulating team than the Yanks in the second half of the year, outdrew them again, this time by the shocking margin of 2,134,185 to 967,715. The hardy little band of Yankee fans enjoyed a summer of modest entertainments. There was a pleasing outburst of long hits by the illustrious Bobby Murcer, who wound up with thirty-three homers. There was a startling doubleheader against Kansas City late in August in which the usually docile Bronxites rapped out forty hits; two days later, in a twi-nighter against Texas, they recorded twenty-six more, for a four-game total possibly unmatched even by the old Yankee Murderers' Row. More often, the script would call for a couple of scratchy runs fashioned by such uncelebrities as Ron Blomberg or Roy White or young Charlie Spikes (a rare new issue for the album of felicitous baseball names) and then defended by earnest but modestly talented infielders like Horace Clarke and Celerino Sanchez—all building to the obligatory scene in the eighth or ninth when the dangerous visiting team would put the tying or winning runs aboard, and Manager Houk, out on the mound, would gesture with his left arm to the bullpen, summoning forth, to a crescendo of happy screaming, the pin-striped white Datsun and its celebrated cargo. As the organ struck up "Pomp and Circumstance," Sparky Lyle, the lefty reliever *sans peur et sans reproche*, would emerge from his cloud-car, hand his jacket to the ball boy, stalk to the mound, and (clamping down on his tobacco wad) fling a few warm-up pitches as the cries of "Dee-fense! Dee-fense!" rose from the bleachers, and then in no time (most of the time) the game would be over and (almost always) won.

Up in Boston, the Red Sox fans seemed to resist such pleasures, even after their team took over first place from the Tigers early in September. Made wary by the Sox' miserable early showing, and perhaps disaffected by a petty and senseless campaign of vilification mounted against the Boston manager, Eddie Kasko, by some of the local sportswriters and radio broadcasters, they kept a certain distance until the evening of September 20. On that night, playing at home, the Beantowners swept a doubleheader from Baltimore, defeating Oriole aces Jim Palmer and Mike Cuellar in succession and, in effect, killing off the old champions for the season. Luis Tiant, walking in from the bullpen to start the nightcap (he threw another shutout), was greeted with a rolling, continuous wave of applause, and after the game was over the writers and venders in Fenway Park could hear the sounds of homeward celebration rising up from the railway bridge and from Kenmore Square, exactly as they did in the great summer of 1967. The triumph was short, for the pursuing Tigers came in the next night and humiliated the Red Sox, scoring four runs in the first inning of a 10–3 game that reduced the Boston lead to .0006 in the standings. Watching these two celebrated powers (both old favorites of mine) that evening, I could detect subtle and contrasting styles and motives of play. Almost surely, the Tigers were driven by a sense of the years descending. With the exception of the left side of their infield—the estimable Brinkman and Rodriguez—this was the same lineup of veterans that had upset the Cardinals in the World Series in 1968; their line soldiers—Kaline, Cash, McAuliffe, Gates Brown, Freehan, Stanley, and Northrup—were all in their thirties now, and they knew that this was a late-season campaign to win, because it was most unlikely that they would ever find themselves in another. The Red Sox offered some old reliables, too—Smith, Petrocelli, and Yastrzemski—but there were a lot of new faces and new hopes on this squad. The following night, the Boston pitcher was a youngster named Lynn McGlothen, who works in a fever of optimistic energy on the mound—all twitches, glances, shrugs, and impatience—and one of the Sox' early runs was initiated by a hit by Carlton Fisk, their rookie catcher. The third and last Sox run came on a rare homer by Yastrzemski—rare because Yaz (who plays first base now) has consciously altered his stroke, after years of diminishing effectiveness, and become a singles hitter. The three runs barely held up in a game that came down to two marvelous moments. In the eighth, the Tigers loaded the bases with none out, and the next batter, Eddie Brinkman, whacked a hard bouncer just over third base, where Rico Petrocelli barely gloved the ball, stepped on third, and threw home in time to complete a double play of Smithsonian rarity. Jim Northrup then hit a fly to short right, which Rick Miller caught in his webbing after a frantic sprint and a slide on his knees, and the Tiger dugout erupted helmets, towels, gloves, and disgust. In the next two days, the teams split the last two games of the set, and broke off the engagement exactly where they had started.

Eight days later, the Red Sox were still holding a bare half-game lead as the two teams, now in Detroit, began the final series of the regular season. The old Tigers, it turned out, still had a couple of bites left. They won the essential first game, 4–1, on the pitching of Mickey Lolich and three hits by Al Kaline, and took over first place. There had been a strange moment in the third inning when the Red Sox' Luis Aparicio stumbled on the way home and then retreated, winding up on third base with another base runner, Carl Yastrzemski, and thus killing a promising inning. The next evening, before a game that the Sox now had to win if they were to avoid extinction, a writer reminded Eddie Kasko that the same embarrassing accident, involving exactly the same base runners, had also happened in Detroit on the very first day of the season, in a game that Lolich also won. Kasko, a quiet and gentle man with a perpetually mournful visage, nodded forlornly and sought comfort in the classics. "I know," he said. "How does that thing go? Oh, yes—'If *ifs* and *buts* were candied nuts, we'd all have a hell of a Christmas.' "

Tiant pitched for Boston, and his opposite was Woodie Fryman, another wonderfully revived elder, who had won nine games for the Tigers after coming over from the Phillies early in August. They had at each other in characteristic style—Tiant wheeling almost toward center field with each pitch and bobbing his head, changing speeds and nicking the corners; Fryman firing quickly, throwing sliders and inside fastballs—and for half the game the only rift in the fabric was a little error that allowed a Boston run in the first inning. The Tigers tied it in the sixth, on a walk, a sacrifice, and a single by Northrup, who waved his cap gaily amid a flurry of confetti when he resumed his place in center field. In the seventh, McAuliffe doubled and then scored on a single by Al Kaline—to an enormous noise, a deluge of noise—and the third and last run came in when Yastrzemski failed to hold on to a little infield chopper off Cash's bat, on which he had a play at the plate. The ball popped loose just in front of the mound, and Yaz, distraught, flung back his head in agony. Another handful of outs, and Detroit had its half-pennant. Yastrzemski wept in the clubhouse, his head hidden in his locker. The loss did seem almost insupportable, for Boston, after this long and exhausting campaign, had achieved very close to nothing—second place in a six-team league. Al Kaline would have wept, too, I believe, if the result had been reversed. He had, in fact, absolutely distinguished himself; the winning blow had been his twenty-second hit in his last forty-four at-bats. During the celebrations in the Detroit clubhouse, somebody mentioned Kaline's extraordinary eyes, which are protuberant and pale and somehow lynxlike. Manager Billy Martin nodded. "He's got sniper's eyes," he said. "He's out to *kill* you."

•

To A fan who had given most of his recent attention to the American League, the first two games of the National League playoffs suggested that the principals were engaged in a different and rather more dangerous sport. Each of the teams—the Cincinnati Reds and the World Champion Pittsburgh Pirates—had entirely flattened the opposition in its half-league by the end of August, and their similar credentials (power, speed, experience, depth, adequate pitching, and enormous competitive pride) had given birth to a smug cliché that one heard in both dugouts: This, in fact if not in name, was the true World Series, between the two best teams in baseball; the subsequent encounter, involving the American League winner, would be an anticlimactic formality. In the opener, at Pittsburgh's Three Rivers Stadium, the Reds' Joe Morgan hit the first pitch to him over the right-field wall. In the bottom of the first, the Pirates banged two singles, a double, and a triple off Red starter Don Gullett, good for three runs. They added two more in the fifth, on a homer by Al Oliver. This was scary baseball. Oliver was one of nine Pirate players to register more than a hundred hits during the regular season; the Mets, by instructive contrast, had had none. The Pirates won the game, 5–1 (a *close* 5–1 game, if that is possible), and the Reds lost their manager, Sparky Anderson, after a fourth-inning line drive by Cincinnati's Cesar Geronimo caromed off the rump of umpire Ken Burkhart, behind first base. Burkhart, even while groveling on the Tartan Turf, called the ball foul, and then quickly added a codicil, expunging Anderson for the energy of his dissent. This drama was positively Sophoclean in its overtones, for Burkhart and Anderson had been among the principals in another autumn catastrophe, during the 1970 World Series, in which Burkhart and a Cincinnati base runner and a Baltimore catcher and a high-chopped ground ball had all mingled in an untidy purée in front of home plate; Anderson lost that appeal, too. After this game, Burkhart, meeting the press in the umpires' dressing room, delicately lowered his towel and revealed a pink contusion about the size of a tea rose on his left haunch. "This was in fair territory," he said, pointing, "but my *hip* was in foul territory, so under the rules the ball was foul."

The following afternoon, the Reds got off the mark even more briskly, as the first five batters smashed out base hits—two singles, three doubles—scoring four runs and eliminating the Pittsburgh starter, Bob Moose, before he could register an out. This not only settled the ball game but offered a useful lesson in the Cincinnati style of winning. It is a system of wonderful simplicity, merely requiring the top three batters to get on base and the next two to drive them home, but rarely has any ball club managed it so effectively over an entire season. The Reds' top three—Pete Rose, Joe Morgan, and Bobby Tolan—got on base an average of five times per game throughout the year (not counting force plays) and scored just over two runs per game—statistics to make any self-respecting pitcher retch. This efficiency was thanks in considerable part to the No. 4 hitter, Johnny Bench (40 homers, 125 runs batted in), and the No. 5 man, Tony Perez (21 homers, 90

RBI). The key part in this assembly was probably Joe Morgan, an assertive and powerful little second baseman, who had arrived from Houston during the winter in a major trade that revivified the Big Red Machine. Here, in the eighth inning, Morgan bashed his second homer in two days; the Reds won, 5–3, and the teams moved along to Cincinnati all even.

I moved along home—not out of a wish to watch less baseball, but more. The encounters I had seen, coupled with the news from the West Coast that the A's had captured the first two games of their playoff with the Tigers in stimulating fashion, suggested to me that we might be in for a rare double festival of baseball, which could best be absorbed on television. The Oakland hostilities had begun with a splendid pitching duel between Mickey Lolich and Catfish Hunter that had gone 1–1 through ten innings; a homer by Al Kaline in the eleventh seemed to settle it, but the A's responded swiftly, scoring the tying run on a pinch single and the winning run after a throw by Kaline skipped past third base. The next game was an easy 5–0 win for the A's, but the participants had been electrified when Dagoberto Campaneris, the veteran Oakland shortstop, after repeated dustings at the plate, tried to even matters by sailing his bat at the Detroit pitcher's skull. He was ruled off the turf for the remainder of the playoffs, amid a fluster of official deplorings that made the moral plain: Plunking an enemy with a thrown ball, rather than a thrown bat, is (a) more efficient and (b) the American Way.

In front of my set, I watched the Pirates take a courageous comeback win from the Reds by 3–2, mostly on some slashing bad-ball hitting by Manny Sanguillen. The next afternoon, the Pirates, now in a position to step into the World Series again, stepped all over their own feet instead, committing three errors and allowing several fly balls to disappear into the sun, all in the course of a dismal 7–1 pasting. Meanwhile, shuffling scorecards and statistics and rosters like a Japanese playground director, I also watched the Tigers (back home after a day off for travel) return to contention with a 3–0, fourteen-strikeout shutout pitched by Joe Coleman.

The next day, Wednesday, we were given an afternoon of baseball unlike any other in the annals of the sport. It was the day on which the playoffs—heretofore only an irritating preamble to the World Series, created to boost baseball's television ratings—suddenly succeeded beyond all expectations. The two games (the fourth for the American League contenders, who had taken a day off for travel, and the deciding fifth for the Reds and Pirates, who had not) were continuously exciting, and the NBC camerawork was alert, subtle, and up to every sudden occasion, thus making it clear that television, at its best, has almost conquered the built-in obstacles involved in covering a spacious, intensely three-dimensional sport in a two-dimensional medium. Vivid closeups—Charlie Finley, the Oakland owner, glowering and chewing his thumb in his box; a ball boy nearly ill with suppressed excitement; Joe Morgan, waiting at the plate for a pitch, pumping his left elbow like a rooster wing—brought us details perhaps missed by most people in the stands, and multiple cameras, catching the play at different levels and distances, showed us more of the pitchers' stuff than the batters seemed to be picking up.

In Detroit, Hunter and Lolich hooked up in another excruciating deadlock, which stood at one run apiece after seven innings, on home runs by McAuliffe and Epstein. The rival pilots, unstrung by possibilities, now indulged themselves in some grotesque overmanaging—Oakland's Dick Williams with a succession of pinch-hitters that effectively stripped his infield of its most capable personnel, and Billy Martin with a wholly uninspired squeeze play that wiped out the potential winning run in the eighth. (Billy Martin loves the squeeze the way a wino loves muscatel.) Oakland brought home two runs in the top of the tenth, but the first two Tiger batters in the inning singled, and then a key force play was missed at second when Gene Tenace dropped the throw; Tenace, a catcher, was playing second because Williams had used up his infielders. Cash walked, to force in the tying run, and Northrup singled in the winner.

Instantly, we were in Cincinnati, in the midst of a taut, quickly played, elegantly pitched game that would decide it all for the National League. The Pirates led from the outset, and in the bottom of the ninth their palm-ball ace, Dave Giusti, came in in relief of Steve Blass, needing only three outs to hold the 3–2 lead. He got none of them. Johnny Bench, leading off, hit the fourth pitch on a frightening parabola into the right-field seats. Tony Perez singled. Denis Menke singled. The expression on Giusti's face (seen in closeup) was almost too stricken, too private to look at. He departed, and his successor, Bob Moose, came in and painstakingly, with infinite care and anxiety, got two outs on fly balls. Foster, running for Perez, had moved from second to third on the first out, and now, with the hordes of the Cincinnati in full cry from the dugout and from all over the enormous park, Moose threw a strike to Hal McRae and then a ball, and then bounced a wild pitch cleanly away from the plate and past his catcher, and the game and the Series and the season were gone for the Pirates.

The final American League game remained, the next afternoon, and it was scarcely less than what had come before. The Tigers scored in the first on a single, a passed ball, and an infield out. The A's tied it in the second on dash and daring—a walk, a stolen base, a sacrifice, a hit batsman, a double steal. The run came at a high price, for Reggie Jackson, the Oakland slugger and leader, severely tore the hamstring muscle of his left leg in a collision at the plate and was carried from the field, finished for the year. The lead run (the winning run, it turned out) came in the fourth on an error, a sacrifice, and a single by Gene Tenace. The pitchers took it from there—Fryman for the Tigers, Blue Moon Odom and then Vida Blue for the A's. In each of the last three innings, the Tigers put the tying run on first base and could not advance him. Their difficulties—the difficulty of all baseball when it is well played—were so evident that announcer Jim Simpson murmured at one point, "This is a game that requires no description." The Detroit elders, who had come so far on so little, died at last because of their lack of speed. (They had stolen only seventeen bases all year.) They were reduced in the end to playing the game one base at a time, which is the least rewarding way to travel the 360 feet around to home. Their demise (with the Oakland players leaping and hugging all by themselves) was the hardest to watch of this hard baseball year.

•

THE SURVIVORS, gathering in Cincinnati for the Series opener, came together in an atmosphere of almost palpable letdown. All the players, it seemed, were less aroused about the games to come than relieved about the ones just past, and as one watched the Reds cheerfully taking their cuts during pregame batting practice it was hard to discount their evident conviction that their most dangerous opponents of the year had already been buried. They looked over at the hairy young A's, in their outlandish green-and-gold-and-white costumes, with a patronizing curiosity that was perhaps shared by the great majority of baseball fans everywhere. Oakland, to be sure, was the best the AL had, but the National, by every comparable measurement, was by far the stronger of the two leagues. The Oakland pitching was good—perhaps even first-class—but Reggie Jackson, the team's only certified slugger, was over there uncomfortably balancing on crutches, and, anyway, who had ever *heard* of a major-league team wearing mustaches? (Charlie Finley's ugly little scheme of paying each of his players to grow a mustache as part of a promotion stunt last June had a cheerful, unexpected result. The players—most of them, at least—liked their new and wildly variegated whiskers and long locks, and remained unshorn through the summer, and in time this eighteen-nineties look became a proud attribute of the squad. During the Series, the young and exuberant and showy A's sometimes suggested a troupe of actors in a road company of *Cyrano de Bergerac*, laughing backstage in their doublets or swaggering a little on the streets after the show. The Reds, by front-office decree, were as clean and barefaced as Kiwanians.) In spite of the imbalance of styles, and the imbalance of talent in the lineups which seemed so strongly to favor the Reds, both teams were equally avid for the reputation and honors that would accrue to the new champion. Over the past two decades, the fall classic has usually offered a match between a famous champion and a new challenger—the Orioles against the Pirates, Reds, and Mets; the Cardinals against the Tigers and Red Sox; the Yankees against almost everybody. Now, relieved of this allegory, we looked at the two clubs with total surmise, wondering not only which would win but whether one of them might not also represent the game's next dynasty.

The sense of mild anticlimax persisted in Cincinnati right through the first game, which the Buttercups (or Bushwhackers, or Pale Feet) won by 3–2. Gene Tenace, the Oakland catcher and, on his record, a rather minor member of the A's entourage, struck a two-run homer off Gary Nolan his first time at bat. The Cincinnati rooters near my seat behind third base smiled at this accident in a rather indulgent manner: these things happen sometimes in baseball, and *their* catcher-slugger, of course, was named Bench. Tenace came up next in the fifth and hit another one out, thus accounting for all the Oakland runs, and this time the hometowners sprang up and cried "Aw, come *onn!*" in unison. Tenace was the first man in history to hit home runs on his first two World Series at-bats. Still, the fans went home in the end only a bit cast down, and the tone of the afternoon was somehow struck by two banners that had been towed over Riverfront Stadium by circling airplanes—"OAKLAND HAS WEIRD UNIFORMS" and "WOMEN'S LIB WILL DESTROY THE FAMILY." The Oakland pitchers, I noticed, had allowed only two walks and a single to those first three Red batters.

The next day (a brilliant, sun-drenched Sunday afternoon),

Johnny Bench had more unwanted practice as a leadoff man, as Catfish Hunter and Rollie Fingers confined the Top Three to a lone single and one free trip to first via an error, and the Goldenrods won again, 2–1. Catfish Hunter, a somewhat unappreciated star (he won twenty-one games in each of the past two seasons, and is one of the few players never to have played a single game in the minor leagues), is a control pitcher of the very first rank, and must usually be scored on in the first couple of innings if he is to be scored on at all. He settled this particular game in the second inning when he struck out the side with two (and eventually three) Reds on base, and in the A's third, left fielder Joe Rudi hit the game-winning solo homer. The hometown crowd, their white-and-scarlet banners drooping, waited in polite but deepening silence for something to cheer about, and their one true yell of the day, in the bottom of the ninth, was suddenly severed when Rudi, in pursuit of a very long drive by Denis Menke, plastered himself belly-first against the left-field wall like a pinned butterfly and somehow plucked down the ball. Later, in their clubhouse, the Reds variously attempted a statesmanlike situation report ("We're a bit flat" . . . "Their offense doesn't impress me" . . . "We're embarrassed, you could say"), but their faces were a little stiff, a little shocked. Tony Perez used both hands to enact for Dave Concepcion a couple of Catfish Hunter's half-speed pitches dipping gently over the corners of the plate. "*Nada!*" he cried bitterly. "*Nada!*"

•

THERE WAS another moment on that same bright Sunday—a moment before the game, which only took on meaning a few days later. In a brief ceremony at the mound, Commissioner Bowie Kuhn presented an award to Jackie Robinson, honoring him for his work in combating drug addiction, and celebrating his arrival, twenty-five years before, as the first black man in the major leagues. Robinson responded, his thin, high voice barely reaching us over the loudspeakers. He was glad to see some of his old Brooklyn friends there—Pee Wee Reese, Joe Black, Red Barber. He introduced his family. He ended by saying that it would be nice to see a black manager standing in the third-base coach's box someday soon. There were handshakes and applause, the party walked away, the microphones were taken down. I had seen Jackie for a minute or two in the tunnel behind home plate—a frail, white-haired old man, with a black raincoat buttoned up to his chin. I remembered at that moment a baseball scene that I had witnessed more than twenty years earlier—a scene that came back to me the following week, when I read about Robinson's sudden death. It was something that had happened during an insignificant weekday game between the Giants and the Dodgers back in the nineteen-fifties. Robinson, by then an established star, was playing third base that afternoon, and during the game something happened that drove him suddenly and totally mad. I was sitting close to him, just behind third, but I had no idea what brought on the outburst. It might have been a remark from the stands or from one of the dugouts; it was nothing that happened on the field. Without warning, Robinson began shouting imprecations, obscenities, curses. His voice was piercing, his face distorted with passion. The players on both teams looked at each other, uncomprehending. The Giants' third-base coach walked over to murmur a question, and Robinson directed his screams at him. The umpire at third did the same thing, and then turned away with a puzzled, embarrassed shrug. In time, the outburst stopped and the game went on. It had been nothing, a moment's aberration, but it seemed to suggest what can happen to a man who has been used, who has been made into a symbol and a public sacrifice. The moment became an event—something to remember along with the innumerable triumphs and the joys and the sense of pride and redress that Jackie Robinson brought to us all back then. After that moment, I knew that we had asked him to do too much for us. None of it—probably not a day of it—was ever easy for him.

•

A COUPLE of hours before the beginning of the third game (which became a rainout), Charles O. Finley, resplendent in a Kelly-green double-knit blazer, got aboard a crowded elevator inside the Oakland–Alameda County Coliseum. When it reached the field level, he stood aside to let the rest of us out, and then turned to the young woman running the elevator. "Listen, dear," he said urgently. "I want you to stop at two on the way back up and pick up the boys with the coffee urns. You got that?" Charlie Finley is a man who must do everything by himself, even when fifty thousand paying customers are at the gates. He is a self-made millionaire, in the insurance business. He bought his ball club by himself and, almost entirely without advice, developed and traded for the players who brought him the championship. (He is also a jock satrap, owning teams in two other sports—the California Golden Seals, of the National Hockey League, and the Memphis Tams, of the American Basketball Association—which he operates and oversees in the same shouldering style.) He designed the A's' uniforms. He designed their style of play. (This year's policy of pinch-hitting for the second baseman as early as the second inning is a Finley invention, and reflects his conviction that baseball should open itself more to pinch-hitting and pinch-running specialists.) He used up nine baseball managers in ten years, and imposes strategy upon the incumbent, Dick Williams, like a Little League daddy. He is a man who must control every situation in which he finds himself, from arranging the seating at a dinner table to personally dispensing the last five hundred World Series tickets behind the Oakland dugout (an area he refers to as "my box"). He brings his team mascot, an enormous mule named Charlie O, to all the A's' public functions, indoors or outdoors. In his relations with his players, he has a fondness for the sudden paternal gesture—an arm around the shoulder and the whispered message that the athlete's contract has just been upped by a few thousand for some deed well done. Last year, Finley tried to persuade Vida Blue to change his first name to True. Later, he publicly presented him with a new Cadillac, but this spring, when Blue held out for a very sizable increase in salary, Finley fought him with such unbridled vehemence that Blue fell into a state of embittered withdrawal that accounted in great part for his disappointing 6–10 record. Mr. Finley believes he enjoys excellent relations with most of his players, and would probably point to his new championship as the best evidence of their happiness. Yet considerable evidence suggests that the A's were united and matured most of all by their shared individual resistance to the Finley style and the Finley presence. During the Series, Reggie Jackson talked to me about this. "The man is insulting and meddlesome," he said. "This team found itself in the summer, but this is not the way to make a team."

Finley has already had a notable influence on baseball (scheduling the weekday Series games at night, as was done this year, is an idea he finally sold to his fellow executives), and now, with a hold on the championship, he will wield more power in the councils of the sport. His prime immediate projects for the game are the addition to the lineup of a designated hitter, who would bat for any other player (probably the pitcher) without requiring him to leave the game, and the use of a bright orange baseball in night games. I hate the first idea, and I would leave the second one up to the players to decide, but both deserve serious testing. Charlie Finley, one comes to realize, is impossible to ignore, like a mule in a ballroom.

•

THE THIRD game, played on a sodden turf and by Pacific Daylight Saving Time, was an austere, nearly eventless affair that finally went to the Reds by a minimal 1–0. The time zone was perhaps the most important element of the game. The action began at five-thirty in the afternoon, which is prime evening tube time in the East and is also the beginning of twilight in California infields in October. The pitchers—Blue Moon Odom for the A's and Jack Billingham for the Reds—were entranced with this crepuscular setting and struck out batters in helpless clusters. The only run of the evening (and only the second Cincinnati run in the past twenty-one innings) almost didn't get into the books, for Tony Perez, rounding third in the seventh inning, slipped on the wet turf and went sprawling —a sudden baseball bad dream—but then got up and tottered home.

The true bad dream for the Reds had been postponed only for a day. In game four, while struggling against the experienced and capable Oakland left-hander Ken Holtzman, they watched incredulously as Gene Tenace deposited another souvenir in the bleachers, in the fifth, to put them down by 1–0. In the top of the eighth, however, Dave Concepcion singled and was sacrificed to second. With two out, Vida Blue came on in relief to face Joe Morgan, and walked him. Bobby Tolan socked Blue's first pitch, a fastball, on a line for two bases and two runs, and Concepcion and Morgan slapped hands happily at the plate. The win would tie the Series, and everything was about to be all right after all. Later—a day or two later—Sparky Anderson remarked that he never truly expects a pinch-hitter to hit safely, so what happened next will probably remain vividly in his mind for months or years to come—a nightmare to be experienced a thousand times, always with the same far-fetched and loathsome outcome. It is the bottom of the ninth, one out. Gonzalo Marquez, an Oakland pinch-hitter, taps a single over second. With the count two and one on Gene Tenace, Anderson summons in a new pitcher, Clay Carroll, who has set an all-time major-league record for saves during the season. Tenace singles. Oakland has two men on, and Don Mincher, a large veteran left-handed swinger, now comes up to pinch-hit for the A's—not a true threat, except that Carroll gets his second pitch up a bit and Mincher eagerly whacks it into right field, tying the game and moving

Tenace to third. Angel Mangual comes up to pinch-hit. Carroll's first pitch to *him* is perfect—a fastball in on the hands. Mangual swings, almost in self-defense, hitting the ball down on the handle and nudging a little bleeder between first and second, which Perez or Morgan cannot quite, either one of them, straining, staggering, get a glove on. The game is gone.

•

Q: YOUR team is trailing, three games to one, in the World Series. It is the top of the first inning of game five, and you are the leadoff batter. What is the best thing to do?

A: Hit the first pitch into the stands for a home run.

The student who got an A on this quiz was Pete Rose, who had heretofore suffered an uncharacteristic eclipse in the Series. Rose is unmistakable on a ball field. He is ardent, entertaining, and unquenchable. He burns by day and by night. He sprints to first base on walks, dives on his belly on the base paths or chasing line drives in the outfield, and pulls in fly balls in left field with a slicing, downward motion that says "There!" At plate, he is the model leadoff man—a medium-sized switch-hitter who, choking the bat and hunching over the plate, can pull the ball with real power or punch it to the opposite field; he scrutinizes every pitch, not just up to the plate but right back into the catcher's glove, and then glares into the umpire's face for the call. He is a great hitter, and only the spring strike this year kept him from his annual quota of more than two hundred hits. (The fans in the left-field bleachers in Oakland, watching Rose in person for the first time, honored him on several occasions with salvos of eggs and vegetables. One of the eggs landed unbroken on the mushy turf, and Rose brought it in as a souvenir to the Cincinnati dugout, where it was eaten by coach Ted Kluszewski.) Tom Seaver says that Pete Rose entirely alters the game when he bats, making it into a deadly personal duel with the man on the mound.

Rose's first-pitch homer off Catfish Hunter announced that the alteration of this fifth game had begun, but it was some time before he got it completely under control. It was a crowded, disheveled sort of game, in which each team successfully employed its various specialties. There was *another* homer by Gene Tenace, good for three runs, in the second inning, and another pinch hit by Marquez—his twelfth in twenty-two such appearances this year. The partisans in Charlie Finley's private preserve, all green-and-yellow in the caps and banners he had provided them, sustained a continuous jubilee, like bullfrogs in a June shower. The A's led by 3–1 and 4–2, but Morgan was walked twice, and each time he whistled around the bases in dazzling style to score on a single by Tolan. It was all tied up in the ninth, then, when Geronimo singled, and was neatly sacrificed to second. An infield error now brought up Rose, this time batting left-handed against Rollie Fingers, the Oakland mound incumbent. Fingers (whose mustache aspires toward the Salvador Dali rococo ideal) had won the previous game in relief, but now he sighed disconsolately, fiddled uncharacteristically, and at last offered up the pitch, which Rose redirected smartly into right field to deliver the winning run. Score for the Top Three for the day: three runs, five hits, two walks, three stolen bases, four runs batted in. Oakland, undiscouraged as always, put on its leadoff man in the home half, and Dave Duncan (a catcher with an Oberammergau coiffure and beard) singled the pinch-runner, Odom, along to third. With one out, Campaneris fouled out to Morgan in very short right field, and after the catch Odom impulsively launched himself down the inviting ninety-foot homestretch. He negotiated eighty-nine feet and six inches of the distance before encountering Johnny Bench and the ball, and then most unhappily got up and prepared to join the rest of us on the somewhat longer journey back to Cincinnati.

•

THE PENULTIMATE meeting was played the next afternoon, a Saturday—also prime viewing time, which meant that the teams were not permitted the customary travel holiday. It was probably just as well, however, for in Riverfront Stadium a bone-chilling easterly suggested that this pastime had already overstayed its season. Vida Blue, given his first start of the Series because of the compressed pitching schedule, did not seem to have his hummer and kept falling behind the Red batters. Bench homered in the fourth, and the Reds sent four men to the plate in the fifth, and five men to the plate in the sixth, and (joyfully falling upon Oakland's second-line pitching) ten men to the plate in the seventh, to wrap up an 8–1 landslide. It was a sad end to Vida's sad year, but there was some satisfaction in watching the Reds' sluggers doing their thing at last. The Cincinnati fans were utterly transported, and with reason: this was the first World Series game to be won by the Reds at home since 1940.

The full seven, then, with a resolution that was still impossible to forecast or guess at. Strangely, no single player had emerged—in the manner of a Clemente, a Brooks Robinson, a Brock—to put his stamp and style on this Series. The closeness of the games and the continuous action on the field almost concealed the fact that the level of play had been less than distinguished. Most of the Cincinnati starting pitchers had been inadequate, both teams had suffered inordinate difficulties in executing the double play, the Oakland pitchers and catcher Gene Tenace had among them surrendered eleven stolen bases, and the teams together were hitting a desultory .203. Still, the original elements of the drama remained, now deepened to a wonderful expectancy—the Oakland pitching and woolly *élan* against the Reds' hitting, speed, and pride. Something would give way here today.

Dick Williams, in an attempt to bolster his hitting and defense simultaneously, moved Tenace to first base, put Duncan behind the plate, and started Angel Mangual in center. (Tenace looked understandably edgy about his new responsibilities. "Tomorrow," he said during batting practice, "I'll probably be playing goalie.") Mangual made a difference in the very first half-inning, when he struck a long drive off Jack Billingham to straightaway center field. Bobby Tolan raced in, absolutely misjudging the play, and then made a leap for the sailing ball, which glanced off his glove and rolled to the fence, with Mangual winding up on third. (Extraordinarily, most of this game seemed to be played at the foot of that center-field fence, 404 feet away.) Gene Tenace, now batting cleanup, pulled a sharp grounder to left that struck the edge of the AstroTurf carpet at the back of the third-base dirt patch and suddenly bounded over Menke's head; and the Yellowlegs, not exactly on merit, had the first run.

Blue Moon Odom, the Oakland starter, has a splendid motion to first base (a gift he has evidently never tried to pass along to his co-workers), and he had stated the night before that no Cincinnati runners would steal on *him*. Now, in the fourth, Pete Rose led off with an enormous smash to center that Mangual one-handed just at the fence. A little startled, Odom walked the swift Morgan, and the crowd began a breathless nonstop shouting: "Go! Go! Go! Go! Go! Go! Go!" Odom would have none of it. Fixing Morgan with a sidewise, over-the-shoulder stare (friends who saw the game on television told me later that the closeups of Odom's face were remarkable), pausing, waiting almost interminably, he whirled and threw to his first baseman five times in succession, twice nearly erasing Morgan. He delivered a ball to Tolan, then made two more pick-off throws, then threw another pitch—a ball—as Morgan flew away to second, where he was cut down, narrowly but plainly, by Duncan's peg. The game, I was suddenly certain, had been won right there.

The Reds were far from done. Tony Perez led off the fifth with a double to the left-field corner, and two successive walks then loaded the bases with only one out. Hal McRae, pinch-hitting, struck the first delivery to him all the way (need it be added?) to the center-field wall, where Mangual made the catch. The score: 1–1. Rose, who had singled in the first, unloaded another rocket to precisely the same spot, and again to no avail. He had now struck two successive clouts, good for a total of more than eight hundred feet, producing two outs. Some baseball games do not yield themselves, even to a Rose.

Billingham had been given up for the pinch-hitter, and Campaneris greeted his successor, Pedro Borbon, with a single. He was sacrificed to second, and Tenace scored him with a double to deep left—and was taken out of the game, to his surprise, for a pinch-runner. (He had won the sports car, clearly, as the top player of the Series, and also became the recipient of a hug and a retroactive raise from the All-father, Charlie Finley.) The next batter, Sal Bando, hit another enormous shot to the battered center-field salient, and this ball landed untouched when Tolan fell at the warning track. The score was 3–1, and Cincinnati's luck had run out.

Pete Rose, leading off for the Reds perhaps for the last time this season, began the eighth with a single off Catfish Hunter, and the despairing Reds rooters hoarsely roused themselves once again. Holtzman, a lefty, came in to pitch to Joe Morgan, a lefty, and the last touch of baseball misfortune now descended on the Reds. Morgan cracked the ball on a low line to right—pulling it so violently, in fact, that Rose had to dodge back to avoid being struck, and then was forced to leap over Mike Hegan, the Oakland first baseman, sprawled in the dirt after his dive for the ball. The ball was in the right-field corner —a sure triple, a certain run, except for that infinitesimal accident at first; Rose came churning around third, with Morgan not far behind, but the ball was on the way in now, and third-base coach Alex Grammas threw up his hands at the last instant, stopping Rose so abruptly that his helmet came flying off. The runners retreated. (Second-guessing, I thought Grammas had made a mistake, but we would never know.) Fingers came in to pitch, and Rose eventually scored on Perez' fly, to bring it to 3–2, but that was all, and a few minutes later the exhausting, searching season was over.

One of the wearers of the green-and-gold in the happy Oakland clubhouse was Rick Williams, the fifteen-year-old son of the victorious manager, whom I had last seen five years ago, when his father piloted the Red Sox to their remarkable pennant. Rick looked only a little younger than most of the whooping and grinning new champions, whose hair and mustaches—now streaming with champagne—had somehow always made them look more boyish than any other big-league team I could remember. Reggie Jackson, in civvies, also had a bottle of champagne. He exchanged hugs and hand-slaps with his teammates, but he had not played in this, the only World Series of his life. In time, he limped unnoticed into another room and sat down to watch a football game on television.

The Reds' clubhouse was utterly quiet. I heard no complaining about the breaks. (Baseball luck is inescapable, and professionals know that in order to win you must dominate the game to the point where it is no longer a factor.) Bobby Tolan, ignoring the reporters, toured the locker room and apologized to every one of his teammates. "I'm sorry I let you mothers down," he murmured. The silence was so profound that three-year-old Pete Rose, Jr., who was carrying a little baseball bat and wearing a miniature version of his father's uniform, kept staring up at the men's faces all around him, trying to understand it. In time, he wandered into the deserted equipment room, where he examined a large bin filled with fresh, untouched ice cubes. Then he assumed a left-handed batting stance and swung his small bat again and again and then again, swinging at an invisible ball—perhaps the only person anywhere at that instant who was ready for more baseball.

4 Stories for a Rainy Afternoon

Summer 1976

THE TARPAULIN is down, and a midafternoon rain is falling steadily. Play has been halted. The lights are on, and the wet, pale green tarp throws off wiggly, reptilian gleams. The scoreboard is lit up, too, bringing us fair-weather scores from other cities, and showing us where this game stood a few minutes ago, when the home-plate umpire threw up his hands to call time and everybody on the field ran for cover. Now the players are back in their locker rooms, and both dugouts are empty. A few fans have stayed in their seats, huddling under big, brightly colored golf umbrellas, but almost everybody else has moved back under the shelter of the upper decks, standing there quietly, behind the seats, watching the rain. The press box is deserted except for a couple of writers knocking out sidebars or an early column; a teletype operator is sitting next to his machine and reading a newspaper. The huge park, the countless rows of shiny-blue wet seats, the long emerald outfield lawns, the rain-spattered tarps—all stand silent and waiting. By the look of it, this shower may hold things up for a good half-hour or more. Time for a few baseball stories.

One story concerns another rain delay, a deluge that interrupted a night game in Baltimore, way back in the nineteen fifties. This happened only a year after the Orioles came to town, in 1954, when the American League franchise in St. Louis was shifted east and the worn-out Browns suddenly became the brand-new Orioles. For a while, everybody in Baltimore was happy about the team, but it became clear within a few weeks that the new uniforms could not alter the abilities of the players who had done so horribly in their previous incarnation. The team finished seventh in its first eastern season, losing one hundred games. A new manager, Paul Richards, came aboard the next year, and he shifted the lineup around a little and tinkered with his pitchers, while the front office put out hopeful reports about better times ahead, but the team went right on losing, and by this time it had also begun to lose its following. On this particular damp midsummer night, the Orioles were behind again (the name of the other team has been forgotten), in a game that had been held up two or three times by brief showers. By the bottom of the ninth, only a few hundred silent, pessimistic fans were still in attendance at Memorial Stadium. A light rain had started again. Unexpectedly, the Orioles rallied. A couple of runs scored, and another base hit drove out the enemy pitcher; suddenly the Orioles had the bases loaded, with the tying run at third base and the winning run at second. The reporters paused over their typewriters, where they had begun their customary irritable or apologetic lead paragraphs for further bad-news stories; a few hoarse cries of hope came out of the stands. The next batter was Clint Courtney, probably the most reliable player on the club. Richards came out of the dugout and whispered in Courtney's ear and whacked him encouragingly on the rump. Clint stepped into the box and scowled at the pitcher through the deepening damp. The count went to two and two. Courtney fouled off a couple of pitches, then there was another ball.

Three and two, and the bases loaded! There was some real yelling from the stands. Now, however, the rain suddenly became a downpour, almost hiding the outfielders from view. The umpire unwillingly called time, the players came in, and the tarps went back on the field.

It rained and rained. The perpetually gloomy Baltimore fans stared up at the sky and nodded their heads disconsolately. The thing would be called, of course, and the score would revert to the bottom of their eighth—another game gone. Nobody went home, though; this one had to be waited out. Midnight struck, and still the rain went on. Then, wonder of wonders, it began to ease up. It lightened to a drizzle, then to a mist, and then stopped. The ground crew appeared and rolled back the tarp. The field had been flooded, and another fifteen or twenty minutes went by while the men worked with rakes and shovels, and scattered sawdust on the mound and in the batters' boxes. The umps came back on the field, and the pitcher returned to the mound and warmed up for a considerable time, as was his privilege. The teams took the field at last, more than an hour after they had left it, and the few dozen surviving fans came down to the front rows and took up a hopeful caterwauling.

The home-plate umpire checked his indicator and looked out at the scorecard. Still three and two. He pointed to the pitcher. Play ball! Courtney stood in, chomped down on his wad of tobacco, waggled his bat, and glared out at the pitcher. The fans screamed. The pitcher got his sign. He went into his stretch, paused, rocked back, and threw. The three base runners were off with his motion, running like jackrabbits. The pitch crossed the heart of the plate. Courtney looked at it, motionless. The ump threw up his hand. Strike three. Everybody went home.

That may not be a story to please every palate. I am fond of it, but I can see that as drama it wants work. Baseball-haters will complain about it for their old, dumb reason: nothing *happens*. But never mind. The best baseball stories are probably appreciated only by true fans, who know the possibilities for unlikelihood, letdown, and wild mischance in their game, which can swing in an instant from morality play to variety show to farce.

Anything can happen in baseball, but it may almost be taken as a rule that the most appalling accidents happen to the worst teams. It was the Mets—the early Mets, of course—who were involved in a play one day at Wrigley Field in which an errant heave from one of their outfielders wound up in the Cubs' ball bag. And it was the Cubs themselves—a similarly gentle and innocuous club—who once were caught up in a calamity undreamed of even in the *Metsungsaga.* On an afternoon in 1959, the Cardinals were the visitors at Wrigley Field, and the batter was Stan Musial. Nobody on base. With the count at three and one, Musial almost offered at the next pitch but checked his swing, and the ball somehow skipped by the Chicago catcher, Sammy Taylor, and went all the way back to the screen. The umpire, Vic Delmore, called ball four, and Musial, unaware of the misplay, trotted toward first. Taylor whirled on Delmore and shouted that the ball had been foul-tipped, and Cub manager Bob Scheffing ran out to back him up. The ball, meantime, was picked up by a ball boy and handed to the Cubs' field announcer, who in those days sat in a chair near the home dugout. Two other Cubs—pitcher Bob Anderson and third baseman Alvin Dark—now made their entrances in the plot, each sprinting in to retrieve the ball. Musial, becoming aware at last of these disturbances, rounded first at full speed and set sail for second. The announcer, horrified to observe that he was somehow an active participant in the National League pennant race, hastily dropped the ball on the ground, where it was seized simultaneously by Anderson and Dark, with Alvin finally winning possession.

Meantime, in another part of the forest—back at home plate—Ump Delmore, frazzled by the importunings of Taylor and Scheffing, suddenly and inexplicably extracted a fresh ball—hereinafter to be known as Ball No. 2—and plopped it into

Taylor's glove. Taylor, spotting Musial on the base path, threw the new pill down to second, a bare instant after Alvin Dark had made the same peg, from well behind him, with Ball No. 1. Musial, sliding into second, saw an unmistakable baseball (it was No. 2) sail untouched past his ear and on into center field. He scrambled up and turned happily toward third, only to be tagged after two or three steps by Ernie Banks, the shortstop, with Ball No. 1. Ball No. 2 was chased down in the outfield by the Cubs' Bobby Thomson, who now threw it wildly past *third* base. But here, at last, both baseballs may be allowed to make their exit, for at this juncture the chief umpire, Al Barlick, who had been working at second base, mercifully threw up his hands, calling time. The ensuing confabulations and plea-bargainings need not be explicated. Barlick's next ruling, which caused the game to be played under official protest by the Cardinals, was that Musial was out at second, because he, Barlick, had seen the tag made there with the ball—or with *a* ball. The game went back a step, then resumed, eventually being won by the Cards, and the sport, once again, survived.

For continuous baseball melodrama, there probably never was a better theater than the Phillies' shabby little park, Baker Bowl, which was finally abandoned in 1938. The field was better suited for a smaller, narrower game—croquet, perhaps—and its very short right-field wall, a bare 270 feet from home, was detested by every pitcher and outfielder in the league. One afternoon in 1934, the starting hurler for the visiting Brooklyn Dodgers was Walter (Boom-Boom) Beck—the nickname was onomatopoetic—and the dangerous starboard garden was being defended by Hack Wilson. Always a robust slugger, Wilson unfortunately got to spend far less time at the plate than he had to put in afield, where he was, to put the matter kindly, less than adequate. Hack was also known to spend an occasional evening at his local tavern, pondering this injustice. On this day, he had experienced a particularly trying afternoon in pursuit of assorted line drives and scorching grounders rifled in his direction off Boom-Boom's deliveries—often getting extra practice as he spun around and tried to field the caroms and ricochets, off that extremely adjacent wall, of the same hits he had missed outward-bound.

The Dodger manager, Casey Stengel, even then accustomed to severe adversity, watched several innings of this before he called time and made his familiar journey to the mound, where he suggested to Beck that he take the rest of the afternoon off. Beck's performance had been perfectly within his genre, but for some reason he was enraged at this derricking, and instead of handing the ball over to Stengel he suddenly turned and heaved it away in a passion. Fate, of course, sent the ball arching out into right field, where Hack Wilson, with his head down and his hands on his knees, was quietly reflecting on last night's excesses and this day's indignities. Boom-Boom's throw struck the turf a few feet away from Wilson, who, although badly startled, whirled and chased manfully after the ball, fielded the carom off the wall, and got off a terrific, knee-high peg to second base—his best fielding play, Casey always said, of the entire summer.

A more recent epochal disorder came in a game played in the Florida Instructional League last year. This time, things began with an outfielder's peg to a rookie catcher (all the players in the Instructional League are rookies), who grabbed the ball and made a swipe at an inrushing, sliding base runner at the plate. As sometimes happens, the catcher missed the tag and the base runner missed the plate. The runner jumped up, dusted himself off, and trotted to his dugout, convinced that he had scored. The umpire made no call either way, which is the prescribed response, and after a moment or two the pitcher and the infielders, analyzing the situation, hurried in and implored the catcher to make the tag.

"What?" said the catcher. "Tag who?"

"The runner, the runner!" they cried, severally. "You missed him. He didn't score. Go tag him!"

"Ah," said the young receiver, the light bulb over his head

at last clicking on. Still holding the ball, he ran eagerly toward the enemy dugout, with the umpire close behind. When the catcher got there, however, he gazed up and down the line of seated fresh-faced rookies without recognizing anyone who looked like a recent passerby. He frowned, then went to one end of the bench and tagged the first two or three men sitting in line. He looked around at the umpire, who was watching with folded arms. The umpire made no sign. The catcher tagged four more players. The ump shook his head almost imperceptibly: nothing doing. Now the erstwhile base runner, seeing the catcher inexorably working up the line toward him, suddenly leaped onto the field and made a dash for the plate. The pitcher, who had been standing bemused near home, screamed for the ball, and he and catcher executed a rundown, more or less in the style of stadium attendants collecting a loose dog on the field, and tagged the man out in the on-deck circle.

•

I HAVE dismissed the Mets too quickly—the progenitors of so many legendary baseball disasters. Some of the legends were true. During the early stages of their terrible first summer, in 1962, their center fielder, Richie Ashburn, suffered a series of frightful surprises while going after short fly balls, because he was repeatedly run over by the shortstop, the enthusiastic but modestly talented Elio Chacon. After several of these encounters, Ashburn took Chacon aside and carefully explained that, by ancient custom, center fielders were allowed full freedom to catch all flies they could get to and signal for. The collisions and near-collisions and dropped fly balls continued exactly as before, and Ashburn eventually concluded that Chacon, who spoke very little English, simply didn't understand what it meant when he saw his center fielder waving his arms and yelling "Mine! Mine! I got it!" Richie thought this over and then went to Joe Christopher, a bilingual teammate on the Mets, and asked for help.

"All you have to do is say it in Spanish," Christopher said. "Yell out '*Yo la tengo!*' and Elio will pull up. I'll explain it to him, too—OK? You won't have any more trouble out there."

"*Yo la tengo?*" Ashburn said.

"That's it," Christopher said.

Before the next game, Ashburn saw Chacon in the clubhouse. "*Yo la tengo?*" Richie said tentatively.

"*Sí, sí! Yo la tengo! Yo la tengo!*" Chacon said, smiling and nodding his head.

"*Yo la tengo!*" Ashburn said. They shook hands.

In the second or third inning that night, an enemy batter lifted a short fly to center. Ashburn sprinted in for the ball. Chacon thundered out after it. "*Yo la tengo! Yo la tengo!*" Richie shouted.

Chacon jammed on the brakes and stopped, happily gesturing for Ashburn to help himself. Richie reached up to make the easy catch—and was knocked flat by Frank Thomas, the Mets' left fielder.

•

INTERESTING BASEBALL happenings sometimes take place away from the field. Consider, for example, the memorable and uplifting public-relations outing made in the mid-sixties by Cy Tatum (this is not his real name). Cy was a remarkable hitter, and he had the good fortune to play for a big-league team in a city close to the town where he had grown up. Like some other players in the majors, he had run into trouble with the law when young, and he had served a few semesters at a state trade school for wayward boys. He mended his ways, went into baseball, and became a great local favorite. One summer when his team was in the process of winning a pennant, its first in many years, somebody in the front office realized what a dynamite PR event it would be if Cy were invited to come back to the trade school and address the boys there. The date was quickly arranged, and Tatum turned up at the appointed time and was introduced by the principal of the school to the full, enraptured student body. Cy spoke eloquently, praising the virtues of the straight-and-narrow path and a level swing at the ball, and sat down, to wild applause.

"Thank you, Cy!" said the principal, coming to the center of the stage. "That was splendid. Now, I know the boys want to ask you a lot of questions, and I wonder if you could give us a few more minutes out of your busy day?"

Cy nodded graciously.

"Fine, fine," said the principal. "Perhaps I could just start things off with a question of my own. I think the boys would be really interested to know what you took when you were at school here. Can you recall, Cy?"

Tatum looked faintly surprised, but he recovered himself quickly. "Mostly," he said, "it was overcoats."

•

Tom LaSorda's story also begins in boyhood. LaSorda, of course, is the long-term third-base coach for the Los Angeles Dodgers who recently was named the successor to Walter Alston as the Dodger manager, after Alston's twenty-third season on the job. LaSorda, it can be proved, is a patient sort of man. He grew up in Morristown, Pennsylvania, and became a serious baseball fan at an early age. When he was twelve or thirteen, he volunteered for duty as a crossing guard at his parochial school because he knew that the reward for this service was a free trip to a big-league ball game—an event he had yet to witness. The great day came at last, the sun shone, and the party of nuns and junior fuzz repaired to Shibe Park, where the Phillies were playing the Giants. Young Tom LaSorda had a wonderful afternoon, and just before the game ended he and some of his colleagues forehandedly stationed themselves beside a runway under the stands, where they could collect autographs from the players coming off the field. The game ended, the Giants came clattering by, and Tom extended his scorecard to the first hulking, bespiked hero to come in out of the sunshine.

"C'n I have your autograph, please, mister?" he said.

"Outta my way, kid," the Giant said, brushing past the boy.

When Tom LaSorda tells the story now, the shock of this moment is still visible on his face. "I couldn't *believe* it," he says. "Here was the first big-league player I'd ever seen up close—the first one I ever dared speak to—and what he did was shove me up against the wall. I think tears came to my eyes. I watched the guy as he went away toward the clubhouse and I noticed the number on his back—you know, like taking the license of a hit-and-run car. Later on, I looked at my program and got his name. It was Buster Maynard, who was an outfielder with the Giants then. I never forgot it."

Seven or eight years went swiftly by (as they do in instructive, moral tales), during which time Tom LaSorda grew up to become a promising young pitcher in the Dodger organization. In the spring of 1949, he was a star with the Dodger farm team in Greenville, North Carolina, in the Sally League, and took the mound for the opening game of the season at Augusta, Georgia, facing the Augusta Yankees. Tom retired the first two batters, and then studied the third, a beefy right-handed veteran, as he stepped up to the box.

The park loudspeaker made the introduction: "Now coming up to bat for the Yankees, Buster May-narrd, right field!"

LaSorda was transfixed. "I looked in," he says, "and *it was the same man!*"

The first pitch to Maynard nearly removed the button from the top of his cap. The second, behind his knees, inspired a beautiful sudden *entrechat*. The third, under his Adam's apple, confirmed the message, and Maynard threw away his bat and charged the mound like a fighting bull entering the plaza in Seville. The squads spilled out onto the field and separated the two men, and only after a lengthy and disorderly interval was baseball resumed.

After the game, LaSorda was dressing in the visitors' locker room when he was told that he had a caller at the door. It was Buster Maynard, who wore a peaceable but puzzled expression. "Listen, kid," he said to LaSorda, "did I ever meet you before?"

"Not exactly," Tom said.

"Did I bat against you someplace, maybe?"

"Nope."

"Well, why were you tryin' to take my head off out there?"

LaSorda spread his hands wide. "You didn't give me your autograph," he said.

Tom LaSorda tells this story each spring to the new young players who make the Dodger club. "*Always* give an autograph when somebody asks you," he says gravely. "You never can tell. In baseball, anything can happen."

5 Season Lightly

July 1973

ONCE A PASTIME, baseball is becoming another national anomaly—an institution that is less and less recognizable as it grows in age and familiarity. The executives of the game, displaying their customary blend of irresolution, impulsiveness, and inflexibility, failed this year even to agree on the basic rules, presenting us with one league of teams playing ten men on a side and another offering the more customary nine. Thus inspired, the leagues have responded with three months of stimulating but inexplicable competition, which has been reflected in team standings of unmatched discombobulation. At times this spring, even the most resilient fan must have felt his grip on things begin to loosen when he opened his morning paper and turned to the good old standings. In mid-May, a full month into the campaign, the six teams in the American League East were separated by the span of a single game. Splendid, total competition, one could conclude, and especially heartening for the supporters of the downtrodden Cleveland Indians and Milwaukee Brewers—until one noticed that every one of the six clubs had lost more games than it had won, and that the race in fact constituted nothing more than a flabby bulge below the waistline of .500 ball. A month later, the American League East *and* West had reached parallel levels of irresolution, having sorted out one clear loser in each division—Cleveland (East) and Texas (West)—and ten other clubs so closely bunched that the standings could be absolutely reversed in the space of a single weekend. Milwaukee, Boston, New York, and Detroit had all taken turns at the top of the East, which most resembled a diorama of heaving stegosauri in a tar pit. Just recently, almost halfway through the long season, the AL East has discovered one club apparently capable of a sustained upright posture—the Yankees, of all people, whose sudden recent successes have brought back unexpected visions of the kind of quiet, well-ordered Yankee summers we all grew up on.

The National League has so far managed a more commonplace arrangement of leaders, contenders, and stragglers, although its certified powers, Cincinnati and Pittsburgh, have been out of the sunshine this spring; the Pirates (who were badly shaken by the death of their great star, Roberto Clemente, in a plane crash last winter) appear to have lost the mysterious group energy that vitalizes winning clubs. The true aristocracy of baseball at present is probably represented by the National League West, which is topped by the Dodgers, with their enormous margin (at this writing) of twenty-one games over the .500 level. The most interesting journey to date has to be that of the Cardinals, who fell into a well by losing twenty of their first twenty-five games, and then instantly resurfaced, looking barely damp, after winning sixteen of their next eighteen.

Back in the AL, the world champion Oakland A's have pushed to the fore after a notoriously languid start; their surprising opposition in the West has come from the Kansas City Royals, a newly muscled entrant that scores runs and gives up runs in thick, juicy clusters. The Royals' main man, John

Mayberry, is an entertaining new slugger whose style at the plate features a forward-spinning airplane-propeller windup with the bat just before the pitch arrives—a perfect replica of Willie Stargell's countdown procedures. If Mayberry has in fact decided to model himself on Willie Stargell, he has picked a superior model. Stargell, I sometimes think, may be one of the last baseball men in whom we can still glimpse the hero. He not only hits the ball often and for great distances—he is currently leading both leagues in home runs—but comports himself in all days and weathers with immense style. I remember watching Stargell in October of 1971, when he was suffering an epochal slump at the plate, brought on in part by painful injuries to both knees. He went hitless through all four games of the playoffs and did scarcely better in the famous World Series against the Orioles, batting in only one run in the seven games. Stargell had led his league in homers that year and had knocked in 125 runs, and he was accustomed to playing a large, even triumphant, part in Pirate affairs, and yet he endured those repeated humiliations at the plate with total composure, trudging back to the dugout after still another strikeout or pop-up without the smallest gesture of distress or despair. I remember coming up to him in the clubhouse after one of those empty afternoons and asking him how it was possible for a proud, intensely competitive man to put up with that kind of disappointment without giving way to anger or explanation. Stargell's four-year-old son, Wilver, Jr., was playing on the floor of his cubicle, and Stargell made a gesture toward him and said, "There's a time in life when a man has to decide if he's going to *be* a man." Later, I realized that this was probably a true Hellenic answer: one couldn't say whether one most admired the principle or the philosopher's way of expounding it.

A few traditions, thank heaven, remain fixed in the summer state of things—the June collapse of the Giants, Gaylord Perry throwing (or not throwing) spitballs, Hank Aaron hitting homers, and the commissioner . . . well, commissioning.

The Giants, after leading the National League West from the very beginning of the season, lost fourteen games out of twenty-seven in the month of June—a pattern as predictable as the spring ascension of Ursa Major. Pitching, as usual, was the problem, and the San Francisco manager, Charlie Fox, confessed, "Our earned-run average looks like the national debt." Gaylord Perry, who formerly did not (or did) throw wet pitches for Charlie Fox, now performs similarly for the Indians, eliciting from American League batters the same howls of outrage that he used to inspire in the National. Bobby Murcer complained so vehemently about the umpires' failure to prosecute Perry for the illegal pitch that he was called in and fined two hundred and fifty dollars by Commissioner Bowie Kuhn. Murcer paid up—and struck a game-winning homer off Perry that night, while the sporting press speculated like Peter Wimseys about the nature of Perry's glop (K-Y Jelly is the leading suspect) and its hiding place (inside the neckband, perhaps) on Perry's person. Perry has professed innocence, but retains his familiar mannerisms—viz.: right fingers to the bill of the cap, to the side of the cap, to the back of the cap, to the right sideburn, to the hair above the right ear, to the hair behind the right ear, to the neck—before delivering each pitch to each quivering batter. Is Perry throwing the spitter? Did the Commissioner's fine constitute an unfair incentive to Bobby Murcer—and if so, should not each slugger on every contending team be similarly docked before going out to face the horrid Perry predilection? Does Gaylord Perry have a tiny vial of water from the Dead Sea concealed inside his eustachian tube? The Supreme Court is expected to rule on these burning issues before their summer recess.

Hank Aaron, now thirty-nine years old, is batting only .221 but has perfected an admirable habit of conservation, since almost half of his hits this year have been homers. His total of 23 to date has brought his lifetime to 696, which means that he is within striking distance this season of Babe Ruth's all-hallowed lifetime mark of 714—a possibility that excites everybody but his fellow townspeople. The Braves' attendance so far strongly suggests that if Hank should waft the record-breaker during a home game the deed will be witnessed by more mediapersons than Atlantans. National League pitchers have already begun to speculate about which one of them will be the victim of No. 715, and thus be propelled into the history books in the manner of a Balaclava cavalryman or a Joe Louis knockee. Commissioner Bowie Kuhn, on hearing of this bullpen chatter, issued a stern warning that he would fine any pitcher guilty of not trying his best to get Aaron out on the historic day. The commissioner has been in splendid moral fettle this year. During spring training, when the news came out that two Yankee pitchers, Fritz Peterson and Mike Kekich, were terminating their marriages in order to make new domestic arrangements with each other's wives, Mr. Kuhn issued an advisory opinion on the matter—not marital counseling, it turned out, but an expression of concern for the image of the game. Fritz Peterson promised the commissioner he would try not to do it again.

•

THE COMING eminence of the Yankees was not detectable during my early calls at the Stadium, where I found the customary acres of empty blue grandstand seats and the customary earnest but unavailing competence on the field. In four of my first seven Yankee games this year, the Bronxites scored no runs at all. This jinx has nothing to do with the Stadium, because I have also seen the Yanks lose just as convincingly on the road. (Cf. against Mickey Lolich in Detroit, May 24: Tigers 4, Yankees 0.) On my first call at Yankee Stadium, the beneficiaries of my whammy were the White Sox, who bashed out thirteen hits and three homers in the course of demolishing Fritz Peterson, 8–4. The day also provided my first look at the American League's new designated hitters—the tenth man in the lineup, who bats in place of the pitcher. The incumbents —Mike Andrews for the White Sox and Jim Ray Hart for the

Yanks—bopped two doubles, two singles, and some line-drive outs, thus running their early DH averages to .429 and .529, respectively, and blunting my moldy-fig objections to the innovations, at least for a time. The other true first, for me and perhaps for everyone there, was the moment in the eighth inning when Yankee catcher Thurman Munson and third baseman Graig Nettles, converging on a bunt by Jorge Orta, made simultaneous bare-handed grabs at the ball and came up holding hands.

I went back the next afternoon and saw the Yankees shut out again, but I cannot take all the credit for the 3–0 loss, since the White Sox pitcher was Wilbur Wood, the knuckleballer, who had unmanned the Yankees on his five most recent outings against them; he beat them four times last year, allowing just two earned runs in thirty-six innings. At the time of this first 1973 visit to the Bronx, the Sox were batting over .300 as a team, and with Wood flipping up his flighty, sailing, fingertip junk, the eventual 3–0 margin looked like a mismatch. Everything about Wilbur Wood is disarming. On the mound, he displays a comfortable expanse of tum and the stiffish-looking knees of a confirmed indoorsman, and thus resembles a left-handed accountant or pastry chef on a Sunday outing. Even the knuckler—which he throws, sensibly, on nearly every pitch—looks almost modest, for it does not leap and quiver like Hoyt Wilhelm's old hooked trout. Like all knuckleballers, Wood works with little strain, and, at the age of thirty-one, he may be just approaching his best years. He pitched 377 innings last year. The Yankee shutout came after Wood had rested for only two days—a frequent custom of his, inaugurated by the iconoclastic Chicago pitching coach, Johnny Sain. After the game, Wood sat comfortably in the corner of the clubhouse and drank several beers and smoked several cigarettes while he talked cheerfully to the reporters in a mild Bahst'n accent (he is from Cambridge), explaining that the only difficult part of his difficult pitch is learning to throw it softer, rather than harder, when he is in trouble. "He has the *perfect* disposition for the knuckleball," Sain said, looking on with evident affection. "He's always like this. He has as fine a control over himself as any athlete I've ever seen."

A few nights later, the visitors to the Bronx were the Orioles, and the two teams—both participants in the stately quadrille then being enacted by the American League East, in which each dancer ascended by degrees to the head of the room and then gracefully gave way to another—played a nearly noiseless encounter: four hits and three runs for the O's, to two hits and guess how many runs for the Yankees. Jim Palmer did not allow any pinstripes to reach second base. The winning blow was a shallow fly-ball home run to the right-field unused-furniture display, and was struck by the Baltimore catcher, Elrod Hendricks, who was up to bat for the second time this season. Hendricks got into the game only because the regular Oriole receiver, Earl Williams, got caught in traffic and was late getting to the ball park. Earl Weaver, the Baltimore manager, said, "He moves in mysterious ways"—apparently not a reference to either catcher. The Orioles, at that point batting .174 for their previous eight games, had apparently resumed the near-total batting slump that afflicted them all last season.

Real spring had come when I next dropped in on the Yanks; the visiting team was the Milwaukee Brewers, who, as it happened, were currently enjoying their turn in first place. It was a lovely, mild night, with several kites aloft in the still-bright Bronxian empyrean, and in the third inning I caught sight of a long, wavery pencil-line of migrating Canada geese far overhead. I pointed out this nonurban marvel to my neighbors in the press box, thus causing them to miss another wonder—a successful pick-off throw to third base by Thurman Munson. Luckily, the Yanks had other entertainments in store for us—four hits in the fourth, a nifty hit-and-run shot by Gene Michael that scored a man all the way from first, and a noisy, cheerful six-run outburst in the sixth. When Yankee starter Steve Kline suffered some arm twinges, Sparky Lyle came in and awed the Milwaukee hitters, at one point striking out five of them in succession with his downer. Munson wound up with a single, a double, a homer, and four runs batted in; the Yanks won by 11–4, and the Brewers gently took up a lower place in the dance.

Unburdened of my jinx, I tried manfully to deepen my appreciation of the Yankees, an experienced if less than dazzling team that had enriched its portfolio over the winter with the acquisition of a pair of tested regulars, Matty Alou and Graig Nettles. I wanted to care about the Yanks—I really did. There is more fan than critic in me, and I take far more pleasure in a game where I can yell for the good guys. I am also a confirmed front-runner, whose loyalty is hardly more selective than that of a Bide-a-Wee puppy. Still, I can't quite attach myself to these Yankees, and to judge by the team's home attendance this year, a lot of other people have been having the same difficulty. I think the problem is ghosts. As every fan knows, one of the strange particularities of our game is the vivid private image we retain of certain players we have seen, players we have watched with intensity. Hours or days after a game—sometimes years after—we recall a name, and in the same instant we *see* the man in perfect midafternoon memory. He doesn't have to be a star or even a regular; all that is required is that we have watched him often enough or with sufficient emotion to make him our own. I can bring back Ed Charles, of the 1969 Mets, as precisely as Ted Williams; I can see Don Mueller or Tommy Byrne as readily as Stan Musial or Warren Spahn. Almost none of the Yankee stalwarts this year (and, to tell the truth, for several years) seem to have this spectral dimension. Bobby Murcer, Roy White, Mel Stottlemyre, Ron Blomberg, Sparky Lyle—I watch them with admiration, but when I come home from the Stadium and go to bed, what I see before sleep is Phil Rizzuto laying down a drag bunt, suddenly dipping the bat down by his belt buckle to tap the ball, and then whirring away down the line; Johnny Mize (a red, melonlike, country-farmer face) hulking over the plate; Yogi

Berra lashing a bad outside pitch to the distant left-field corner; Allie Reynolds, in heavy trouble, glaring down at the hitter; or Joe DiMaggio motionless in the sunlight in center field, with his hands on his knees. Among the contemporary Yankees, only Thurman Munson has impinged on my picture show: stubborn, solid, dust-smeared, he straddles the plate, awaiting the arriving peg and an on-rushing enemy base runner, with his meaty arms and fat glove still casually at rest at his side—the catcher in a classic attitude, just before battle. This year's Yankees have good power (Munson, Nettles, Murcer, Blomberg), fair defense, pretty good starting pitchers (Peterson, Stottlemyre, Doc Medich), firm direction (Ralph Houk), and irresolute competition (Detroit, Milwaukee, et al.); all they need now is an exorcist.

•

AMERICAN LEAGUE attendance is actually up a trifle, which is happy news indeed, and it is almost a certainty that the AL den leaders will claim that the designated-hitter innovation is responsible. I doubt this—partly because the only significant AL gate increases are in Milwaukee, California, Kansas City, and Chicago, where the local teams have only lately sprung into contention, and partly because I cannot imagine many hundreds of new fans suddenly clustering in to watch a .230 or .240 hitter strut his stuff. The truth is that, taken together, the anointed new men in the lineups have not been able to hit the ball any better than the eight other regulars—which is to say not well at all. They *have* outhit the pitchers-*cum*-pinch-hitters they replaced by a margin of .237 to .169. The real gain has been in home runs; the designees have hit out 107 so far, as against a full season's total of 48 by the 1972 pitchers and pinch-hitters. It is probably useless to complain at length about the league's shiny new thingummy, which was officially proclaimed a success almost on opening day, but one cannot forget that the game—the game itself, as played out there between the foul lines—has been wrenched out of shape. Gone now—in one league, at least—is that ancient and unique concept of a player's total individual accountability, the requirement that he engage in and be measured at every aspect of this difficult sport. Vanished, too, is the strategic fulcrum of baseball—the painful decision about pinch-hitting for your pitcher when you are behind in late innings—and gone with it is the fans' pleasure in vociferously sharing in and second-guessing this managerial bind. Now the game is farther away from us all, less human and less fun, and suddenly made easy. The DH was voted in after a minimal trial in the minors by executives who seem to believe that perpetual action is the name of this game, too, and who wish to make their sport resemble all other sports. Most of all, they are in the grip of what can be called the television state of mind—the conviction that all entertainments are the same and thus in absolute competition with each other, and that anything less than a No. 1 rating is clear warning that you must alter your product radically or prepare to throw it away.

For two decades, the central affliction of big-league baseball has been its sagging batting averages. Last year, the cumulative National League average stood at .248, and the American League at .239. These are figures to be taken seriously by any baseball fan or baseball magnate not just because they indicate that the game is declining in pleasure and energy but because they suggest that today's big-league stars are less capable than their famous predecessors. It is this unspoken belief that has the most serious effect upon the game's national popularity, and yet it is probably false. In every sport where comparable performances can be fairly measured—track and swimming come to mind—the modern athlete regularly and overwhelmingly exceeds the best marks recorded twenty or thirty years ago. There is no reason to assume that the strength and capabilities of contemporary baseball players are an exception. The hitting drought, then, is almost certainly due to a number of technical alterations in the game—night baseball, bigger ball parks, bigger infielders' gloves, the slider, the size and strength of today's pitchers, and the vastly increased and more effective use of relief pitchers. The redress should be minimal and precise—a further alteration of the strike zone, a livelier baseball, a more visible baseball, a shaving of the dimensions of the plate. By some means, baseball must bring back its long-lost hero, the .350 hitter—who is, in all likelihood, the same deserving young slugger now struggling so earnestly to maintain himself at .275. The designated-hitter ruling simply misses the point: it is the *batters* who have been killing the game at the plate, not the pitchers. The DH is a hype.

•

WRIGLEY FIELD, in Chicago, is a splendid argument against baseball chic. Built in 1914, it was originally intended as the home park for the Chicago Whales, of the outlaw Federal League, but has served instead, of course, as the honored family mansion of the Cubs. No Monday night games will be televised from Wrigley Field this summer (or any other summer soon), because the Cubs' owner, Philip K. Wrigley, has as yet found no reason to install floodlights in the park. He believes that baseball is a sunshine game, best played by athletes who can see both the top and bottom halves of a baseball in flight, and best enjoyed by a family audience, and he has absolutely resisted the game's first and most radical alteration. With one exception, all the other major-league clubs now play the great majority of their games at night; a good many of them—the Dodgers, the Astros, and the Royals, for example—schedule *all* their home games, except for Sundays or holidays, at night. At least half of the Giants' home games are held in the afternoon, because in the evening their stadium, Candlestick Park, is comfortably habitable only by penguins. A mere handful of the other teams, including the Mets and the Indians, have made any attempt to hold some vestige of balance between day and night games and their dissimilar audiences. With baseball's declining attendance figures, the question of whether the game should continue to throw itself wholly and perpetually into competition with prime-time television and other night entertainments is no longer a dated or insignificant issue.

P. K. Wrigley is not entirely unadaptable. In contrast to many of his competitors, who severely restrict the telecasting of their teams' home games in order to compel fans toward the turnstiles, Wrigley has decreed that all the Cubs' home engagements are to be televised. This particular convenience, to be sure, is enjoyed by Wrigley himself, who never attends a game at Wrigley Field; an intensely private man, he recently told a Chicago reporter that he was sometimes tempted to drop in on his team but always thought better of it because he knew that too many ushers would fuss over him. The Wrigley eccentricities are endlessly discussed in high baseball circles, mostly because the Cubs' attendance has remained so healthy over the years; last season, the Cubs and their downtown rivals, the White Sox, both finished second in their divisions, and yet the Cubs' afternoon audience was a shade larger than the Sox' nightpeople—1,299,163 to 1,177,318. Chicago is a terrific baseball town.

I happily renewed acquaintance with the Cubbies and their habitat in early June, during two weekday-afternoon games against the Dodgers. Wrigley Field is one of the few remaining enclosures that still merit the title of "ball park"—a grassland enclosed by an ancient red brick wall and a gentle, curving, spacious sweep of stands, two levels high along the foul lines, that is surmounted by a low, shadowy pavilion roof. Unlike many of the surviving original stadiums, the place is handsomely tended and painted—an estate that matches the charms of the Petit Palais of the East, Fenway Park. In the outfield, the brick wall is entirely overgrown with ivy and rises toward elevated banks of bleacher seats. In 1969, when the Cubs led the league for most of the distance—only to fall disastrously before the onrushing Mets in September—the bleachers were inhabited by vociferous, beery, baiting hordes wearing yellow hardhats; the left-field pack was sometimes led in organized cheering by a Cub relief pitcher named Dick Selma. After a

Cub victory, everyone waited to scream in unison when Ron Santo performed a happy leap and click of the heels as the Cubbies streamed out to their clubhouse in left field. This year, most of the hardhats are gone, the bleachers are filled to overflowing with teen-agers, and Ron Santo has given up his *entrechats*. The Cubs, who lost so bitterly under their old manager, Leo Durocher, are winning in more modest, and perhaps more mature, fashion under his successor, Whitey Lockman, who took the helm last summer. The club's fixed stars—Santo, Billy Williams, Glenn Beckert, Don Kessinger, Fergie Jenkins—are, in truth, a bit more than mature, and Lockman has so far performed a subtle orchestration of his famous elders and eager juniors. The first thirteen wins by the Cub pitching staff this year were recorded by ten different pitchers, and second baseman Glenn Beckert was rested six times during the course of a twenty-six-game hitting streak. Whitey Lockman is cheerful, low-key, and approachable, and, as more than one Chicago fan has observed, enjoys the enormous initial advantage in his new job of not being Leo.

My appreciation of the Cubs was at first deflected by the visiting team, the Dodgers, who, having just completed the most successful May record of any club this year, arrived in Chicago leading the league in both batting and pitching and were, in fact, ascending rapidly toward their suite at the Top o' the West. They bolted from the mark in the first game, jumping on Fergie Jenkins for four lightning-fast runs in the first, mostly thanks to a homer propelled completely out of the park by Ron Cey, the Los Angeles third baseman. (A stiff breeze was blowing out toward center field—a frequent local meteorological phenomenon that causes National League pitchers to mutter in their sleep.) Cey, a compact, bunchily muscled youngster with a wad of sandy hair protruding from his helmet, was a stranger to me, as were the new second baseman—a jackrabbit named Dave Lopes—and the catcher, Joe Ferguson, who was the current league leader in runs batted in. Ferguson and Cey have solved the Dodgers' perennial problems at their respective positions. In the third inning, Ferguson helped to fashion a run by flicking a dandy hit-and-run single to right, deposited so precisely that Glenn Beckert, the Chicago second baseman, fell to his knees in his attempt to reach the ball as it hopped through the spot he had just vacated. All the Dodgers seemed transported with confidence, bashing out fifteen hits in a runaway 10–1 win. The Cubs were flat. In the fifth, their right fielder, José Cardenal, ran down a long drive by Willie Davis, which he seemed to glove just as he got to the center-field wall; looking around happily, with his arms still deep in the ivy, Cardenal was startled to see Davis streaking past second, and only then discovered the ball lying behind his left foot: triple.

The Cubs kept their self-possession, winning the next day. (One-game losing streaks have been their specialty this year.) They amputated another potential big first inning by the visitors with a fine peg and relay to third, wiping out Ferguson, who had overrun the bag by a foot or two, and then came back to knock out Don Sutton with two runs in the fifth and with four more in the sixth; along the way, we were given a picture double play—a lovely pastoral by the Chicago-school Old Masters, Beckert and Kessinger. The Cubs won, 6–4, surviving a ninth-inning scare by the scary Dodgers, and Cubs fans—opinionated adult critics with the sparrowlike alertness of old Brooklyn fans, and *swarms* of youngsters, including perhaps every eleven-year-old boy in the greater Chicago area—nearly split themselves in appreciation. I was grateful, too—for these fans and these teams, and for Mr. Wrigley. The day before, there had been a brief rain delay in the seventh inning—a mild shower that held things up for about twenty minutes. The people down front came up under the roof, and the ground crew put the tarp on and took it off and then put it on again, and some of the teen-age couples stayed in their seats, squashing happily together under newspapers and pieces of plastic. The little kids, their hair plastered down with rain, ran about in the aisles with their heads cricked back, catching rain in their open mouths. The organist kept playing ("Raindrops Keep Fallin' on My Head"), and the rest of us stayed in our seats and stretched and waited—no place to go, and nothing to hurry for—and in time the sun came out and lit up the wet, deep-green grass in the outfield. It was nothing —a summer moment, but part of other summers, too.

•

BASEBALL, WE sometimes need reminding, is meant to be played by the young. This homely truth came back to me during some illustrated lectures by the visiting Giants at Shea Stadium. Although on the decline (this was mid-June, and the team had just lost three straight to Montreal), the San Francisco touring kindergarten, the youngest team in the majors, still included Dave Kingman, who is twenty-four, along with five .300 hitters among their regulars, and a dazzling new outfield—Gary Matthews, Garry Maddox, and Bobby Bonds—whose averages came out to twenty-four (age), .331 (batting), and 9.4 (hundred-yard dash, unofficial). I am a lifelong Giants fan, and since I understand that the unique quality of my club (even more distinctive than the June swoon) is its habit of discovering outstanding young baseball talent and then perversely trading it away (Willie McCovey, Orlando Cepeda, Jose Pagan, Gaylord Perry, the three Alou brothers, etc.), I looked on these new prodigies with what I can only call anticipatory nostalgia, as I prepared to say goodbye to them even in the act of saying hello. They did look dashing, particularly in the first game against the Mets. In the third inning, shortstop Chris Speier darted to his right to scoop up a grounder and somehow released the ball, all in the same instant, back over his shoulder to second base, in time for a force. A moment later, Gary Matthews ran back in deep left field for Felix Millan's long drive, made a twisting, last-second leap, and plucked back the ball after it had cleared the bullpen fence. Speier, who is twenty-three, has range and a tremendous arm, and is something like a continuous surprise on the field.

With the fading of Brooks Robinson, he is almost my favorite infielder.

The Mets persevered, dropping that first game by 2–1 and then capturing the brief series with 5–4 and 3–1 wins. They are, however, a team now so afflicted with injuries, bad luck, weak hitting, and disappointing pitching (especially by the bullpen) that even their victories are almost dispiriting. Their injury list, this year as last year, encompasses almost the entire club roster, and the current absence of Bud Harrelson, out with a broken wrist, has finally extinguished the last, low fires of 1969. No team can be blamed for injuries, but the Mets are suffering just as much from a plain dearth of talent; when compared with other clubs in their league—not just the Dodgers and Giants but also the likes of the new Phillies—they are a team truly without prospects.* One of their problems, it must be admitted, is Willie Mays, who is now, at forty-two, the oldest player in the National League and has so far resisted the clear evidence that he should retire. He plays sporadically, whenever he is well and rested, and gives his best, but his batting reflexes are gone, and so is his arm. In that opening game against the Giants, the first San Francisco run came in on a long double to the left-center-field fence struck by young Ed Goodson, the Giants' third baseman. Mays chased down the ball at the fence, picked it up, and unexpectedly flipped it to his left fielder, George Theodore, an innocent spectator of the action. Theodore was so surprised that he bobbled the ball for an instant before making the throw, far too late, to third. I had never seen such a thing. Theodore was given an error, but the horrible truth of the matter was that Mays was simply incapable of making the play. In the bottom of the same inning, Mays grounded out to short, and his batting average for the year slipped below .100. He has subsequently done a little better—.202, with three

* All absolutely true, and the fact that the Mets later in 1973 won their divisional title and then the National League pennant and very nearly won the World Series should not detract from the brilliance of this appraisal.

homers, at this writing—but his failings are now so cruel to watch that I am relieved when he is not in the lineup. It is hard enough for the rest of us to fall apart quite on our own; heroes should depart.

•

JULY 4: Boston at N.Y. (2): Ah, friends, can this be the real thing at last? The Yanks, in first place at the traditional mid-season milepost, in a holiday doubleheader against their ancient enemies the Red Sox! Our boys (strengthened by the recent purchase of two strong and combat-tested starting pitchers, Pat Dobson and Sam McDowell) have run off a record of 30–15 since May 20, winning fourteen of the last fifteen at home. How *about* that, fans? Yes, the crowds have materialized at last, in thickening numbers, and the Fourth is to be their reward—the first proper baseball celebration in the Bronx in almost a decade . . . and also the last Fourth here for some years to come, while the old ballyard is closed for major alterations. So come *on*, everybody. Nothing can spoil this day!

Well, almost nothing. As it turned out, our hosts for the afternoon, having gone to such pains to provide us with a memorable party, first dropped the watermelon off the back of the truck and then forgot to bring the fireworks—losing the first game by 2–1, on errors, and the second by 1–0, on vapid hitting. A miserable Fourth, in short, for most of the 41,693 of us who made the scene. The crowd itself was the only happening of the day—a hoarse, eager, sweating, half-dressed multitude that cheered hopefully and then derisively, that ate and drank without cease, flew paper airplanes, scattered trash, dropped showers of beer from the upper deck, set off salvos of firecrackers and ashcans, got into fights, roused itself again and again for shouted encouragement, and lapsed at last into irritated torpor. Handmade banners flew from the railings ("We Love You Bobby #1" for Bobby Murcer; "BA Boomer" for Ron Blomberg, who was leading the league in batting), and there were heads visible along the back wall of the very top deck—the sure sign of a huge, old-fashioned Stadium crowd, right out of the nineteen forties or fifties. All began eagerly and happily, with the home-team hitters—almost dangerous now, in our renewed and hopeful estimation—swinging for some hard, deep outs off the Boston starter, Ray Culp, and with Mel Stottlemyre setting down the visitors without strain. In the fourth inning, a wonderful baying of pleasure welcomed Bobby Murcer's low homer into the right-field bullpen—a Yankee run that would have earned a longer commemoration if its unique nature had been appreciated at the time. The hot, damp afternoon wore along, and the audience, preoccupied with feeding its face and mopping its brow, sustained an uninterrupted cheerful racket, a deep undertow of noise, that suggested little anxiety about the difficult event at hand. Then, in the top of the ninth, Stottlemyre gave up a leadoff single to Reggie Smith—the cue, of course, for the Datsun and Sparky Lyle, the fabled reliever. Yastrzemski singled on Lyle's second pitch. Cries of "Dee-fense! Dee-fense!" from the top deck—a plea now utterly ignored by the Yankees. Cepeda dropped a tiny, unsurprising bunt in front of the plate that Thurman Munson somehow kicked away. Petrocelli fanned, but with the bases still loaded, Fisk rapped a bouncer to Nettles, who seemed to consider various options—Throw home? Step on third and then throw to first?—and finally chose the wrong one: a peg to second in time for one out but not nearly in time for the essential relay to first. That throw got away from Blomberg, who chased down the ball, saw Yastrzemski sprinting in from third, and bounced a wild heave past Munson which allowed the second run to score. Disaster. The Yanks, in their half, put their lead runner aboard, but Matty Alou's pinch-hit bunt was too deep, ruining the sacrifice, and a few minutes later, the shouting was over—a game literally thrown away.

The nightcap was a game of Still Pond No More Moving, featuring some impressive pitching by the Yanks' Doc Medich and the Red Sox' Roger Moret, and a lone score in the fifth, a mini-run fashioned out of a walk to Rick Miller, a stolen base, and a little single by Yastrzemski. The Yanks' hitting, so boisterous in recent weeks, had fallen away to a mutter—six scattered and unferocious blows—and the run-famished crowd stared out at some of the out-of-town scores now going up on the board: St. Louis 11, Pittsburgh 3; Baltimore 6, Milwaukee 4; Baltimore 10, Milwaukee 7. Those two Oriole wins could move them up to within two games of the Yankees.

Firecrackers were banging and popping all over the park now, and there were some boos for the Yankee hitters. Empty seats were beginning to show up. I got up and wandered around, in search of some action and a breeze. From the back of the lower deck, I watched that old and wonderful New York baseball panorama—the Stadium playing field viewed as a narrow, skyless slot of intense green, framed between the black of the overhanging mezzanine above and the black of the seated crowd below: a game-vista that an auto mechanic might have from under a stalled DeSoto. I kept going, and sat down at last in an empty seat way out in Section 34, beyond the foul pole. From here, I looked out across the immense distances of deep left field—Gionfriddoland—and on to the distant, tiny figures of the players. From this vantage, the infielders' throws over to first swooped and dipped at odd angles, and whenever a batter hit a ball there was a pause long enough to measure—*one . . . two*—before the high, thin sound reached us. The crowd out here was quieter—mostly older men sitting alone, with a space of a few seats and rows between each of them. One of them was holding a radio to his ear. Then a man down in front of me stood up and came slowly up the aisle, folding his *News* under his arm. "Ah, well," he said as he came by. He was quite right; we could forget this particular day. There was a lot of this season still to come, still plenty of baseball for us to watch and care about in the weeks ahead. It was time to head home.

6 Three for the Tigers

September 1973

MAX. It is lunchtime at Gene & Georgetti's Restaurant, on North Franklin Street in downtown Chicago. It is the middle of the week, and the place is pretty full. A lot of businessmen eat here: Bloody Marys, chopped sirloin or the veal scallopini, salad, coffee, shoptalk. At one table—a party of three—somebody mentions the St. Louis Browns, the old American League baseball club that moved to Baltimore in 1954 and became the Orioles. A man rises from a nearby table, approaches the threesome, and bows. "Excuse me, gentlemen," he says. They look up. He is a sandy-haired, bright-eyed man—still a bit below middle age, one would guess—with a small cigar in his hand; his eyeglasses are in the new aviator-goggle style. "Excuse me," he says again, smiling cheerfully. "I just overheard one of you mention the old St. Louis Browns, and I'm sure you would all like to be reminded of the lineup of the 1944 Brownies, which, as you will recall, was the only Browns team ever to win the AL pennant, and which lost that World Series, of course, to their hometown rivals, the Cardinals, in six games. It was one of the two World Series, in fact, in which both participating teams came from west of the Mississippi River. The Browns' regular lineup in 1944 went: catcher, Frank Mancuso; first base, George McQuinn; second base, Don Gutteridge; third base, Mark Christman . . ." He runs through the eight names (one of the least celebrated lineups in the history of the game), adds starting pitchers Jack Kramer, Sig Jakucki, Bob Muncrief, and Denny Galehouse and, for good measure, throws in a second-string catcher named Red Hayworth. "You probably remember," he says, still smiling, "that Red Hayworth and the regular catcher, Frank Mancuso, both had brothers who were also major-league catchers and, in both cases, *better* catchers. Thank you." He bows and departs.

The three men at the table look at one another, and then one of them calls after their informant. "Hey!" he says. "Do you come from St. Louis?"

"No," says the stranger. "Detroit."

He sits down at his table again, but he has stopped smiling. He has just remembered that he lives in Chicago now—away from Detroit, away from the Tigers.

•

BERT. A little after nine-thirty on a Monday morning in June, Bert walks into his ground-floor office in Oak Park, Michigan, which is a suburb on the north side of Detroit. His name is on the door: "Bert Gordon, Realty." He says good morning to his secretary and to his assistant, Barbara Rosenthal, and goes on into his own office, which looks out on a parking strip and, beyond that, onto Greenfield Road. He sits down at his desk, leans forward and takes off his shoes, and slides his feet into a pair of faded blue espadrilles. Then he swings his swivel chair to the right, so that he is facing a desk-model calculator on a side table, and punches out on it the numbers "2922" and "1596." The first figure is the total number of days of President Nixon's two terms in the White House; the second is the number of days the President has served to date. He hits another button, and the answer slot at the top of the machine offers up "54.62" in illuminated green numbers. Bert is a member of the Michigan Democratic State Central Committee, and he has just figured (as he figures every weekday morning) the expired percentage of President Nixon's two terms of office. Now Bert clears the machine and punches out the numbers "9345" and "2806." (Since Friday morning, the first number has gone up by seven and the second by one: Al Kaline, the veteran star outfielder for the Detroit Tigers, hit one single in seven official times at bat against the Minnesota Twins over the weekend.) The machine silently presents another set of green numbers; today Kaline's lifetime major-league batting average stands at .3000267. Bert sighs, erases the figure, and picks up his telephone. He is ready to start his day.

•

DON. Don and his wife, Susan, are attending a performance of *The Marriage of Figaro* by the touring Metropolitan Opera company at the Masonic Temple Auditorium in Detroit. They are both very fond of the theater, and they go to a play or an opera whenever they can manage it. As usual, Don has bought seats near the back of the balcony, where he knows the radio reception is better. The two of them are following the opera attentively, but Don is also holding a small transistor radio up to his left ear. (He is left-eared all the way.) Through long training, he is able to hear both the opera and (because of the good reception) the voice of Ernie Harwell, the sports broadcaster for Station WJR, who is at this moment describing the action at Tiger Stadium, where the Brewers are leading the Tigers 1–0 in the top of the fourth. A woman sitting directly behind Don and Susan is unable to restrain her curiosity, and during a recitative she leans forward and taps Don on the shoulder.

"Excuse me," she whispers. "I was just wondering what you're listening to on that little radio."

Don half turns in his seat. "Simultaneous translation," he whispers.

•

In this country's long love affair with professional sports, the athlete has more and more come to resemble the inamorata—an object of unceasing scrutiny, rapturous adoration, and expensive adornment—while the suitor, or fan, remains forever loyal, shabby, and unknown. Sports fans are thought of as a mass—statistics that are noticed only when they do not fall within their predicted norms—but the individual fan (except for a few self-made celebrities, like Hilda Chester, the Ebbets Field bell ringer, or the Knicks' Dancing Harry, or the Mets' folding-sign man) is a loner, a transient cipher, whose streaks and slumps go unrecorded in the annals of his game. Every sport, however, has its great fans as well as its great athletes—classic performers whose exceptional powers set them apart from the journeyman spectator. They are veterans who deserve notice if only for the fact that their record of attachment and service to their game and their club often exceeds that of any player down on the field. The home team, in their belief, belongs to them more than to this passing manager or to that arriviste owner, and they are often cranky possessors, trembling with memory and pride and frustration, as ridiculous and touching as any lovers. These rare ones make up a fraction of every sporting audience, but they seem to cluster more thickly in the homes of the older, well-entrenched franchises. The three Detroit nonpareils are a vivid constellation of contemporary baseball fandom: Maxwell H. Lapides, a businessman who went to work last spring as a vice-president of a national collection agency in Chicago, thus painfully exiling himself from his friends and his ball team; Bertram Gordon, whose real-estate agency specializes in finding and leasing business and shopping-center locations in the areas of thickening population outside the central city; and Dr. Donald N. Shapiro, a distinguished oral surgeon. They are intimate friends, united by their ages (middle to upper forties), their similar backgrounds and styles of life, their neighboring families, their Jewishness, and their wit and intelligence, but most of all by their consuming passion for the Detroit Tigers. None of the three is willing to accept the cheerfully patronizing tone that nonsporting friends and relatives usually direct toward the baseball-bitten; none of the three, for that matter, regards himself as a baseball fan at all. "Right from the beginning, I have been a Tiger fan and nothing else," Max Lapides said this summer. "Other men can happily go to ball games wherever they happen to find themselves—not me. My interest is the Tigers. They are the sun, and all the twenty-three other teams are satellites. You can't begin to understand or appreciate this game unless you have an intense involvement."

Dr. Donald Shapiro, in spite of the demands imposed by his successful and extensive practice, by his family (he is married and has three children), by his writing for medical and dental journals, by his sideline in theatricals (he played a small part in a Hollywood gangster film shot in Detroit last winter), by his weekend career as a highly competitive Class A tennis player, and by his voluminous, wide-ranging reading, manages to keep abreast of the Tigers' news almost inning by inning throughout their 162-game season. Evenings, friends at his house or at their own have taught themselves to ignore the fact that his left ear, like van Gogh's, is of no immediate social use; in the spring, when a good many ball games are played in the afternoon, Shapiro tries to schedule his surgical appointments in hospital operating rooms that he knows to have an acceptable interior Harwell-level. (Sinai Hospital has the worst reception in Detroit.) When all else fails, he calls his baseball friends, and Bert Gordon has come to recognize the sound of Don's telephone voice, blurred with haste and a surgical mask, asking, "How're we doing?" One afternoon in 1970, Bert answered his phone and heard Don whisper, "This is probably a violation of every professional canon, but I can't help it. Guess who I've got in the chair!"

"Who?" said Bert.

"Chet Laabs!"

"*Chet Laabs!*"

"Chet Laabs!"

They hung up. (Chet Laabs, a chunky, unremarkable outfielder, played for the Tigers from 1937 to 1939.)

This kind of belonging brooks no alternatives. "When I'm listening to a game, there is nothing that annoys me as much as somebody who clearly doesn't care coming up to me and smiling and saying 'How's it going?' " Don says, "*How's it going!* Why, don't they understand that for a real fan it's always a matter of suffering and ecstasy? What we're involved with here is exaltation!"

Bert Gordon, in turn, detected a crucial slight in the midst of a recent bridge-table conversation, and demanded, "How come you're a bridge authority and your partner's an art aficionado but I'm a baseball nut?"

Bert and Don are lifelong friends who grew up in the near-northwest section of Detroit and graduated from Central High together in the class of 1942. Max Lapides, who is forty-five years old—three and a half years younger than the others—did not live in the same neighborhood, and thus the triumvirate was not completed until early in the nineteen sixties, although they have subsequently established the fact that they were fellow witnesses, usually in person, of innumerable famous moments in Tiger history: Goose Goslin's championship-winning single in the ninth inning of the sixth game in the 1935 Series; an unknown thirty-year-old rookie named Floyd Giebell outpitching Bob Feller in Cleveland on the second-to-last day of the 1940 season to nail down the pennant for Detroit; Rudy York and Pinky Higgins hitting two-run homers in the same inning against the Reds in the Series that fall; Earl Torgeson stealing home in the bottom of the tenth inning to defeat the hated Yanks in 1955; Joe DiMaggio hammering a grounder that broke George Kell's jaw—and Kell picking up the ball and stepping on the bag to force the runner from second before collapsing in front of third base. Don and Max met at last in 1960, when a friend in common brought them together at a dinner party, having assured each one beforehand that the other was a Tiger fan of surpassing tenacity and knowledge. Both of them, of course, utterly ignored the proffered *bona fides*, and the marriage very nearly expired on the spot. Late in the evening, however, the two chanced to arrive at the drinks table together. Don Shapiro, regarding Max with evident distrust, ventured a minute opening. "R.L.," he said.

"R.L.?" returned Max.

Don nodded, watching his man.

"Why, Roxie Lawson," said Max. (Roxie Lawson was a right-handed pitcher for the Tigers in the mid-thirties.) "Of course."

They fell into each other's arms.

In recent years, the three-way entente has deepened in complexity, ritual, and affection. Max Lapides, who has regularly attended about thirty or thirty-five Tiger home games every year, often to the extent of going to the park alone ("He even likes a night game against the Texas Rangers in the last week of September," says Bert Gordon), has been an energizing catalyst for the three, organizing baseball dates and tickets, nudging baseball memories, berating the Tiger management, comparing active and erstwhile ballplayers, inventing bets and interior games, finding causes for contention and laughter. Since each of the three friends sustains an almost permanent state of transcendental baseball meditation, they are forever making and sharing new discoveries. Last year, for instance, Bert startled Max with the sudden announcement that Aurelio Rodriguez, the present Tiger third baseman, is the only major-league infielder with all five vowels in his first name.

Max and Bert are telephone addicts, and have made several thousand calls to each other in the past four or five years (Bert: "Think how many if we *liked* each other!"), mostly to exchange baseball talk. In a recent call, Max baited Bert for having inexplicably forgotten that Don Heffner had played in six games for the Tigers in 1944, long before beginning his tenure as a Detroit coach. "Now we're even for Milt Bolling, right?" he said. "It must be a *year* you haven't let me up because I forgot Milt and Frank Bolling played together that once for us in the fifties." In time, they went on to bubble-gum cards. "I never saw the Waners, because they were in the wrong league, but I know how they each looked up at the plate," Max said. "Both were lefty hitters, of course, but Lloyd held the bat sort of out in front of him when he was up, and Paul's bat was tipped sideways and back. That's the way it was on my cards, anyway. Listen, what were the worst baseball cards you used to have—you know, the ones you always had so many of you couldn't get rid of them? . . . Harlond Clift? Oh, yes, my God, you're right, Bert! I'd absolutely forgotten. But with me it was always too many Hudlins. Willis Hudlin, the old Cleveland twirler—right? I think I had a hundred Willis Hudlins. . . . What were the *best* baseball cards? You mean like the Gehringers and . . . Oh, the rarest ones. Let me see. . . . I guess they were so rare I never got one. I mean, I can't remember. Probably some good ballplayer on a terrible team. Somebody on the old Athletics who'd get overlooked there. Like—oh, like Bob Johnson. You remember him—Indian Bob. He used to *kill* us. . . . I think we talked about this once already, but let's talk about it some more, OK?"

By agreement among the three, Max holds the post of official historian, Don is entrusted with tactics, and Bert is the statistician, though none of them is reticent about intruding upon another's turf of expertise. Like most long-term fans, they are absolutely opposed to the American League's new designated-hitter rule, but Bert Gordon may be the first classicist to point out that the addition of the tenth man means that the pregame public announcement of the team lineups now takes 11.1 percent longer to complete than it did last year. His avidity for figures seems to remove him a little from the day-to-day adventures of his team, but he keeps his Kaline statistics warm, and this summer he spent a good many hours extrapolating the day on which Kaline would pass Charlie Gehringer as the player with the third-highest number of base hits (behind Ty Cobb and Sam Crawford) in Tiger history. Early in June, Bert settled on August 17 as the likely date for the event, but later revised it to August 9; the epochal Kaline hit actually came on August 8—a single against Oakland that was probably appreciated more quickly and more deeply by Bert Gordon than by the man who struck it. Bert polishes such Tiger events and figures in his mind—the unmatched Ty Cobb records; Harry Heilmann's odd-year batting championships, in 1921, '23, '25, and '27; Denny McLain's startling 31-6 year in 1968—but the one Tiger record he believes to be absolutely unassailable was made in an afternoon game on June 21, 1970, when a modestly talented Tiger infielder named Cesar Gutierrez hit safely in seven consecutive times at bat. "For one thing, you have to send fifty-five men to the plate in the game before the thing even becomes statistically possible," Bert said recently. "Why, only two men in the entire history of this game, out of all the thousands and thousands that have played big-league ball, have ever gone seven for seven. Just think about that for a minute." He lit a Lucky Strike and thought about it for a minute, humming happily under his breath. "You know something about that Gutierrez?" he said, and an enormous laugh convulsed him. "Oh, boy, was he ever *lucky!*" *

* Bert Gordon's pleasure in the Gutierrez miracle was expunged on September 16, 1975, when Rennie Stennett, second baseman for the Pittsburgh Pirates, went seven for seven against the Chicago Cubs, in a game at Wrigley Field that the Pirates won by the score of 22–0. Gutierrez had set his mark in a twelve-inning game, but Stennett's seven straight hits—four singles, two doubles, and a triple—came in the regulation distance; actually, Stennett wrapped up his day's work in *eight* innings, and then was allowed to sit out

Max Lapides, by his own careful, historian's estimate, has attended at least twelve hundred Tiger games. Looking back from this Everest over a baseball landscape of almost forty years, he still has no difficulty in selecting the greatest Tiger games of his time; in the spring of 1967, acting out of a pure, Thucydidean sense of duty, he wrote a considerable monograph on the two—or, in strict fact, three—battles that remained brightest in his memory. (Today, he has said, he might have to add either the fifth or the seventh game of the 1968 World Series, when the Tigers came back from an almost hopeless disadvantage to defeat the Cardinals for the World Championship.) On the night of June 23, 1950, playing at home, the Tigers gave up four home runs to the Yankees in the first four innings, to fall behind by 6–0; in their half of the fourth they hit four home runs of their own, including a grand slam by pitcher Dizzy Trout, altogether good for eight runs. Homers by Joe DiMaggio and Tommy Henrich again put the visitors ahead, by 9–8, but Hoot Evers won the thing with a two-run inside-the-park homer in the bottom of the ninth. This Waterloo—eleven homers, sixty-two total bases, all nineteen runs the result of home runs—still holds a number of all-time baseball records (perhaps including "Frightened Pitchers, Most"), but Max's true fanly preference falls upon quite a different game, a two-part event of almost total austerity that began on July 21, 1945, when the Tigers and the Athletics played a twenty-four-inning, 1–1 standoff in Philadelphia. (Max Lapides happened to see this afternoon of mime because he had just begun his freshman year at the University of Pennsylvania. He also happened to see every game played by the Tigers at Shibe Park during his undergraduate years. Later in the summer of 1945, he and a college friend took a train to

the ninth. The next day, Stennett singled on his first two trips to the plate and then at last popped out, after nine straight safeties. The first (and only other) seven-for-seven performance was achieved in 1892 by Wilbert Robinson, of the Baltimore Orioles, which was at that time a National League club. Gutierrez—as Bert now sometimes murmurs to himself—still holds the American League consecutive-hit record for one game.

Washington to see a significant series between the Tigers and the Senators, who were then neck and neck in the pennant race; the students slept on park benches, subsisted on hot dogs and cornflakes, and saw five games in three days.) That 1–1 game was rescheduled for September 12, 1945, and again the Tigers and Athletics froze at 1–1 after nine innings, and then at 2–2 after eleven. The A's won at last, in the sixteenth inning, and Max's precise and admirable account—his prose style may owe something to a press-box titan of his boyhood, H. G. Salsinger, of the Detroit *News*—concludes ringingly:

> It was a fatal move. The exhausted Dazzler [Dizzy Trout] had nothing left—even in the dark shadows of Shibe Park. . . . Next came the troublesome Estalella, always a thorn in the Tiger paw. . . . Roberto and Diz battled to a full count and then, swinging late in the murky dusk, the Cuban sliced a sharp line drive to the right-field corner. Cullenbine, shading center field for the righthanded batter, never had a chance as Smith raced around to score the winning run and wrap up the "longest game" in baseball history after forty innings of play.
>
> Two days later, whatever justice there was for the Tigers came when Leslie Mueller defeated the Athletics 1–0 in a five-inning game, while allowing only two hits.

•

On a Saturday morning late last May, Bert Gordon and Don Shapiro drove to the Detroit Metropolitan Airport to meet Max Lapides, who was returning from Chicago to attend his first Tiger game of the year with his old friends. Max's wife and their two young daughters were staying in their Detroit home, in the suburban Birmingham section, until the end of the school year, so Max's exile was still leavened by weekend paroles. On the way to the airport, Bert and Don considered the awful possibility that Max might someday be converted to the White Sox, but the subject died of unlikelihood, and in time the two began comparing some Tiger managers. Red Rolfe (1949–52), it was agreed, had been decent; Fred Hutchinson (1952–54) had been sound but touched with temper; Charlie Dressen (1963–66) had been deep in knowledge but past his prime. Surprisingly, the vote for the best manager since Mickey Cochrane (1934–38) went to the incumbent, Billy Martin, who had taken an aged Tiger team into the playoffs the previous fall, and who had the same seniors currently, if barely, at the top of their division again. "He's winning ball games," said Don, "and that's absolutely all that counts."

"Plus he's exciting," said Bert. "This is the first time since I was eleven years old that you see a Tiger base runner go from second to third on a fly ball."

Another passenger inquired about Mayo Smith, the pilot who brought the Tigers to within one game of a pennant in 1967, and who won it all the following year. There was a painful pause, and then Don Shapiro, the resident strategist, said, "Listen, there were times when Mayo Smith was managing, and he would call in somebody from the bullpen, and I would know who he had chosen and I knew that he was going to be wrong. I knew the game was down the drain, and so did everybody else in the ball park. Why, that sense of impending disaster was so strong you could almost chart it. It was palpable. And then the disaster would happen. Mayo Smith absolutely lacked that mystical foreknowledge of baseball events, and as a manager you *have* to have that. Oh, this man was a monkey on my back for so long, and the worst part of it was that everybody loved Mayo Smith, because he was such a nice guy and such a charming guy. Mayo the nice poker companion, Mayo the great drinking companion—nobody had anything bad to say about him, and it was all absolutely true except for one thing: the man was overwhelmingly inept. Oh, boy, I hated that man, and I hated myself for hating him. I probably would have *killed* him if I'd run into him in '67 after he blew the pennant for us." The Tigers lost a famous three-way race on the last day of the 1967 season, when the Red Sox won the pennant by beating the Minnesota Twins while the Tigers lost the second game of a doubleheader to the California Angels at home. "That last game, he did everything wrong," Don went on. "He let our pitcher stay in, and I was standing up on my seat screaming, 'Take him out! Take him out!' I was blind with rage. I can still see what happened next—that pitch coming in to the Angels' Fregosi, and Fregosi getting ready to hit it—and I can see the ball going through the hole between short and third, and I can see the man coming around third to put them ahead. And then, like everybody else in this town, I can still see Dick McAuliffe, in the ninth, hitting into only his second double play of the entire season, to end it all. Listen, I'm like a dying man; I can see that whole game flashing before my eyes. It was like a scene out of Fellini, because right in back of me this guy is sitting there and listening to a *football* game—it was a Sunday, and football was on—and his radio is blaring football as the runner is rounding third base, and Mayo Smith is standing there, riveted to that post of his, holding up the dugout." He shook his head and laughed hollowly. "That was the day I came home and went down in the basement and broke all our flowerpots."

Bert, from the front seat, said, "Think about something happier. Think about 1968."

"The trouble with you is you don't suffer enough," Don said.

"I don't *suffer* enough!" said Bert, shouting with laughter. "I'm Jewish, I'm short, I'm fat, I'm poor, I'm ugly—what else do you want me to suffer?"

"That's all true," Don said, looking at his friend affectionately. "A man like you probably can't bear the necessary onus of suffering. After all, this isn't just a game of ours. It isn't just a preoccupation. It isn't an obsession. It's a—well, it's a—"

They said it together: "It's an obsession."

At the airport, Max was met and hugged, and the car aimed back toward the ball park. Suddenly, it was a party.

"Everything is fine, I guess," Max said. "Only, I miss my friends, now I'm with them again. I like this so much I may do it every week. But things are not fine back there, really. Listen, the other night when we beat the Yanks I turned on the TV in Chicago and the guy forgot to give the Tigers' score. He absolutely forgot. I couldn't get to sleep until four in the morning. Nobody knew. You pick up the morning paper in Chicago, and it says, 'N.Y. at Detroit (n.).' I mean, doesn't a man have a Constitutional right to the box scores?" He said that he was sometimes able to pick up Ernie Harwell on his car radio. "It only happens a little bit outside the city, on the north side," he added. "Sometimes it's only a snatch of the game broadcast, with a lot of static, but I can always tell from Ernie's voice how we're doing. Anyway, that's how come we bought the new house in Highland Park—so I can get the broadcasts and be closer to drive to all the Tiger games in Milwaukee. Fortunately, my wife likes the area."

At the ball park, the three friends sat in their accustomed place, in Section 24, between first and home; Tiger Stadium is an ancient, squared-off green pleasance, and the view was splendid. None of the three bought scorecards. ("The thing to do," Bert said, "is *remember*.") The World Champion Oakland A's, who had barely beaten out the Tigers in a violent five-game playoff the previous fall, were the opposition, and a modest but enthusiastic audience was filling up the nearby seats. Don Shapiro has a dark, vivid face—a downturned mustache, some lines of pain, some lines of hope—and he now looked about with satisfaction and clapped his hands. "Well!" he said. "Well, well. What could be nicer than this? I mean that. I really mean it. I'm supremely happy. I like this park even better than my Eames chair." He caught sight of the Oakland starting pitcher, Ken Holtzman, warming up, and his face fell. "*Uh*-oh," he said. "A very tough man, and now I've got some ethnic problems, too. A Jewish pitcher against our guys."

The game was a quiet, almost eventless affair for the first few innings, but Don was a restless spectator, twisting and bending in his seat, grimacing, groaning occasionally, leaping up for almost every enemy out. In the fifth, Gene Tenace, the Oakland first baseman, hit a home run into the left-field stands, and Shapiro fell back into his seat. He stared at the concrete floor in silence. "God damn it," he muttered at last. "This is *serious.*" The A's added two more runs off the Detroit starter, Woodie Fryman, but in the bottom half the Tigers put together two singles, a walk, and a third single, by Bill Freehan, the Detroit catcher, to tie it up, and the party was delighted.

"That was a good little rally," Max said. "Just right. Lots of running, and we have a tie."

"Yes, I don't like that *one* big blow," Bert said.

Don, watching the game and his emotions simultaneously, announced, "I'm elated. I'm back to my original state of anxiety. But listen, Max, we're lucky they decided to pitch to Freehan."

"Yes," Max said. "First of all, I would walk him. But then I absolutely don't throw him any kind of up pitch like that."

Jim Northrup, the Tiger right fielder, came up to the plate in the sixth, and Bert said, "I still don't see why this guy doesn't hit about .380."

"We've been saying that for ten years," Don said.

Northrup flied out, and Rodriguez stood in. Bert cried, "Au-reeli-*oh!*"

"See, here's another one," Max said. "This guy hit nineteen homers one year, and everybody called him a home-run hitter. They've been waiting ever since."

"He hit *nineteen?*" said Bert.

"Yes, for the Angels."

"Not for us, of course."

"Aurelio has a lazy bat," Don said. "He doesn't whip that bat."

"Frank Bolling had a lazy bat, too," Max said.

"You can't remember Milt Bolling?" Bert said.

Rodriguez hit a two-run home run to left, and Max, waving his arms and laughing, cried, "Exactly what I said! He's a great home-run hitter. I always knew it. Anyway, Williams should have taken out Holtzman. The man was dying out there—anybody could see it."

In the eighth, however, the Oakland designated hitter, Deron Johnson, jumped on a pitch by a Detroit reliever named Tom Timmerman and drove it high into the left-field seats. The game was tied. There was an enormous silence, and Don Shapiro, holding his head, stood up and turned his back on the field. "I knew it," he said. "I *knew* it!" He swayed slightly. "Oh, listen to that damned organ, will you? They're playing funeral selections." (Another bitter cause: In 1966, Don and Max directed a barrage of letters at the Tigers' general manager, Jim Campbell, protesting the installation of an organ at the stadium. Max wrote, "Baseball games are baseball games, and vesper services are vesper sarvices." Don wrote, "Who in hell wants to hear 'Funiculi Funicula' in the middle of a Tiger rally?" Max wrote, "The object of a ball game for the fan is not to be entertained. It is to win." The organ was not removed.)

Rich Reese, leading off the bottom of the eighth, was walked, and hopes revived noisily. Dick Sharon stood in, and Max said, "He should bunt, but we have the worst bunting team in history."

"It's an absolute must-bunt situation," Don agreed. Last year, Don mailed a lengthy letter to Billy Martin outlining a new defense for the must-bunt, which involved sending the second baseman to charge the plate on the right side of the diamond, instead of the traditional move by the first baseman. Don's plan quoted from his correspondence with the Michigan State baseball coach, Danny Litwhiler, who had devised the new play. No answer came from Martin, but his response, relayed later to Don, was "I don't go for that funny stuff."

Here, in any case, Sharon did bunt, and was safe when first baseman Tenace muffed the ball. A moment later, Northrup smacked a triple for the go-ahead runs—good enough, it turned out, for the game. The Tigers won, 8–5, and Don, on his feet and clapping, had brightened perceptibly. "I was never worried for an instant," he said. A moment later, he added, "Well, that's a lie. My trouble is I tend to view these games viscerally. Baseball gives me that endogenous epinephrine. I'm hooked on my own adrenaline."

•

DETROIT IN the nineteen-thirties had few visible civic or economic virtues, but it just may have been the best baseball town in the country. The Tigers—a dangerous and contentious team built around the power hitting of the enormous Hank Greenberg, and around Charlie Gehringer and Mickey Cochrane and, later, Rudy York, and around the pitching of Schoolboy Rowe, Tommy Bridges, and, later, Bobo Newsom—did not win nearly as often as the lordly Yankees, but victory, when it came, was treasured. There was a pennant in 1934 (the first since 1909), a championship in 1935 (the first ever for Detroit), and another pennant in 1940. At his home on Tuxedo Avenue, young Don Shapiro, listening to games over Station WWJ in the afternoon, tried to work magic spells to make the Tigers win: twenty-eight baby steps across his bedroom without losing his balance could bring Gehringer a hit (not quite pure magic, since Gehringer's batting average between 1933 and 1940 was .336). The Ernie Harwell of those Piltdown days was Ty Tyson, for Mobil Oil and "The Sign of the Flying Red . . . Horse!," who called Greenberg "Hankus-Pankus" and Schoolboy Rowe "Schoolhouse" or "Schoolie." ("For a pitcher, Schoolie is sure pickin' 'em up and layin' 'em down.") Whenever they could, Don and Bert and their friends took the Trumbull Avenue streetcar at noontime to the ball park, then called Navin Field, and stood beside an iron gate on the corner of National Street, behind home plate. In time, the gate rolled up, to a great clattering of chains, and a Tigers' supervisor would conduct a mini-shape-up ("You and you and you and *you* over there") for the job of assistant ushers. The designees took up their posts in the outer reaches of the upper deck, beyond the uniformed regulars, and returned batting-practice fly balls and dusted seats and, between times, eyed the Olympians on the field: not just Greenberg and Gehringer and Rowe but the others—Marv Owen and Gee Walker and Elon Hogsett and Pete Fox, and batboy Whitey Willis and trainer Denny Carroll and groundskeeper Neil Conway. A lot of the players lived in apartment houses out on Chicago and Dexter Boulevards, or Boston and Dexter, and if you walked out there and waited long enough, you could sometimes pick up an autograph. The game and the players must have seemed very near in those days. Once, in 1936, when Don Shapiro was twelve years old, he played catch with Tiger first baseman Jack Burns, who split Don's left thumb with a throw; the wonderful stigma—a white cicatrix on the first knuckle—is still visible.

Bert Gordon's father, a rabbi, was a passionate fan who sometimes got his tickets through the Detroit Council of Churches, which provided free seats for the clergy. "I'd be sitting beside him at the park, and I'd say 'Father—' and the whole section would turn around," Bert said recently. He laughed, and went on, "My father was a city man—like all our fathers, I guess. He never went fishing, or anything. It was baseball that was the bond between us. Baseball was the whole thing. I don't think anybody can imagine the terrific importance of Hank Greenberg to the whole Jewish community then. He was a god, a true folk hero. That made baseball acceptable to our parents, so for once they didn't mind if we took a little time off from the big process of getting into college. And then, of course, Hank Greenberg was so big and so handsome—a handsome giant. Plus he didn't change his name. I can remember Rosh Hashanah, or some day like that, in 1938, when Hank was going after Babe Ruth's record of sixty home runs in a season. Of course, nobody in the synagogue could go near a radio that day, but somebody came in late from the parking lot with a report about the game, and the news went through the congregation like a *wind*."

Don kept a scrapbook that summer, pasting up Greenberg's

pictures and box scores and headlines ("HANK'S NINE DAYS AHEAD!"). Under one photograph of Greenberg swinging a bat, he penciled "There she goes!" and under the headline "HANK NEEDS FOUR HOMERS IN NINE GAMES TO TIE" he wrote "Two bits he does it!" He was wrong; Hank hit fifty-eight, falling shy of the record by two. A year or two earlier, Greenberg had accepted an invitation to dinner with some friends of his who had a house in Max Lapides' part of town, and word was sent out that he would shake hands with the neighborhood kids. The excited juniors lined up (in their sweatshirts with Greenberg's number 5 inked on the back, and carrying, nearly all of them, first basemen's mitts), but Max was not among them, for he had broken a leg a few days before and was forbidden to get out of bed. He cried himself to sleep that night, but he was awakened by his father turning on the light and ushering Hank Greenberg into the room. The sudden visitor was so enormous, Max recalls, that he had to duck his head to get through the door. Greenberg sat on Max's bed and talked to him for half an hour. Before he left, he took out a pen and signed Max's cast and then, seeing a copy of Max's favorite baseball book—*Safe!*, by Harold Sherman—on the bedside table, he signed that, too.

"In our household, we used to talk about only three things—current events, the Jewish holidays, and baseball," Max has said. "You have to try to remember how much easier it was to keep up with all the baseball news back then. For us, there were just the Tigers and the seven other teams in the American League, so we knew them by heart. All the games were played in the afternoon, and none of the teams was in a time zone more than an hour away from Detroit, so you got just about all the scores when the late-afternoon papers came. You could talk about that at supper, and then there were the stories in the morning papers to read and think about the next day. Why, in those days we knew more about the farms than I know about some of the West Coast teams right now. By the time a Hoot

Evers or a Fred Hutchinson was ready to come up from Beaumont, we knew all about him."

Max's father, Jack, did not need Hank Greenberg to introduce him to baseball. *His* father, in turn, had been a butcher in Rochester, New York, and young Jack Lapides had often made the morning rounds in the family cart and then sat next to his father in a saloon and studied the pictures of the baseball players of the day—with their turtleneck uniforms and handlebar mustaches—up above the big, cool bar mirror. Jack Lapides had a laundry business in Detroit, and by the nineteen thirties he had arranged things well enough so that in the stirring seasons of 1934 and 1935 he was able to attend every single Tiger home game and many on the road. "My father used to take me to fifty or sixty games a year," Max recalled this summer, "and I recently became aware that between us we encompassed just about the entire history of big-league ball in this century. He went to most of the games every year right up to the end of his life, in 1967. I'd met Don by then, and in those last few years he would come along with us, too."

Don Shapiro's father, a tallow merchant, knew nothing about baseball, but one of Don's uncles was a junk dealer who owned a semipro team in Lapeer, Michigan; and even as a very young boy, Don was sometimes allowed to sit on the bench with the players. That was enough—more than enough—to start it all for him. Don has a vivid and affectionate memory of Jack Lapides. "He was a very formal man, a reserved sort of man," he said not long ago, "and I can still see him sitting up there in the stands, in his coat and collar and tie, with one hand on the railing in front of him. He kept me and Max on our toes. 'Pay attention, boys,' he always said. 'This is a serious business.' "

•

It is another Saturday, the last day in June, and Max is back from Chicago again, to be with his family and his Tigers and his Tiger friends. This time, it has been decided, the game will be watched on television, and the three meet for lunch at Bert's big, comfortable house in Huntington Woods. Before lunch, Max and Don throw a baseball back and forth in Bert's backyard; according to custom, each is wearing the top half of a gray Tiger road uniform. The name on Don's back, above the number 42, is SZOTKIEWICZ; Max is 21, ZEPP. The shirts, which are both beautifully pressed, were gifts from Ernie Harwell, who extracted them from the Tiger clubhouse after the brief, almost unnoticed careers of two Tiger foot soldiers—Kenny Szotkiewicz and Bill Zepp—had come to a close. (Harwell, who is a friend and admirer of Don Shapiro, telephoned Don from Cleveland one afternoon late in the 1966 season, and asked if he would care to work out with the Tigers before their game with the Indians that evening. Don canceled his appointments, flew to Cleveland and suited up, was introduced to Tiger manager Frank Skaff—who may have been a trifle surprised to find that the "prospect" Harwell had promised him was a slight, forty-two-year-old oral surgeon—and then warmed up with Don Wert, Ray Oyler, Willie Horton, and the rest. In photographs of the event, which hang on the wall of Don's living room, the ballplayers look bemused, but the prospect is ecstatic.) Max begins throwing harder now, and Don, who has a catcher's mitt and is wearing a Tiger cap on backward, goes into a crouch. Max's motion is a little stiff, but you can see in it the evidences of a fair high-school ballplayer. Don handles his glove elegantly, coming up smoothly and in one motion after each pitch and snapping the throw back from behind his shoulder. He is smiling. He caught briefly for the University of Michigan varsity and, later, on a Sixth Service Command team in Chicago. The ball is beginning to pop in the gloves, and Bert, umpiring from behind the invisible mound, expresses concern for his wife's borders. Max pauses for breath and reminds everyone of a similar pregame workout some years ago when a small protective sponge fell out of

Don's glove. "All he could say was 'These hands. These golden hands.' From catcher to surgeon in one second."

"Throw the ball," says the catcher-surgeon.

"Knuckler," says Max.

"Hey!" says Don. "Not bad. Again."

The next knuckleball sails over Don's head and through the hedge.

"OK, that's it," Bert declares, calling the game. "Zena will kill me."

"Listen," Don says as they troop toward Bert's sun porch. "I think my arm is coming back. I really mean that. Wouldn't that be *something*, to get my arm back after all this time?" He notices that a lacing on his mitt has come loose, and he stops to tie it up. "Goddam dog," he murmurs.

The Tigers, who have recently lost eight straight and have slipped to fifth place, are playing the rising Orioles, but they score two unearned runs off Mike Cuellar in the first inning, and in the second Mickey Stanley hits a home run. The Tiger pitcher is a big, strong-looking young right-hander named Mike Strahler. The friends sit in easy chairs in Bert's study, with plates of sandwiches and salad in their laps. Zena Gordon, Bert's wife, brings around seconds. Brian Gordon, Bert's younger son, who is sixteen, comes in and watches for an inning or two and then wanders out again. The Gordons' other son, Merrill, is away at his summer job. He is a Michigan State sophomore, who wants to become a forester; he does not care about baseball. "He thinks it's a lot of men running around in funny suits," Bert explains. Bert used to take Merrill to games, but the summer Merrill was eleven years old he finally got up the nerve to tell his father that baseball meant nothing to him. "Everything you do in life, you do so that your son will go to ball games with you, and then he doesn't want to," Bert says now. He makes a joke of it, but at the time the news shook him so severely that he himself hardly went to the ball park for two years. "If my family wanted to be home, I wanted to be home with them," he says. Max Lapides has two daughters, who are seven and eleven; he says he can't tell yet about them and baseball. Don's son, Alan, who is fifteen, is crazy about baseball. He catches for a team called the Rangers in his suburban Colt League, and he watches the Tigers with something of his father's unhappy intensity. Still, there are no streetcars that run from his house to the ball park, and it is almost certain that he will never discover a baseball world that is as rich and wide as his father's. "You know what I really wish?" Alan said to Don one day last spring. "I wish I had friends like yours."

The wives of the three friends apparently accept their husbands' zealotry and their arcane closed company; indeed, they have no choice, since they cannot enter it on anything like even terms, and none of them, in truth, is much of a fan. Max and Sissi Lapides used to go to several games together each year, but then during one Yankee game, with the score tied at 6–6 in the eighth inning, Max noticed that his wife was quietly reading a book under her program, and it was thenceforth agreed that their interests in the pastime were not really comparable. Sue Shapiro is an admitted front-runner, who gets excited about the Tigers only when they are doing well. "Don is a fan," she said recently. "It's a fact of his life, so I have no trouble with it at all."

The game at Bert's house glides along, with the Tigers leading the Orioles by 4–1 after the fifth, and everything apparently in hand; the lighted figures move distantly on the screen, the room deepens in shadow, and the men lean back in their big chairs and let the baseball lull them. There is nothing to be concerned about except Kaline's average (computed today by Bert on a pocket calculator), and now, after his second unsuccessful trip to the plate, the figures slip at last to .2994788, and Al Kaline is no longer a lifetime .300 man. It is sad; this may be Kaline's last year. Then, a bit later, Eddie Brinkman singles, and Tiger first-base coach Dick Tracewski slaps him on the rump as he stands on the bag. Max Lapides says, "I wonder who holds the lifetime record for handing out most pats on the ass."

"It has to be Crosetti," Bert says instantly. "All those years he stood there in the third-base box for the Yankees and slapped all those big guys as they came around. He must be ahead by thousands."

"A true piece of baseball trivia!" Max shouts.

"You can't *say* 'baseball trivia,' " Don says. "It's a contradiction in terms. It's antithetical. We don't use the word 'trivia.' "

"OK, then," Max says. "OK—how about 'A Compendium of Little-Known Facts'?"

•

WE CANNOT quite leave these friends here—three aging men, laughing together still, but too comfortable with their indoor, secondhand sport, and too much like the rest of us. Perhaps this sort of unremarkable fandom is what is ahead for them now; perhaps not. Bert Gordon, who worries about his health, goes to fewer and fewer night games. "You get older," he says. "It gets colder." Max Lapides, much happier in his Chicago job than he was in the old one in Detroit, has less time to call Bert with a baseball stumper in the middle of the morning. "I'm beginning to change a little," he confessed recently. "Sometimes I even put an old player on the wrong team by a year or two. I sometimes think that after the big years of '67 and '68 I couldn't really stay intense *all* summer about the Tigers if they were playing under-.500 ball again. I'm looking at it all from farther off, I guess." The Lapides family now lives in Highland Park, Illinois, where the new school year is just beginning; by next April the late Tiger scores will bother Max a little less. The Tigers, in any case, have just about slipped from contention for this year; now in third place, behind Baltimore and Boston, they trail the division-leading Orioles by seven games—a margin that, according to Bert's calculator, will require them to play at an .864 clip throughout September (plus a helpful Baltimore slump to a .500 level) in order to bring about another miracle. The friends have also lost Billy Martin, who, despite their stamp of approval, was recently fired as the manager of the Tigers. It's been a hard season. No matter; these three men should be remembered in full summer, and at their home ball park, for it is there that they, like a few other great fans in other cities, made their game into something resembling a private work of art. It is a modest genre, to be sure, and terribly dated now, but still perhaps not one to be put aside too quickly. At the very least, these gentle prodigals have used their sport to connect themselves to their fathers and to their boyhood and to their city—the inner city that they long since lost and left—and also to connect themselves to friends with whom they could share a passion, a special language, and an immense private history. Baseball has been a family to them.

Don Shapiro, perhaps the most intricate of the three, may be the only one who will not change—the last to give up that mad, splendid hope of one absolutely perfect season: one hundred and sixty-two straight wins for his Tigers. Late last May, Don went to a night game against the Oakland A's, and after eight and a half innings the score still stood at 0–0. Mickey Stanley led off the ninth for the Tigers with a single, and Gates Brown came up to bat. "He's got to bunt. He's *got* to!" Don said, watching the field intently. "He's got to bunt, but he can't. Just wait and see." He was right; Brown swung away and singled to right, sending Stanley to third, as vast sounds of joy rose in the night. Oakland changed pitchers, and Duke Sims struck out. Tony Taylor batted for Cash, and on the one-and-two count Stanley set sail for the plate at full career, and Taylor, bunting on the suicide squeeze, fouled the ball off and was out.

"I don't *believe* it!" Don cried hoarsely. "They've lost their minds down there! They're trying to kill me. They're doing it on purpose. If they don't do it, I'll have to kill myself."

Dick McAuliffe then struck out, taking the called third

strike without moving his bat from his shoulder, and the rally and the inning ended. Don, who had been standing and clutching his temples, now sat down and buried his head in his arms. He shuddered, and at last forced himself to look out at the emerald field. "If we lose, this is the worst game I ever saw," he announced.

• • •

FOLLOWING THE Tigers has not become any easier since this report was written. Kaline and Cash and Northrup and McAuliffe and other stalwarts have departed; the team finished third in its division in 1973, and dead last in 1974 and 1975. Thanks to some new stars like Ron LeFlore and Mark Fidrych, they moved up to fifth place in 1976 but finished twenty-four games behind the division-winning Yankees. The three great fans, it is comforting to report, have changed much less than their team. Max Lapides, now entirely at home in Chicago, has not turned to the White Sox or the Cubs for solace. He follows the Tigers as best he can, sometimes calling Bert for a good long catch-up on the team, and he goes to every Tiger game within reach. Two years ago, in June, he arranged things so that he was able to drive to Milwaukee and back on three successive days—a total of more than five hundred miles—to watch a Tigers-Brewers series. The Tigers lost the first game, 8–4; on the second day, they dropped a doubleheader, 5–0 and 4–2; they also lost the last game, 5–4.

President Nixon resigned from office on August 9, 1974, thus relieving Bert Gordon of one of his self-imposed morning tasks; the last reading on Bert's calculator showed that Mr. Nixon had surrendered 30.62970 percent of his White House tenancy. Bert's other vigil ended in October 1974, when Al Kaline retired. Shortly before game-time on the afternoon of the Tigers' final home game that year, Bert suddenly realized that he was missing his last chance to see Kaline in action. He jumped in his car and raced for Tiger Stadium. He turned on the car radio and heard Ernie Harwell describe Kaline's first turn at bat in the game; he parked in his regular lot and was hurrying across Michigan Avenue to the ball park when he heard the crowd roar that greeted Kaline's second appearance. Bert went in and happily took his seat, and for an inning or two he did not notice that Kaline had left the lineup after that second time up—left it for good. "I got up and went home," Bert said later. "There wasn't even anybody there I could *tell* about it. It was the story of my life." The next morning, in his office, he punched out the final Kaline numbers: 10,116 at-bats, 3007 hits, for a lifetime batting average of .2972518.

Since then, Bert has suffered the diminution of Cesar Gutierrez at the hands of Rennie Stennett, and one day last summer, when he was idly skimming the box scores, it suddenly came to him that Ed Figueroa, the Yankee pitcher, has all five vowels in his *last* name. "Goodbye, Aurelio," Bert wrote in a letter to Max. "I still can't believe the whole thing."

Don Shapiro gave up on the Tigers in the terrible season of 1975, when they lost 102 games and finished 37½ games behind the division-leading Red Sox. "I hated myself," he says, "but I couldn't help it. They were literally killing me." Last year, when the young Tigers suddenly began knocking off the Yankees and the champion Red Sox in surprising fashion, Don allowed himself to be won back. He called me late in the summer and told me that he and Bert were going to Tiger Stadium that night. "This Mark Fidrych is pitching," he said, "and he's got a little color, you know. At least, I think he does—we're not used to that sort of thing here in Detroit, so it's hard to tell. And Ralph Houk [the incumbent Detroit manager] is so lackluster that it has this deadening effect on everybody, especially me. But I'm getting optimistic again, I think. I really am. The fires are being stoked."

7 Mets Redux

October 1973

All sporting memories are suspect—the colors too bright, the players and their feats magnified in our wishful recapturing. The surprising rally or splendid catch becomes incomparable by the time we fight free of the parking lot, epochal before bedtime, transcendental by breakfast. Quickly, then, before we do damage to the crowded and happy events of the late summer and early autumn, it should be agreed that this was not absolutely the best of all baseball years. The absorbing, disheveled seven-game World Series that was won by the defending Oakland A's, who had to come from behind to put down the tatterdemalion Mets, was probably not up to the quality of the seven low-scoring games contested by the A's and the Cincinnati Reds last year, or even comparable to three or four other classics we have been given in the past dozen Octobers. As for the Mets, the general rejoicing over their deserved victory in their league did not match the passions or disbelief of 1969, when the Amazin's did it all first and better; these 1973 Mets finished their season with a won-lost percentage of .509, the lowest ever recorded by a winner or demiwinner in either league. Not a vintage year, then, but not a vapid one by any means. Both the league playoffs went to the full five games, as they did last year, with the Orioles and the Reds going down bitterly at the very end. The unforgiving brevity of these Championship Series, which can sink a proud summer flagship in the space of three unlucky afternoons, is just beginning to be understood by the players, who now look on them with far more concern and apprehension than they do the World Series. It was during the playoffs, it will be remembered, when the Mets' and Reds' squads threw themselves to scuffling and punching in the infield dirt, when showers of trash came out of the left-field stands of Shea Stadium, and when the Met fans, at the very pinnacle of their joy, fell into hysteria and violence. All of this, to be sure, made for some wonderfully eventful and discussable days and weeks—a time in which baseball almost seemed to return to its central place in our autumn attention.

There were many fresh discoveries and speculations to be found in the season's statistics. Nolan Ryan, the California Angels' fireballing right-hander, and an ex-Met (*there's* a speculation!), struck out 383 batters, to erase (by one whiff) Sandy Koufax's old one-season record. The White Sox, early leaders in the American League West, collapsed after an injury to their star slugger, Dick Allen, and attained a startling low when two of their pitchers, Wilbur Wood and Stan Bahnsen, became twenty-game losers in the same season. The Yankees, leading their division at the All-Star Game break, lost drearily and implacably through August and September, and finished seventeen games off the pace; in the end, they also lost not only their manager, Ralph Houk, who resigned and moved along, probably to pilot the Tigers next season, but their ball park, which will be closed for alterations for the next two years. Suddenly the poorest of poor cousins, the Yankees will now have to share Shea Stadium with the National League Champion Mets—their first clear shot at likableness in forty years.

The season-long assault mounted by Hank Aaron against Babe Ruth's lifetime total of 714 home runs—perhaps the most widely memorized figure in baseball—utterly captivated the sporting press. Aaron's progress was so numbingly over-reported that the real news was not his season-ending total of 713, one shy of the Babe, but the fact that he was able to function at all on the field in the presence of a hovering daily horde of newsmen, network camera crews, photographers, publicity flacks, souvenir hunters, advertising moguls, league officials, and other assorted All-American irritants and distracters. All those magazine cover stories, wire-service bulletins, and breathlessly updated daily figures were curious indeed, because Aaron's splendid consistency at the plate and his remarkable athletic longevity have made his arrival at the sacred plateau very nearly inevitable for the past two or three years. Since there was no immediate time element in this particular achievement, the story had none of the tension and excitement of, say, Roger Maris's attack on Ruth's one-season mark of sixty homers. The next couple of clicks on the Aaron meter will come in April or May, then, and the only cause for concern will be whether the new numbers and the old hoopla will not somehow again obscure the kind of man and the kind of ballplayer Hank Aaron is. Observers back from the Atlanta tent show have told me that Aaron sustained a three-month-long attack on his privacy and concentration with absolute patience and good humor. Playing under these conditions, at the age of thirty-nine, he enjoyed an exceptional season at the plate—40 home runs and a batting average of .301. Skipping the second games of doubleheaders and afternoon games played after night games, he struck his 40 round-trippers in only 392 official at-bats—a rate of production exceeded only six times in baseball history. Let it be noted, too, that Aaron and Ruth and Willie Mays, who retired last month with 660 homers to his credit, are the only three ballplayers to attain even 600 lifetime home runs; the next nearest, Harmon Killebrew, is more than a hundred back of Mays, with 546. Aaron's over-.300 season—his fourteenth in twenty years in the majors—was achieved despite a miserable start; from June 15 on, he batted .354. A wonderful year, then, but very nearly an ordinary one for Hank Aaron. His cumulative home-run totals have been ticked off, year after year, with almost machinelike regularity. Never hitting as many as 50 in a single season, he has averaged (since his first three warm-up seasons) very close to 36 or 37 per year for every three-year span over the past seventeen seasons; that level is actually up a bit in the past five years, when he has averaged 40 per year. To look at this another way, he notched his 100-homer marks in his fourth, seventh, tenth, thirteenth, fifteenth, eighteenth, and twentieth summers. Next summer, his twenty-first (showing us, as always, the perfect daily temperament for this most daily of all sports, and that familiar grooved, elegant, iron-wristed, late, *late* swing), he not only will pass the Babe in homers but will probably also move up to first place in times at bat and runs batted in, adding these to his present records of most extra-base hits and most total bases. What else? Well, one more statistic: Hank Aaron, soon to possess the No. 1 record attainable in his sport, also ranks No. 1 alphabetically; his is the very first name on the all-time roster of the thousands and thousands of players recorded in big-league box scores. Figuring the odds against *that* meaningless wonder should take us all a good way along toward spring training.

•

The Mets—ah, the Mets! Superlatives do not quite fit them, but now, just as in 1969, the name alone is enough to bring back that rare inner smile that so many of us wore as the summer ended. The memory of what these Mets were in midseason and the knowledge of what they became suggest that they are in the peculiar position of being simultaneously overrated and patronized in our recollection. Their microscopic winning margin at the end of the regular season and their frightful, groaning struggles to get their chin up over the .500 bar should not obscure their startling march from the bottom to very nearly the top of the baseball world in the space of two months. This sustained burst of winning, stouthearted play took them to within a single game of the world championship, though they appeared to have been frighteningly outmanned all along the way. They were lucky and persevering and optimistic, but far less inspired by their own unlikelihood than the startled young heroes of '69 were. This time was a lot harder. "I've never known a season that was any more work than this one," shortstop Bud Harrelson said one night near the end. "We played our asses off. *No one* in this club had an easy year, and almost every game—even the big wins—seemed like hard, hard work. We deserve everything we get this time." Rusty Staub, just after his splendid four-hit, five-runs-batted-in performance in the fourth game of the World Series, soberly explained that it was the result of "concentration and hard work," and Wayne Garrett, after an essential September win over the Pirates, made a pushing, snowplow gesture with both hands and said, "Games like this—all these games—you've got to . . . *wedge* it out."

In the middle of August, hard work did not appear to offer much of an answer. Dead last in their division, the Mets were a team flattened by injuries and abandoned by their fans. At one time or another, eight of their players were on the disabled list. Catcher Jerry Grote broke his wrist. Bud Harrelson broke his hand and then his breastbone. Left-handed ace Jon Matlack was struck by a line drive and suffered a hairline fracture of the skull. John Milner, Cleon Jones, Rusty Staub, George Theodore, and Willie Mays were sidelined with ailments, and ace reliever Tug McGraw, with an earned-run average over the past two seasons of 1.70, was suddenly and mysteriously unable to get anybody out—and, in the words of Manager Yogi Berra, "if you ain't got a bullpen, you ain't got nothin'." Yogi himself was said to be on the way out—a charming relic, insufficient in ideas and words. His one tenet was the repeated and miserably evident observation that the Mets had not yet made their move.

The first tiny stirring was McGraw's good outing against the Giants on August 11—in a game the Mets finally lost in the thirteenth inning. On August 18, Bud Harrelson, the infield's main man, returned to the lineup, and the Mets whacked the powerful Reds by 12–1. That began the time of hard labors—a close, heartening win or two, a terribly discouraging loss—but now the pitching (Seaver, Matlack, Koosman, George Stone, and McGraw and rookie Harry Parker in the bullpen) was clearly terrific at last, and everybody knew that if this club was going to go anywhere it would be on its pitching. Weirdly, though the Mets were still twelve under the .500 level late in the month, they trailed the division-leading Cardinals by a mere six and a half games. On the last day of August, the Mets climbed over the Phillies and into fifth place. Belief ("You gotta be-leeve!"—*The Sayings of Chairman McGraw*) had begun.

In September, the NL East was a crowded and dangerous tenement. The Cardinals led for a while and then gave way to the Pirates, who had made a hunchy late change of managers, replacing Bill Virdon with his predecessor, Danny Murtaugh. The Cubs, a team of elders that had wasted an enormous early-summer lead, had still not expired, and in among them all was the true surprise of the year—the Montreal Expos, who were suddenly getting wonderful pitching from a rookie named Steve Rogers and from relief man Mike Marshall, and some long-ball hitting by a former Met, Ken Singleton. On September 7, the Mets won a chilly, edgy doubleheader in Montreal by 1–0 and 4–2; the nightcap was 1–1 through fourteen innings, and that Met run had come in after Expo infielder Pepe Frias dropped an easy pop fly. The next day, Steve Rogers outpitched Seaver, winning 3–1, and the ravished, wintry Montreal fans dreamed their *drapeau* dreams again.

A week later, the Mets beat the Cubs, 4–3, at Shea on a suicide squeeze bunt by Jerry Grote. They were in fourth place, but only two and a half games behind the first-place Pirates, and the five immediately upcoming games with Pittsburgh—two away and then three back at home—would settle *something*. An insupportable something, perhaps, for the Pittsburgh sluggers bombed Tom Seaver that opening Monday, winning by 10–3, and then the next night the Pirates led again, by 4–1, in the top of the ninth. Here, however, the Mets pushed across five runs—the essential hits coming from benchpersons Jim Beauchamp and Ron Hodges. Since Tug McGraw had already completed his evening's outing, Yogi now entrusted this trembling lead to Bob Apodaca, a youngster just one day up from the minors, who instantly walked the first two major-league batters of his life, and was succeeded by Buzz Capra, who gave up a sacrifice, a run-scoring infield out, an intentional walk, an unintentional walk, and (to Manny Sanguillen, with the bases loaded) a strike, three balls, and, at excruciatingly long last, the fly-ball out that ended the game. Every Met, from that evening on, claimed that this was the inning that did it all.

Back to Shea then, and a brisk, heartening 7–3 Metsian victory that brought them to third place, one and a half back. Heartening because Cleon Jones, their brooding and enigmatic left fielder, whacked two homers and drove in five runs. Jones, one of the streakiest hitters imaginable, had apparently ended his season-long unstreak. The next night, the Mets came from behind three times, scoring one run each time, to tie at 3–3—more hard work—but then suddenly the sea parted, as it did so often in 1969, and one could sense that this week was going to be shining and famous. In the top of the thirteenth, the visitors' Richie Zisk singled off Ray Sadecki, and then Dave Augustine rocketed a deep, high sailer over Cleon Jones' head in left; the ball, descending implacably toward the bullpen, struck the very top of the fence—a fraction of an inch shy of a home run—and rebounded on a line into Cleon's grasp.

Startled, Jones whirled and threw to Garrett, who relayed to Ron Hodges at the plate, who collided with the sliding and truly startled Richie Zisk and tagged him out. One knew—one *knew*—that Hodges would then drive in the winning run in the bottom of the same inning.

This kind of baseball electrification changes everything, and the Pirates never looked like the same team after that ricochet. At Shea the next night, you could see fans—and, in their dugout, Pirates, too—pointing to the landmark spot just above the "5" in the middle of the "358" sign on the fence, where the Augustine carom shot had struck. Wayne Garrett then singled on the first Pittsburgh pitch of the evening, and the Mets ripped out eight hits and six runs in the first three innings, providing Tom Seaver with his first easy ride in weeks. An enormous crowd, most of them trooping in late after an epochal traffic jam, came to roar in exultation, and there were Met hits that bounced up into the faces of Pirate infielders and through the pitcher's legs and off the bag at third base, and there were resounding homers by Milner and Garrett and Staub, and the fans shouted "We're No. 1!" and Jane Jarvis played "You're the Top" on the organ, and the sign man held up a sign that said "ENTER AT YOUR OWN RISK!" and the scoreboard showed that Montreal had lost again—their fifth straight defeat—and when it was over (Mets 10, Pirates 2), the Mets really *were* No. 1: the first team in baseball history to go into first place and arrive at the .500 level on the same evening in September.

From then on—a week and a little more—every Met fan was caught up in a double sport, simultaneously catching the out-of-town news on the scoreboard and watching the dangerous business at hand. It was a time of almost continuous baseball excitement—hazard and reward, silence and shouted relief—from which each of us could select games and moments to store away: Matlack fanning the first three batters of the day, all swinging, and then utterly stifling the Cardinals in a swift, almost eventless 2–0 shutout; an enormous Sunday conviviality as the biggest crowd of the year celebrated a come-back 5–2 win over the Cards, nailed down at last by Garrett's triple and Cleon's homer and sterling long relief by Parker and short relief by Tug McGraw and the cheerful air full of wind-blown paper and hundreds upon hundreds of migrating mon-arch butterflies; Willie Mays Night—he was retiring at last, at the end of the season—with speeches and tears and awk-wardness and felicity (Willie, wiping his eyes: "I look at the kids over here, and the way they're playing and the way they're fighting for themselves, and that say one thing to me: 'Willie, say goodbye to America' "), and finally the release of the game, against Montreal and Steve Rogers, a 2–1 bleeder won twice by Cleon Jones, first with a homer and then with a breathtaking running catch in the deepest left-field corner, to save two runs; and then the sad, heavy letdown of an ominous loss to the Expos in the last regular-season game at Shea, with Seaver tired and wild and gone after two, and the Mets' fine comeback from a five-run deficit all for nothing, and the sud-denly revived awful doubt (with the cushion down to a bare half game) about whether there would be any more baseball back here this autumn after all.

The crucial final weekend, it will be remembered, was not so crucial after all, because the Pirates miserably and helpfully lost three close games in a row while the Mets waited through two rainouts in Chicago, and by the time play finally resumed there on Sunday the four barely breathing contenders—and the distant, astounding possibility of a five-way final tie—seemed to offer only a statistical menace. Matlack lost a painful 1–0 duel with the Cubs' Rick Reuschel, but then Koosman had a happier time of it in the nightcap—an error-filled 9–2 affair that finally did in the Cubs, as Montreal expired, too, in Pitts-burgh. Tom Seaver pitched the clincher in the rain on Monday —6–4 over the Cubs (with whole sectors of the wet, shining stands there absolutely empty)—and Cleon fittingly hit an-other home run (his seventh in eleven days), and McGraw fittingly got the save (his twelfth, plus four wins, in his last seventeen outings), and the champagne corks flew at last. A final scoreboard study suggests that four teams certainly lost this tattered half pennant but that the fifth just as surely won it. From mid-August on—after August 20, that is—the Cardinals (who finished second, one and a half games back) won 18 games and lost 20, while the terrible exertions of the Pirates, Expos, and Cubs brought them respective records of 21-21, 20-20, and 19-19—deadly, dead-even ball. The Mets, by contrast, went 27-13 after August 20, including 21 victories in their last 29 games, which translates out to .675: championship work in any league.

•

SINCE IT was clear to this experienced fan that the opening games of the American League playoffs between the Oakland A's and the Baltimore Orioles would offer a not-to-be-missed collision between the two best pitching staffs in baseball, I hopped the Metroliner to Baltimore, confidently postponing the Mets and Reds until the Shea Stadium part of their playoffs —and thereby missing, it turned out, the two best-pitched games of the month. In Baltimore, on an incomparable autumn afternoon and before the customarily comparable hometown crowd, Jim Palmer, the presiding Oriole right-hander, fanned six Oakland batters in the first two innings and went on to whiff six more in the course of shutting out the hairy green-and-gold defending champs by 6–0. This result was not wholly unexpected, since Palmer had won twenty-two games this year (it was his fourth straight twenty-game season) and his earned-run average of 2.40 was the best in his league. Dick Williams, the Oakland cogitator, attempted to counter these odds by opening with Vida Blue, the third-best of his three twenty-game winners. The presence of Blue, a southpaw, would deprive the Birds of Rich Coggins and Alonza Bumbry, two swift rookie outfielders, who both batted well above .300 this year, but who, being lefties, regularly played only against right-handed pitchers. This was typical baseball strategy, deeply moving in its beauty and profundity, and almost typical in its results: Baltimore batted around in the first inning, driving out Vida and scoring four runs, two of which were registered by Bumbry's and Coggins' replacements. Palmer's only difficulties were with his control—he threw more than 150 pitches—and with a terrifying line single by Oakland's Reggie Jackson, which he barely deflected, throwing himself backward on the mound just before it struck him in the face.

The next afternoon, Bumbry and Coggins combined in the first inning to help fashion a Baltimore run, and in the top of the third Bumbry gathered himself at the foot of the left-field fence—staring up and tensing and poising like a cat about to leap onto a bureau—and ascended perfectly to pluck back Sal Bando's drive just as it was departing the premises. Bando found balm for this disappointment by knocking two subsequent pitches a good deal higher and deeper, both well beyond Bumbry's reach and into the seats; the second of these was the fourth Oakland homer of the afternoon, and was sufficient to do in the Oriole pitcher, Dave McNally, on the wrong end of an eventual 6–3 score. Catfish Hunter, the splendid Oakland ace (he was 21-5 this year), gave us a characteristically low-key winning performance—working in and out, flicking the corners, tugging on his oversized cap between pitches, and, in the hard places, striking out batters with his dipping curve.

What I was missing was even better, of course. By the time I got back to my hotel-room TV set on the first afternoon, it was the seventh inning in Cincinnati, and I found that, for the first time in weeks, Tom Seaver's fastball was alive and well. He was leading by 1–0 and had fanned nine batters, and within a minute or two he added numbers ten and eleven. My heart sank. Seaver's hummer comes in to a batter about letter-high; at its best, it is very nearly untouchable, and the way Tom throws it past a hitter—with his powerful body dropping low and driving forward at the instant of delivery—is one of the ornaments of modern baseball. He relies heavily on the fastball on its good days, always seeming to challenge a batter to beat his best with one blow. As strategy, this is straightforward, courageous, and stubborn—and also, in view of Seaver's record and proud nature, probably unarguable. It is extremely scary to watch, and sometimes, in the late innings of a low-score game against a team of proud and famous sluggers, *too* scary. With one out in the eighth, Pete Rose hit a homer; with one out in the ninth, Johnny Bench hit another, to win it.

When I caught up with the Mets again the next afternoon (this time via a tiny TV set perched in a corner of a Union News Company stand in Baltimore's dusty, ancient Pennsylvania Station), they were engaged in another character-builder, once again leading by a bare 1–0 in the seventh. The pitcher was Matlack, who looked even more commanding than Seaver had the day before; his fastball was riding in on the fists of the right-handed Cincinnati batters, and he was pouring over some scimitarlike curves as well. Between innings, I exchanged glances with some fellow Met freaks in the little crowd of standees, and we shook our heads wordlessly: not enough runs. Wrong again. In the top of the ninth, the Mets put together two walks and a tiny fusillade of singles, most of them just over second base, for four more runs and the game and the tie—and, now, some solid hope.

Another squeaker seemed insupportable, and Rusty Staub took care of *that* quickly the next afternoon, at Shea, with a first-inning home run over the Manufacturers Hanover sign in center, and a second-inning home run above the right-field auxiliary scoreboard. The latter poke came while the Mets were happily batting around, and a little later Jerry Koosman drove in a run with his second hit of the afternoon, and the Reds began throwing the ball away in rather discouraged fashion, and the score went to 9–2, and the Gotham hordes were laughing at the Cincinnati pitchers. This kind of breaking apart is perfectly commonplace, of course, though not perfectly or equally acceptable to all participants. And so in the top of the fifth, Bud Harrelson, airborne in the middle part of a lovely 3-6-3 double play, came down a bit heavily on the sliding Pete Rose, and Pete Rose came up a trifle irritably with an elbow, and then Bud and Pete were rolling and punching in the dirt, and all 53,967 of us came to our feet shouting. First the benches emptied and then the bullpens, with the galloping Met battalion being led—*ta-ra!*—by Teddy R. McGraw. As ancient custom dictates in these matters, there was a great deal of milling and shouldering but really not much doing—until Cincinnati relief man Pedro Borbon fetched New York relief man Buzz Capra an unexpected clout on the right temple, to which Capra (who had not worked since mid-September) responded vigorously but with understandably poor control. In time, they all streamed slowly off the field, and Borbon, discovering a Met cap on his head (it was Capra's), furiously snatched it off, bit it, tore it in half, and flung it away. Eventually, Pete Rose resumed his post in left field, to an accolade of garbage and abuse (he outweighs Harrelson by forty or fifty pounds, and Bud is . . . well, *ours*), but when a whiskey bottle plumped to the ground near him, he sensibly withdrew, and Manager Sparky Anderson waved his troops from the untidy field. Shouting and chaos, but no baseball. Then spake the president of the tribe of the Nationals, the goodly Chub Feeney, and so it came to pass that forth from the home dugout emerged a holy company—Yogi, Cleon, Rusty, Tom, and, yea, Willie himself—and right swiftly did they hie themselves toward the troubled multitudes, and sweetly did they remind them, with upraised arms and pleading visages, of the hospitality and courtly good will owed the visiting gentle knights, and also of the score, which stood so fairly for the forces of right and good, and of the power of dark-garbed arbiters to erase and reverse such a score in the face of undue hubbub. And lo! the multitudes were hushed and the play resumed and the memorable foolishness at last concluded.

In the batting cage the next afternoon, the trailing Reds seemed loose and cheerful, while the Mets, now only a game away from the pennant, looked pale and grim. Some of the

Reds stared up at the new banners unfurling in the upper deck —"ROSE IS A WEED," "THIS ROSE SMELLS," and others less elegant—and Johnny Bench murmured, "The best thing you can do is get Pete Rose mad." This Rose had led his league (for the third time) with a batting average of .338, rapping out 230 hits (his sixth 200-hit season); by instructive contrast, Felix Millan established a new club record for the Mets this year with 185 hits. When play began, the left-field pack again bayed vociferously at Rose, but then the tension of the game caught everyone up, and a remarkable quiet descended. It was 1–0, Mets, but then 1–1 after Tony Perez' homer in the seventh—a waiting, silent sort of game, too close for pleasure. Tug McGraw came on in relief of George Stone and repeatedly pitched himself into terrible difficulties, loading the bases in the ninth and again in the tenth—and somehow wriggled free, helped in no small part by the Reds' inordinate difficulties when bunting. Twice, Tug tiptoed past the wolves' lair at the top of the Cincinnati batting order, releasing screeching cries of hope from the upper decks, but the Met hitters were being utterly smothered by the Cincinnati relief men. In the eleventh, with two out and two on, the visitors' Dan Driessen poled a line drive deep to right; Rusty Staub, running hard, hard, pulled the ball in over his left shoulder and collided heavily with the wall, falling onto his back with the ball still clutched in his glove. Enough Tug for this day, clearly, and when Pete Rose came up in the twelfth, the new pitcher was young Harry Parker. Rose had been on base three times without result, but this time he made sure, whacking a high fastball out over the right-field fence and under the scoreboard. He circled the bases with his right fist held high.

The finale, the tie breaker, was less good as a game, better as a pageant. Rusty Staub, his right shoulder damaged by his smash into the wall, was replaced by Eddie Kranepool, the only surviving Met from the original 1962 light-opera company, and nobody present could have been entirely surprised to see the bases loaded when Eddie stepped up in the first inning, or absolutely astounded when he rapped the first pitch to him on a line into left field for two runs. It was going to be that kind of an afternoon. Tom Seaver, without his fastball this time, pitched with restraint and intelligence—curves, sliders, hard work. The Reds labored, too, and Pete Rose doubled and then came around to tie the score in the fifth. Minutes later, Garrett doubled and then Jones doubled and Milner walked, and the bases were loaded, and Willie Mays—yes, of course, *that* kind of day—batted for Kranepool. Overswinging, fooled by the pitch, Willie hammered the ball straight into the dirt (or perhaps off the plate itself), so that it bounded high up in the air and came down, thirty feet up the third-base line, far too late for Clay Carroll, the unhappy pitcher, to make a play anywhere, and another run was in. It was the shortest heroic blow in memory, but, as Mays suggested after the game, box scores and record books do not show the distance of hits, or their luck. Two more runs ensued, and in the sixth Tom Seaver hit a double that Pete Rose ran and dived in the dirt for, all in vain, and then Tom came around and scored, of course—7–2 now—and grins and cheers and smiles and hugs and handshakes broke out everywhere, and all of us believed.

Somehow it should have ended there, when the scoring stopped, but there were three more innings to be played, which is a long time to put off a party. The cries of joy became chants, the shadows deepened, and there were clouds of paper on the grass, and sudden ripping sounds in the stands as strings of firecrackers went off. The ninth began, and the waves of waiting celebrants pushed forward in the lower stands, filling up the lower aisles and crowding the railings. There was some enormous urgency visible here—a yearning for the field itself, a need to belong to this event in a deeper way. A temporary fence out beyond the home dugout collapsed with a tearing noise, and then there was a long, tension-filled wait as some frightened wives in the official Cincinnati party were led from their overrun box seats and out through the visitors' dugout. It *was* frightening, in a way, and so was the enormous horde let loose by the final out, and the sight of Reds and Mets alike (Tug McGraw from the mound, Pete Rose from the base path) running and dodging, as if for their lives, through hundreds upon hundreds of grasping hands, past hundreds of passionate, shouting faces. Streamers and papers (and one sudden red flare) and other things came down from the upper deck, and then a great cloud of dust rose and hung over the entire field as chunks of turf began to be torn up and taken away. This sort of riotous unleashing has almost grown into an institution in our sports in recent years, and what one makes of it all probably depends on what each of us thinks about a great many complex matters, the very least of which is baseball. Cincinnati manager Sparky Anderson, for instance, was disappointed that the police did not take matters in hand, and he said, "Can you imagine this happening in America?" The answer to *that*, at least, seems easy.

•

THE CONVENTION opened gently in Oakland. Both clubs, recovering from playoffs of bruising intensity, were plainly glad to be in the World Series at all, and they regarded each other with congratulatory speculation. (The A's had won an eleven-inning squeaker over the Orioles' Mike Cuellar; had lost 5–4, going down before a shocking five-run Baltimore rally; and then had taken their flag on a 3–0 shutout by Catfish Hunter.) Any other outcome of the playoffs would have produced teams that had already faced each other in a recent World Series, but A's vs. Mets was new and promising. I was grateful, too, to have the defending champs back—the grand White Shoes, with their cheerful dash, their proud quarrelsomeness, and the vivid quality of their play. The A's were probably an even better club than they had been the previous October, with deeper pitching, more speed, and some useful new second-line players purchased with the customary sudden midseason disbursement of cash by owner Charles O. Finley. Their fine young center fielder, Bill North, who had stolen fifty-three bases, was out with a sprained ankle, but this was less of a handicap than the sidelining of Reggie Jackson in last year's Series. This year, Reggie had just concluded a brilliant season —32 homers, 117 RBIs and a certain coming award as the Most Valuable Player in his league. The Mets, we could all see, were outmanned again.

In the opener, the Oakland left-hander Ken Holtzman pitched extremely well and won, while Jon Matlack pitched even better and lost. The day contained a bare few minutes of news. Matlack, falling to a 3–2 count on Holtzman in the third, came in with a fastball that Holtzman rapped into left field for two bases—and a vivid concurrent editorial on the designated-hitter artifice. Bert Campaneris now hit an easy roller to second, which the almost infallible Felix Millan missed cleanly, for an error and a run; it seemed to me that Campaneris's burning speed up the line distracted Millan. That same threat now distracted Matlack, who caught Campy leaning the wrong way at first but flung his pick-off throw high, allowing Campaneris to motor safely along to second, from where he scored Oakland's second and final run, on a single by Joe Rudi. The Mets responded in the next half—a double by Cleon Jones, a run-scoring single by John Milner—but then Reggie Jackson, playing center field for the first time this year, got a splendid jump on Jerry Grote's line drive and made a dazzling, going-away catch, to amputate the only Met hopes of the day.

Having been given a canapé for the opener, we came back the next day for a gigantic goulash of mistakes and wonders that the Mets finally won, 10–7, in twelve innings. It was the longest World Series game in captivity, and one that absolutely defies elucidation. (A friend of mine, driving his wife and children from New Hampshire to New York City that afternoon, tuned in to the game on the car radio, grateful that it would help pass the early miles of the trip; the entertainment concluded four hours and thirteen minutes later, exactly at his apartment door.) The excessive happenings included several fly balls falling untouched out of the dazzling California cerulean for extra-base hits, homers by Garrett and Jones, triples by Campaneris and Bando and Jackson, five Oakland errors, four cannonlike hits by Reggie Jackson, Willie Mays stumbling on the base path, Willie Mays falling twice in the outfield, three hit batsmen, twelve A's left on base, fifteen Mets left on base, 49,151 disbelieving fans. The sway of the game went first toward the hometowners, who led early by 3–1 and would have led by more except for a misbegotten squeeze play; then toward the Mets, who put six straight men aboard in the sixth, scurrying around the bases on looped hits and little hoppers and an appalling wild throw past the plate by pitcher Darold Knowles; then back to the A's again, who tied the game at 6–6 by bringing across two runs with two out in the ninth inning. The Mets displayed gallantry of their own, to be sure, surviving a bad call at the plate (I still think) by umpire Augie Donatelli that cost them a run in the tenth, and the excruciating tension that falls upon the visiting team in an extra-innings free-for-all like this. In the end, the thing seemed to come down to a clear confrontation between a classic undermanager and an inveterate overmanager. Yogi Berra stayed with his ace reliever, McGraw, for six full innings, during which time he surrendered the tying ninth-inning runs; Tug, as usual, was both tough and brilliant—sighing heavily, cocking his chin at the enemy hitter, staring in for the sign, plucking the ball from his upheld glove like a cup from a tray, and then firing the screwball over the top for the strikeout.

Endless games produce endless possibilities, and so the twelfth brought us Willie Mays up at bat with two out and two on; he broke the tie with another bounced single—barely over the pitcher's head this time, and barely through second. It was the last hit and last triumph of his career. Jones singled, and the next two Met batters hit sure outs to second baseman Mike Andrews, who misplayed them both—a grounder right through the wickets, a terrible throw to first—allowing the last three Met runs to come in. Andrews is not known as a fielder, but he was there because Dick Williams, the impatient Oakland manager, had used up two better second basemen along the way. Tom Seaver summed things up a few minutes later in the Mets' clamorous clubhouse. "You couldn't write a book about this one that would tell anybody how to play this game," he said.

There is some temptation to omit any mention of the two central figures of the third meeting, back at Shea Stadium, since neither of them was in uniform. The Mets lost the game by 3–2 in eleven innings, but most of the emotion of the evening centered on the errant and unfortunate Mike Andrews, who was languishing at his home in Peabody, Massachusetts, and on Charles O. Finley, the Oakland vizier, who had subjected Andrews to a medical examination immediately after the conclusion of the twelve-inning debacle and had then dropped him from the squad. The vindictiveness of this maneuver exceeded several low marks previously held by the excessive Mr. Finley, and this time his troops came to the very edge of mutiny. Fortunately, the commissioner quickly restored Andrews, and Manager Williams held a camp meeting for his players, at which he declared his own coming voluntary retirement and total disaffiliation with Finley and the A's after the end of the season. This may seem a curious form of encouragement for a team in the very midst of a World Series, but it should be understood that the vivid, what-the-hell morale of the A's has always been built out of a shared abhorrence of the man at the top. They display the utter unity of a pack of ragged and sequestered Dickensian schoolboys, and Charlie Finley is their Gradgrind.

In the game—which was played on a subarctic evening—the Mets burst from the mark with a leadoff homer by Garrett, a single by Millan, and an exquisite wrong-field hit-and-run poke by Staub. Catfish Hunter now let the second run slip in on a wild pitch, but then slammed the door shut for good. Tom Seaver, his opposite, struck out nine Oaklands in the first five innings, and then, suddenly bereft of his fastball, was whacked for some frightening line drives in the sixth, somehow surrendering only one counter. Campaneris became the tying run in the eighth: a single, a steal of second off Tom's big motion and a super-slide under Grote's super-peg, a trip home on Joe Rudi's single. In the eleventh, after a succession of frigid agonies, Campy happened again. Met relief man Harry Parker walked Ted Kubiak but fanned Angel Mangual, swinging, with a pitch that utterly fooled Jerry Grote as well. The passed ball put Kubiak on second and brought Campaneris to the plate; he whistled a single up the middle, sending Kubiak and, shortly thereafter, all the rest of us home.

Two misapprehensions about this heartbreaker seem possible—that Seaver should have done better, and that the visitors' win was somehow undeserved, because of the Mets' mistakes. Seaver came into this game after 307 innings of work this season—an enormous and exhausting burden for a man who throws as hard as he does. Furthermore, he had never fully recovered from the tender right shoulder that afflicted him in September. Pitching well under all conditions is one hallmark of a $140,000-a-year pitcher, and Tom, at far less than his best, very nearly pulled off a masterpiece—giving up two runs on seven hits, twelve strikeouts, and one walk. Oddly enough, the last figure suggests the aspect of Seaver's pitching that most awes his fellow professionals. Most big-league hurlers never record a full season in which their combined total of walks and hits given up is lower than the total number of innings they have worked. Among the great fastball pitchers, Walter Johnson accomplished this feat nine times, Sandy Koufax four times, and Grover Cleveland Alexander three. Seaver did it this summer for the third time in his brief seven-year career, which puts him in pretty good company. As for the quality of the Oakland victory, it might be noted that this strategy of waiting for small errors (Seaver's failure to hold Campaneris close to first, Grote's passed ball) and then having the right man on the spot to capitalize (Campaneris, Rudi, Campaneris again) was the killing habit, the essential technique of victory, that kept the Yankees on top for more than four decades.

Subtleties were dispensed with the next night, which produced enormous ovations for three heroes—Rusty Staub, who hit a three-run homer in the first, a two-run single in the fourth, and two subsequent safeties; Jon Matlack, who surrendered three grudging hits and one unearned run; and Mike Andrews, miraculously restored, who was sent up to bat in the eighth (ah, there, Charlie Finley!) and shortly trotted back to the dugout in the midst of the loudest and longest accolade ever bestowed upon a pinch-hitter grounding into an infield out. The Mets won by 6–1, retying the Series. Staub's socko performance at the plate was achieved in spite of the shoulder injury he had sustained in the penultimate playoff game, which still made it impossible for him to throw overhand. He was also the only person on the frigid premises in bare-armed décolletage—not an affectation for a player who had survived three seasons in Montreal, where, as he explained later, outfield weather conditions can be toughening, sometimes even requiring the ingestion of a little cognac after a night game. For Mr. Finley, the evening must have seemed a mite draggy. When he stood up for the visitors' seventh-inning stretch, the Mets' folding-sign man flashed him a "SIT DOWN, YA BUM!," and when Andrews came up to bat in the eighth, there were rolling, defiant waves of applause from every part of the park. Finley clapped a bit, too, and then waved his green-and-gold banner. Caligula never had a night like that.

The last winter exercise—the final game in New York, and the coldest baseball game in my memory—offered various perceptions and rewards. This Series, though more crowded and eventful than a samurai drama, had not yet brought us a single game of top quality; between them, the two clubs had so far committed thirteen errors (with a good many other transgressions going forgiven) and had left eighty-four men on base. Strangely, the Mets had outhit the dangerous A's, who had yet to record a homer; the Mets had won the two free-hitting affairs and, strangest of all, had lost the two close ones because of poor defense. Now we were owed something better. The business at hand began in lively fashion when Rusty Staub, batting against Vida Blue in the bottom of the first, knocked off a burning line foul that entered my part of the mezzanine like a SAM missile and caught a late-coming male patron in the back of the right thigh. He sagged to the steps, while nearby patrons explained, "Staub hit that! Staub did it!" The fan looked pained but ecstatic, like a man who has just received a personal message from Jove.

Something better began almost at once—some rabbit-quick infield plays by Bud Harrelson; some darting, quite uncharacteristic fastballs by Jerry Koosman, who said later that the dry, cold air made it impossible for him to grip the ball properly for his meal-ticket pitch, the curve. Jerry also solved the Campaneris problem, with a terrific double-leaning, Warren Spahn pick-off move in the third inning which caught Dagoberto a full eight feet off the bag. Meanwhile, Cleon Jones, who eats up Vida Blue pitches like M & Ms, had whanged a double to the left-field fence and scored on a little eye-hit by John Milner. Blizzards of torn-up paper took wing, rising to vast heights in the windy dark, to the accompaniment of deep, mittened sounds of joy. The chilly air and the pleasure and closeness of the game kept us shivering in our serapes and ski masks and steamer rugs and quilts, and in time there were bits of paper in everybody's hair, on everybody's shoulders. The wind rushed up out of the entrance tunnels, lifting the plastic bunting and making the homemade fan banners on the railings flap like laundry, and sometimes, when the cheering faded for a moment, you could hear the stadium itself groaning and creaking like a great ship in the night.

Koosman threw a shutout, it turned out, winning by a bare 2–0, and there were swift plays afield to keep us shouting and pointing—Felix Millan running at full speed away from the plate and pulling down a shallow fly at the last instant between two inrushing outfielders; a heart-stopping leap and catch by

Joe Rudi as he crashed into the left-field barrier; Bud Harrelson making wonderful stops and throws all over his spacious rangeland. Once, he robbed Reggie Jackson with an effortless scoop and force-play toss from directly behind second base; Reggie stopped dead in the base path and stared at him incredulously: What are you doing over *there*, man? Then McGraw came in and twice put on the tying runs with walks, and twice survived rifled line-drive outs (Jesus Alou, disgusted, sent his green batting helmet spinning into the air), and the upper decks cried "Dee-fense! Dee-fense!" and Tug pitched out, and in the ninth, all together for the last time this year, we sang "Good-byyye, Char-lee, we hate to see you go-oh-oh!" in a deafening chorus, and the Mets were ahead in the World Series.

•

I DID not go back to Oakland. After the winter party in the stands, and after seeing the exuberant cheerfulness in the Mets' clubhouse that night, which almost suggested a Series victory celebration, I decided that Finleyland could not contain deeper rewards. What I secretly feared, of course, was almost exactly what came to pass. In game six, Tom Seaver, with very little left but guile (it seemed to me, watching via television), gave up run-scoring doubles to Reggie Jackson in the first inning and again in the third (with an Oakland runner scoring all the way from first because Rusty Staub still could not throw), and a third A's run came across on still another Met error, by Don Hahn this time. Somehow, the Mets kept it close, but Darold Knowles (in relief of Hunter) came in and fanned Rusty, with two runners aboard, on three fiery fastballs, to nail down the game, 3–1, and tie the Series for the last time. The next day, the A's won the big game, 5–2, as Jon Matlack's almost unparalleled streak of sustained great pitching came to an end. In collecting his first six outs of the day, he completed forty-two innings in which he had surrendered exactly one earned run. Now, in the third, in the space of a bare minute or two, Holtzman doubled and Campaneris homered on the very next pitch; Rudi singled and, after an out, Reggie Jackson homered to deepest right-center field—four hits, four runs, one World Championship. The moment Jackson hit his shot, he dropped his bat at his feet and stood stock-still at the plate, watching the ball go, more or less in the style of Sir Kenneth Clark regarding a Rembrandt. I thought he could be forgiven this gesture; he was, after all, the big gun of the A's, and he had shot us down in the end.

Everyone could be forgiven, it seemed. The Mets' super pitching had finally been worn away (Matlack's last two starts had been on three days' rest), and Oakland had won with its power, its depth, and its own fine pitching (their two top relievers, Rollie Fingers and Darold Knowles, had a combined earned-run average of 0.45 over twenty innings). The Oakland victory represented the first back-to-back championship by any team since the 1961–62 Yankees, and I could not think of any pennant winner in the interim that deserved the title more. If the renewed championship seemed an undue reward for the likes of Mr. Finley, it was the only conceivably sufficient compensation for his mistreated schoolboys. As for the Mets—ah, the Mets! What can one feel for them but gratitude for such a season of prizes, for a summer that lasted, in the end, just two afternoons too long?

8 Landscape, with Figures

July 1974

It's quiz time, Mr. and Mrs. John Q. Fan, and here we go with a brainteasing assortment of baseball stumpers! Are you a *real* baseball fan? Do you enjoy matching wits with the savants of the press box, with the Figger Filberts who keep watch over the precious "stats" of the game, and with the hoary historians of the onetime National Pastime? No? Oh, come on—say yes. Good for you! Now get out your pencils and scratch pads, and away we go! Just one little thing before you step up to the plate. . . . This time, in order to squeeze a little more fun out of our quiz, we're going to bring you the answers first, instead of the questions. Got that? Play ball!

A: Hank Aaron.

Q (*no peeking!*): Who is the current major-league leader in lifetime home runs, and also the lifetime leader in total bases and extra-base hits, and the holder of the second-highest lifetime marks for runs batted in and times at bat, and of the third-highest lifetime marks for hits, runs, and games played (with a good chance to move up a notch or two in some of these categories before the end of this season), and the man who with the first swing of his bat in the 1974 campaign tied the previous lifetime-home-run record (the hallowed 714 hung up forty years earlier by the Sultan of Swat, Babe Ruth) and then surpassed that record, and so attained something close to the ultimate sports transfiguration (plus uncounted hundreds of thousands of dollars' worth of publicity and commercial sponsorships), by striking his seven-hundred-and-*fifteenth* round-tripper in Atlanta at 9:07 P.M. on April 8, 1974, in his second time at bat in his team's hometown opener, thus transporting 53,775 Atlanta Braves fans (on hand in prayerful hope of witnessing the historic four-ply blow live and in person), as well as several hundred national- and local-media persons, and the gratified Atlanta Braves' owners and front-office nabobs (who had earlier suffered over the horrid possibility that the billion-dollar poke might come to pass, like its immediate predecessor, in some ball park other than the all too rarely occupied confines of Atlanta Stadium), and simultaneously pleasing several million fans and (to be sure) idly curious nonfans watching by national television, who then saw the game stopped in its tracks for almost a quarter of an hour of handshakes, hugs, encomiums, plaque presentations, photos, and assorted ceremonials (and had the opportunity, a few minutes later, to see the whole business, from pitcher's fateful windup to politician's fervent speechifying, repeated on a taped replay, under the auspices of an entirely different and extremely forehanded commercial sponsor), and who eventually (in much diminished numbers) resumed watching the game at hand—the Braves, by the way, vs. the Los Angeles Dodgers—perhaps then noticing that a large part of the outfield in Atlanta had been painted (in the style of a pro-football field) to represent a map of the United States, executed in red and white stripes, and also noticing that the stands in Atlanta were almost vacant within an inning or two after the awaited event, and then possibly sighed a deep sigh occasioned by a private and quite uncharacteristic feeling of anticlimax and ennui, and hoped (against hope) that at last the real business of baseball (which is the playing of games, rather than the celebration of history) and the rest of the season might now be allowed to proceed—as, indeed, thank goodness, it has?

Did you get all that right, quiz players? Way to *go!* More coming up in a minute.

•

IT HAS been a strange season so far, beginning with such a sudden shout, and in retrospect it appears that Hank Aaron's finest feat this year was the swiftness with which he accomplished his necessary business, thus saving himself and the rest of us from the embarrassment of waiting for an inevitability. That seven-hundred-and-fifteenth homer was a fixed target, of course, and its attainment is more a landmark than a true event. There is something warming and elegant about Hank Aaron's long conservation of his powers, but lifetime records lack urgency. This was not a sudden prodigy, like batting over .400 or hitting sixty home runs in a single season. Babe Ruth was prodigious; Bad Henry is—well, historic. Most of us sensed some of this, and these differences should not be lost in the current rush of Aaron fame and money and publicity. It was understandable that the baseball establishment should look on Hank's feat as a fabulous PR opportunity, since the new record so clearly suggests that modern baseball, despite all secret fears to the contrary, is at least as good as, and maybe even better than, baseball in the Babe's day. This is not provable, and it is not the point. Hank Aaron has not really defeated Babe Ruth, but he has accomplished something far more difficult and significant. He has defeated the averages.

The statistics of baseball form the critical dimensions of the game. Invisible but ineluctable, they swarm and hover above the head of every pitcher, every fielder, every batter, every team, recording every play with an accompanying silent shift of digits. The true, grinding difficulty of this sport is to be found in its unwinking figures, and ballplayers on the field are in competition not just with the pitchers and sluggers of the opposing team but with every pitcher or batter who ever played the game, including their past selves. Some aspects of fielding are not perfectly measurable, and good or bad managerial thinking is similarly obscure, but each pitcher and hitter is absolutely without illusion about the current level of his professional competence and the likely curve of its continuation. The red-hot spring hitter *knows* he will not stay up there at .472; the averages will get him. The veteran knows he will break out of his 0-for-22 slump—but when, *when?* At night, in his hotel room on the road, the manager rereads the day's new cumulative team stats and thinks about his not so dazzling rookie outfielder: the figures spell Tulsa. In the next room, a thirty-two-year-old pitcher slowly rubs his aching shoulder and silently reruns his numbers (ERA 3.81; W 5—L 8; HR 12; CG 0), which are beginning to say something to him about his next year's salary and his chances of a ten-year-man's pension. Only the superstar, with his years of averages and numbers safely banked in the record books, has longer thoughts —perhaps about his precise eventual place in the history of this game, and about the players (some of them now old, some of them now dead) who at this moment bracket his name in the all-time totals. His figures may have begun to spell another destination: Cooperstown. None of this is secret; none of it is hard to understand. The averages are there for us all to read and to ponder, and they admit us to the innermost company of baseball. On that same evening, the true fan, comfortably at home with his newspapers and *The Sporting News* and his "Official Baseball Guide"'s and his various record books and histories, notes the day's and the week's new figures, and draws his conclusions, and then plunges onward, deeper into the puzzles and pleasures of his game.

•

A: Jim and Gaylord Perry.

Q: Which pair of brothers have together pitched the most winning games in the major leagues?

Ah, friends, this one hurts. The answer here is a brand-new one—a mark hung up on April 23 of this year, when Gaylord Perry, on his way to a dazzlingly successful early season, won his second game of the year for the Cleveland Indians. Gaylord, now thirty-five, has subsequently run his record to 14–1, and tops all pitchers in both leagues with an earned-run average of 1.27. His achievement so far is curious as well as astounding, since he seems to have abandoned the infamous spitball with which he used to fan so many batters, enrage so many managers, and mystify so many umpires. Faced with a new ad-hoc (and *con*-Gaylord) ruling this year which permits an umpire to call an automatic ball on any pitch that appears even faintly perspiring in its flight, and to eject a hurler for a second offense, Perry (or so he claims) has gone to a fork ball that behaves very much like its damp cousin as it crosses the plate—that is, like a diving pelican. Wet or dry, Gaylord Perry deserves homage, but one cannot entirely help wishing that he had stayed down on the family farm in Williamston, North Carolina, this summer. The new brother-pitcher record—composed of Gaylord's pre-1974 lifetime mark of 177 wins, plus his first two this year, and Jim Perry's 194, plus his first this year (also for the Indians)—erased an ancient mark much beloved of press-box historians and other baseball loonies: the 373 victories scored by Christy and Henry Mathewson. The latter sibling was not quite as effective as his celebrated bro, having appeared in a total of three games for the Giants during the seasons of 1906 and 1907, during which he ripped off a lifetime mark of zero wins and one defeat. That sum, carefully added to Christy's 373, had topped all comers until now. There was a brief further flurry this spring when some statistical mole discovered that *three* brothers—Dad and John and Walter Clarkson—pitching in baseball's Pleistocene era, had put together a lifetime conglomerate of 386 wins. But the Perrys have now topped that, too, and the last word on the foolish matter may have been said by a visiting baseball writer at Shea Stadium last month who murmured, "Cy Young and his sister have still got them all beat."

•

A: Al Benton and Bobo Newsom and (in a way) Satchel Paige.

Q: Name two (or three) pitchers who pitched to both Babe Ruth and Mickey Mantle.

Benton's and Newsom's careers as hurlers encompassed both 1934 and 1952, which were, respectively, Ruth's last and Mantle's first full years in the majors. Paige is perhaps subject to challenge, since the big leagues' old racial barriers made it impossible for him to pitch against the Babe in anything but exhibition games.

A: Dan Brouthers, Nick Altrock, Bobo Newsom, Mickey Vernon, Early Wynn, Ted Williams.

Q: How many players can you name whose active careers spanned at least four calendar decades?

An infuriating question, answerable only by zealots wearing bottle-bottom eyeglasses who have wasted their lives groveling in the fine print of the baseball record books. Brouthers, a Hall of Fame slugger and first baseman, appeared in his first big-league game in 1879 and his last in 1904. Newsom's career stretched from 1929 to 1953, Vernon's and Williams' from 1939 to 1960, Wynn's from 1939 to 1963. Nick Altrock's span is 1898 to 1924, or maybe even 1933, but he barely merits inclusion, since most of his appearances after 1912 (he was a left-handed pitcher) were token affairs—an inning or two per year. He may be remembered by a few elders (including this scribe) as a beloved long-time coach with the Senators who used to team with Al Schacht in a clown act between the games of doubleheaders in baseball's sunshine days.*

* A new, if tainted, addition to the four-decade set is Minnie Minoso, who was coaching for the White Sox last year when he was activated, at the age

More infuriation?

A: Dodgers, Cubs, Browns, Senators, Red Sox, Senators, Browns, Tigers, Browns, Tigers, Senators, Dodgers, Browns, Senators, Dodgers, Athletics, Senators, Yankees, Senators, Giants, Athletics, Senators, Athletics.

Anybody got the question? Oh, come on, this one is easy.

Q: Name in order all the major-league teams for which Bobo Newsom pitched. (Or, variantly, name the pitcher who served more terms as a Senator than Strom Thurmond.)

A: c, King Kelly; 1b, Ted Kluszewski; 2b, Harvey Kuenn; 3b, George Kell; ss, Don Kessinger; of, Willie Keeler, Al Kaline, Ralph Kiner; p. Sandy Koufax, Tim Keefe, Jim Kaat, Jerry Koosman.

Q: Name an all-time-best lineup of players with names beginning with "K."

No single answer is right here, but this is a game that can be played for hours on end among badly bitten fans or, solo, by insomniac baseball freaks in the darkest hours of the night. Utterly useless disputes and time-wasting reveries can ensue, thus providing some of the true secret rewards of fandom. Your team, of course, can play for any letter of the alphabet; if you start with "C," for instance, it is possible to come up with an All-Hall-of-Fame lineup. "K" is more rewarding than one might think at first, however. It isn't easy to relegate Chuck Klein, Charlie Keller, Harmon Killebrew, Ken Keltner, Tony Kubek, or Highpockets Kelly to the bench, as I have done, but with pinch-hitters like that, one probably doesn't need a very deep bullpen: Jim Konstanty, Ray Kremer,

---

of fifty-three, into a designated hitter. This was a gate-hype, of course, thought up by Chicago owner Bill Veeck. A self-proclaimed current aspirant to this strange brotherhood is Ron Fairly, the veteran National League outfielder and first baseman, who was purchased from the Cardinals by the Oakland A's late last summer. Fairly, who came up with the Dodgers in 1958, is in excellent shape; he will only be forty-one years old when the opening day of the 1980 season comes along, which suggests that a little good luck and three comfortable summers in a designated-hitter's rocking chair should see him home.

Ellis Kinder, and Alex Kellner. (Harvey Kuenn, incidentally, never did play second base, but my manager, Eddie Kasko, is not afraid to experiment a little with a lifetime .303 hitter like Harv.) Let's add Eddie Kranepool to the club, for good luck, and the back-up catcher, of course, is Clyde Kluttz. Probably I have left somebody out. If you need a little help in scouting him, take along Paul Krichell.

And just one more—absolutely the final one.

A: Three feet seven inches.

Q: How tall was Eddie Gaedel, the midget whom Bill Veeck sent up to bat as a pinch-hitter for the St. Louis Browns against the Tigers on August 19, 1951?

Gaedel walked, of course (which was the whole idea), and the rules of the game were instantly changed to prohibit such high unseriousness. The story is not complete, however, unless one adds:

A: Pearl du Monville. (Yes, I know, I know, but this is part of the same question. Stop complaining.)

Q: Name the midget who was signed up to pinch-hit for a big-league team in James Thurber's *Saturday Evening Post* story "You Could Look It Up," published a full decade before Veeck's coup.

You could look it up.

•

THIS INTERROGATIVE outburst has been inspired by the recent publication of two significant (and significantly different) volumes of baseball records. One is the long-awaited new edition of *The Baseball Encyclopedia* (Macmillan; $17.95), which attempts to update the epochal first edition, of 1969. The other is *The Sports Encyclopedia: Baseball* (Grosset & Dunlap; $5.95 paperback, $14.95 in the regular edition), which presents the essential data of the game in year-by-year rather than biographical fashion. Macmillan's original *Baseball Encyclopedia* was recognized almost from the instant of its publication as the most accurate and rewarding book of baseball records ever compiled. The original edition (let's call it "Mac I") had its beginnings in the mid-nineteen-sixties, when a group of young computer scientists who had allied themselves as Information Concepts, Inc., approached Robert Markel, an executive editor at Macmillan, and suggested that it was high time that the new capabilities of computer science be permitted to go to work on the vast, almost oceanic depths of essential baseball statistics that had accumulated over the years. They had found the perfect partner, for Markel had previously published a number of original and most successful sports books, including *The Glory of Their Times*, by Lawrence S. Ritter, which is a glowing re-creation of the early days of big-league baseball as told by some surviving Nestors of the game. Markel was enthusiastic about the new proposal, and became even more enthusiastic when he learned that ICI had independent financial backing that would begin to support the enormous costs of programming the work and building the essential data bank—a Fort Knox of stats. The ICI planners—notably, two men named Paul Funkhouser and David S. Neft—had in mind an eventual computerization of baseball that would hook up the scoreboards in all the big-league parks to a single central electronic brain, which would also pick up and print and store all the statistics of the game as they happened. In computer circles, this is known as "real-time" work. It could also be called dream-time work, for the costs of the scheme were admittedly phenomenal, and organized baseball is not known for its instant response to brand-new ideas or to unexpected financial disbursements of any nature. In any case, the cost of the preparation of the data for Mac I sailed right through the independent financial backing and up into the hundreds of thousands of dollars, effectively postponing the advent of ICI as an instantaneous electronic sports colossus, but not before it had provided Macmillan with a data bank of incomparable value and interest. The primary source of the data was the daily "official sheets" of baseball statistics kept by the American League (since 1905) and by the National League (since 1902). For corroborative evidence and for the statistics of all the nineteenth-century contests, the compilers consulted local libraries and ancient newspaper files, and the precious records of famous baseball students like the late Lee Allen, the official historian of the Baseball Hall of Fame at Cooperstown, and John Tattersall, a Philadelphia steamship executive. (Tattersall has compiled a history of every home run ever struck in major-league competition, including the inning, the number of men on base, and the pitcher.) All this digging yielded a formidable body of figures (the first-draft specifications came to eight thousand pages), and included a few corrections of famous old individual statistics: Ty Cobb's hallowed Most Hits was raised from 4,191 to 4,192, as the result of two previously overlooked games he played in 1906.

Mac I came out in the fall of 1969, to instant success. Priced at twenty-five dollars, it eventually sold some fifty thousand copies in the bookstores, plus another fifty or sixty thousand via book clubs and mail orders. It is an elegantly organized, beautifully printed and laid-out volume of 2,337 pages, containing (among a great many other things) a statistical summary of the changing team averages over the years; a summary of individual leaders in batting, pitching, fielding, and so on; a year-by-year roster of all the teams and their players and statistics (the dates, here and elsewhere, go back to the National League of 1876, and also include vanished big leagues like the Players League, the American Association, the Union Association, and the outlaw Federal League); an alphabetical roster of every major-league player and his batting record; an alphabetical roster of all pitchers and their pitching records; a register of managers; and a description of every World Series game, with accompanying data. The book, in short, was a self-certifying classic that made its fortunate purchasers wonder how they and the game had ever got along without it. My own copy, its spine lettering almost worn away by my ceaseless browsings and burrowings, is now kept under lock and key, for the volume is irreplaceable.

Irreplaceable, alas, despite its official replacement, Mac II, which came out in June. My first misgivings about the new edition were instantaneous when I noticed that the price had been dropped to $17.95 and the number of pages cut by more than a third, to 1,532. How, I wondered, could anyone have enforced a diet upon a book that carried an additional five years of new players and new records? One could understand the need to keep the price of the new book beneath a range acceptable only to independently languid bibliophiles, but the attempt at a more popular price suggested that the current editors of the work did not understand the necessary dimensions and classic purposes of a basic reference work. The makers of Mac II have skimped and shaved, sometimes sensibly but more often oddly or arbitrarily or thoughtlessly. New listings of no-hit games and Hall of Fame members are welcome, and so are descriptions of the new Championship Series games, which were first played after Mac I. Gone, however, is the essential year-by-year roster of all the teams and all their players—the section in Mac I that most warmed and pleased old fans, since it repopulated the playing fields of their recollection with long-forgotten batteries, ancient double-play combinations, and nearly vanished bench-warmers. (Hello, Gene Desautels! *Ave*, Russ van Atta!) Gone from each player's statistical biography are mentions of important injuries and of years lost to military service. Gone, appallingly, are his accompanying World Series figures—as if these were somehow not germane to the man's total performance.

What this means in terms of day-to-day usefulness is dismaying. I can imagine, for example, a young fan spending an hour or two musing over Ted Williams' lifetime records. How good *was* the Splendid Splinter? In the new volume, he would not be able to learn that Williams missed out on some 450 games of major-league action because of his military service in 1943–45, and some 250 more games for the same reason in 1952–53. Extrapolating his prime-season figures, the sprout might have discovered that this duty time represented a possible loss of 160 career home runs, which would have brought Williams to a lifetime total of 681—right up there in Aaron-Ruth country.

When *was* it that Dizzy Dean had his toe broken by a line drive in an All-Star Game, and then ruined his arm forever by pitching before it was quite healed? When was Eddie Waitkus shot by that unknown female admirer? How many World Series games did it take for Lou Brock to steal his record-breaking fourteen bases? When, and for whom, did Rogers Hornsby play in the World Series? Why did Sandy Koufax quit so suddenly? Why did Nemo Gaines require special permission to attempt a career in the majors? How many at-bats did Walter Alston have in the majors? How tall was Eddie Gaedel? Mac I says; Mac II either doesn't say or mumbles. It's a pity.*

* Further bad-tempered complaints of mine about Mac II have been deleted here, for good reason. In the spring of 1976, Macmillan brought forth a third edition of *The Baseball Encyclopedia,* which restores almost all of the unfortunate omissions and economies of Mac II. The year-by-year team rosters are back, and so are the full records of players with less than twenty-five major-league at-bats (thus preserving for the ages the news that Walter Alston's lifetime batting record was one at-bat and no hits). Individual World Series batting records have also reappeared, although only in summary form. Furthermore, Mac III contains some brand-new data—a club-by-club all-time roster of players and managers, and a greatly expanded section listing lifetime leaders in most conceivable batting and pitching attainments, which in itself provides fuel for many long nights of hot-stove musings. Here, for instance, one finds the names of all the 139 players with a lifetime batting average of .300 or better (Rod Carew, with .328, is in twenty-eighth place; Pete Rose, at .310, is eightieth); here are the 117 players with more than a thousand runs batted in; here are the leaders in most strikeouts per times at bat, with Reggie Jackson, Bobby Bonds, and Dick Allen in hot competition for the number-one spot. Farther along, we find all 70 pitchers who won more than 200 games (Jim Kaat, with 235 wins, leads the active members); all 96 pitchers (from Walter Johnson on down to Bobo Newsom) who threw 30 shutouts or more; and Nolan Ryan leading all pitchers—all pitchers *ever*—in two separate lifetime categories: most strikeouts per nine innings (9.58), and fewest hits per nine innings (6.25). And so on.

This latest edition of *The Baseball Encyclopedia* has gone up to 2,142 pages, and it is miraculously priced at twenty-five dollars. The principal editor of this restored classic, Mr. Fred Honig, now ranks somewhere near

The Grosset & Dunlap volume, which turned up about the same time as Mac II, is a reference work built primarily around the old yearbooks of the game—every name and every offensive statistic of every season. Career averages are to be found in five "era summaries," and several ingenious codes supply much of the quirky individual details that Mac II has dropped. The "career-interruption" code, for instance, lists seventy-three separate forms of bad news, including "LA—Leg amputated"; "SU—Suspended for hitting or abusing umpire"; "JL—Returned to Japanese league"; and "JA—In jail for assault." The printing and paper and typography are not up to the quality of the Macmillan volumes, but there are a number of counterweighing innovations, possibly even including the sizable and rather fervently written descriptions of each major-league season and its happenings. The best new material here is some averages I have never seen before, including lifetime *differences* in winning percentages for pitchers and the winning percentages of the teams they played for. The simple lifetime percentages for pitchers, for instance, find Jim Palmer first on the list of currently active players, with .682, and Tom Seaver second, with .640. The lifetime difference list, by contrast, places Bob Gibson and Juan Marichal at the top of the active list, and Palmer and Seaver don't show up on it at all. Here, too, at last, are the very first comparative performance figures for black, white, and Latin players, which confirm what has so far been only broadly perceptible: a huge overall increase in numbers of black and Latin players since 1947 (but a much smaller one among pitchers); batting averages, slugging averages, and stolen bases notably higher for nonwhite players than for whites; a clustering of black and Latin stars at the top levels of baseball accomplishment. These figures, as *The Sports Encyclopedia: Baseball* counsels, open enormous areas of speculation that should be explored with care and in the company of sociologists and other experts.

---

the top on the all-time list of friends of baseball, and seems to be the ideal curator for the essential future editions.

The new reference book, primarily intended for paperback sale, is also the work of Robert Markel, now the editor-in-chief at Grosset & Dunlap, who reunited David Neft and some of the other ICI alumni to put together a different sort of "Fan's Companion." The data bank compiled for Macmillan was no longer available to them, of course, and the figures in the new work were put together by hand—with a resulting proof-reading bill of ten thousand dollars and oculists' fees as yet unknown.

•

A FEW moving figures have been observed amid the digit-thickets. On a sunny afternoon in the middle of April, I welcomed the Red Sox in their first visit to the Yankees' sublet, Shea Stadium, and watched Mel Stottlemyre beat Luis Tiant, 2–1, in a game that was full of early-season false hints. The young Bosox, who had dropped Orlando Cepeda and Luis Aparicio at the end of spring training, showed none of the speed and power and confidence that subsequently distinguished their campaign this year, and the two Yankee scores came about as the result of malfeasances—a wild peg to first by the Boston catcher, and a hit batsman and bases-loaded walk by Tiant. (Tiant, who has the most entertaining and effective move to first base of any right-hander, did not pick anybody off this day. Once, I congratulated him on this highly specialized talent, and he grinned and said, "Oh, my father he had a much better move than me. [Tiant *père* was a celebrated Cuban hurler of his day.] He say he used to strike out batters with it.") Further evidences of springtime were the three straight singles rapped out by Yankee third baseman Graig Nettles. Normally a docile batsman, Nettles was enjoying an almost Faustian prosperity at the plate, which eventually brought him eleven home runs in the month of April, tying a league record. He was at a loss to explain this. "I don't know," he said in the clubhouse. "I'm just seeing the ball better, or *something.*" He looked embarrassed—the proper expression of a player waiting for the averages to bite him.

A month later, there were a lot of new Yankee faces in the dugout, as the result of a wave of late trades by Yankee president Gabe Paul. One old Yankee face, Ralph Houk, was on hand in his fresh guise as the Detroit manager; he seemed genuinely touched by the wave of boos that greeted him as he carried out his lineup card. None of the Yankees, new or old, could do much with Mickey Lolich, who set them down with three hits and won by 5–2. Chris Chambliss, the large new first baseman whom the Yankees had just acquired from Cleveland, swung mightily and smote several eleven-hop infield grounders. It was the fourth straight Yankee loss.

The next visiting southpaw observed by me was Mike Cuellar, of the Orioles, who even outdid Lolich, surrendering two hits and a single run. This was late May, and the Yanks, now engaged upon an entirely different five-game losing streak, had fallen to last place. They looked dispirited, especially while swinging against Cuellar's junky screwballs and curves. At its best, Cuellar's attack on the plate reminds one of a master butcher preparing a standing roast of beef—a sliver excised here, a morsel trimmed off the bottom, two or three superfluous swishes of the knife through the air, and then a final slice of white off the ribs: *Voilà!*

I caught the Orioles again a few days later, by television, when I saw the Kansas City Royals inflict frightful indignities on Jim Palmer, the Baltimore ace. Palmer, last year's Cy Young Award winner in the American League, was gone after two and two-thirds innings, having surrendered seven hits and five runs. It was his sixth loss of the year, against two wins, and his record has subsequently gone to three and eight. He is suffering from a bad elbow. Mike Cuellar is still capable of some excellent outings, as I had observed, but he is thirty-seven years old and cannot last for many more summers. Dave McNally, the third member of the celebrated Baltimore corps of starters, is currently bumping along at 7-6 and a 4.30 ERA, and it may well be that this marvelous triumvirate is nearing the end of its reign. Before it goes, attention and honor should be paid.

McNally, a left-hander, came up to the Orioles from the minors in 1962, at the age of twenty; Palmer, who is right-handed, arrived in 1965, also at the age of twenty, although he was to spend the better part of the 1967 and 1968 seasons in the minors, recovering from an arm injury. The trio was completed at the beginning of the 1969 season when Cuellar, a veteran already in his thirties, came over from the Astros. In the five full seasons since then, the three pitchers have won 297 games while losing 150—a winning percentage of .664, which puts them up among the most effective and famous three-man staffs in history. These would include Eddie Lopat, Allie Reynolds, and Vic Raschi, who won 307 games and lost 143 (or .682) for the Yankees between 1948 and 1953; Bob Lemon, Early Wynn, and Mike Garcia, whose nine-year record for the Indians from 1949 to 1957 was 473-293, or .617; and, going back a bit, Lefty Grove, George Earnshaw, and Rube Walberg, who toiled together for Connie Mack's Athletics from 1928 to 1933: 344-169, good for .670. No other more recent corps of starters suggests itself.

A more spectacular and perhaps fairer way to measure these splendid inner teams is to compare their cumulative performance during their three *peak* years together—a performance that in each case resulted in at least one pennant for the pitchers' clubs. It comes out this way:

	Years	*W–L*	*Pctg.*	*ERA*
Grove Earnshaw Walberg	1929–31	197–78	.716	3.43
Lopat Reynolds Raschi	1949–51	167–81	.673	3.45

	Years	*W–L*	*Pctg.*	*ERA*
Lemon Wynn Garcia	1952–54	188–96	.662	2.93
Palmer McNally Cuellar	1969–71	188–72	.723	2.89

Those Athletics' records, it should be explained, mean mostly Grove. His three-year stats for the selected time were 79 wins and only 15 losses, and an earned-run average of 2.47. Looking back to earlier times, one finds some dazzling three-year, three-man totals for games won—196 for Ed Walsh, Frank Smith, and Doc White, of the 1907–09 White Sox; 197 for Christy Mathewson, Rube Marquard, and Jeff Tesreau, of the 1912–14 Giants; and 231 for Mathewson, Joe McGinnity, and Dummy Taylor, of the 1903–05 Giants. Since old-time hurling staffs included very few relief pitchers, most of the pitchers of the era worked many more innings than modern stars do, and absorbed more losses, with consequent damage to their winning percentages.

•

So FAR this summer, Met-watching has been an excruciating pastime, especially when one remembers the tenacity and verve of the same club last autumn. At this writing, the World Series runners-up are in last place in the East, with the worst record in their league—worse than the Padres'. Ten games behind and fourteen games below the .500 level would suggest a summer best forgotten if it were not for the fact that their division again lacks a consistent leader. At less than their top form, the Mets have always looked abysmal. Their good years have been built on splendid pitching, from both starters and relievers; an airtight defense; and a patient attack that rarely produces more than the minimum necessary runs—in sum, a little twenty-one-jewel mechanism that works perfectly or not at all. The Mets have also never won without a top performance from Tom Seaver, and Seaver, in sixteen starts, stands at 4–6, with an earned-run average of 3.64; he is second in the league in strikeouts, and first in homers given up—fifteen.

I have watched Seaver work three times this year—a big, dominant win over Montreal, a sudden late-inning loss to the Giants on a three-run homer conked over the center-field fence at Shea by Gary Matthews, and a middling no-decision performance against the Reds. He has looked overpowering at times, the genuine Tom Terrific (during one twelve-inning outing in Los Angeles he fanned sixteen Dodgers), and decidedly ordinary at others. He has a formidable pitching intelligence, and knows how to employ all the talents he possesses on any given day, but this year he has sometimes been let down by his big strikeout pitch, the high fastball. (As we all know, the high hummer that is even a fraction short often ends up in the parking lot.) Seaver claims that his arm has never felt better, but it may be that he is suffering more than he wants to admit from a sciatic hip, which recently caused him to miss several starts. He may be at the time when we should begin to speculate about his future.

Seaver has had seven years in the majors to date, winning 135 games and losing 76 (up to 1974), with an ERA of 2.38. He has led the league three times in strikeouts (also registering the lowest ERA in each of those three years). Last summer, he pitched the Mets to a pennant and won his second Cy Young Award, but he was admittedly an arm-weary pitcher in the late going. He is twenty-nine years old. This is still young for a ballplayer, but not quite so young, the records suggest, for a strikeout pitcher. Hal Newhouser, the Tigers' left-handed star of three decades ago, twice led his league in strikeouts and twice in ERA, and averaged close to three hundred innings pitched for six years, but was finished as a winner at the age of twenty-nine. Sudden Sam McDowell, while with the Cleveland Indians, kept his fastball for six years, five times topping the American League in whiffs, and then declined rapidly, never recording a significant winning season after the age of twenty-eight.

Robin Roberts, not exactly a flamethrower, lasted for nineteen years in the majors. He, too, had six top seasons—winning more than twenty games per year (and pitching over three hundred innings) from 1950 to 1955. He performed capably after that, but he was a much diminished pitcher after the age of twenty-nine. Bob Feller was a nonpareil fastball pitcher for seven years (not including a four-year wartime interruption)—seven years tops in Ks, five years tops in innings pitched and games won. But players who batted against him always mention the fact that Feller also possessed a magnificent curve, and it was this pitch that kept him in the majors for eighteen years; the fastball was in decline by the time he entered his thirties.

There is some evidence to the contrary, as well—famous iron-arms who threw hard and fast for a decade or more: Walter Johnson (twelve times the league strikeout leader, the last time in his thirty-seventh year), Dazzy Vance (who also led in strikeouts at the age of thirty-seven), Warren Spahn, Bob Gibson. And then, unforgettably, there is Sandy Koufax, who toiled ineffectively for six years, then gave us six astounding summers—five years tops in ERA, four years tops in strikeouts, three years tops in games won, no-hitters in four consecutive seasons—and then vanished like a spent rocket, his arm gone at the age of thirty.

It is certainly not suggested here that Seaver's career is nearing its conclusion, or even that he is in decline as a consistent big winner. He is, however, at a stage in his professional life where he may soon have to become a different kind of pitcher—a process that is always extremely interesting to watch. It may be that the flaring Seaver fastball is about to disappear—gone, not so mysteriously, after some two thousand big-league innings and eighteen hundred whiffs. Let it go. Seaver seems to have the skills and temperament to stay on top, one way or another, for years to come—and here, too, the records are helpful. In 1927, Grover Cleveland Alexander, then forty years old, won 21 games for the Cardinals and lost only 10; he pitched 268 innings and fanned no more than 48 batters. There is more than one way to skin the game of one o' cat.*

•

A GOOD many of the surprises and spectacles of this season have eluded me. So far, I have not caught up with the surprising Phillies and their suddenly terrific third baseman, Mike Schmidt; with the surprising Texas Rangers and their league-leading run-producer, Jeff Burroughs; or with the briefly surprising Milwaukee Brewers, whose shortstop, Robin Yount, is eighteen years old.

I did get away for one quick field trip to Chavez Ravine, where the Dodgers, leading the National League West by eight games in early June, had put together some statistics that seemed about to go right off the top of the charts—an eight-game lead over the Reds, a .700 winning percentage, league-leading batting totals of .284, fifty-seven homers, sixty-four stolen bases, and an average of ten base hits per game. (Their pinch-hitters as a group were batting. 324.) The Dodger pitching stats showed league-leading totals in earned-run average (2.82) and complete games and shutouts. Four of their pitchers —Tommy John, Charlie Hough, Andy Messersmith, and Doug Rau—were clustered at the top of the league's won-lost records, with a combined mark of 26-6, and one of their

* Tom Seaver continued to have an unhappy time of it in 1974, finishing with a record of 11-11, but he quickly resumed his pedestal at the top of his league the following year, when he wound up at 23-11 and took home his third Cy Young Award. My anxieties about the Seaver fastball were happily premature, for he struck out over two hundred batters in 1974, '75, and '76, thus establishing a significant new record: nine consecutive seasons of two hundred whiffs or more. Pete Rose, a devout student of pitching, is of the opinion that Seaver's fastball is still the prime article and that Seaver is still the paramount pitcher in the National League. Last summer, one could see that Tom was going to his breaking stuff earlier in a game than he used to, and that he was throwing the hummer less often but perhaps to greater effect than ever.

catchers, Steve Yeager, had caused the invention of a new stat, inasmuch as he had yet to play in a losing game, and stood at 24-0 for the year.

First place is a nice neighborhood—large family crowds of happy front-runners (whose expressions bore none of the anxieties and irritable passions of the Metsian-fan face), Pacific evening sunshine slanting across the capacious and beautiful O'Malley palazzo (with some Eastern results, already up on the scoreboard, suggesting the terrible struggles of the other clubs to keep up), and smiles and youthful shouts in the clubhouse. Steve Garvey, the powerful and extremely polite young first baseman who was leading the league in runs batted in, said, "This kind of big jump at the start makes every game a whole lot easier. We know we can win a different way every night—thirteen to nothing, or one to nothing, or everything in in the bottom of the ninth. You can hardly wait to get to the ball park every day."

I asked Walter Alston about this year and last, when the Dodgers lost an early lead of eight and a half games and finally gave way to the onrushing Cincinnati Reds. Alston, now in his twenty-first year at the Dodger helm and a man of mountainous calm, murmured, "The difference is that last year we had three regulars who were playing their first full year in the majors [third baseman Ron Cey, second baseman Davey Lopes, catcher Joe Ferguson]. Garvey was playing first for the first time, and we were still trying to make a big-league shortstop out of Bill Russell. Young players can get down on themselves—a little slump, a few injuries—and the pitchers are tougher the second or third time around. But we've been through all that together, and we know what it's like now. Experience is more valuable than anything you can buy—except maybe Jim Wynn."

Jimmy Wynn, the stubby and mightily muscled Dodger center fielder, has been leading the league in homers all summer, and in a recent series against the Padres he bashed out thirteen hits in eighteen times at bat. In this case, however, sudden success is probably less attributable to a statistical anomaly than to plain gratitude. Wynn came over to the upwardly mobile Dodgers last winter in a trade from the hapless Astros, and was thus relieved of his discouraging long-term work of trying to slug balls into the seats through the mudlike imprisoned air of the Astrodome.

"I'm happy to be here in every way I can think of," he said to me. "Winning makes you happy all day—you know that? I also like the fans. They were nice to me from the first day I played here."

I asked him how he had done in the Dodgers' home opener, against the Padres.

"I did all right—three for five. A home run."

What about the next day?

"One for three."

What about the third day?

"Three for five." He smiled. "Well, I guess I *helped* those fans a little. Made it easier for them to be happy with me."

Happiness abounding—except that the Dodgers, of course, lost the two games I had come for, going down before the admirable Cardinals, 1–0 and 6–3, on successive nights. Andy Messersmith surrendered four meager singles in the opener, but he was up against young Lynn McGlothen, the combative right-hander whom the Cards picked up from the Red Sox last winter. McGlothen has a fine, quick curve and an impatient, gimme-that-ball manner that are reminiscent of his new teammate Bob Gibson. Steve Yeager, behind the plate for the Dodgers, helped break his own undefeated streak when he inadvertently tipped Lou Brock's bat in the sixth, putting Brock on base with what was to become the only run of the evening.*

* I failed to mention here the only certifiably historic sight of my baseball summer—a steal of second base by Lou Brock, in the eighth inning. The theft, Brock's fortieth of the year, was a typically efficient piece of Brockery, but it did not alter the score or the game. There was no way for me to know, of course, that Lou was on his way to a new all-time record of 118 stolen bases in one season. Like statesmen or actors, celebrated stats are not easy to recognize in their youth.

The next evening, all sorts of misadventures befell the Dodgers —a two-run homer by the Cards' Joe Torre; some stout pitching by another Red Sox alumnus, John Curtis; a dismaying outing by the Dodger starter, Don Sutton (who has been badly off form of late); and a Lou Brock line-drive triple that was utterly misjudged by Jimmy Wynn in center field. Afterward, Walt Alston, probably quoting Agamemnon, said, "The averages are beginning to even up a little. There's still a long way to go." Flying home, I tried to figure out my own stats— 4,902 miles flown, round-trip, for a total of three Dodger runs observed, or a run-per-mile average of .000612.

Two nights later, back at Shea Stadium, predictability returned when the Mets, crippled and down on their luck, lost to the Dodgers by 3–2. Tommy John gave up six hits and ran his record to 10-1; Jon Matlack gave up six hits and ran his to 5-4. Misery abounding. The winning run, it turned out, was surrendered in the ninth inning by Tug McGraw, just off the disabled list, who thereby kept his earned-run average for the year at an even 9.00. The last out of the night was a strikeout by Mike Marshall, the indefatigable relief man whom the Dodgers picked up from Montreal this year. Marshall (a stocky, heavily sideburned veteran who is a Ph.D. candidate in physiology) toweled his face after the game and said, "Sure, we've had a fantastic start, but I'm glad there's still a long way to go. This is the time of year when baseball is most exciting. I enjoy it. The hitters are ready now, and the pitchers at their best. June, July, and August—this is the best part of the baseball year."

•

JUNE, JULY, August . . . How to salute this season in its passage, except with a further and final selection from *The Baseball Encyclopedia*—this time not in numbers? Come, let us have a little music, a quiet coda of baseball names upon the summer air.

Carden Gillenwater. Alban Glossop. Johnny (Hippity) Hopp. Donie Bush, Guy Bush, Bullet Joe Bush. Alpha Brazle.

Jimmy Ring. Dupee Shaw. Buck (Leaky) Fausett. Estel Crabtree. Victory Faust. Chief Yellowhorse. Emil Yde.

Mordecai Peter Centennial (Three-Finger) (Miner) Brown.

Saturnino Orestes Arrieta Armas (Minnie) Minoso.

Calvin Coolidge Julius Caesar Tuskahoma (Cal) McLish.

Flint Rhem. Bibb Falk. Jewel Ens.

Urban Shocker. Urbane Pickering.

Dummy Deegan, Dummy Murphy, Dummy Hoy, Dummy Taylor, Silent John Titus, and Silent George Twombly.

Sunny Jim Bottomley.

Dutch Ruether, Dutch Leonard, Dutch Leonard, Dutch Hartman, Dutch Wilson, Germany Schaefer, Heinie Manush.

Dusty Miller. Zack Wheat. Hod Lisenbee.

Robert Barton (Dusty) Rhoads. William Clarence (Dusty) Rhodes. James Lamar (Dusty) Rhodes. John Gordon (Dusty) Rhodes. Charlie Rhodes.

Fielder Jones. Orator Shaffer. Socks Seibold. Shoeless Joe Jackson. Tillie Shafer. Dolly Stark. Sadie McMahon.

Kitty Brashear, Kitty Bransfield, Rabbit Maranville, Rabbit Warstler, Pig House, Possum Whitted, Chicken Wolf, Doggie Miller, and Hank (Bow Wow) Arft.

Frank Chance, the Peerless Leader.

Spec Shea, the Naugatuck Nugget.

Roger Bresnahan, the Duke of Tralee.

Vic Raschi, the Springfield Rifle.

Arlie Latham, the Freshest Man on Earth.

Amos Rusie, the Hoosier Thunderbolt.

Welcome Gaston. Eppa Rixey. Garland Buckeye.

Hank Aaron. Babe Ruth.

9 How the West Was Won

October 1974

THE SUMMER's immense business is at last shut down, the Oakland A's stand bemedaled as the three-time champions of the world and first-time champions of California, and the sound of baseball silence is upon the land. The World Series, in which the familiar green-and-yellow team—Sal and Reggie and Joe, Rollie and Ken and Campy and Cat, and all the other dashing Octobermen—knocked off the young Dodgers in five games, and the preceding league playoffs, which both concluded in four, were mercifully brisk and decisive. They constituted the only visible signs of economy in a season of excess, which must now be sorted out somehow. O for a Muse of fire! Or, rather, O for a competent certified public accountant, who at least might begin to bring order out of the untidy profligacy of baseball news and records and races, baseball achievement and failure and unlikelihood, that made the late summer and early fall of 1974 so crowded and busy and ridiculously entertaining for us all. On the chance of such help, we can at least pick out a few preliminary clips and jottings from this year's crowded files.

NOTES FOR A STONECUTTER: Hank Aaron, who started off briskly with those two April home runs that took him past Babe Ruth's ancient roadmark of 714, concluded his labors for the year with 20 homers, or 733 lifetime. This year, he also took over first place on the all-time roster for games played (3,076) and times at bat (11,628), and added to his first-place figures for lifetime total bases (6,591) and extra-base hits (1,429). Aaron is retiring from the Atlanta Braves, but if he succeeds with his reported plan to sign on with the Milwaukee Brewers as a designated hitter, he will have a clear shot next year at Ruth's first-place standard of 2,217 runs batted in. Aaron has now passed Ty Cobb as the holder of more lifetime batting records than anyone in baseball history.

LEGS: Lou Brock, of the Cardinals, stole 118 bases this summer, thus wiping out the old one-season mark of 104 thefts held by Maury Wills. Brock's pursuit of the new record was a macrocosm of one of his accelerated journeys between first and second base. After a good early-season jump, he stole 18 bases in June, 17 in July, 29 in August, and 24 in September. He was caught stealing 33 times. Brock is thirty-five years old, and he estimates that he is two or three feet slower between bases than he was at his youthful peak, which suggests that the real contest on the base paths is mostly cerebral and strategic—the runner's experience versus the pitcher's nerves. The other essential ingredients for the remarkable new record were Brock's batting average of .306 for the year (he had to get on some base in order to set about stealing the next one) and the batting judgment and protection provided by the next man in the Cardinal lineup, Ted Sizemore. Watching Lou Brock taking a lead off first base is the best fun in baseball.

ARMS: Mike Marshall, the muscular, muttonchopped relief man for the Los Angeles Dodgers, appeared in 106 games for the year, thus wiping out his own previous one-season mark of 92, which he set last year with the Expos. To judge by his effectiveness (15 wins, 21 saves, an earned-run average of 2.42), his combativeness, and his habit of pitching batting practice for the Dodgers after just one day of idleness, he is perfectly capable of raising this mark by twenty or thirty games, if Walter Alston and the Dodger starters should so require.

Nolan Ryan, the California Angels' fireballer, pitched his third no-hit game in two years, attaining a lifetime level reached by only five other pitchers. (Sandy Koufax notched four.) Ryan also struck out nineteen batters in a single game, to tie a record previously held by Steve Carlton and Tom Seaver. Ryan, however, did this *three times* this year. He struck out more than three hundred hitters (376) in a single season for the third time. One of his deliveries was timed by an electronic device at 100.8 miles per hour, which exceeded Bob Feller's old speed mark (recorded on a different machine) of 98.6 mph. Another Ryan pitch struck Red Sox second baseman Doug Griffin above the ear, retiring him from competition for two months; the next game in which Griffin faced Ryan, he hit two singles. No award or trophy for courage was offered to either man.

Ryan was one of nine American League pitchers to achieve twenty wins this year—a new record mostly attributable to the designated-hitter artifice, which allows starting pitchers to stay in a game until their ears are knocked off. In the American League, the traditional level of pitching effectiveness probably should now be raised from twenty to twenty-five games—a more exclusive neighborhood, inhabited this summer only by Ferguson Jenkins and Catfish Hunter.

ARRIVAL: The day after the regular season ended, Frank Robinson was named manager of the Cleveland Indians. He is the first black manager in the majors, and the belated, much publicized appointment confirms the inflexibility and down-home cronyism that still pervade most of the business side of baseball—a world in which black executives and women executives are equally invisible. Commissioner Bowie Kuhn and the two league presidents had pressured the clubs to make such an appointment, and after it happened Kuhn said, "I don't think that baseball should be exceptionally proud of this day. It's been long overdue." Robinson, who will take over a feeble and (to judge by its play in late September) demoralized club, will have his work cut out for him, but he is qualified for the job. He was a true team leader during his six years with the Orioles, where his manager was Earl Weaver, one of the best and most accessible baseball thinkers of our time. Robinson has also managed the Santurce Crabbers in Puerto Rico for five winter seasons, and an observer of his performance there has told me that he was unexcitable, tough, and effective, not hesitating on occasion to take down such superstars as Reggie Jackson (who is black) and such prima donnas as Dave Kingman (who is white). Frank Robinson is probably even qualified to become the first black manager in the majors to be fired.

DEPARTURES: Dick Allen, the highest-paid player in the game, at $225,000 per year, announced his retirement from the White Sox at the age of thirty-two. He may change his mind and return to baseball; he may not. No one knows what Dick Allen will do next, probably not even Dick Allen. He has been an odd and enigmatic eminence—a great hitter and superior fielder who disdained or ignored every aspect of baseball except occasionally the actual playing of it, the game on the field. He could scarcely bear to give his attention to spring training, to the press, to bus and plane schedules, or, in the end, even to batting practice. Unsurprisingly, he exhausted the patience of several managers and owners, but when at last he was traded to Chicago, in 1972, his new manager, Chuck Tanner, announced that any private drumbeat heard by Dick Allen was perfectly acceptable to him, since Allen was obviously the best player anywhere. Allen responded with one splendid season—a .308 average, 37 homers, and 113 RBIs—which won him his only Most Valuable Player award. The next year, he broke a leg, and since then his other preoccupations—late hours, breeding race horses, silence, indifference—have kept him from the almost limitless baseball heights that could have been his. It is a strange, sad business. Although he quit the sport with two weeks remaining in the season, his thirty-two home runs were tops in his league this year.

Al Kaline retired, after twenty-two memorable years with the Tigers. Here there should be no gloom. On September 24, Kaline rapped out a single and a double against the Orioles and thus surpassed his announced final goal in baseball—3,000 lifetime hits. He finished up with 3,007, which places him eleventh on the all-time list of hitters—a most distinguished gentlemen's club. In temperament and talent, he was almost exactly the opposite of Dick Allen. Never a superstar or a true slugger (his lifetime batting average is a shade under .300), he seemed always able to play at a level very close to the peak of his ability, and the fealty he aroused was almost religious in its ardor. The week after the season ended, I received a four-page letter about him from one of his lifelong fans, a professor at the University of Michigan, who said, among other things, "He did everything perfectly—fielding, throwing, running, judgment, bunting, advancing runners, hitting the ball. . . . I am sorry to see him go, because he may be the last of the complete ballplayers." I heard almost the same words from Eddie Kasko, the former Boston manager and now a super-scout for the Red Sox, who added, "I even liked watching him take outfield practice. He did the whole thing, every part of the game, the way it should be done. If he was throwing to third, say, he would line up his body, take the ball just right, and get off the throw like a picture. You *enjoyed* it." (Not until this summer, by the way, did I suddenly become aware of the marvel of Al Kaline's name. Somewhere in the world, I wonder—perhaps in Spain—could there be an outfielder named A. Cid?)

DISCORD: It was a famous year for fights—commotions in the stands, embroilments on the field, scuffles in clubhouses, ructions on the road. Early in the summer, some fans celebrated Beer Night at the Cleveland ball park with such energy that it cost the Indians a forfeited game; on the last night of the season, Pittsburgh fans celebrated a pennant by showering visiting Cub outfielders with obscenities and empty bottles. The contumelious world-champion A's staged a main-event clubhouse one-rounder between outfielders Reggie Jackson and Bill North, which sidelined catcher (and would-be peacemaker) Ray Fosse for half the season. The Yankees may have lost their chance at a pennant when an alcoholic battle between two second-line players in the lobby of the Pfister Hotel, in Milwaukee, resulted in an injury to Bobby Murcer (also a noncombatant) which kept him out of a late-season game that the Yankees had to win.

Most baseball scuffles, of course, are purely entertaining. On September 22, in Busch Stadium, the visiting Cubs were batting in the ninth against the Cardinals in a critical game, then tied at 5–5. The Cardinals' pitcher was their ace reliever, Al Hrabosky, who has the habit of withdrawing from the mound between deliveries and walking halfway to second base, where he holds visible converse with himself until he attains a point of confidence and batter-hatred that will allow him to return and offer up the next pitch. On this edgy occasion, the Cub batter, Bill Madlock, waited until Hrabosky had completed his psychic countdown, and then reversed the process, walking halfway to his dugout and turning his back on the field while he tapped dirt from his shoes and muttered mutters. Plate umpire Shag Crawford observed this parody and then briskly ordered Madlock back to his place of business. Madlock protested, and so did the Cub manager, Jim Marshall. Crawford signaled to Hrabosky to proceed. Hrabosky threw at the unguarded plate, and Crawford called a strike—an automatic call, under the rules. Hrabosky, delighted, got the ball back and fired again, just as Madlock and the on-deck Cub hitter, José Cardenal, *both* leaped into the batter's box. Crawford signaled "No pitch" and turned to adjudicate matters, at which point the Cardinal catcher, Ted Simmons, punched Madlock in the face. Chaos. Asked later what Madlock had said that had proved insupportable to him, Simmons replied, "He didn't say anything. I didn't like the way he was *looking* at me."

LONGIES: On September 11, the Mets and the Cardinals played a seven-hour-and-four-minute game at Shea Stadium, which the Cardinals won, 4–3, at 3:12 A.M., in twenty-five innings. The home-plate ump was Ed Sudol, who also called balls and strikes during a twenty-three-inning Mets game in 1964 and a twenty-four-inning Mets game in 1968. There is no time and a half, by the way, for umpires.

On September 21, the Red Sox defeated the Orioles, 6–5, in ten innings, in a game that consumed six hours and twenty-seven minutes because of rain delays. The winning pitcher, Bill Lee, went the full distance. The loss dropped the Orioles out of first place.

On September 25, the Cardinals beat the Pirates, 13–12, in eleven innings. The Pirates scored three runs in the top of the eleventh; the Cardinals scored four runs in the bottom half. The victory moved the Cardinals into first place and dropped the Pirates to second.

On September 27, the Orioles defeated the Brewers, 1–0, in seventeen innings, in a game that lasted four hours and twenty-eight minutes. The winning run scored on a bunt. The victory moved the Orioles into a one-game lead in their division.

As it happened, all these deformed contests were important games—evidence of the grudging competition in the pennant races that were fought down through the final weeks and days and hours of the season in the two Eastern divisions. During the final month, the Cards and the Pirates exchanged the lead in the National League East four times and tied at the top four times; the Pirates' final one-and-a-half-game margin was achieved by means of four wins over the Cardinals out of six harsh head-to-head September games—that, plus a passionate kiss of fortune bestowed on them in the last of the ninth inning of their very last game of the season: with two out and the Cubs leading by 4–3, Pirate pinch-hitter Bob Robertson struck out, swinging, but Cub catcher Steve Swisher failed to hold the ball. He then hit Robertson on the back with his peg toward first, allowing the tying run to score from third. The Pirates won it in the tenth.

•

SEPTEMBER IN the AL East began with the Red Sox still in their summerhouse at the top of the division but already in the grip of a frightful batting catatonia that eventually resulted in ten defeats in twelve games (including seven shutouts) and, on September 5, the end of their lead. The startled inheritors of first place were the Yankees, who had been doing some streaking of their own—twelve wins out of fourteen games, including six in a row. A clear marvel, but not the only one, as it happened, for here came the Orioles, suddenly the winners of ten straight, including an astounding five successive shutouts, four of them thrown by the celebrated ancients of their pitching corps.

Any appreciation of the Yankees must be clouded by our knowledge that their adventurous summer voyage fell just short of its goal. The headshakings and forebodings of the nonbelievers and Yankee-haters proved to be correct—not quite enough pitching, not enough speed, not quite enough talent around second base, not enough power (for most of the season the club was last in the league in both home runs and stolen bases), not quite enough *anything* to win, even in an admittedly weak division. Yes, but who cared about any of that back when it all seemed to be happening? Wasn't that the whole point, the real joy of it? These Yankees were a cobbled-up team of retreads, trade bait, and disappointed regulars. The new manager, Bill Virdon, was hired only when the original appointee, Dick Williams, became legally estopped from the job. But never mind; it all came together somehow, at least for a few days. The crowds and the screaming and the banners ("YES, WE CAN!") burst forth in Shea Stadium once again, this time for the new tenants, and some optimist discovered that the club did lead the league in at least one category—sacrifice flies. In the second week of September, the team took to the road and won successive series in Boston, Baltimore, and Detroit. In the eleventh inning of the second game in Boston, Sandy Alomar saved everything with an astounding dive, stop, and throw from short right field that thwarted the winning Red Sox run; Alex Johnson, a brand-new Yankee, then won the game with a homer in the twelfth. In Baltimore, young Mike Wallace made his first American League start and shut out the Orioles and Jim Palmer, 3–0. In Detroit, the Yankees wrapped up the trip by scoring ten runs against the Tigers in each of the last two games, and came home two and a half games in front of the pack. Yes, it seemed, they could!

No, they couldn't. The home stand opened against the Orioles, and the trio of veteran Baltimore pitchers, perfectly accustomed to taking difficult matters in hand in late summer, now utterly suppressed the arrivistes with three beautifully pitched complete-game victories—4–0 for Palmer, 10–4 for Mike Cuellar, 7–0 for Dave McNally—and Baltimore took over the lead by a half game. The visitors offered instructive lessons in power, in defense (notably some wizard catches in center by Paul Blair, of the kind he has been making for a decade now), and—well, in baseball itself. In the second game, Bobby Grich led off the fourth inning with a walk and then was sent along to third on a hit-and-run single by designated hitter Tommy Davis, who stroked the ball precisely behind Sandy Alomar as the second baseman dashed over to cover second; Grich scored a moment later. In the sixth, Grich again led off with a walk, and this time Davis improved on his microsurgery, rapping the hit-and-run, two-and-two pitch a bare yard behind Alomar's heels, as Sandy once again jammed on the brakes and attempted a backward dive at the ball. Nothing in baseball is prettier than this, and no one does it better than Davis. Seven runs now swiftly ensued—and so did my absolute conviction that the Yankees could not win this pennant. The Orioles' clubhouse was a merry place on these evenings, for the team had revived its Kangaroo Court—a traditional buffoonery staged after each Baltimore victory. The judgeship this year went to catcher Elrod Hendricks (Frank Robinson was the Mr. Justice Marshall of his time), who presided with perfect unfairness and the assistance of a sawed-off, magenta-colored bat stub. "Cases" were loudly brought against various players—Mark Belanger for being overambitious on the base paths, Brooks Robinson for an error, Coach Billy Hunter for some invented malfeasance—and suitable booby prizes (an ancient, silver-painted spike shoe, a broken-down glove) were awarded and one-dollar fines assessed. "Vote!" the entire team would shout. "Vote! Vote!" and Hendricks, brandishing his bat, would roar out the guilty verdict: "One! Two! Three! Whop!" The Orioles were loose.

The Yanks were not quite done. They swept a four-game home series from the Indians and were back in first by a single game when the Red Sox came to Shea on September 24 and won both games of a wintry twi-night doubleheader. That was the stunner. Luis Tiant, the venerable Cuban master, threw a six-hit, 4–0 shutout in the opener, thereby achieving his twenty-first win, after five successive defeats. (Exactly one month earlier, he had been the first pitcher in the majors to win his twentieth game of the season, and the Sox had been comfortably ahead. "In baseball," he said now, puffing a post-game cigar as he soaked his arm in ice water, "you don't know *nothin'*.") The Bosox won the nightcap by 4–2 as the Yankees and their fans both began to come apart a little. Bobby Murcer fell on the base paths and was tagged out, and there were two errors by the Yankee infield and an unearned Boston run. On the scoreboard, the Orioles, playing at home, trailed for a time, but then they came back and beat the Tigers and took over first again (for good, this time, it turned out), and the shivering, unsatisfied 46,448-man crowd at Shea fell into disputation and anger, showering the field with firecrackers and old tennis balls. In the seventh, the game was stopped for several minutes while squads of special police separated the participants in three or four violent and prolonged fistfights and pulled them, writhing, from the stands. This was September baseball—or a part of it, at least. There was something cold and miserable about it, beyond the pain and disappointment of watching a whole, long summer's work going for nothing. Winter was coming. Both clubhouses were quiet that night. Bobby Murcer, asked about the violent fans, said, "I don't blame 'em. Tonight, I wanted to get up there and whale with them."

•

THE NEXT Saturday—a cool, drizzly afternoon—I began a vigil in front of my television set, and tried to keep up with things. Less than a week of baseball remained. The Cardinals and the Cubs were scheduled for Channel 4 on the NBC Game of the Week, the Yankees were away for a doubleheader in Cleveland on Channel 11, and the Mets were entertaining the Pirates at Shea on Channel 9, so most of the contenders were available to me. The Yanks sprang away to a quick 2–0 lead over Gaylord Perry, on a homer by Ron Blomberg, and out in Chicago, on a gloomy day, the Cub and Cardinal pitchers worked two quick scoreless innings. Switching channels, I became aware of distractions. On Channel 7, Texas Tech was leading Texas in football—a possible upset there—and on Channel 5 W. C. Fields was suddenly visible at work in a grocery store. Could it be? It was: Channel 5 was running a super Fields movie, *It's a Gift.* On Channel 4, Cub pitcher Rick Reuschel knocked down Ken Reitz with a pitch, then fanned him. On 11, Pat Dobson put away the Indians one-two-three, throwing mostly sliders. On Channel 5, Fields wrapped up a five-cent order of chewing gum with paper and string while a customer shouted "Where are my *kumquats?*" On Channel 4, Reuschel walked Ted Simmons. It was beginning to rain out there in Chicago. On Channel 9, they were taking off the tarpaulin at Shea—a delayed start. On Channel 7, Texas Tech had gone up by 26–3. Back on Channel 5, W. C. Fields called out to a blind man, "Sit still, Mr. Muckle, honey!" but Mr. Muckle blundered into an enormous display rack of light bulbs. I could not tarry. Back to Channel 11, where Elliott Maddox ripped a double down the left-field line. The Indians held a mound conference and decided to pitch to Ron Blomberg ("Which I like to see," Phil Rizzuto announced), and Blomberg hit his second home run into the right-field upper deck, for a 5–0 Yankee lead. On Channel 5, Baby LeRoy hit Fields on the elbow with a can of clams. On Channel 9, the Pirates were leading, 1–0. On Channel 4, NBC had given up on the delayed Game of the Week and was offering a costume drama in its place: Tyrone Power, wearing tights, was in prison. Someone was asking him to sign a confession of heresy; Power smiled enigmatically. On Channel 9, Pittsburgh manager Danny Murtaugh yelled at an umpire. On Channel 5, W. C. Fields groaned as he attempted to go back to sleep on a porch swing up on a third-floor balcony; a man on the ground was calling up to him asking for someone named Carl LaFong. "Carl LaFong!" he shouted. "Large 'C,' small 'a,' small 'r,' small 'l,' large 'L,' small 'a,' large 'F,' small 'o' . . ." On Channel 7, Texas Tech kicked off to Texas, and the ball went right out of the end zone. I looked out my study window and saw that it had cleared up a little, and took my son out to the park for a quick snootful of air.

When we got back, Richie Zisk was in the act of hitting a homer for the Pirates off Tug McGraw on Channel 9, and the Pirates were leading the Mets by 6–1. The scoreboard at Shea showed that the Yankees had won their first game against the Indians, 9–3. The game in Chicago had resumed, with the Cubs ahead by 4–3 in the seventh; NBC had blown it. W. C. Fields had vanished from Channel 5. Apparently, Channel 11 was not going to telecast the second Yankee game; an Abbott and Costello program was on instead. The Orioles would not play until evening. . . .

Three nights later, again encamped at the tube, I watched the Yankees lose to the Brewers, 3–2, in Milwaukee, thus delivering the divisional pennant to the Orioles. It was terrifically cold in Milwaukee, and the stands were almost deserted. In the bottom of the eighth, a long drive to right field was misplayed by Maddox and Piniella, and the Brewers tied the game at 2–2. The ball could have been caught by Bobby Murcer, the regular right fielder, but he was absent because of the injury he had suffered in that senseless hotel-lobby scuffle. None of the Yankee telecasters explained this; baseball announcers work for the club and are not encouraged to give out bad news. On this evening, however, their obligatory ebullience faded to whispers in the tenth inning, when the Brewers put the game and the Yankees away at last.

•

THE PLAYOFFS were swift, tasty, light—a confection of baseball pleasures. I went first to Pittsburgh, and repeated a favorite autumn stroll of mine—over the Fort Duquesne Bridge to Three Rivers Stadium, with the water taxis churning up the sparkling Allegheny below, the sound of a band playing somewhere, the eager early arrivals filing along quietly together, and our expectation almost visible in the soft sunshine. Most of all, I looked forward to watching the Dodgers, a young and wonderfully talented club that had led its division all year and had fought off a scary challenge by the Cincinnati Reds that was a good deal too reminiscent of the late charge to which Los Angeles succumbed the summer before. This year, the Reds had closed to within a game and a half of the Dodgers on September 15, but a grand-slam homer by Dodger outfielder Jimmy Wynn beat them that day and, it turned out, broke them for the year. The Dodgers had pitching and speed and power—they led their league in homers and collective earned-run average—and absolute self-confidence. The Pirates' record, by contrast, was built on plain hitting—by warm young bats like Richie Zisk and Al Oliver, and heavy boppers like Willie Stargell and Richie Hebner. Their pitching, never much to admire, had been weakened by the loss of Dock Ellis. The Dodgers, however, had not won a game in Pittsburgh all year.

All such speculation dwindled away and became perfectly useless in the course of the next couple of hours, as the Dodgers' starter, Don Sutton, shut out the Pirates, 3–0, with four bare singles. It was a sight to remember—a fine pitcher working nine innings at a pinnacle of knowledge, strength, delicacy, and control, and so dominating the event that everything else that happened on the field became nearly superfluous. The Dodgers, for the record, scored once in the second, on a pair of singles and a pair of walks off Pirate starter Jerry Reuss, and twice in the ninth, on three hits and a stolen base. Sutton, a right-hander, was not overpowering; he gave up one walk and struck out six. Above all, perhaps, he was intelligent, adjusting every pitch to the precise situation and batter at hand, controlling the corners, throwing patterns—up and in, out and away, curve and fastball and slider—and reaffirming the enormous imbalance between hurler and hitter that makes baseball look so difficult when pitching is at its prime. Afterward, Sutton admitted that no more than four of his deliveries had disappointed him. "I'd like to write this game down in a textbook and use it for the rest of my career," he said. The performance could not have come as a total surprise to him, however, since it was his tenth victory in a row and his fourteenth in his last fifteen games. I had previously seen Sutton at Dodger Stadium in June, when he was suffering through a frustrating and depressing slump. Manager Walter Alston had left him alone, permitting him to work out his problem while he absorbed six consecutive losses. "It's just some little mistake," Alston told me at the time. "Probably his body is not in exactly the right position over his leg when he delivers. It's puzzling, but you have to be patient. Pitching is a subtle thing."

A few more Dodgers got into the act the next afternoon, when a 5–2 win for the visitors put the unhappy Pirates into a very deep hole. (Three losses in the Championship Series means elimination, of course, and so far in the series' six-year history a two-game deficit has invariably proved fatal.) Andy Messersmith, the Dodgers' only twenty-game winner this year, continued the starvation of the Pirate sluggers, giving up nothing but singles. The golden Californians won in characteristic style, getting on the board in the first inning with a ringing single by their young first baseman, Steve Garvey (a picture-book hitter, who batted .312 this year, knocking out 200 hits and delivering 111 runs), and then breaking the game open in the eighth with three runs. Third baseman Ron Cey started things off with his second successive double (he was four for five on the day, with nine total bases), and then shortstop Bill Russell laid down a perfect, killing bunt to the left side, which catcher Manny Sanguillen threw hopelessly to third base. Then Crawford bonked a little handle-hit over the drawn-in infield, and Mota singled and Lopes singled, and Sanguillen added a wild pickoff throw—five successive hits and a little luck, too, but the Pirates had clearly been cracked apart by the pressure of speed and eager, winning baseball. Cey's outburst at the plate also looked lucky, until one noticed that he had driven in ninety-seven runs in the season—one more than Willie Stargell.

I now bade farewell to the two NL squads, who were off to Chavez Ravine for the rest of their exercises. (The Pirate bats, it will be recalled, came alive there one afternoon, for a 7–0 Pittsburgh victory, in which Stargell and Hebner homered. The following day, the Dodgers took the pennant with a gruesome 12–1 laugher.) My next engagement was the renewal of the A's-Orioles playoff rivalry in Baltimore—by now an autumn event nearly as heartwarming and as poorly attended as an Ivy League football game. The teams here were back from the West tied at one game apiece; the Orioles, finding Catfish

Hunter uncharacteristically wild and high, had whacked him for three homers and a 6–3 victory, and had then been stopped cold by Ken Holtzman, 5–0.

The pitching matchup in game three looked unfair—Jim Palmer, whose Championship Series record for the Orioles was four victories and no defeats, against Vida Blue, who had never won a playoff game or a World Series game, being 0-2 in each category. Everyone knew Vida's pattern—blinding heat for a time, then a slight lapse in concentration, a few walks, a reduction of speed in favor of control, then a couple of telling base hits, and, all too often, another game gone. Absolutely true, except that here in Baltimore it didn't happen. Instead, it was Vida nonstop; Vida burning with concentration and impatience; Vida overpowering everything and everyone, including himself; Vida wall-to-wall. He threw 101 pitches, all but six of them fastballs, gave up two singles, struck out seven batters, walked none, and came in with a 1–0 victory in less than two hours. It was another nearly awesome performance, but one that bore almost no relation to Sutton's game; one felt that the two pitchers might have been engaged in different sports. For that matter, there was still a third splendid and courageous effort—Jim Palmer's losing four-hitter. Palmer has been afflicted with an injury to the ulnar nerve in his pitching arm this year, and he now throws very few fastballs. All the same, he went the distance, too, facing only two more batters than Blue did, and the game eventually turned on a brief personal duel between him and Sal Bando in the fourth, when Bando fouled off several pitches and then lined a home run into the left-field stands. "I should have walked him," Palmer murmured afterward. Manager Weaver, summing up Blue's great game, said, "Our best shot against him was ball four, and he never threw it all day."

Pitching is very nearly the whole story in the playoffs, and so it was again on the final afternoon. A one-hitter *must* be a pitching story, even if that hit is accompanied by eleven walks, even if the other team wins, and even if everyone in the stands is driven absolutely bananas by the anxiety and emptiness and disappointment of it all. Mike Cuellar, the Oriole junk man, is a famously slow starter, so no one was much surprised when he walked the bases loaded in the first inning before recording the third out. On this day, however, he never did find his accustomed groove on the outer fringes of the strike zone. Hunching his shoulders and growling at the home-plate umpire, he threw an intolerable number of near-misses and full counts, until at last, with two out in the fifth, he walked Bando, walked Jackson, threw a wild pitch, walked Rudi on purpose, walked Tenace by mistake, and was gone, responsible for no hits and no satisfaction. The other Oakland run came in the seventh, on the team's only safety—a double by Jackson that scored Bando all the way from first. Catfish Hunter and Rollie Fingers kept the door closed on the Orioles until the ninth, when a walk and two singles brought in the first Baltimore counter in thirty innings. But, with the tying run on third base and the Oriole fans screaming and weeping and pleading, Fingers fanned Don Baylor, to win the game, 2–1, and wrap up the third straight Oakland pennant. California, here we came.

•

THE SERIES was called to order before the largest (and perhaps happiest) crowd in the history of Dodger Stadium, and in the midst of the liveliest kind of advance speculations. The Dodgers' team statistics for the year were the best in their league, overall, while the World Champions presented more clouded data: the finest pitching (by far) in the AL but a flaccid .247 team batting average (twenty-five points below the Dodgers'). The All-Cal final offered an even more vivid difference in personalities and living styles. The Dodgers—somehow personified by their shining new star Steve Garvey—were young, modest, articulate, polite, intelligent, optimistic, brave, clean, reverent . . . They very much suggested a UCLA or USC varsity baseball team, and the campus image was reinforced by their gentle, fatherly manager and by a front office (or dean's office) that liked to talk about an ineffable, enlightened, shared motivation pervading and guiding the entire organization—a spirit known as "Dodger Blue." The two-time-champion A's were something else—whiskery veterans, grown men, distinct and famously quarrelsome personalities, stars who were motivated by their own reputations and the team's fame and success but also, quite openly, by money. Their manager, Alvin Dark, had brought the team home in spite of the players' known fondness and respect for his predecessor, Dick Williams, and their bitterness over the meddling of owner Charles O. Finley, which had caused Williams to give up the reins. Dark, who is a devoutly religious Baptist, had not had an easy summer of it ("You couldn't manage a meat market!" team captain Sal Bando said to him one day), and there were other causes for contention, including Finley's latest *coup de tête:* the signing and use of an athelete who had never played a day in organized ball until he joined the A's. He was Herb Washington, a world-class professional sprinter, whom Finley, via Dark, employed frequently as a pinch-runner. Finley, the inventor and promulgator of the designated hitter, is now campaigning to admit designated base runners to the game, and Washington was his showpiece, or puppet. Learning the rudiments of the game as he went along, Washington stole twenty-nine bases this summer, and was caught stealing sixteen times—not a useful percentage. The company line on Washington, repeated at frequent intervals by Alvin Dark, was "He won eight games for us this year"—to which various old regulars responded with a muttered "Yeah, and how many games did he take us out of?"

This dispute, however, barely quivered the needle on the Oakland seismic scale, and in spite of the North-Jackson imbroglio, there had been some late-summer whispers that the A's were growing more peaceable and cuddlesome. This horrid possibility was done away with, however, when it was revealed that ex-Oakland infielder Mike Andrews had just sued Finley for two and a half million dollars over his forced retirement during last year's Series, that Catfish Hunter had commenced legal steps to force his contract release by Finley for nonpayment of fifty thousand dollars in deferred salary, and that Oakland pitchers Rollie Fingers and Blue Moon Odom had engaged in a clubhouse battle on the very eve of the Series: five stitches in Rollie's scalp and a sprained ankle for Odom. The Oakland AC was ready to play ball.

The opener, which the defending champions won by 3–2, was a busy and absorbing affair, crowded with events and mistakes and discussable baseball. There was Reggie Jackson taking up exactly where he left off in the seventh game of last year's Series—with a terrific near-line-drive home run muscled over the left-field fence in the second inning. There was Oakland pitcher Ken Holtzman, batting in his very first game of the year, rapping a double to left—his third two-bagger in his last four Series games; he proceeded to third on a wild pitch by Andy Messersmith, and was scored on a dandy suicide-squeeze bunt by Campaneris. Dodger dash brought in their first counter: Davey Lopes, on base after a Campaneris error, flew away to second as Bill Buckner bounced a single over first, and when Jackson bobbled the ball ever so briefly in right, Lopes steamed all the way around and easily beat the throw to the plate. The winning Oakland run, in the eighth, was pieced together out of a single, a sacrifice, and a terrible throwing error by Ron Cey. The young Dodgers, as flashy as they were fallible, scored again in the ninth, on a homer by Jimmy Wynn, and had the tying run aboard when Catfish Hunter, of all people, came in to relieve Fingers and fanned Ferguson for the final out. The Los Angeles fans went home stimulated and perhaps insufficiently troubled. In addition to the costly Dodger error and the costly wild pitch, there had been a mystifying failure of strategy after the Dodgers placed their first two batters on base in the second inning and again in the third; in neither case was there any attempt to bunt them along, and none of the four base runners scored.

Perhaps it didn't matter. It didn't seem to the next afternoon, when Don Sutton and Vida Blue faced each other before the same enormous, sun-drenched multitudes, and the home side reversed things, winning by 3–2, for a split on the weekend. It was a quiet, minimal sort of game for most of the distance, with Sutton, now in quest of his twelfth successive win, having a bit the better of things. Vida, down by a bare run, gave up a single to Garvey in the sixth and then tried to throw an inside fastball past Ferguson, who redirected it over the fence in dead center field, exactly between the two "395" markers. Blue threw up his hands in despair. Oakland loaded the bases in the eighth after a fielding error by Dodger shortstop Russell, but Russell now took North's hopper behind second, sprinted over and stepped on the bag, and got off a straining, anxious heave toward first, which Garvey backhanded on a short hop, for an inning-ending, Little League DP. A livelier finale was still to come. In the ninth, Oakland scored twice, on a hit batsman, an accidental, checked-swing double to left by Jackson, and a solid single by Joe Rudi. Reliever Mike Marshall fanned Tenace, whereupon Mr. Finley, suddenly aware of a vivid opportunity to trot his new hobbyhorse, ordered Herb Washington to run for Rudi. Washington now represented the tying run, and Marshall, who is known as perhaps the fastest pick-off gun in the West, sourly eyed him over his shoulder, exactly like Bat Masterson registering the arrival in town of still another uppity gunsel from the prairies. He stepped off the mound three times as Washington, swinging his arms between his knees in a nervous, amateurish fashion, took up a minimal lead. Marshall then spun and fired, Garvey made the tag, umpire Doug Harvey threw up his arm, and Washington, figuratively shot between the eyes, lay twitching in the dust, as 55,989 Los Angelenos cried "Ah-HAH!" in one single splendid shout.

Up in Oakland, two nights later, a pattern began to show itself—not just the third successive 3–2 score (this one in favor of the A's) but something woven more subtly into the texture of these games. Some miserable Dodger luck was part of it: two whistling Los Angeles line drives were hit directly at Oakland infielders and converted into instant double plays. Contrariwise, with two Oakland men on base and two out in the third inning, Reggie Jackson barely topped a pitch by Dodger starter Al Downing, nubbing it feebly but luckily up the first-base line; Jackson flung his bat away in disgust and raced for first, closely accompanied by Joe Ferguson (on this day the Dodger catcher), who lunged for the ball and saw it dribble off the end of his glove for an error. A run was in, and then Rudi hit a single up the middle that barely skipped under Lopes' glove, good for another run, and only the third Oakland run—a trifling walk-sacrifice-and-single affair—was earned. Catfish Hunter gave up two solid solo homers—to Buckner and Crawford ("I had some friends here from North Carolina," Hunter said afterward, "and they'd never seen a home run, so I gave 'em a couple")—but somehow it was Oakland that was now ahead in the Series. It was almost unfair. Bad baseball luck, however, can usually be contained or nullified by perfect defense, but these careless young Dodgers were letting the genie out of the bottle.

Charles O. Finley, it must be added, did not fail to intrude himself into the proceedings. During that third game, we could all watch him leading the hometown hordes in banner-waving, or, up on his feet, joining in the fervent singing of "God Bless America" during the seventh-inning stretch. Then, too, the public-address system announced that Mr. Finley himself could be observed in his box, next to the Oakland dugout, *in the very act* of placing a call to President Ford, in which he invited him to come and throw out the first ball at one of the remaining Series games. The President said sorry, he was busy, but thanks anyway, and moments later we watched Charlie calling up ex-President Nixon in San Clemente—with the same result. The crowd loved it. (Charles O. Finley, I have began to think, may be the last of the true populists.) Then, the next day, Finley abruptly benched and enraged Gene Tenace just before game time, replacing him in the lineup with another protégé and discovery of his, also named Washington

—in this case, Claudell Washington, a twenty-year-old rookie outfielder, who, by the looks of him, may become one of the best left-handed hitters in baseball. (Charles O. Finley, I have concluded, is never boring.)

Game No. 4, both managers had stated in advance, would be the core of the Series, and its core inning, it turned out, was the bottom of the sixth. The Dodgers were leading by then, 2–1, thanks to a triple by Bill Russell; Ken Holtzman had accounted for the Oakland score with another personal editorial on the subject of the designated hitter—this time, a home run. In Dodger retrospect, the Oakland sixth may have turned on a trifling mistake by Andy Messersmith, who made a bad pick-off throw that allowed North to move along to second base, with none out. Or perhaps it was Bando's lucky, blooped, wrong-field single to right (his first hit of the entire Series), or possibly the unfortunate walk to Jackson that came next. Nothing much could be done about the surprising but excellent sacrifice bunt that Joe Rudi now laid down (Rudi *bunting?*), which in turn, of course, required an intentional walk to the next man, and set up the only solid blow of the rally—a pinch single by Jim Holt. There was hardly anything to the whole business, then, except that four runs were in (Was that right—*four?*) and the game, now somehow at 5–2, was nearly gone. It vanished forever in the top of the ninth, on a fantastic sliding, lunging stop by Oakland second baseman Dick Green, who flipped to Campaneris from the dirt to begin a double play. These A's knew how to play this hard old game.

The pattern continued right to the end—a pattern of nearly forgivable little Dodger errors or youthful lapses in judgment, and deadly, coldly retributive play by the old and now doubly renewed champions. This was not in the end a distinguished World Series, because of the losers' multiple mistakes, but rarely has any of these October seminars offered so many plain lessons in winning baseball, or such an instructive moral drama about the uses of baseball luck and the precision with which experienced, opportunistic veterans can pry open a tough, gnarled, closed-up game and extract from it the stuff of victory. In that fifth and final game, Dodger catcher Steve Yeager committed a throwing error in the very first inning, allowing Bill North to move along to third, and to score, a moment later, on a sacrifice fly. Ray Fosse's homer off Don Sutton made it 2–0, but the Dodgers responded, bravely and necessarily, in the sixth—a pinch double by Tom Paciorek, a walk, a fine sacrifice bunt, a fly ball, and a single by Garvey (his eighth hit of the Series). The game was tied, 2–2.

The next bit of Dodger bad luck (or bad play) was not instantly recognizable, for it began with a brief flurry of violence—a small shower of debris and bottleware from the left-field stands directed at outfielder Bill Buckner, which delayed the game for perhaps six minutes. The Dodger pitcher was now Marshall again, and curiously he failed to continue warming with his catcher during the delay, which was his privilege—and, it turned out, his bounden duty. The tiny omission was observed by the leadoff Oakland hitter, Joe Rudi, who cogitated the matter and concluded that Marshall's first pitch to him would not be anything fine and delicate like a curve but probably a fastball. He guessed right, pulled the trigger, and deposited Marshall's delivery in the left-field seats, for the last run of the year, and the last and best baseball lesson, too: Thinking wins ball games. The last big *play* of the year came a moment later, in the eighth, when Dodger leadoff man Buckner whanged out a solid single and watched it slip away from center fielder Bill North. Not content with this free trip to second, he turned the bag and raced madly on toward third, as Reggie Jackson, backing up, swiftly scooped up the ball and fired to the relay man, Dick Green, who whirled—the runner was by now no more than five feet away from third base—and cleanly cut down Buckner with a low, perfect throw to Bando, while Jackson and North exchanged delighted double-slaps back out there at the beginning of it all. It was a play to remember (the throw from the outfield to third base is always one that sticks in memory), a play to carry us through the winter. Bill Buckner, I am sure, will remember it much longer than that, and so, too, will Walter Alston, and so will Sal and Reggie and Joe, and Rollie (who had been chosen as the most valuable player in the Series) and Dick and Campy and Catfish, and the other green-and-yellow champions, who now so clearly deserve our praise and gratitude and whatever other rewards they can extract from their inventor and tormentor and unique leader, Charlie Finley. Nor will Alvin Dark forget. In the lathery, liquid Oakland dressing room, Bando grabbed Alvin by the arm and pulled him up on the interviewers' rostrum. "Come on *up* here, Skip," he said, grinning. "You couldn't manage a meat market!"

10 Sunny Side of the Street

April 1975

It was raining in New York—a miserable afternoon in mid-March. Perfect. Grabbed my coat and got my hat, left my worries on the doorstep. Flew to Miami, drove to Fort Lauderdale, saw the banks of lights gleaming in the gloaming, found the ballpark, parked, climbed to the press box, said hello, picked up stats and a scorecard, took the last empty seat, filled out my card (Mets vs. Yankees), rose for the anthem, regarded the emerald field below (the spotless base paths, the encircling palms, the waiting multitudes, the heroes capless and at attention), and took a peek at my watch: four hours and forty minutes to springtime, door to door.

The journey and the arrival and then a few innings of mild, meaningless baseball would have been more than enough for my first day of spring training, but this particular evening promised a treat. It was the middle meeting of a three-game set between the Yankees and the visiting Mets, and the starting pitchers were Catfish Hunter and Tom Seaver. The ball park was sold out, and there were rows of standees three or four deep along the fences in left and right field. Yankee manager Bill Virdon and Met manager Yogi Berra contributed to this sudden party by starting their first-stringers—two lineups that looked to be very close to the teams that would take the field four weeks later, on opening day. Both New York front offices had been avid participants in an off-season of exceptionally complex trading activity, and as I studied the old names and the new names I had written on my scorecard, I sensed myself already awash in the kind of deep-water baseball speculation that usually becomes possible only in August or September. Among the new Mets were Del Unser (a useful if unbrilliant center fielder who had come over from the Phillies as part of a trade that had taken away Tug McGraw) and Joe Torre, who was with the Cardinals last year—a lifetime .300 hitter and a former Most Valuable Player, now thirty-four years old and well past his peak but perhaps still better than any previous Met third baseman. Starting in left field was Dave Kingman, a tall free-swinger and erstwhile (very recently erstwhile) Giant, who had just been picked up for $125,000 in a straight cash deal. Last of all, most of all, there was Tom Seaver, the Mets' champion, who would be trying out the sciatic hip that afflicted him all last summer—a disability now tentatively but anxiously regarded as cured by rest and osteopathy.

The Yankee alterations were even more noticeable. Gone was the familiar and overburdened Bobby Murcer, who had been dealt to the Giants for another outfielder—another *kind* of outfielder—Bobby Bonds, a swift, powerful, mercurial and not altogether reliable courser, who had never quite attained the superstar status expected of him. Thurman Munson, the Yankee catcher, would be making his first appearance of the year and would be testing the damaged forearm that limited his effectiveness last year. And best of all, there was Catfish Hunter, the ex-Oakland ace, a twenty-game winner over four consecutive seasons, last year's American League Cy Young Award winner (he was twenty-five and twelve, with an earned-run average of 2.49), undefeated in Seven World Series games, et cetera, et cetera, who was cut free from the A's last December by an arbitrator's decision, as a result of Oakland owner Charles O. Finley's failure to make payments on a deferred portion of his salary. Thus suddenly empowered to sell his fealty and right arm to the highest or most attractive bidder, Hunter settled upon the Yankees, after receiving unimaginable cajoleries ("You want Helen of Troy, Cat? Listen, we'll fix Helen up with a beautiful annuity and throw in a li'l old Dodge Charger for her, and . . .") from almost every other club, for a sum in the neighborhood of three and a half million dollars in salaries and deferrals and shelters and other considerations, to be paid over the next five years, and more. Inevitably, some sportswriters have begun to refer to him as Goldfish Hunter.

Beyond these individual athletic and fiscal histories was the interesting business of the two clubs themselves and their impending summer-long fight for the affections of the same enormous and demanding baseball audience—the battle of Shea Stadium, the war for New York. There has been nothing quite like this since the departure of the Giants and the Dodgers, for the swift decline of the once mighty Yankees in the past decade and the even more precipitous ascent of the darling Mets had seemed utterly independent of each other. Now a big-city baseball reversal may be in progress, with the young and star-enriched Yankees, who were a close second in their division last year, apparently the possessors of the best pitching and the best outfield in their half-league, on the rise; and with the aging Mets, pennant winners in 1973 but a fifth-place club last year, apparently in pitching difficulties and thus possibly in very bad trouble indeed. This spring meeting was part of a good subway summer to come.

The game began, and baseball replaced speculation. Hunter in pinstripes was about the same as Hunter in green and gold—the flowing hair, the flowing motion, the big, oversize cap resettled between each pitch. Seaver, too, restored memory—the cold, intelligent gaze; the unwasteful windup; the sudden forward, down-dropping stride off the rubber. He struck out two of the first three Yankee batters, without really trying his fastball. Now, with one out in the top of the second, Dave Kingman stood in for the Mets, occasioning a small hum of interest because of his height, which is six feet six inches, and his batting style, which is right-handed, tilted, and uppercutting. The hum was replaced by an explosion of sustained shouting as Kingman came around on a high Hunter change-up, caught all of the ball—every inch and ounce of it—with his bat, and drove it out of the park and out of the lights in a gigantic parabola, whose second, descendant half was not yet perceptible when the ball flew into the darkness, departing the premises about five feet inside the left-field foul line and about three palm trees high. I have never seen a longer home run anywhere.

There were further entertainments and events—two hits by Munson; the Mets winning the game, 3–0, on sterling shutout pitching by Seaver and his young successors, Craig Swan and Rick Baldwin; and *another* homer by Kingman, also off Hunter—this one a high, windblown fly just over the fence, giving him a total of four round-trippers in his first five games as a Met. He also fanned weakly on his last two times up. In the fourth inning, Joe Torre took a backward step near third base as Bobby Bonds came down the base path from second (there was no play on him), and somehow severely sprained his right ankle. It was an inexplicable, almost invisible little accident that nonetheless ruined Torre's spring, and the kind of pure bad luck that can sometimes darken a club's entire season.

Nothing, however, could touch or diminish Kingman's first shot. Catfish Hunter, after his stint, sat in the training room with his shoulder encased in an ice bag and his elbow in a bucket of ice water, and reminisced cheerfully about other epochal downtowners he had given up. There had been a preseason one by Willie McCovey and perhaps, years ago, a Mickey Mantle five-hundred-footer. Mantle, now a Yankee springtime coach, could not remember it. "I know I never saw one longer than this," he said. Bill Virdon guessed that the ball had flown an additional two hundred and fifty feet beyond the fence, into an adjacent diamond, which might qualify it as a simultaneous homer and double: a six-base blow. The Yankees were still talking about the home run the next day, when Hunter told Ron Blomberg he hoped he hadn't hurt his neck out there in left field watching the ball depart. Others took it up, rookies and writers and regulars, redescribing and amplifying it, already making it a legend, and it occurred to me that the real effect of the blast, except for the memory and joy of it, might be to speed Catfish Hunter's acceptance by his new teammates. There is nothing like a little public humiliation to make a three-and-a-half-million-dollar executive lovable.

That night, the press clustered thickly around Kingman in the visiting clubhouse. He is a shy, complicated young man, twenty-six years old, and he seemed embarrassed by his feat, although he was noted for similar early-season tape-measure blows while with the Giants, as well as for his strikeouts. "I'm just trying to win a job here," he said. "I'm putting home runs and strikeouts out of my mind. They're not in my vocabulary." Well, yes. Every spring is a new beginning, especially for a ballplayer with a new team, but in his three and a half major-league seasons to date, Dave Kingman has hit 77 home runs while striking out 422 times—once for every three trips to the plate—and his batting average is .224.

Rusty Staub, dressing in front of his locker, looked over at the tall newcomer and the eight or ten writers around him, and laughed. "The trouble with you, Dave," he called over, "is you're just having a slow start. You'll get going once the season rolls along."

•

SPRING TRAINING is all hope. Hope is the essential, for every club and every player. Walt Williams, a black thirty-one-year-old journeyman outfielder, started for the Yankees in the

Mets game the next afternoon, playing second base. He has had nine years in the majors, mostly with the White Sox; he hit .304 one season. Last year, however, his batting fell off to an abysmal .113, and he ended the season with the Yanks as a pinch-runner. He claims that he had an incorrect prescription in his eyeglasses. This year, he thought about the incoming Yankee talent and decided that his chances as an outfielder were "poor or none." He received permission from Bill Virdon and general manager Gabe Paul to try to make the club as an extra infielder. The day before, he had played second in a B game against the Texas Rangers, and had made three hits, including a home run, and had been involved in a double play. Walt Williams is five feet six inches tall, with the shoulders and chest of a heavyweight prizefighter. At the plate, he stands with his arms and shoulders raised high, peering at the pitcher over his left biceps, and waggles the bat fiercely. While playing in Chicago, he was called No-Neck Williams—a name he does not like. He runs everywhere, runs out everything. He talks fast, in explosions of words, and smiles ceaselessly. It is impossible not to like him. Before the game, he said, "Listen, I'm just like a rookie in the infield, only I've got better hands than the average infielder. I'm a lifetime .280 hitter. Forget about last year—just throw it out. Aren't too many guys going to outhit me. Truthfully, after last year I was going to go and play in Japan. I planned on winning the batting championship there. Then I got a little fan mail, letters that said 'Don't go,' so I came and talked to Gabe about being an extra infielder. Those letters made me feel good. Listen, I *know* I can play second, but can I show them in time? When did I last play second base? Before yesterday? Oh, my, I think it was when I was about seventeen."

In the game (which the Yanks won, 7–6), Walt Williams hit a single and a double, ran out everything, started one double play with a tag on the base path, and made an error when he dropped the ball in his eagerness to start another. In the clubhouse, panting and pouring sweat from the postgame squad sprints, he said, "I made a mistake out there—changed my mind at the last minute. But I think I showed them something. I know I can play this game. I *know* it."

There are two utility infielders, Eddie Leon and Fred Stanley, already on the Yankee roster, and reserve infielders are kept on mostly for their steady gloves and their experience. But Walt Williams is hopeful; he has no other choice.

POSTCARDS

SAW Eddie Kranepool hit three singles today, against the Yanks. Eddie Kranepool always hits. Last year, he hit an even .300. Eddie will always be a Met. Mrs. Payson loves him, and, besides, why would you ever get rid of him? Eddie has it made. He has twelve years in as a major leaguer, twelve years on the pension. Eddie Kranepool is thirty years old. Good old Eddie.

•

RON BLOMBERG came up the steps from the clubhouse and into the dugout, and saw a *Times* reporter reading the Mets' press pamphlet. "Hey," he said, "can I see that for a minute?" "Sure," the writer said, tossing it to him. "Don't drop it." Blomberg nearly did drop it. "Jesus!" he muttered. Terrible hands. Bill Virdon said, "You got him thinking." Everyone nearly died laughing. . . . Maybe you had to *be* there.

•

PITCHERS ARE expected to do a lot of running in the spring. They sprint in groups of three or four along the outfield fence, from one of the foul lines to center field. They stop and rest, then run back. If the sun is out, they stop in the little slab of shade along the fence and bend over, with their heads down and their hands on their knees, and pant like dogs. This happens in every camp every day. Hundreds of pitchers running and panting.

•

WATCHED Los Angeles taking batting practice before the next game at Fort Lauderdale. A young Dodger was looking at three girls sunning themselves behind home. Coach Monty Basgall said, "Get out of the stands; you're married now."

The ballplayer said something short.

"You still married?" Basgall asked.

"I think so. Why?"

"I don't know," Basgall said. "I figure you for the kind's going to get married three, four times."

•

BOBBY BONDS, sitting on a trunk in the clubhouse before the Dodger game, talking about his old Giant teammate Dave Kingman: "If you see him hit two singles, it's amazing. If he's making contact, the ball's going to go. You know he's a great bunter? People don't know everything about him. . . . I'm the DH today. Never did *that* before. What does the DH do when he isn't up swinging? . . . It's funny—I looked over at the Dodgers there today and I didn't get that old feeling. We used to be so up for those games. They really counted."

STRAIGHT ARROWS

A SLIM, tan, dark-eyed young man with a very thin mustache turned up in the Yankee clubhouse. He was not in uniform, but most of the Yankee regulars came over to shake his hand. "Hey," they said. "Way to go. I just heard. Go get 'em there, now." He was Ray Negron, a nineteen-year-old Queens resident, who was a Yankee batboy last year. This winter, he was taken on by the Pirates in the second round of the free-agent draft, and now he was on his way to report to Pirate City, in

Bradenton, for the opening day of minor-league training camp. He hopes to play second base with the Pirates' Class A club, in Charleston, South Carolina.

"Leaving home yesterday was the hardest thing I ever did in my life," he said. "Everybody came to the airport to see me off. My father, my mother, my two sisters, my grandfather, my girl friend, and me—everybody was there, everybody was crying. I'm not afraid of what will happen. I know I can pick it in the infield, so the only question is whether I can hit the pitching. I'm very thrilled. This is what I've wanted all my life. Being around the big leaguers last year on the Yankees got my attitude together. Watching guys like Alex Johnson and Lou Piniella made me learn to be positive. Before last year, I was a sure out. Couldn't hit, couldn't win. Since then, I've hit over .500 in every league I've been in. I know how hard a major leaguer has to work, so I'm ready. I told my girl, Barbara, I wouldn't see her until September, no matter what happens. I said, 'You go out, have a good time. You're free. But if you want to wait, I'll be waiting, too. I'll wait for you in September.' " He looked down at the floor, suddenly shy.

•

STEVE GARVEY, the young Dodger first baseman, shook hands with two New York writers near the batting cage. Last year, he batted .312, hit 21 homers, and knocked in 111 runs, and was voted Most Valuable Player in the National League. Garvey's hair is short and neat, and he is always clean-shaven. He is friendly and extremely polite. "It was a busy winter for me," he said. "I spoke at thirty-five or forty lunches and dinners, and made sixty or seventy appearances in all. I also did PR work for Pepsi-Cola. I missed being with my family, but on the whole it was a very satisfying experience. It was a real opportunity for me to be a good-will ambassador for baseball and for the club. There were a lot of father-and-son dinners and YMCA affairs, so there was the opportunity to influence young people, to show them there are people in the world they can look up to and pattern their lives after. The kids do listen to you—I was amazed. I think they're ready to get away from the antiheroes of the nineteen sixties and move on to the heroes of the seventies. Anyway, I don't care if they listen or not, because I believe this and I practice it in my life. Excuse me for a second, please. It's my turn to bat."

He stepped into the cage. The writers watched him in absolute silence.

•

RANDY TATE, a tall young right-handed pitcher, was throwing hard on the mound at Huggins-Stengel Field, the Mets' training headquarters in Saint Petersburg. He was being watched by Rube Walker, the Mets' pitching coach, and by a videotape camera. There was a long orange-colored electric cord snaking across the field from the sidelines to the machine, which bore the name Video Logic. It was a cool, bright morning, and the grass was still dark with dew and early shadow. Rube Walker shook his head and called Tate in from the mound. His place was taken by Jon Matlack. "Seven minutes, Jon babe," Walker said.

Tate pulled on a silky blue warm-up jacket and joined Rube Walker beside the machine. The camera operator began the playback, and we all watched Tate pitching in slow motion on the little screen. "You still think you're pushin' off the rubber?" Rube said. "You call that pushin' off? Look at that. This machine does the trick, Randy. I could talk to you about it all day, but this damned machine don't lie. Run it back again."

Huggins-Stengel is a modest double diamond in the middle of one of the Saint Petersburg public parks. The field is surrounded by trees. There is a lake out beyond right field, and a tiny strip of bleacher seats next to the low clubhouse building. An old-fashioned water tower behind home plate. On this morning, there were about thirty spectators sitting in the stands; some of them were watching the infield workout, and some were reading newspapers. There were six or eight schoolboy ballplayers there, wearing sneakers and pale-blue pinstriped uniforms with "Cardinals" across the shirtfronts in blue script. Birds were twittering. It was so quiet that when one of the coaches tapped a grounder out to a shortstop you could hear the sound the ball made as it hit the infield grass.

Del Unser was inside the batting nets, out in left-field foul territory. He stood about ten feet in front of the plate, making things harder for himself, and swung left-handed against the characterless offerings of the pitching machine. Phil Cavarretta, the Mets' batting coach, stood behind him, with his arms folded. Cavarretta has a deeply tanned face and white hair. The machine stopped, and Unser and Cavarretta began collecting the dozens of balls scattered about the rope enclosure; they looked like park attendants picking up after a holiday. They reloaded the machine and then dusted it with a rosin bag. "I turned this wrist just a little and opened up on it," Unser said, picking up his bat again. Cavarretta nodded. "If I keep my hands back, I can bail on a pitch and still hit the ball," Unser said.

"You're damn right you can," Cavarretta said.

Randy Tate began throwing again, and I walked back and stood beside Rube Walker, behind the backstop. Rube watched a few more pitches. "He ain't doin' a damn thing different," he murmured to himself. "How am I going to get *through* to him?"

In time, batting practice began, with coach Joe Pignatano throwing from behind a low screen on the mound. Jay Kleven, a young nonroster catcher, hit two pop flies to center, and coach Eddie Yost said, "Try to loosen up that top hand, Jay. Just throw the bat at the ball."

Kleven hit a liner over second base.

"That's it," Yost said. "Good!"

The next pitch broke down sharply over the plate, and everyone cried, "Spitter! Hey, a spitter!"

"Aw, it just got a little wet on the grass," Piggy said, laughing.

•

I DROVE downtown to Al Lang Field, the ancient, iron-beamed park where the Mets and the St. Louis Cardinals play their home games in the spring. The White Sox, who had come up from Sarasota to play the Mets that day, were taking batting practice, observed from behind the batting cage by their manager, Chuck Tanner, and by Harry Walker, a special-assignment scout for the Cardinals. The Cards were off in Lakeland for a game against the Tigers, but Walker was here. He was wearing a faded Cardinal road uniform, and he was talking earnestly to Tanner. From time to time, he pointed to a batter in the cage and then touched Tanner's arm or pointed to his knees. He held up an imaginary bat and cocked his hands and hips and swung the bat forward in different planes, talking all the while. Tanner watched his batters, but he nodded as Walker went on talking. A number of players and writers looked at this tableau in delight.

Harry Walker is a tall, deep-bellied man who has at various times managed the Cardinals, the Pirates, and, most recently, the Houston Astros. As a player, three decades ago, he was known as Harry the Hat; he won the National League batting title in 1947, with an average of .363. He is Dixie Walker's brother. Harry Walker is reputed to be one of the finest theoreticians of hitting in baseball, and several players who have come under his tutelage have given him credit for an increase of twenty or thirty points in their batting averages—astounding figures, for batting is considered the most difficult of all athletic techniques to learn or to teach. Some other players, however, have admitted that they found it impossible to take advantage of Walker's wisdom, simply because they could not force themselves to stay within earshot of him—to go on listening to the hundreds of thousands of words that pour from Harry Walker every day. Harry Walker talks like a river.

He is easily capable of as many words per hour as Hubert Humphrey or Buckminster Fuller—which is to say that he is in the Talkers' Hall of Fame. A few summers back, one of the Houston infielders is reported to have said to a teammate, "I'm worried about Harry. He's a natural .400 talker, and these last few days he ain't talked more than about .280."

Three years ago, before an Astros-Dodgers game in Los Angeles, I casually asked Harry Walker why his young pitchers and catchers seemed to be giving up so many stolen bases to enemy runners. Harry Walker has no casual answers, and his reply, which took the better part of twenty minutes, encompassed the American public-school system, permissiveness in the American home, Dr. Spock, our policies in Vietnam, great pick-off deliveries of various right-thinking pitchers of the past, the high rate of divorce in America, umpiring then and now, the inflated American economy, the exorbitant current bonuses paid to young baseball prospects, taxation, growing up in the Great Depression, how to protect home plate with your bat during the run-and-hit, and various other topics. At one point I recall his crying, "Whah, hell-fahr, when Ah was goin' after mah battin' title in '47 and Ah got the sign to lay down the bunt 'cause we was down a run late in the game and needed to move that runner up, Ah didn't come stormin' and hollerin' back to the dugout to tell the old man how much Ah wanted mah at-bats in order to qualify for that title and whah Ah'd ruther have hit away, and Ah didn't slam mah battin' helmet down on the ground like those kids do here today. No, sir! Whah, God damn it, we din' even *have* any battin' helmets back then!"

Here, in time, the Mets and the umpires and the fans appeared, and the batting cage and Harry Walker were taken off the field, and the game began, and the visitors demolished the Mets, in a somnolent, sun-filled time-killer, by 10–4. Jerry Koosman pitched three good innings, and Randy Tate pitched, too, and gave up five runs and six hits; I am not a camera, but it seemed to me that Tate was still not driving off the rubber.

Between these two hurlers, there was an appearance by a good-looking Mets sprout named Jeff Grose, who is only two years out of high school. Grose, a southpaw, showed us a live fastball and a smooth, high-kicking motion, and he hid the ball behind his hip while on the mound, like Sandy Koufax. He seemed poised, but he was working a little too quickly, and he gave up three hits and a run in his first inning of work. In the next inning, his fastball began missing the corners. He kept falling behind the hitters, and then forcing things and overthrowing to make up for it. He gave it a battle, though. With two out and a run in, he went to three and two, saw the next pitch barely tipped foul, then threw the fourth ball way inside, to load the bases, then swiftly walked in another run and gave up a single, and was lucky when Rusty Staub threw out a base runner at the plate. It was painful to add up his totals: four runs, six hits, and four walks in two innings. Spring training is good young pitchers falling behind on the count and then disappearing until next year.

POSTCARDS

Saw the Phillies beat the Cards at Al Lang Field by 1–0, in a game illuminated by wind, sun, and young baseball stars. The newcomers include twenty-three-year-old Alan Bannister, a swift Phillie outfielder, and twenty-one-year-old Keith Hernandez, the new Cardinal first baseman, who batted .351 last year in the American Association. Before the game, I saw the Cards' Reggie Smith and the Phillies' Dave Cash in earnest conversation near the batting cage. As I walked by, Reggie was saying, "And the rest I got in tax-exempts."

•

Al Lang Field is to be demolished next fall, and a more modern ball park will be built on the same site. It seems a pity, since the stands, which look like a leftover segment of Ebbets

Field, perfectly match the style and antiquity of the fans. And what will happen to the ushers? When an Al Lang usher escorts an elderly female fan to her seat, it is impossible to tell who is holding up whom.

•

"Pick it" is this year's "in" baseball phrase. It means playing the infield well. Ken Reitz, the Cardinal third baseman, can really pick it.

•

Talked to John Curtis, the tall, intelligent left-handed pitcher who came over to the Cardinals from the Red Sox two years ago. I told him I had a vivid recollection of a night game at Yankee Stadium two years ago, in July, in which he had shut out the Yankees by 1–0, and had retired the last batter on a pop-up with the bases loaded in the bottom of the ninth. He remembered it, too, of course. "That one-and-two change-up I threw to Felipe Alou in that spot was the best pitch of my life," he said.

Curtis had an off year last season, and this campaign will be an important one for him. I have heard it said that he may be too gentle a man to become a big winner in the majors.

VETERAN

The speaker is Ray Sadecki, thirty-four, who is beginning his fifteenth year as a major-league pitcher. His lifetime totals are 129 victories and 127 losses, and an earned-run average of 3.77. His best year was 1964, when he won twenty games for the Cardinals and also won a World Series start. The next year, he slipped to six and fifteen. He has also pitched for the Giants and, in the last five years, for the Mets. He was sent back to the Cards last winter, as part of the Joe Torre trade. He sat in the dugout at Al Lang Field one afternoon, wearing a bright-red warm-up jacket, and talked about baseball. He has a quizzical, amused expression and an easy manner. He is left-handed.

"It seems to take me every single day of the spring season to get ready now," he said. "I make all the same moves, but I come up a little short. Then, of course, when the season starts, a man like me who isn't a front-line pitcher anymore has to do all his training all over again, throwing on the sidelines. You get caught in those rainouts and before you know it you've only pitched two or three innings in three weeks. The most starts I had with the Mets was twenty, and the least was two. You get to know all the conditions, all the possibilities. You know about that year when I lost fifteen games, right after my best year? Well, a man has to be pitching pretty well to get the *chance* to lose fifteen.

"Every time I'm traded, I figure the other club wants me. I went once for a pretty fair player named Orlando Cepeda. This trade from the Mets—you know they had to make it. Getting a chance at Torre doesn't mean they dumped me. The thing about trades is it's an opportunity for most players. An awful lot of trades end up helping the people involved. Look at Nolan Ryan. Look at Dave Cash. Torre came over to this club from Atlanta and won an MVP. Too many people get it wrong and think, 'Boy, what a rotten thing to do.' Fans don't understand trades.

"The only tough part about being traded—the worst part—is when it happens during the season. Seventy-two hours to report. Your family is all upset, your wife has to do all the moving. You walk into your new dugout and they're playing the anthem. Hell, when I went over to the Giants I walked out onto the mound, and Tom Haller and I had to get together on our *signs*. A pitcher and a catcher need a lot of time to get used to each other.

"I'm a completely different kind of pitcher than I was when I was with this club the last time. But I don't figure I'm down here to let them see what I can do. They're looking at the young pitchers. I got together with Red [Schoendienst, the Cardinal manager] and Barney [Schultz, the pitching coach], and said I'll get ready in my own time. I pitched two and two-thirds yesterday. They weren't the best ever, but they were just right for me. I'm just where I want to be. That's what spring training is for. Anyway, we all know about a pitcher who gets hammered all spring and then walks out there on opening day and nobody can touch him. Another one has it the other way around—once the bell rings, he can't get anybody out. It's awful hard to make a decision about people in the spring. I've been out there at times in March and couldn't do *anything*. I embarrassed myself. But you can't start throwing harder and mess yourself up. That's what a kid will do. It's the last week or so of training that counts. That's when you'll see a pitcher try things he hasn't done all spring. He's getting ready for that first start. You can't pay much attention to what happens down here. Putting on these games has always seemed to me sort of a distraction. I think that most of the players are less cooperative with the press in spring training because of this—because you can't go telling the writers, 'Look, don't pay any attention to what I did.'

"It's the young players I'm sorry for. It's awful hard for a rookie to make a ball club in the spring. If you're a pitcher, you've pretty well got to throw all scoreless innings. If you're a batter, you've got to hit about .400. Even so, they'll all say, 'Hell, it's only spring training.' Spring is hard on people."

•

THE CACTUS LEAGUE consists of four small ball parks attached to a ribbon of motels, moccasin shops, trailer sales lots, and Big-Boy burger stands in and around Phoenix, Arizona—plus outlying baseball stockades in Tucson, Yuma, and Palm Springs, California. (The air service to Palm Springs, where the Angels train, is sketchy, and when one of the Phoenix-area clubs—the Cubs, say—plays there, the visitors can count on a good twelve hours, round-trip, in which to study the desert from the windows of their bus.) The motels are functional to the spring baseball scene. Generally, they feature an enclosed central swimming pool and lawn and patio, plus restaurant and bar and dance floor and shuffle courts and lobby and coin-operated electronic Ping-Pong games, all of them variously patronized by players, managers, league executives, front-office people, writers, scouts, and fans, and attendant wives, children, babies, parents, in-laws, girl friends, hookers, and Baseball Annies. (Lounging at poolside one morning, I noticed a nearby gathering of cheerfully forward, heavily tanned ladies, of indeterminate age and affiliation. I asked a fellow writer about them. "Groupies," he said. "They've been coming here for years and years. They used to hang out with the players, then with the coaches. Now I think they're umpire groupies.")

The Giants' park, Phoenix Municipal Stadium, is an agreeable, half-sunken field, with a concrete grandstand offering a prospect of distant mountains, a nearby highway, and, in between, several weirdly twisted, buttelike rock formations suggesting dinosaurs or Boschian damned souls or Horace Stoneham's baseball hopes. The Giants, by general consensus, in recent years have led their league in finding and developing the greatest talent and then employing it to the smallest possible ends. This year, they have come up with another one of their nearly irresistible Spring Specials—a new (almost) manager, a lineup stripped of last year's disappointing stars, and a stimulating catalogue of young arms and great wheels. Gone is the charming, moody skipper, Charlie Fox, who plainly lost control of things last summer and was replaced in midcampaign by the calm and approachable Wes Westrum. Gone are the high-strung, well-paid Bobby Bonds and Dave Kingman. A veteran hot-dog second baseman, Tito Fuentes, was sent to the Padres in return for a new hot dog, Derrel Thomas.

The pitching staff is young and strong but without a true stopper—with the possible exception of a second-year fireballer named John D'Acquisto. The holdover regulars afield, including Chris Speier and Garry Maddox and Gary Matthews, have dash but not much power, and there is a terrific catching prospect named Marc Hill.

I watched this bright-eyed entering class in action against the World Champion A's, whom they defeated by 7–2, thus pleasing an underflow crowd of 2,802 and persuading me that another summer of high, dashed hopes was in the making at Candlestick Park. Steve Ontiveros, a former outfielder, does not exactly pick it at third base for the Giants; in the fourth inning, he played a one-hopper by Joe Rudi off his shoulder, and he later threw the ball away while attempting an easy double play. (The Giants have had forty-six third basemen since they came to the Coast in 1958.) The A's, for their part, seemed to be suffering from similar tinkering. Joe Rudi, the best defensive left fielder in the American League, has been moved to first base in order to make room for Claudell Washington, who is a fine hitter but cannot field much. He played a fly ball by Matthews into a double and later threw behind a runner. The best poke of the day was a triple in the fifth by Bobby Murcer—a Murcer Special into the deepest right-field corner. A week or two earlier, Bobby had delivered himself of a bad-tempered public blast against the Yankees for shipping him off to San Francisco in the Bonds trade, but now, after the game, he appeared to be in splendid humor, as befits a man currently batting .500. I asked him if the trade might not in fact be one of those that ended up helping both principals. "Don't know," he said. "Ask me in September."

•

THE MOST heavily reported news at the Indians' camp in Tucson this spring was fundamentally unreportable—the fact that Frank Robinson, the new Cleveland manager, is black. Like several dozen visiting scribes before me this year, I sought him out in his office at Hi Corbett Field (where he was lunching on two Cokes and some saltines crumbled into a cup of soup), shook hands, asked him some questions, and concluded that he was going about his duties in a responsible if inescapably predictable fashion. He admitted to some innovations—no team curfew, the appointment of two team captains (one white, one black; or, rather, as Robinson put it, one an outfielder and one an infielder)—and said he had turned over a great deal of detail work to his coaches, so that he might have more time to watch and get to know his players. "I want things done right," he said. "That is, I want them done my way."

He hadn't had time to do much batting himself, and thus prepare himself for his additional duties as a designated hitter. Robinson spoke with alternate gravity and humor, exuding the same sense of weight and presence I have always observed in him. We chatted a little, and then I said goodbye and wished him luck, and made room for three more out-of-town reporters, who had come for the same unspoken and unspeakable purpose: How does a black manager manage? What is black managing? How does it, uh, *feel* to be the first black manager?

It was nice and hot in Tucson, and I sat in the stands that afternoon and caught some rays. There was a grove of trees out beyond center field, and the distant outfield fences were covered with old-style billboards—Jim Click Ford, Coors Beer, Ralph Hays Roofing, Patio Pools. (Arizona outfields are spacious, to make room for the great distances that fly balls carry through the dry, desert air; a few years ago, in Mesa, Curt Blefary ducked away from an inside pitch, and the ball struck his bat and flew over the right-field fence for a homer.) Two veteran flingers, the Indians' Fritz Peterson and the Angels' Chuck Dobson, had at each other, with the visitors enjoying all the best of things. The Angels have only speed and pitching, and their left fielder, Mickey Rivers, a skinny blur on the base paths, stretched two routine singles into doubles. In the California fourth, Cleveland center fielder George Hendrick fielded a single and threw the ball over the cutoff man's head. The Indians, who have insufficient pitching, may have a long summer of it.

There was a good mix taking the sun in the stands that day: high-school girls with long, clean hair; a lot of young men—probably students at the University of Arizona—with beards and tanned bare chests and cutoff jeans and silver bracelets; and, of course, old folks. At one point, somebody behind me said, "I understand they gave Homer a pacemaker, but it was sort of out of pace with his heart." A pause, and then "Oh, well, Homer has more money than Carter has little pills."

Just before I left, in the seventh, I recorded a personal baseball first: Most Fans Seen Wheeling a Bicycle up Aisle of Grandstand—1.

•

FRIENDS HAVE told me that they find the Oakland A's insufferable. I find this a mystery. The three-time World Champions have not only more talent but more interesting troubles and more lively conversationalists than anybody else around. This year, their problems may be sufficient to keep them from their customary October rendezvous, for Charlie Finley's fiscal irresiliency has cost them not only Catfish Hunter but the services of their second baseman, Dick Green, a twelve-year veteran who retired rather than accept Finley's kind of emolument for another year.

I had heard about the infamous conditions at the home park of the A's, in Mesa, but I was still not quite ready for the dim, cluttered, corridorlike room there that serves as the champions' clubhouse. Team trunks were stacked everywhere, and sweatshirts hung from the overhead pipes and rafters. There was one fan, and the place suggested nothing so much as a migrant-labor-camp barracks. Joe Rudi must have seen my expression, because he laughed and said, "You know how it is with

Charlie—first-class all the way." (Finley, it should be added, was not on hand; he rarely comes to Arizona—or, for that matter, to Oakland.)

In the past, the captain of the A's, Sal Bando, has been more gentle about his employer than most of his teammates, but this spring he emerged the loser in a vituperative salary arbitration, and he has joined the bad-mouth majority. Finley won four of six arbitration cases this year; whatever the issues, the effect of this was to deny real raises, after a third world championship, to Bando, Ken Holtzman, Ray Fosse, and Reggie Jackson.

"Until this year," Bando said to me, "I found it hard to understand how low and upset he could make a player feel. Now I understand. The big thing is his lack of respect for other people, and the lack of communication in the whole organization. I said last winter that the front office was a one-man show, and he used this as an excuse to call in the press and demean me. [Finley stated, among other things, that his team captain was the eleventh-best third baseman in the league.] To me, this is like a car dealer buying time on TV and saying he has the worst cars in town. No wonder people don't come to see us play. We win on this team only because each of us has a sense of pride—which is exactly what he wants to take away from us. Winning is what holds this team together."

Winning and, he might have added, great baseball and, inexplicably, great good cheer. In spite of their celebrated squabbles, the A's have always struck me as having the most ebullient dugout in the game. On this afternoon, Bando finished his Finleyan discourse by suddenly leaping off the bench and tipping Pat Bourque's cap over his eyes and grabbing the ball he was about to catch in warm-up. Then young Phil Garner, the rookie who will replace Green at second base this year, came down the steps and said, "My luck's really runnin' good. My wife went to the doc this morning, and he said the baby isn't coming until July. And . . . well, he said it sounds like there's more than one heartbeat in there."

Bourque and Ray Fosse and Rollie Fingers took up the topic with alacrity.

"*Uh*-oh! You better get Charlie on the phone right now. Tell him you're holding out for more. Play on his sympathy."

" 'More than one'? Listen, that doesn't mean two, does it? Think about that a little, Phil."

"Yes, if your wife's been messin' with those fertility pills, you'd better get out there and hit about .310 this year and a hundred and fifty runs batted in. At *least!*"

In the game that day, against the Padres, Phil Garner made three errors. The A's had other troubles, too—including Reggie Jackson running his spring average to one for fifteen, or .066—but Gene Tenace hit a homer and a double, and Bando and Claudell Washington and Ted Kubiak doubled, too, and the miserable A's cheerfully won the game, 4–2.

POSTCARDS

A GROUP of big-league scouts—Dario Lodigiani, Al Hollingsworth, Haywood Sullivan, and some others—turned up at most of the games I saw. Apparently by agreement, they always seemed to come to the same games, and they always sat together, watching the play and writing notes in their notebooks. Reminded you of Second World War spies taking their apéritifs together at Estoril.

•

SPOTTED Alvin Dark's car parked outside Rendezvous Park, in Mesa—a big, mocha-colored Imperial LeBaron, with Florida plates and two rear bumper stickers. "A's, World Champions" was on the left side and "Jesus Is Coming Soon! Every Knee Shall Bow" on the right. Dark, the Oakland manager, is a direct man. Last winter, he mailed several revivalist tracts to Ron Bergman, who covers the team for the Oakland *Tribune*. Bergman is Jewish.

•

Rollie Fingers, watching the Padres take infield practice: "There's that Hernandez, at short. I'll never forget that year he had five hundred and something at-bats and drove in twelve runs."

Ray Fosse: "*What?* That's impossible."

Fingers: "Look it up."

I looked it up. The year was 1971. Enzo Hernandez drove in twelve runs in 549 trips to the plate.

•

Before an Indians-Brewers game at Sun City, Gaylord Perry, the Cleveland pitcher who is starting his fourteenth year in the majors, spotted Del Crandall, who put in sixteen years as a player and is starting his fourth year as the Brewers' manager.

"Hey there, Big Del," Perry said. "I see we made it to another year."

"Yeah," Crandall said. "Let's hope it don't run out on us."

•

March was winding down, and my holiday was nearly over. The penultimate stop was a Giants-Brewers night game, which I witnessed from the stands in the company of seventy or eighty members of the Giants Boosters Club. Surrounded by orange-and-black caps and buttons and pennants, I yelled for every San Francisco grounder and fly ball, and felt a lively sense of accomplishment over the eventual 3–1 win by the Good Guys. As one might imagine, given their team's recent record, the Boosters don't know the meaning of quit. There are some four thousand of them in all, mostly season-ticket holders at Candlestick Park, and a lot of them sign up for road trips, too, accompanying their boys to Los Angeles or as far as the East Coast, and even once to Japan. The Boosters are middling-old, and not many of them, I noticed, keep score. This is not a sign of amateurish fandom, however; the Boosters are too busy simultaneously yelling and socializing to do any writing. All Giants are addressed, *fortissimo*, by their first names, but some criticism is permitted within the family, too. After Ontiveros threw out a Milwaukee base runner, a woman next to me leaned over and murmured, "Every time Steve throws the ball, I shudder." At one point, I asked another lady near me what she thought about the recent news that Juan Marichal, the longtime Giants mound ace, had signed up with the Dodgers. She pondered the question, and then said, "Well, I'm sort of sorry for Juan. You can't tell me he *liked* doing that."

The winning two-run Giants rally, sparked by a Derrel Thomas double, interrupted a lengthy discussion of home states ("You're from *Montana?* Why, I was born in Butte. . . ."), and then we all anxiously discussed the Giants' relief pitcher David Heaverlo, who was summoned in to protect the lead. Heaverlo, a young nonroster flinger, was so delighted at being invited to camp this year that he shaved all the hair off his head. Tonight, it turned out, he was throwing nothing but BBs out there. "Heave her low, Heaverlo!" we shouted, and he did, and we went home hoarse but happy.

On, then, the next afternoon, for the Indians and the Brewers, at Sun City. This is a retirement community, a vast walled city of low, white bungalows, which, viewed from the nonvantage point of the ceaseless desert plain, looks as big as Benares. The ball park appears to have been dug out of one end of a parking lot—an arrangement I finally understood when I realized that it allowed all the fans to walk down to their seats; a number of them spared themselves even this minimal strain by watching the proceedings from parked golf carts. On this particular day, however, there were a good many younger adults and children mixed in with the geezers—Easter-vacation visitors, perhaps. Hank Aaron, baseball's most celebrated active codger, started for the home team as the designated hitter, and began a six-run Milwaukee outburst in the fourth with a single off Gaylord Perry. Aaron batting and

Perry pitching would make a terrific energy-conservation poster.

The afternoon had begun with wind and threatening low clouds. As the game wore on, the clouds began to break up, but the wind blew and blew. The clear desert air became dusty-red, and later that afternoon there were reports of forty- and fifty-mile-an-hour gusts nearby. The wind began to blow away the ball game. Three fly balls got up into the river of air above us and sailed out beyond the fence for homers; one of them was a grand slam. The sun came out at last, and the sun and the wind made me restless, and I got up and walked out to the deepest part of the stands along the right-field foul line and sat down. There was a flagpole on an embankment above me, and the great wind had nailed the two flags in the air up there—the Arizona state flag under the Stars and Stripes—making them stand out like planks. There was no one near me but a couple of county cops in brown uniforms, and three boys and one girl in jeans and T-shirts and sneakers—they looked about ten or twelve years old—and, just down below us, a young Cleveland pitcher and bullpen catcher, sitting motionless on folding chairs in their warm-up jackets.

My trip was ending, and I was beginning to feel sad about it. In these ten days on the road, it had become clear to me that there is almost no reason for the spring baseball schedule. Most baseball people I had talked to seemed to agree with Ray Sadecki that only the pitchers really needed the full six weeks in which to prepare themselves; Frank Robinson told me that the games were an interruption and that he could have used the same time to better advantage for straight instruction. Strangest of all, it seemed to me, was the fact that the baseball establishment has hardly ever tried to promote spring-training games, or to inflate them beyond their evident usefulness as a publicity device. They are still called exhibitions. Spring baseball, I had to conclude, continues for the strangest of all possible reasons—because everyone enjoys it. It is a relic—sport pure and simple, or the closest we can come to that now. Sport for the joy of it.

I watched the end of the game from there. The warm wind ruffled our hair and rattled the outfield fence, and from time to time bits of peanut shells and pieces of popcorn flew by us, airborne. Nobody said anything. Spring was over, or part of it. Dazed with sun and wind, we stared back at the distant players and the silent movements of the game.

POSTCARD

WALT WILLIAMS made the team. He was on the Yankees' twenty-five-man roster that went north to start the regular season—in part because of the club's decision to cut loose its ailing longtime pitching ace, Mel Stottlemyre. Randy Tate had a splendid late-spring record and began the season as the Mets' No. 4 starting pitcher. Ray Sadecki hung on with the Cardinals, but it was a near thing. His earned-run average for the training season was 9.00. Spring, as he said, is hard on people.

• • •

LATE POSTCARD

WALT WILLIAMS got the job done in the 1975 season, just as he promised he would. He appeared in eighty-two games for the Yankees, batted .281, and qualified as a ten-year man in the major-league pension plan. Last summer, he played for the Nippon Ham Fighters, in Japan, where he batted .288 and ran out everything. Ray Negron's hopes were not similarly rewarded. He worked hard at Pirate City and impressed the Pittsburgh organization with his eagerness and character, but he could not hit professional pitching. He was cut loose early in the season, and thus got home to see his girl friend Barbara long before September. Ray Sadecki suffered more midseason trades in 1975, moving from the Cardinals to the Braves, and from the Braves to the Kansas City Royals, while accumulating an overall record of four wins and three losses and an earned-run average of 4.03. Last year, he pitched for the Milwaukee Brewers, finishing with marks of 2–0 and 3.86. Del Crandall, the Milwaukee manager, was fired at the end of the 1975 campaign. He took a year-round job as public relations director for a California medical group, but when spring training came around again he discovered that it was impossible for him to stay away from baseball, and he signed on to manage the Salinas Angels, in the Class A California League.

11 Gone for Good

June 1975

THE PHOTOGRAPH shows a perfectly arrested moment of joy. On one side—the left, as you look at the picture—the catcher is running toward the camera at full speed, with his upraised arms spread wide. His body is tilting toward the center of the picture, his mask is held in his right hand, his big glove is still on his left hand, and his mouth is open in a gigantic shout of pleasure. Over on the right, another player, the pitcher, is just past the apex of an astonishing leap that has brought his knees up to his chest and his feet well up off the ground. Both of *his* arms are flung wide, and he, too, is shouting. His hunched, airborne posture makes him look like a man who just made a running jump over a sizable object—a kitchen table, say. By luck, two of the outreaching hands have overlapped exactly in the middle of the photograph, so that the pitcher's bare right palm and fingers are silhouetted against the catcher's glove, and as a result the two men are linked and seem to be executing a figure in a manic and difficult dance. There is a further marvel—a touch of pure fortune—in the background, where a spectator in dark glasses, wearing a dark suit, has risen from his seat in the grandstand and is lifting his arms in triumph. This, the third and central Y in the picture, is immobile. It is directly behind the overlapping hand and glove of the dancers, and it binds and recapitulates the lines of force and the movements and the theme of the work, creating a composition as serene and well ordered as a Giotto. The subject of the picture, of course, is classical—the celebration of the last out of the seventh game of the World Series.

This famous photograph (by Rusty Kennedy, of the Associated Press) does not require captioning for most baseball fans or for almost anyone within the Greater Pittsburgh area, where it is still prominently featured in the art collections of several hundred taverns. It may also be seen, in a much enlarged version, on one wall of the office of Joe L. Brown, the general manager of the Pittsburgh Pirates, in Three Rivers Stadium. The date of the photograph is October 17, 1971; the place is Memorial Stadium, in Baltimore. The catcher is Manny Sanguillen, of the Pirates, and his leaping teammate is pitcher Steve Blass, who has just defeated the defending (and suddenly former) World Champion Baltimore Orioles by a score of 2–1, giving up four hits.

I am not a Pittsburgher, but looking at this photograph never fails to give me pleasure, not just because of its aesthetic qualities but because its high-bounding happiness so perfectly brings back that eventful World Series and that particular gray autumn afternoon in Baltimore and the wonderful and inexpungible expression of joy that remained on Steve Blass's face after the game ended. His was, to be sure, a famous victory—a close and bitterly fought pitchers' battle against the Orioles' Mike Cuellar, in which the only score for seven innings had been a solo home run by the celebrated Pirate outfielder Roberto Clemente. The Pirates had scored again in the eighth, but the Orioles had responded with a run of their own and had brought the tying run around to third base before Blass shut them off once and for all. The win was the culmination of a stirring uphill fight by the Pirates, who had fallen into difficulties by losing the first two games to the Orioles; Steve Blass had begun their comeback with a wonderfully pitched three-hit, 5–1 victory in the third game. It was an outstanding Series, made memorable above all by the play of Roberto Clemente, who batted .414 over the seven games and fielded his position with extraordinary zeal. He was awarded the sports car as the most valuable player of the Series, but Steve Blass was not far out of the running for the prize. After that last game, Baltimore manager Earl Weaver said, "Clemente was great, all right, but if it hadn't been for Mr. Blass, *we* might be popping the corks right now."

I remember the vivid contrast in styles between the two stars in the noisy, floodlit, champagne-drenched Pirate clubhouse that afternoon. Clemente, at last the recipient of the kind of national attention he had always deserved but had rarely been given for his years of brilliant play, remained erect and removed, regarding the swarming photographers with a haughty, incandescent pride. Blass was a less obvious hero—a competent but far from overpowering right-hander who had won fifteen games for the Pirates that year, with a most respectable 2.85 earned-run average, but who had absorbed a terrible pounding by the San Francisco Giants in the two games he pitched in the National League playoffs, just before the Series. His two Series victories, by contrast, were momentous by any standard—and, indeed, were among the very best pitching performances of his entire seven years in the majors. Blass, in any case, celebrated the Pirates' championship more exuberantly than Clemente, exchanging hugs and shouts with his teammates, alternately smoking a cigar and swigging from a champagne bottle. Later, I saw him in front of his locker with his arm around his father, Bob Blass, a plumber from Falls Village, Connecticut, who had once been a semipro pitcher; the two Blasses, I saw, were wearing identical delighted, nonstop smiles.

Near the end of an article I wrote about that 1971 World

Series, I mentioned watching Steve Blass in batting practice just before the all-important seventh game and suddenly noticing that, in spite of his impending responsibilities, he was amusing himself with a comical parody of Clemente at the plate: "Blass . . . then arched his back, cricked his neck oddly, rolled his head a few times, took up a stance in the back corner of the batter's box, with his bat held high, and glared out at the pitcher imperiously—Clemente, to the life." I had never seen such a spirited gesture in a serious baseball setting, and since then I have come to realize that Steve Blass's informality and boyish play constituted an essential private style, as original and as significant as Clemente's eaglelike pride, and that each of them was merely responding in his own way to the challenges of an extremely difficult public profession. Which of the two, I keep wondering, was happier that afternoon about the Pirates' championship and his part in it? Roberto Clemente, of course, is dead; he was killed on December 31, 1972, in Puerto Rico, in the crash of a plane he had chartered to carry emergency relief supplies to the victims of an earthquake in Nicaragua. Steve Blass, who is now thirty-three, is out of baseball, having been recently driven into retirement by two years of pitching wildness—a sudden, near-total inability to throw strikes. No one, including Blass himself, can cure or explain it.

•

THE SUMMER of 1972, the year after his splendid World Series, was in most respects the best season that Steve Blass ever had. He won nineteen games for the Pirates and lost only eight, posting an earned-run average of 2.48—sixth-best in the National League—and being selected for the NL All-Star team. What pleased him most that year was his consistency. He went the full distance in eleven of the thirty-two games he started, and averaged better than seven and a half innings per start—not dazzling figures (Steve Carlton, of the Phillies, had thirty complete games that year, and Bob Gibson, of the Cards, had twenty-three) but satisfying ones for a man who had once had inordinate difficulty in finishing games. Blass, it should be understood, was not the same kind of pitcher as a Carlton or a Gibson. He was never a blazer. When standing on the mound, he somehow looked more like a journeyman pitcher left over from the nineteen thirties or forties than like one of the hulking, hairy young flingers of today. (He is six feet tall, and weighs about one hundred and eighty pounds.) Watching him work, you sometimes wondered how he was getting all those batters out. The word on him among the other clubs in his league was something like: Good but not overpowering stuff, excellent slider, good curve, good change-up curve. A pattern pitcher, whose slider works because of its location. No control problems. Intelligent, knows how to win.

I'm not certain that I saw Blass work in the regular season of 1972, but I did see him pitch the opening game of the National League playoffs that fall against the Cincinnati Reds, in Pittsburgh. After giving up a home run to the Reds' second batter of the day, Joe Morgan, which was hit off a first-pitch fastball, Blass readjusted his plans and went mostly to a big, slow curve, causing the Reds to hit innumerable rainmaking outfield flies, and won by 5–1. I can still recall how Blass looked that afternoon—his characteristic, feet-together stance at the outermost, first-base edge of the pitching rubber, and then the pitch, delivered with a swastikalike scattering of arms and legs and a final lurch to the left—and I also remember how I kept thinking that at any moment the sluggers of the Big Red Machine would stop overstriding and overswinging against such unintimidating deliveries and drive Blass to cover. But it never happened—Blass saw to it that it didn't. Then, in the fifth and deciding game, he returned and threw seven and one-third more innings of thoughtful and precise patterns, allowing only four hits, and departed with his team ahead by 3–2—a pennant-winning outing, except for the fact that the Pirate bullpen gave up the ghost in the bottom of the ninth, when a homer, two singles, and a wild pitch entitled the Reds to meet the Oakland A's in the 1972 World Series. It was a horrendous disappointment for the Pittsburgh Pirates and their fans, for which no blame at all could be attached to Blass.

My next view of Steve Blass on a baseball diamond came on a cool afternoon at the end of April this year. The game—the White Sox vs. the Orioles—was a close, 3–1 affair, in which the winning White Sox pitcher, John McKenzie, struck out seventeen batters in six innings. A lot of the Sox struck out, too, and a lot of players on both teams walked—more than I could count, in fact. The big hit of the game was a triple to left center by the White Sox catcher, David Blass, who is ten years old. His eight-year-old brother, Chris, played second, and their father, Steve Blass, in old green slacks and a green T-shirt, coached at third. This was a late-afternoon date in the Upper St. Clair (Pennsylvania) Recreation League schedule, played between the White Sox and the Orioles on a field behind the Dwight D. Eisenhower Elementary School—Little League baseball, but at a junior and highly informal level. The low, *low* minors. Most of the action, or inaction, took place around home plate, since there was not much bat-on-ball contact, but there was a shrill nonstop piping of encouragement from the fielders, and disappointed batters were complimented on their overswings by a small, chilly assemblage of mothers, coaches, and dads. When Chris Blass went down swinging in the fourth, his father came over and said, "The sinker down and away is *tough*." Steve Blass has a longish, lightly freckled face, a tilted nose, and an alert and engaging expression. At this ball game, he looked like any young suburban father who had caught an early train home from the office in order to see his kids in action. He looked much more like a commuter than like a professional athlete.

Blass coached quietly, moving the fielders in or over a few steps, asking the shortstop if he knew how many outs there were, reminding someone to take his hands out of his pockets. "Learning the names of all the kids is the hard part," he said to me. It was his second game of the spring as a White Sox coach, and between innings one of the young outfielders said to him, "Hey, Mr. Blass, how come you're not playing with the Pirates at Three Rivers today?"

"Well," Blass said equably, "Im not *in* baseball anymore."

"Oh," said the boy.

Twilight and the end of the game approached at about the same speed, and I kept losing track of the count on the batters. Steve Blass, noticing my confusion, explained that, in order to avert a parade of walked batters in these games, any strike thrown by a pitcher was considered to have wiped out the balls he had already delivered to the same batter; a strike on the 3-0 count reconverted things to 0-1. He suddenly laughed. "Why didn't they have that rule in the NL?" he said. "I'd have lasted until I was fifty."

Then it was over. The winning (and undefeated) White Sox and the losing Orioles exchanged cheers, and Karen Blass, a winning and clearly undefeated mother, came over and introduced me to the winning catcher and the winning second baseman. The Blasses and I walked slowly along together over the thick new grass, toting gloves and helmets and Karen's fold-up lawn chair, and at the parking lot the party divided into two cars—Karen and the boys homeward bound, and Steve Blass and I off to a nearby shopping center to order one large cheese-and-peppers-and-sausage victory pizza, to go.

•

Blass and I sat in his car at the pizza place, drinking beer and waiting for our order, and he talked about his baseball beginnings. I said I had admired the relaxed, low-key tenor of the game we had just seen, and he told me that his own Little League coach, back in Connecticut—a man named Jerry Fallon—had always seen to it that playing baseball on his club was a pleasure. "On any level, baseball is a tough game if it isn't really fun," Blass said. "I think most progress in baseball comes from enjoying it and then wanting to extend yourself a little, wanting it to become more. There should be a feeling of 'Let's go! Let's keep on with this!' "

He kept on with it, in all seasons and circumstances. The Blasses' place in Falls Village included an old barn with an interestingly angled roof, against which young Steve Blass played hundreds of one-man games (his four brothers and sisters were considerably younger) with a tennis ball. "I had all kinds of games, with different, very complicated ground rules," he said. "I'd throw the ball up, and then I'd be diving into the weeds for pop-ups or running back and calling for the long fly balls, and all. I'd always play a full game—a made-up game, with two big-league teams—and I'd write down the line score as I went along, and keep the results. One of the teams always had to be the Indians. I was a *total* Indians fan, completely buggy. In the summer of '54, when they won that record one hundred and eleven games, I managed to find every single Indians box score in the newspapers and clip it, which took some doing up where we lived. I guess Herb Score was my real hero—I actually pitched against him once in Indianapolis, in '63, when he was trying to make a comeback—but I knew the whole team by heart. Not just the stars but all the guys on the bench, like George Strickland and Wally Westlake and Hank Majeski and the backup third baseman, Rudy Regalado. My first big-league autograph was Hank Majeski."

Blass grew up into an athlete—a good sandlot football player, a second-team All-State Class B basketball star, but most of all a pitcher, like his father. ("He was wilder than hell," Blass said. "Once, in a Canaan game, he actually threw a pitch over the backstop.") Steve Blass pitched two no-hitters in his junior year at Housatonic Regional High School, and three more as a senior, but there were so many fine pitchers on the team that he did not get to be a starter until his final year. (One of the stars just behind him was John Lamb, who later pitched for the Pirates; Lamb's older sister, Karen, was a classmate of Steve's, and in time she found herself doubly affiliated with the Pirate mound staff.)

The Pittsburgh organization signed Steve Blass right out of Housatonic High in 1960, and he began moving up through the minors. He and Karen Lamb were married in the fall of 1963, and they went to the Dominican Republic that winter, where Steve played for the Cibaeñas Eagles and began working on a slider. He didn't quite make the big club when training ended in the spring, and was sent down to the Pirates' Triple A club in Columbus, but the call came three weeks later. Blass said, "We got in the car, and I floored it all the way across Ohio. I remember it was raining as we came out of the tunnel in Pittsburgh, and I drove straight to Forbes Field and went in and found the attendant and put my uniform on, at two in the afternoon. There was no *game* there, or anything—I just had to see how it looked."

We had moved along by now to the Blasses' house, a medium-sized brick structure on a hillside in Upper St. Clair, which is a suburb about twelve miles southeast of Pittsburgh. The pizza disappeared rapidly, and then David and Chris went off upstairs to do their homework or watch TV. The Blass family room was trophied and comfortable. On a wall opposite a long sofa there was, among other things, a plaque representing the J. Roy Stockton Award for Outstanding Baseball Achievement, a Dapper Dan Award for meritorious service to Pittsburgh, a shiny metal bat with the engraved signatures of the National League All-Stars of 1972, a 1971 Pittsburgh Pirates World Champions bat, a signed photograph of President Nixon, and a framed, decorated proclamation announcing Steve Blass Day in Falls Village, Connecticut: "Be it known that this twenty-second day of October in the year of our Lord 1971, the citizens of Falls Village do set aside and do honor with pride Steve Blass, the tall skinny kid from Falls Village, who is now the hero of baseball and will be our hero always." It was signed by the town's three selectmen. The biggest picture in the room hung over the sofa—an enlarged color photograph of the Blass family at the Father-and-Sons Day at Three Rivers Stadium in 1971. In the photo, Karen

Blass looks extremely pretty in a large straw hat, and all three male Blasses are wearing Pirate uniforms; the boys' uniforms look a little funny, because in their excitement each boy had put on the other's pants. Great picture.

Karen and Steve pointed this out to me, and then they went back to their arrival in the big time on that rainy long-ago first day in Pittsburgh and Steve's insisting on trying on his Pirate uniform, and they leaned back in their chairs and laughed about it again.

"With Steve, everything is right out in the open," Karen said. "Every accomplishment, every stage of the game—you have no idea how much he loved it, how he enjoyed the game."

That year, in his first outing, Blass pitched five scoreless innings in relief against the Braves, facing, among others, Hank Aaron. In his first start, against the Dodgers in Los Angeles, he pitched against Don Drysdale and won, 4–2. "I thought I'd died and gone to Heaven," Blass said to me.

He lit a cigar and blew out a little smoke. "You know, this thing that's happened has been painted so bad, so tragic," he said. "Well, I don't go along with that. I know what I've done in baseball, and I give myself all the credit in the world for it. I'm not bitter about this. I've had the greatest moments a person could ever want. When I was a boy, I used to make up those fictitious games where I was always pitching in the bottom of the ninth in the World Series. Well, I really *did* it. It went on and happened to me. Nobody's ever enjoyed winning a big-league game more than I have. All I've ever wanted to do since I was six years old was to keep on playing baseball. It didn't even have to be major-league ball. I've never been a goal-planner—I've never said I'm going to do this or that. With me, everything was just a continuation of what had come before. I think that's why I enjoyed it all so much when it did come along, when the good things did happen."

All this was said with an air of summing up, of finality, but at other times that evening I noticed that it seemed difficult for Blass to talk about his baseball career as a thing of the past; now and then he slipped into the present tense—as if it were still going on. This was understandable, for he was in limbo. The Pirates had finally released him late in March ("outrighted" him, in baseball parlance), near the end of the spring-training season, and he had subsequently decided not to continue his attempts to salvage his pitching form in the minor leagues. Earlier in the week of my visit, he had accepted a promising job with Josten's, Inc., a large jewelry concern that makes, among other things, World Series rings and high-school graduation rings, and he would go to work for them shortly as a traveling representative in the Pittsburgh area. He was out of baseball for good.

•

PITCHING CONSISTENCY is probably the ingredient that separates major-league baseball from the lesser levels of the game. A big-league fastball comes in on the batter at about eighty-five or ninety miles an hour, completing its prescribed journey of sixty feet six inches in less than half a second, and, if it is a strike, generally intersects no more than an inch or two of the seventeen-inch-wide plate, usually near the upper or lower limits of the strike zone; curves and sliders arrive a bit later but with intense rotation, and must likewise slice off only a thin piece of the black if they are to be effective. Sustaining this kind of control over a stretch of, say, one hundred and thirty pitches in a seven- or eight-inning appearance places such excruciating demands on a hurler's body and psyche that even the most successful pitchers regularly have games when they simply can't get the job done. Their fastball comes in high, their curves hang, the rest of their prime weapons desert them. The pitcher is knocked about, often by an inferior rival team, and leaves within a few innings; asked about it later, he shrugs and says, "I didn't have it today." He seems unsurprised. Pitching, it sometimes appears, is too hard for *anyone*. Occasionally, the poor performance is repeated, then extended. The pitcher goes into a slump. He sulks or rages, according to his nature; he asks for help; he works long hours on his motion. Still he cannot win. He worries about his arm, which almost always hurts to some degree. Has it gone dead? He worries about his stuff. Has he lost his velocity? He wonders whether he will ever win again or whether he will now join the long, long list—the list that awaits him, almost surely, in the end—of suddenly slow, suddenly sore-armed pitchers who have abruptly vanished from the big time, down the drain to oblivion. Then, unexpectedly, the slump ends—most of the time, that is—and he is back where he was: a winning pitcher. There is rarely an explanation for this, whether the slump has lasted for two games or a dozen, and managers and coaches, when pressed for one, will usually mutter that "pitching is a delicate thing," or—as if it explained anything—"he got back in the groove."

In spite of such hovering and inexplicable hazards, every big-league pitcher knows exactly what is expected of him. As with the other aspects of the game, statistics define his work and—day by day, inning by inning—whether he is getting it done. Thus, it may be posited as a rule that a major-league hurler who gives up an average of just over three and a half runs per game is about at the middle of his profession—an average pitcher. (Last year, the National League and the American League both wound up with a per-game earned-run average of 3.62.) At contract-renewal time, earned-run averages below 3.30 are invariably mentioned by pitchers; an ERA close to or above the 4.00 level will always be brought up by management. The select levels of pitching proficiency (and salary) begin below the 3.00 line; in fact, an ERA of less than 3.00 certifies true quality in almost exactly the same fashion as an over-.300 batting average for hitters. Last year, both leagues had ten pitchers who finished below 3.00, led by Buzz Capra's NL mark of 2.28 and Catfish Hunter's 2.49 in the AL. The best season-long earned-run average of the modern baseball era was Bob Gibson's 1.12 mark, set in 1968.

Strikeouts are of no particular use in defining pitching effectiveness, since there are other, less vivid ways of retiring batters, but bases on balls matter. To put it in simple terms, a good, middling pitcher should not surrender more than three or four walks per game—unless he is also striking out batters in considerable clusters. Last year, Ferguson Jenkins, of the Texas Rangers, gave up only 45 walks in 328 innings pitched, or an average of 1.19 per game. Nolan Ryan, of the Angels, walked 202 men in 333 innings, or 5.4 per game; however, he helped himself considerably by fanning 367, or just under ten men per game. The fastball is a great healer.

At the beginning of the 1973 season, Steve Blass had a lifetime earned-run average of 3.25 and was averaging 1.9 walks per game. He was, in short, an extremely successful and useful big-league pitcher, and was understandably enjoying his work. Early that season, however, baseball suddenly stopped being fun for him. He pitched well in spring training in Bradenton, which was unusual, for he has always been a very slow starter. He pitched on opening day, against the Cards, but threw poorly and was relieved, although the Pirates eventually won the game. For a time, his performance was borderline, but his few wins were in sloppy, high-scoring contests, and his bad outings were marked by streaks of uncharacteristic wildness and ineffectuality. On April 22, against the Cubs, he gave up a walk, two singles, a homer, and a double in the first inning, sailed through the second inning, and then walked a man and hit two batsmen in the third. He won a complete game against the Padres, but in his next two appearances, against the Dodgers and the Expos, he survived for barely half the distance; in the Expos game, he threw three scoreless innings, and then suddenly gave up two singles, a double, and two walks. By early June, his record was three wins and three losses, but his earned-run average suggested that his difficulties were serious. Bill Virdon, the Pirate manager, was patient and told Blass to take all the time he needed to find himself; he reminded Blass that once—in 1970—he had

had an early record of two and eight but had then come back to finish the season with a mark of ten and twelve.

What was mystifying about the whole thing was that Blass still had his stuff, especially when he warmed up or threw on the sidelines. He was in great physical shape, as usual, and his arm felt fine; in his entire pitching career, Blass never experienced a sore arm. Virdon remained calm, although he was clearly puzzled. Some pitching mechanics were discussed and worked on: Blass was sometimes dropping his elbow as he threw; often he seemed to be hurrying his motion, so that his arm was not in synchronization with his body; perhaps he had exaggerated his peculiar swoop toward first base and thus was losing his power. These are routine pitching mistakes, which almost all pitchers are guilty of from time to time, and Blass worked on them assiduously. He started again against the Braves on June 11, in Atlanta; after three and one-third innings he was gone, having given up seven singles, a home run, two walks, and a total of five runs. Virdon and Blass agreed that a spell in the bullpen seemed called for; at least he could work on his problems there every day.

Two days later, the roof fell in. The team was still in Atlanta, and Virdon called Blass into the game in the fifth inning, with the Pirates trailing by 8–3. Blass walked the first two men he faced, and gave up a stolen base and a wild pitch and a run-scoring single before retiring the side. In the sixth, Blass walked Darrell Evans. He walked Mike Lum, throwing one pitch behind him in the process, which allowed Evans to move down to second. Dusty Baker singled, driving in a run. Ralph Garr grounded out. Davey Johnson singled, scoring another run. Marty Perez walked. Pitcher Ron Reed singled, driving in two more runs, and was wild-pitched to second. Johnny Oates walked. Frank Tepedino singled, driving in two runs, and Steve Blass was finally relieved. His totals for the one and one-third innings were seven runs, five hits, six bases on balls, and three wild pitches.

"It was the worst experience of my baseball life," Blass told me. "I don't think I'll ever forget it. I was embarrassed and disgusted. I was totally unnerved. You can't imagine the feeling that you suddenly have no *idea* what you're doing out there, performing that way as a major-league pitcher. It was kind of scary."

None of Blass's appearances during the rest of the '73 season were as dreadful as the Atlanta game, but none of them were truly successful. On August 1, he started against the Mets and Tom Seaver at Shea Stadium and gave up three runs and five walks in one and two-thirds innings. A little later, Virdon gave him a start in the Hall of Fame game at Cooperstown; this is a meaningless annual exhibition, played that year between the Pirates and the Texas Rangers, but Blass was as wild as ever and had to be relieved after two and one-third innings. After that, Bill Virdon announced that Blass would probably not start another game; the Pirates were in a pennant race, and the time for patience had run out.

Blass retired to the bullpen and worked on fundamentals. He threw a lot, once pitching a phantom nine-inning game while his catcher, Dave Ricketts, called the balls and strikes. At another point, he decided to throw every single day in the bullpen, to see if he could recapture his groove. "All it did was to get me very, very tired," Blass told me. He knew that Virdon was not going to use him, but whenever the Pirates fell behind in a game, he felt jumpy about the possibility of being called upon. "I knew I wasn't capable of going in there," he said. "I was afraid of embarrassing myself again, and letting down the club."

On September 6, the Pirate front office announced that Danny Murtaugh, who had served two previous terms as the Pirates' manager, was replacing Bill Virdon at the helm; the Pirates were caught up in a close, four-team division race, and it was felt that Murtaugh's experience might bring them home. One of Murtaugh's first acts was to announce that

Steve Blass would be given a start. The game he picked was against the Cubs, in Chicago, on September 11. Blass, who had not pitched in six weeks, was extremely anxious about this test; he walked the streets of Chicago on the night before the game, and could not get to sleep until after five in the morning. The game went well for him. The Cubs won, 2–0, but Steve gave up only two hits and one earned run in the five innings he worked. He pitched with extreme care, throwing mostly sliders. He had another pretty good outing against the Cardinals, for no decision, and then started against the Mets, in New York, on September 21, but got only two men out, giving up four instant runs on a walk and four hits. The Mets won, 10–2, dropping the Pirates out of first place, but Blass, although unhappy about his showing, found some hope in the fact that he had at least been able to get the ball over the plate. "At that point," he said, "I was looking for even a little bit of success—one good inning, a few real fastballs, anything to hold on to that might halt my negative momentum. I wanted to feel I had at least got things turned around and facing in the right direction."

The Mets game was his last of the year. His statistics for the 1973 season were three wins and nine defeats, and an earned-run average of 9.81. That figure and his record of eighty-four walks in eighty-nine innings pitched were the worst in the National League.

•

I WENT to another ball game with Steve Blass on the night after the Little League affair—this time at Three Rivers Stadium, where the Pirates were meeting the Cardinals. We sat behind home plate, down near the screen, and during the first few innings a lot of young fans came clustering down the aisle to get Steve's autograph. People in the sections near us kept calling and waving to him. "Everybody has been great to me, all through this thing," Blass said. "I don't think there are too many here who are thinking, 'Look, there's the wild man.' I've had hundreds and hundreds of letters—I don't know how many—and not one of them was down on me."

In the game, Bob Gibson pitched against the Pirates' Jerry Reuss. When Ted Simmons stood in for the visitors, Blass said, "He's always hit me pretty good. He's really developed as a hitter." Then there was an error by Richie Hebner, at third, on a grounder hit by Ken Reitz, and Blass said, "Did you notice the batter take that big swing and then hit it off his hands? It was the swing that put Richie back on his heels like that." Later on, Richie Zisk hit a homer off Gibson, on a three-and-two count, and Blass murmured, "The high slider is one of *the* hittable pitches when it isn't just right. I should know."

The game rushed along, as games always do when Gibson is pitching. "You know," Blass said, "before we faced him we'd always have a team meeting and we'd say, 'Stay out of the batter's box, clean your spikes—anything to make him slow up.' But it never lasted more than an inning or two. He makes you play his game."

A little later, however, Willie Stargell hit a homer, and then Manny Sanguillen drove in another run with a double off the left-field wall ("*Get* out of here!" Steve said while the ball was in flight), and it was clear that this was not to be a Gibson night. Blass was enjoying himself, and it seemed to me that the familiarities and surprises of the game had restored something in him. At one point, he leaned forward a little and peered into the Pirate dugout and murmured, "Is Dock Ellis over in his regular corner there?" but for the most part he kept his eyes on the field. I tried to imagine what it felt like for him not to be down in the dugout.

I had talked that day to a number of Blass's old teammates, and all of them had mentioned his cheerfulness and his jokes, and what they had meant to the team over the years. "Steve's humor in the clubhouse was unmatched," relief pitcher Dave Giusti said. "He was a terrific mimic. Perfect. He could do Robert Kennedy. He could do Manny Sanguillen. He could do Roberto Clemente—not just the way he moved but the way he talked. Clemente loved it. He could do rat sounds—the noise a rat makes running. Lots of other stuff. It all made for looseness and togetherness. Because of Steve, the clubhouse was never completely silent, even after a loss." Another Pirate said, "Steve was about ninety percent of the good feeling on this club. He was always up, always agitating. If a player made a mistake, Steve knew how to say something about it that would let the guy know it was OK. Especially the young guys—he really understood them, and they put their confidence in him because of that. He picked us all up. Of course, there was a hell of a lot less of that from him in the last couple of years. We sure missed it."

For the final three innings of the game, Blass and I moved upstairs to general manager Joe Brown's box. Steve was startled by the unfamiliar view. "Hey, you can really see how it works from here, can't you?" he said. "Down there, you've got to look at it all in pieces. No wonder it's so hard to play this game right."

In the Pirates' seventh, Bill Robinson pinch-hit for Ed Kirkpatrick, and Blass said, "Well, *that* still makes me wince a little." It was a moment or two before I realized that Robinson was wearing Blass's old uniform number. Robinson fanned, and Blass said, "Same old twenty-eight."

The Pirates won easily, 5–0, with Jerry Reuss going all the way for the shutout, and just before the end Steve said, "I always had trouble sleeping after pitching a real good game. And if we were home, I'd get up about seven in the morning, before anybody else was up, and go downstairs and make myself a cup of coffee, and then I'd get the newspaper and open it to the sports section and just—just soak it all in."

We thanked Joe Brown and said good night, and as we went down in the elevator I asked Steve Blass if he wanted to stop off in the clubhouse for a minute and see his old friends. "Oh, no," he said. "No, I couldn't do that."

•

After the end of the 1973 season, Blass joined the Pirates' team in the Florida Instructional League (an autumn institution that exists mostly to permit the clubs to look over their prime minor-league prospects), where he worked intensively with a longtime pitching coach, Don Osborn, and appeared in three games. He came home feeling a little hopeful (he was almost living on such minimal nourishments), but when he forced himself to think about it he had to admit that he had been too tense to throw the fastball much, even against rookies. Then, in late February, 1974, Blass reported to Bradenton with the other Pirate pitchers and catchers. "We have a custom in the early spring that calls for all the pitchers to throw five minutes of batting practice every day," he told me. "This is before the rest of the squad arrives, you understand, so you're just pitching to the other pitchers. Well, the day before that first workout I woke up at four-thirty in the morning. I was so worried that I couldn't get back to sleep—and all this was just over going out and throwing to *pitchers*. I don't remember what happened that first day, but I went out there very tense and anxious every time. As you can imagine, there's very little good work or improvement you can do under those circumstances."

The training period made it clear that nothing had altered with him (he walked twenty-five men in fourteen innings in exhibition play), and when the club went north he was left in Bradenton for further work. He joined the team in Chicago on April 16, and entered a game against the Cubs the next afternoon, taking over in the fourth inning, with the Pirates down by 10–4. He pitched five innings, and gave up eight runs (three of them unearned), five hits, and seven bases on balls. The Cubs batted around against him in the first inning he pitched, and in the sixth he gave up back-to-back home runs. His statistics for the game, including an ERA of 9.00, were also his major-league figures for the year, because late in April the Pirates sent him down to the Charleston (West Virginia) Charlies, their farm team in the Class AAA International League. Blass did not argue about the decision; in fact, as a veteran with more than eight years' service in the majors, he had to agree to the demotion before the parent club could send him down. He felt that the Pirates and Joe Brown had been extraordinarily patient and sympathetic in dealing with a baffling and apparently irremediable problem. They had also been generous, refusing to cut his salary by the full twenty percent permissible in extending a major-league contract. (His pay, which had been ninety thousand dollars in 1973, was cut to seventy-five thousand for the next season, and then to sixty-three thousand this spring.) In any case, Blass wanted to go. He needed continuous game experience if he was ever to break out of it, and he knew he no longer belonged with a big-league club.

The distance between the minors and the majors, always measurable in light-years, is probably greater today than ever before, and for a man making the leap in the wrong direction the feeling must be sickening. Blass tries to pass off the experience lightly (he is apparently incapable of self-pity), but one can guess what must have been required of him to summon up even a scrap of the kind of hope and aggressive self-confidence that are prerequisites, at every level, of a successful athletic performance. He and Karen rented an apartment in Charleston, and the whole family moved down when the school year ended; David and Chris enjoyed the informal atmosphere around the ball park, where they were permitted to shag flies in batting practice. "It wasn't so bad," Blass told me.

But it was. The manager of the Charlies, Steve Demeter, put Blass in the regular starting rotation, but he fared no better against minor-leaguers than he had in the big time. In a very brief time, his earned-run average and his bases-on-balls record were the worst in the league. Blass got along well with his teammates, but there were other problems. The mystery of Steve Blass's decline was old stuff by now in most big-league-city newspapers, but as soon as he was sent down, there was a fresh wave of attention from the national press and the networks; and sportswriters for newspapers in Memphis and Rochester and Richmond and the other International League cities looked on his arrival in town as a God-given feature story. Invariably, they asked him how much money he was earning as a player; then they asked if he thought he was worth it.

The Charlies did a lot of traveling by bus. One day, the team made an eight-hour trip from Charleston to Toledo, where they played a night game. At eleven that same night, they reboarded the bus and drove to Pawtucket, Rhode Island, for their next date, arriving at about nine in the morning. Blass had started the game in Toledo, and he was so disgusted with his performance that he got back on the bus without having showered or taken off his uniform. "We'd stop at an all-night restaurant every now and then, and I'd walk in with a two-day beard and my old Charleston Charlies uniform on, looking like go-to-hell," Blass said. "It was pretty funny to see people looking at me. I had some books along, and we had plenty of wine and beer on the bus, so the time went by somehow." He paused and then shook his head. "*God*, that was an awful trip," he said.

By early August, Blass's record with Charleston was two and nine, and 9.74. He had had enough. With Joe Brown's permission, he left the Charlies and flew West to consult Dr. Bill Harrison, of Davis, California. Dr. Harrison is an optometrist who has helped develop a system of "optometherapy," designed to encourage athletes to concentrate on the immediate physical task at hand—hitting a ball, throwing a strike—by visualizing the act in advance; his firm was once retained by the Kansas City Royals baseball team, and his patients have included a number of professional golfers and football players. Blass spent four days with him, and then rejoined the Pirates, this time as a batting-practice pitcher. He says now that he was very interested in Dr. Harrison's theories but that they just didn't seem to help him much.

In truth, nothing helped. Blass knew that his case was desperate. He was almost alone now with his problem—a baseball castaway—and he had reached the point where he was willing to try practically anything. Under the guidance of pitching coach Don Osborn, he attempted some unusual experiments. He tried pitching from the outfield, with the sweeping motion of a fielder making a long peg. He tried pitching while kneeling on the mound. He tried pitching with his left foot tucked up behind his right knee until the last possible second of his delivery. Slow-motion films of his delivery were studied and compared with films taken during some of his best games of the past; much of his motion, it was noticed, seemed extraneous, but he had thrown exactly the same way at his peak. Blass went back and corrected minute details, to no avail.

The frustrating, bewildering part of it all was that while working alone with a catcher Blass continued to throw as well as he ever had; his fastball was alive, and his slider and curve shaved the corners of the plate. But the moment a batter stood in against him he became a different pitcher, especially when throwing a fastball—a pitcher apparently afraid of seriously injuring somebody. As a result, he was of very little use to the Pirates even in batting practice.

Don Osborn, a gentle man in his mid-sixties, says, "Steve's problem was mental. He had mechanical difficulties, with some underlying mental cause. I don't think anybody will ever understand his decline. We tried everything—I didn't know anything else to do. I feel real bad about it. Steve had a lot of guts to stay out there as long as he did. You know, old men don't dream much, but just the other night I had this dream that Steve Blass was all over his troubles and could pitch again. I said, 'He's ready, we can use him!' Funny . . ."

It was probably at this time that Blass consulted a psychiatrist. He does not talk about it—in part out of a natural reticence but also because the Pirate front office, in an effort to protect his privacy, turned away inquiries into this area by Pittsburgh writers and persistently refused to comment on whether any such therapy was undertaken. It is clear, however, that Blass does not believe he gained any profound insights into possible unconscious causes of his difficulties. Earlier in the same summer, he also experimented briefly with transcendental meditation. He entered the program at the suggestion of Joe Brown, who also enrolled Dave Giusti, Willie Stargell, pitcher Bruce Kison, and himself in the group. Blass repeated mantras and meditated twice a day for about two months; he found that it relaxed him, but it did not seem to have much application to his pitching. Innumerable other remedies were proposed by friends and strangers. Like anyone in hard straits, he was deluged with unsolicited therapies, overnight cures, naturopathies, exorcisms, theologies, and amulets, many of which arrived by mail. Blass refuses to make jokes about these nostrums. "Anyone who takes the trouble to write a man who is suffering deserves to be thanked," he told me.

Most painful of all, perhaps, was the fact that the men who most sympathized with his incurable professional difficulties were least able to help. The Pirates were again engaged in a close and exhausting pennant race fought out over the last six weeks of the season; they moved into first place for good only two days before the end, won their half-pennant, and then were eliminated by the Dodgers in a four-game championship playoff. Steve Blass was with the team through this stretch, but he took no part in the campaign, and by now he was almost silent in the clubhouse. He had become an extra wheel. "It must have been hell for him," Dave Giusti says. "I mean *real* hell. I never could have stood it."

When Blass is asked about this last summer of his baseball career, he will only say that it was "kind of a difficult time" or "not the most fun I've had." In extended conversations about himself, he often gives an impression of an armored blandness that suggests a failure of emotion; this apparent insensitivity about himself contrasts almost shockingly with his subtle concern for the feelings of his teammates and his friends and his family, and even of strangers. "My overriding philosophy is to have a regard for others," he once told me. "I don't want to put myself over other people." He takes pride in the fact that his outward, day-to-day demeanor altered very little through his long ordeal. "A person lives on," he said more than once, smiling. "The sun will come up tomorrow." Most of all, perhaps, he sustained his self-regard by not taking out his terrible frustrations on Karen and the boys. "A ballplayer learns very early that he can't bring the game home with him every night," he said once. "Especially when there are young people growing up there. I'm real proud of the fact that this thing hasn't bothered us at home. David and Chris have come through it all in fine shape. I think Karen and I are closer than ever because of this."

Karen once said to me, "Day to day, he hasn't changed. Just the other morning, he was out working on the lawn, and a couple of the neighbors' children came over to see him. Young kids—maybe three or four years old. Then I looked out a few minutes later, and there was a whole bunch of them yelling and rolling around on the grass with him, like puppies. He's always been that way. Steve has worked at being a man and being a father and a husband. It's something he has always felt very strongly about, and I have to give him all the credit in the world. Sometimes I think I got to hate the frustration and pain of this more than he did. He always found something to hold on to—a couple of good pitches that day, some little thing he had noticed. But I couldn't always share that, and I didn't have his ability to keep things under control."

I asked if maintaining this superhuman calm might not have damaged Steve in some way, or even added to his problems.

"I don't know," she said. "Sometimes in the evening—once in a great while—we'd be sitting together, and we'd have a couple of drinks and he would relax enough to start to talk. He would tell me about it, and get angry and hurt. Then he'd let it come out, and yell and scream and pound on things. And I felt that even this might not be enough for him. He would never do such a thing outside. Never." She paused, and then she said, "I think he directed his anger toward making the situation livable here at home. I've had my own ideas about Steve's pitching, about the mystery, but they haven't made much difference. You can't force your ideas on somebody, especially when he is doing what he thinks he has to do. Steve's a very private person."

•

STEVE BLASS stayed home last winter. He tried not to think much about baseball, and he didn't work on his pitching. He and Karen had agreed that the family would go back to Bradenton for spring training, and that he would give it one more try. One day in January, he went over to the field house at the University of Pittsburgh and joined some other Pirates there for a workout. He threw well. Tony Bartirome, the Pirate trainer, who is a close friend of Steve's, thought he was pitching as well as he ever had. He told Joe Brown that Steve's problems might be over. When spring training came, however, nothing had altered. Blass threw adequately in brief streaks, but very badly against most batters. He hit Willie Stargell and Manny Sanguillen in batting practice; both players told him to forget it. They urged him to cut loose with the fastball.

Joe Brown had told Blass that the end of the line might be approaching. Blass agreed. The Pirate organization had been extraordinarily patient, but it was, after all, in the business of baseball.

On March 24, Steve Blass started the second game of a doubleheader against the White Sox at Bradenton. For three innings, he escaped serious difficulty. He gave up two runs in the second, but he seemed to throw without much tension, and he even struck out Bill Melton, the Chicago third baseman, with a fastball. Like the other Pirates, Dave Giusti was watching with apprehensive interest. "I really thought he was on his way," he told me. "I was encouraged. Then, in the fourth, there were a couple of bases on balls and maybe a bad call by the ump on a close pitch, and suddenly there was a complete reversal. He was a different man out there."

Blass walked eight men in the fourth inning and gave up eight runs. He threw fifty-one pitches, but only seventeen of them were strikes. Some of his pitches were close to the strike zone, but most were not. He worked the count to 3–2 on Carlos May, and then threw the next pitch behind him. The booing from the fans, at first scattered and uncomfortable, grew louder. Danny Murtaugh waited, but Blass could not get the third out. Finally, Murtaugh came out very slowly to the mound and told Blass that he was taking him out of the game; Dave Giusti came in to relieve his old roommate. Murtaugh, a peaceable man, then charged the home-plate umpire and cursed him for the bad call, and was thrown out of the game. Play resumed. Blass put on his warm-up jacket and trotted to the outfield to run his wind sprints. Roland Hemond, the general manager of the White Sox, was at Bradenton that day, and he said, "It was the most heartbreaking thing I have ever seen in baseball."

Three days later, the Pirates held a press conference to announce that they had requested waivers from the other National League clubs, with the purpose of giving Blass his unconditional release. Blass flew out to California to see Dr. Bill Harrison once more, and also to visit a hypnotist, Arthur Ellen, who has worked with several major-league players, and has apparently helped some of them, including Dodger pitcher Don Sutton, remarkably. Blass made the trip mostly because he had promised Maury Wills, who is now a base-running consultant to several teams, that he would not quit the game until he had seen Mr. Ellen.

Blass then returned to Bradenton and worked for several

days with the Pirates' minor-league pitching coach, Larry Sherry, on some pitching mechanics. He made brief appearances in two games against Pirate farmhands, and threw well. He struck out some players with his fastball. After the second game, he showered and got into his Volkswagen and started north to join his family, who had returned to Pittsburgh. It was a good trip, because it gave him time to sort things out, and somewhere along the way he decided to give it up. The six-day waiver period had expired, and none of the other clubs had claimed him. He was encouraged about his pitching, but he had been encouraged before. This time, the fastball had been much better, and at least he could hold on to that; maybe the problem had been mechanical all along. If he came back now, however, it would have to be at the minor-league level, and even if he made it back to the majors, he could expect only three or four more years before his effectiveness would decline because of age and he would have to start thinking about retirement. At least *that* problem could be solved now. He didn't want to subject Karen to more of the struggle. It was time to get out.

•

OF ALL the mysteries that surround the Steve Blass story, perhaps the most mysterious is the fact that his collapse is unique. There is no other player in recent baseball history—at least none with Blass's record and credentials—who has lost his form in such a sudden and devastating fashion and been totally unable to recover. The players and coaches and fans I talked to about Steve Blass brought up a few other names, but then they quickly realized that the cases were not really the same. Some of them mentioned Rex Barney, a Dodger fastball pitcher of the nineteen forties, who quit baseball while still a young man because of his uncontrollable wildness; Barney, however, had only one good year, and it is fair to say he never did have his great stuff under control. Dick Radatz, a very tall relief pitcher with the Red Sox a decade ago, had four good years, and then grew increasingly wild and ineffective. (He is said to have once thrown twenty-seven consecutive balls in a spring-training game.) His decline, however, was partially attributable to his failure to stay in shape. Von McDaniel, a younger brother of Lindy McDaniel, arrived suddenly as a pitcher with the Cardinals, and disappeared just as quickly, but two years' pitching hardly qualifies as a record. There have been hundreds of shiningly promising rookie pitchers and sluggers who, for one reason or another, could not do their thing once they got up to the big time. Blass's story is different. It should also be understood that his was not at all the somewhat commonplace experience of an established and well-paid major-league star who suffers through one or two mediocre seasons. Tom Seaver went through such a slump last summer. But Seaver's problems were only relatively serious (his record for 1974 was 11-11), and were at least partly explicable (he had a sore hip), and he has now returned to form. Blass, once his difficulties commenced, was helpless. Finally, of course, one must accept the possibility that a great many players may have suffered exactly the same sort of falling off as Blass for exactly the same reasons (whatever they may be) but were able to solve the problem and continue their athletic careers. Sudden and terrible batting and pitching slumps are mysterious while they last; the moment they end, they tend to be forgotten.

What happened to Steve Blass? Nobody knows, but some speculation is permissible—indeed, is perhaps demanded of anyone who is even faintly aware of the qualities of Steve Blass and the depths of his suffering. Professional sports have a powerful hold on us because they display and glorify remarkable physical capacities, and because the artificial demands of games played for very high rewards produce vivid responses. But sometimes, of course, what is happening on the field seems to speak to something deeper within us; we stop cheering and look on in uneasy silence, for the man out there is no longer just another great athlete, an idealized hero, but only a man—only ourself. We are no longer at a game. The enormous alterations of professional sport in the past three decades, especially the prodigious inflation of franchises and salaries, have made it evident even to the most thoughtless fan that the play he has come to see is serious indeed, and that the heart of the game is not physical but financial. Sport is no longer a release from the harsh everyday American business world but its continuation and apotheosis. Those of us (fans and players alike) who return to the ball park in the belief that the game and the rules are unchanged—merely a continuation of what we have known and loved in the past—are deluding ourselves, perhaps foolishly, perhaps tragically.

Blass once told me that there were "at least seventeen" theories about the reason for his failure. A few of them are bromides: He was too nice a guy. He became smug and was no longer hungry. He lost the will to win. His pitching motion, so jittery and unclassical, at last let him down for good. His eyesight went bad. (Blass is myopic, and wears glasses while watching television and driving. He has never worn glasses when pitching, which meant that Pirate catchers had to flash him signals with hand gestures rather than with finger waggles; however, he saw well enough to win when he was winning, and his vision has not altered in recent years.) The other, more serious theories are sometimes presented alone, sometimes in conjunction with others. Answers here become more gingerly.

He was afraid of injury—afraid of being struck by a line drive.

Blass was injured three times while on the mound. He cracked a thumb while fielding a grounder in 1966. He was struck on the right forearm by a ball hit by Joe Torre in 1970, and spent a month on the disabled list. While trying for his twentieth victory in his last start in 1972, he was hit on the point of the elbow of his pitching arm by a line drive struck by the Mets' John Milner; he had to leave the game, but a few days later he pitched that first playoff game for the Pirates and won it handily. (Blass's brother-in-law, John Lamb, suffered a fractured skull when hit by a line drive in spring training in 1971, and it was more than a year before he recovered, but Blass's real pitching triumphs all came after that.)

He was afraid of injuring someone—hitting a batter with a fastball.

Blass did hit a number of players in his career, of course, but he never caused anyone to go on the disabled list or, for that matter, to miss even one day's work. He told me he did not enjoy brushing back hitters but had done so when it was obviously called for. The only real criticism of Blass I ever heard from his teammates was that he would not always "protect" them by retaliating against enemy hitters after somebody had been knocked down. During his decline, he was plainly unable to throw the fastball effectively to batters—especially to Pirate batters in practice. He says he hated the idea of hitting and possibly sidelining one of his teammates, but he is convinced that this anxiety was the result of his control problems rather than the cause.

He was seriously affected by the death of Roberto Clemente.

There is no doubt but that the sudden taking away of their most famous and vivid star affected all the Pirates, including Steve Blass. He and Clemente had not been particularly close, but Blass was among the members of the team who flew at once to Puerto Rico for the funeral services, where Blass delivered a eulogy in behalf of the club. The departure of a superstar leaves an almost visible empty place on a successful team, and the leaders next in line—who in this case would certainly include Steve Blass—feel the inescapable burden of trying to fill the gap. A Clemente, however, can never be replaced. Blass never pitched well in the majors after Clemente's death. This argument is a difficult one, and is probably impossible to resolve. There are Oedipal elements here, of course, that are attractive to those who incline in such a direction.

He fell into a slump, which led to an irreparable loss of confidence.

This is circular, and perhaps more a description of symptoms than of the disability itself. However, it is a fact that a professional athlete—and most especially a baseball player—faces a much more difficult task in attempting to regain lost form than an ailing businessman, say, or even a troubled artist; no matter how painful his case has been, the good will of his associates or the vagaries of critical judgment matter not at all when he tries to return. All that matters is his performance, which will be measured, with utter coldness, by the stats. This is one reason that athletes are paid so well, and one reason that fear of failure —the unspeakable "choking"—is their deepest and most private anxiety. Steve Blass passed over my questions about whether he had ever felt this kind of fear when on the mound. "I don't think pitchers, by their nature, allow themselves to think that way," he said. "To be successful, you turn that kind of thought away." On the other hand, he often said that two or three successive well-pitched games probably would have been all he needed to dissipate the severe tension that affected his performances once things began to go badly for him. They never came.

The remaining pieces of evidence (if, indeed, they have any part in the mystery) have been recounted here. Blass is a modest man, both in temperament and in background, and his success and fame were quite sudden and, to some degree, unexpected. His salary at the beginning of 1971—the year of his two great Series wins—was forty thousand dollars; two years later it was ninety thousand, and there were World Series and playoff checks on top of that. Blass was never thought of as one of the great pitchers of his time, but in the late sixties and early seventies he was probably the most consistent starter on the Pirate staff; it was, in fact, a staff without stars. On many other teams, he would have been no more than the second- or third-best starter, and his responsibilities, real and imagined, would have been less acute.

I took some of these hard questions to Blass's colleagues. Danny Murtaugh and Bill Virdon (who is now the Yankees' pilot) both expressed their admiration for Blass but said they had no idea what had happened to him. They seemed a bit brusque about it, but then I realized, of course, that ballplayers are forever disappearing from big-league dugouts; the manager's concern is with those who remain—with today's lineup. "I don't know the answer," Bill Virdon told me in the Yankee clubhouse. "If I did, I'd go get Steve to pitch for me. He sure won a lot of big games for us on the Pirates."

Joe Brown said, "I've tried to keep my distance and not to guess too much about what happened. I'm not a student of pitching and I'm not a psychologist. You can tell a man what to do, but you can't *make* him do it. Steve is an outstanding man, and you hate to quit on him. In this business, you bet on character. Big-league baseball isn't easy, yet you can stand it when things are going your way. But Steve Blass never had a good day in baseball after this thing hit him."

Blass's best friends in baseball are Tony Bartirome, Dave Giusti, and Nelson King (who, along with Bob Prince, was part of the highly regarded radio-and-television team that covered the Pirate games).

Tony Bartirome (*He is forty-three years old, dark-haired, extremely neat in appearance. He was an infielder before he became a trainer, and played one season in the majors—with the Pirates, in 1952*): "Steve is unique physically. He has the arm of a twenty-year-old. Not only did he never have a sore arm but he never had any of the stiffness and pain that most pitchers feel on the day after a game. He was always the same, day after day. You know, it's very important for a trainer to know the state of mind and the feelings of his players. What a player is thinking is about eighty percent of it. The really strange thing is that after this trouble started, Steve never showed any feelings about his pitching. In the old days, he used to get mad at himself after a bad showing, and sometimes he threw things around in the clubhouse. But after this began, when he was taken out of a game he only gave the impression that he was happy to be out of there—relieved that he no longer had to face it that day. Somehow, he didn't show any emotion at *all*. Maybe it was like his never having a sore arm. He never talked in any detail about his different treatments—the psychiatry and all. I think he felt he didn't need any of that—that at any moment he'd be back where he was, the Blass of old, and that it all was up to him to make that happen."

Dave Giusti (*He is one of the great relief pitchers in baseball. He earned a BA and an MA in physical education at Syracuse. He is thirty-five—dark hair, piercing brown eyes, and a quiet manner*): "Steve has the perfect build for a pitcher—lean and strong. He is remarkably open to all kinds of people, but I think he has closed his mind to his inner self. There are central areas you can't infringe on with him. There is no doubt that during the past two years he didn't react to a bad performance the way he used to, and you have to wonder why he couldn't apply his competitiveness to his problem. Karen used to bawl out me and Tony for not being tougher on him, for not doing more. Maybe I should have come right out and said he seemed to have lost his will to fight, but it's hard to shock somebody, to keep bearing in on him. You're afraid to lose a friend, and you want to go easy on him because he is your friend.

"Last year, I went through something like Steve's crisis. The first half of the season, I was atrocious, and I lost all my confidence, especially in my fastball. The fastball is my best pitch, but I'd get right to the top of my delivery and then something would take over, and I'd know even before I released the ball that it wasn't going to be in the strike zone. I began worrying about making big money and not performing. I worried about not contributing to the team. I worried about being traded. I thought it might be the end for me. I didn't know how to solve my problem, but I knew I *had* to solve it. In the end, it was talking to people that did it. I talked to everybody, but mostly to Joe Brown and Danny and my wife. Then, at some point, I turned the corner. But it was talking that did it, and my point is that Steve can't talk to people that way. Or won't.

"Listen, it's tough out there. It's hard. Once you start maintaining a plateau, you've got to be absolutely sure what your goals are."

Nellie King (*A former pitcher with the Pirates. He is friendly and informal, with an attractive smile. He is very tall —six-six. Forty-seven years old*): "Right after that terrible game in Atlanta, Steve told me that it had felt as if the whole world was pressing down on him while he was out there. But then he suddenly shut up about it, and he never talked that way again. He covered it all up. I think there *are* things weighing on him, and I think he may be so angry inside that he's afraid to throw the ball. He's afraid he might kill somebody. It's only nickel psychology, but I think there's a lost kid in Steve. I remembered that after the '71 Series he said, 'I didn't think I was as good as this.' He seemed truly surprised at what he'd done. The child in him is a great thing—we've all loved it —and maybe he was suddenly afraid he was losing it. It was being forced out of him.

"Being good up here is *so* tough—people have no idea. It gets much worse when you have to repeat it: 'We know you're great. Now go and do that again for me.' So much money and so many people depend on you. Pretty soon you're trying so hard that you can't function."

I ventured to repeat Nellie King's guesses about the mystery to Steve Blass and asked him what he thought.

"That's pretty heavy," he said after a moment. "I guess I don't have a tendency to go into things in much depth. I'm a surface reactor. I tend to take things not too seriously. I really think that's one of the things that's *helped* me in baseball."

A smile suddenly burst from him.

"There's one possibility nobody has brought up," he said. "I don't think anybody's ever said that maybe I just lost my control. Maybe your control is something that can just go. It's no big thing, but suddenly it's gone." He paused, and then he laughed in a self-deprecating way. "Maybe that's what I'd like to believe," he said.

•

On my last morning with Steve Blass, we sat in his family room and played an imaginary ball game together—half an inning of baseball. It had occurred to me that in spite of his enforced and now permanent exile from the game, he still possessed a rare body of precise and hard-won pitching information. He still knew most of the hitters in his league, and probably as well as any other pitcher around, he knew what to pitch to them in a given situation. I had always wanted to hear a pitcher say exactly what he would throw next and why, and now I invited Blass to throw against the Cincinnati Reds, the toughest lineup of hitters anywhere. I would call the balls and strikes and hits. I promised he would have no control problems.

He agreed at once. He poured himself another cup of coffee and lit up a Garcia y Vega. He was wearing slacks and a T-shirt and an old sweater (he had a golfing date later that day), and he looked very young.

"OK," he said. "Pete Rose is leading off—right? First of all, I'm going to try to keep him off base if I can, because they have so many tough hitters coming up. They can bury you before you even get started. I'm going to try to throw strikes and not get too fine. I'll start him off with a slider away. He has a tendency to go up the middle and I'll try to keep it a bit away."

Rose, I decided, didn't offer. It was ball one.

"Now I'll throw him a sinking fastball, and still try to work him out that way. The sinking fastball tends to tail off just a little."

Rose fouled it into the dirt.

"Well, now we come back with another slider, and I'll try to throw it inside. That's just to set up another slider *outside*."

Rose fouled that one as well.

"We're ahead one and two now—right?" Blass said. "Well, this early in the game I wouldn't try to throw him that slow curve—that big slop off-speed pitch. I'd like to work on that a couple of times first, because it's early and he swings so well. So as long as I'm ahead of him, I'll keep on throwing him sliders—keep going that way."

Rose took another ball, and then grounded out on a medium-speed curveball.

Joe Morgan stood in, and Blass puffed on his cigar and looked at the ceiling.

"Joe Morgan is strictly a fastball hitter, so I want to throw him a *bad* fastball to start him off," he said. "I'll throw it in the dirt to show it to him—get him geared to that kind of speed. Now, after ball one, I'll give him a medium-to-slow curveball and try to get it over the plate—just throw it for a strike."

Morgan took: one and one.

"Now I throw him a *real* slow curveball—a regular rainbow. I've had good luck against him with that sort of stuff."

And so it went. Morgan, I decided, eventually singled to right on a curve in on the handle—a lucky hit—but then Blass retired his next Cincinnati hitter, Dan Driessen, who popped out on a slider. Blass laid off slow pitches here, so Sanguillen would have a chance to throw out Morgan if he was stealing.

Johnny Bench stood in, with two out.

"Morgan won't be stealing, probably," Blass said. "He won't want to take the bat out of Bench's hands." He released another cloud of cigar smoke, thinking hard. "Well, I'll start him out with a good, tough fastball outside. I've got to work very carefully to him, because when he's hot he's capable of hitting it out anytime."

Ball one.

"Well, the slider's only been fair today. . . . I'll give him a slider, but away—off the outside."

Swinging strike. Blass threw another slider, and Bench hit a line single to left, moving Morgan to second. Tony Perez was the next batter.

"Perez is not a good high, hard fastball hitter," Blass said. "I'll begin him with that pitch, because I don't want to get into any more trouble with the slider and have him dunk one in. A letter-high fastball, with good mustard on it."

Perez took a strike.

"Now I'll do it again, until I miss—bust him up and in. He has a tendency to go after that kind of pitch. He's an exceptional offspeed hitter, and will give himself up with men on base—give up a little power to get that run in."

Perez took, for a ball, and then Blass threw him an intentional ball—a very bad slider inside. Perez had shortened up on the bat a little, but he took the pitch. He then fouled off a fastball, and Blass threw him another good fastball, high and inside, and Perez struck out, swinging, to end the inning.

"Pretty good inning," I said. "Way to go." We both laughed.

"Yes, you know that *exact* sequence has happened to Perez many times," Blass said. "He shortens up and then chases the pitch up here."

He was animated. "You know, I can almost *see* that fastball to Perez, and I can see his bat going through it, swinging through the pitch and missing," he said. "That's a good feeling. That's one of the concepts of Dr. Harrison's program, you know—visualization. When I was pitching well, I was doing that very thing. You get so locked in, you see yourself doing things before they happen. That's what people mean when they say you're in the groove. That's what happened in that World Series game, when I kept throwing that big slop curveball to Boog Powell, and it really ruined him. I must have thrown it three out of four pitches to him, and I just *knew* it was going to be there. There's no doubt about it—no information needed. The crowd is there, this is the World Series, and all of a sudden you're locked into something. It's like being plugged into a computer. It's 'Gimme the ball, *boom!* Click, click, click . . . *shoom!*' It's that good feeling. You're just flowing easy."

12 The Companions of the Game

September 1975

The San Francisco Giants, it seems, are about to be sold to some Japanese businessmen. The news, which appeared in the *Times* late last month, was somehow both startling and boring —instant antipodal emotions that only stories about quintuplets or the business side of sports arouse in me. The *Times*' account was a blurry, hedging affair, beginning with a denial by the Giants' front office of the reported deal, followed by several paragraphs explaining why it probably would go through. It was generally known, of course, that the club has been in financial difficulties for several years, and earlier this summer its president, Horace C. Stoneham, announced that his controlling share of the National Exhibition Company (which is the team's florid, nineteenth-century corporate handle) was up for sale. A San Francisco-based group, headed by a real-estate man named Robert A. Lurie and including the National League president, Chub Feeney, who is a nephew of Stoneham's, and Bill Rigney, a former Giant manager, had been talking with Stoneham, but the Japanese offer of seventeen million dollars—for the club, its minor-league affiliates, and some baseball and hotel properties at the Giants' spring-training headquarters in Phoenix, Arizona—is apparently a good deal higher than any other bids so far.* The sale, in any case, will require the approval of the other National League owners, who will vote on the matter sometime after the World Series.

As a lifetime Giants fan whose passionate boyhood attachment had been slowly cooled by the departure of my heroes from the Polo Grounds in 1958, by the decline and eventual retirement of Willie Mays, and by the pale neutrality of middle age, I tried to summon up a semblance of outraged xenophobia at the news of the possible Toyotafication of my old team and my old pastime, but it became clear to me in the same instant that I simply didn't give a damn. Big-league baseball is a commercial enterprise, and the business of Japan, as Calvin Coolidge probably meant to tell us, is business. There was a time when the ownership of a ball team by a hometown brewer or chewing-gum family did not seem an especially important part of its public identity, but in the past twenty years eight of the original sixteen big-league clubs have been sold (and in some cases resold and re-resold) to new business interests, while eight new clubs have been born, four of which have later changed hands. As a result, the financial adventures of some teams are almost better publicized (and often a good deal more interesting) than their achievements in the pennant race. A typical modern ball team is operated coldly and from a distance, just like any other conglomerate subentity with interesting tax-depletion build-ins and excellent PR overtones. Their owners and operators are men whose money derives from, and whose deepest loyalties adhere to, insurance companies, broadcasting chains, oil wells, whiskey manufacture, real-estate sales, trucking and shipping lines, quick-lunch

* It was, in fact, a great deal lower, since the Japanese sportsmen never let anyone see the color of their yen, and the deal fell through. For the true further adventures of Mr. Lurie and the elusive San Francisco franchise, see page 336 *et seq*.

chains, and the like, and it doesn't seem to make much difference if one of the teams should now land in the portfolio of some enterprising visitors whose hero is Sadaharu Oh instead of Babe Ruth, and whose cash comes from the marketing of *sake* or electronic calculators or sushiburgers.

For all that, there is one aspect of the sale of the Giants that seems worth attention, worth caring about, and that is the departure of Horace Stoneham from baseball. The Stoneham family has owned the Giants ever since Horace's father, Charles A. Stoneham, purchased the club, in 1919, in partnership with a New York City magistrate named Francis X. McQuade and the team's famous manager, John J. McGraw. Charles Stoneham, who held the majority interest in the team, died in 1936, and Horace Stoneham, then thirty-two years old, succeeded him, thus becoming the youngest club president in baseball history. The Stoneham family has *been* the Giants for more than half a century, for it has had no other business in that time. Along with Calvin Griffith, of the Minnesota Twins (formerly the Washington Senators), Stoneham is the last of the pure baseball men, the owners who owned nothing but their team and cared for nothing but the game. (Tom Yawkey, the longtime Red Sox owner, is of the same breed, but he is also the possessor of a sizable fortune.)

In recent years, it has been the custom for men at baseball gatherings to talk about Horace Stoneham with affectionate and patronizing sadness. "I *like* Horace," the conversation always begins. "Hell, everybody likes him, but . . ." The sentence trails off, and the speaker shakes his head in the manner of a young lawyer who has undertaken to bring order out of his mother's checkbook. Nothing has gone right for Stoneham in recent years, but there was a time when he had his share of success. His Giants have won five pennants, a world championship, and one divisional title. He has hired winning managers. In his father's time, he recommended the selection of McGraw's successor, Bill Terry, who captured a world championship in his first year at the helm, and in 1948 he snatched

Leo Durocher from the despised Brooklyn Dodgers. Stoneham was capable of risky and decisive moves, such as the house-cleaning in 1949, when he traded away the stars of a popular but nonwinning Giants club—Johnny Mize, Walker Cooper, Sid Gordon, Willard Marshall, and Buddy Kerr—to make room for Eddie Stanky and Alvin Dark and the others who would, under Durocher, fashion the marvelous winning summers of 1951 and 1954. The Giants' scouts and farms delivered up some true stars—Monte Irvin, Willie Mays, Willie McCovey, Juan Marichal, and Orlando Cepeda—and estimable front-liners like Sal Maglie, Whitey Lockman, Bobby Thomson, Larry Jansen, the Alou brothers, Gaylord Perry, and Bobby Bonds. Until quite recently, in fact, the Stoneham record has been one of the better ones in baseball, a high-risk business in which true dynasties are extremely rare.

The Dodgers, to be sure, were far more successful than Stoneham's club in the last decade of their co-tenancy of New York, and when the two clubs moved west, in 1958, the disparity widened. The Los Angeles Dodgers have won five pennants and three World Series since their relocation, and the extraordinary season-long outpouring of fans to Dodger Stadium, which regularly tops the home-attendance figures of all other clubs, has made the team the most profitable franchise in baseball. For the San Francisco Giants, it has been quite the other way. The team was idolized in its first few summers, drawing one million eight hundred thousand customers in its first season in Candlestick Park, and there was a famous pennant (and very nearly a world championship) in 1962. From the day Candlestick opened, however, it was plain that its site and its design were disastrous. Its summer-long icy winds and swirling bayside fogs, which often made the act of watching a ball game into something like an Eskimo manhood ritual, have become an old, bad local joke. These discouragements, coupled with five straight second-place finishes between 1965 and 1969, cut attendance in half by 1970, a particularly heavy falloff coming in 1968, when the A's established residency across the Bay. Since then, the proximity of the two clubs has clearly strained the limited audience and the dim baseball fealty of the area, but the A's, now three-time world champions, have had much the better of it. Last year, the A's drew 845,693, while the Giants, who finished fifth in their division, drew 519,991—the worst in either league.*

The most riveting difference between the Oakland A's and the San Francisco Giants is not, however, in their comparative records or attendance figures but in their owners. Indeed, the temperament and reputation of the two men are at such utter removes that they almost seem to represent polarities of human behavior, and their presence in the same business and the same metropolis suggests nothing so much as fictional irony flung off by Ayn Rand. Charles O. Finley, the owner of the A's, is a relative newcomer to baseball, who has in a short time achieved an extraordinary success, and perhaps even greater notoriety. He is a self-made man, a millionaire insurance salesman, who has built a formidable championship club by relying almost exclusively on his own intelligence, quickness, hunches, and energetic dealing. He is a great promoter, with a perfect inner instrument attuned to the heat of the crowd, the glare of the event, and he is an instinctive and embarrassing self-aggrandizer. He is an innovator who has disturbed the quiet, dim halls of baseball and altered the game irrevocably. As an executive, he takes a personal hand in all the daily details of his club, including the most minute decisions on the field, and he swiftly disposes of managers and subalterns who cannot abide his meddling. The A's headquarters, in the Oakland-Alameda County Coliseum, consists mainly of empty offices. Most of the time, Finley follows his team by telephone from an office in Chicago, either plugging into a local radio broadcast or being provided with a running play-by-play account of the action by someone on the scene. Baseball as occasion—the enjoyment and company of the

* The trend continued in 1975, when the A's drew 1,075,518 for the season, against the Giants' 522,919.

game—apparently means nothing to him. Finley is generally reputed to be without friends, and his treatment of his players has been characterized by habitual suspicion, truculence, inconsistency, public abasement, impatience, flattery, parsimony, and ingratitude. He also wins.

Horace Stoneham is—well, most of all he is not Charlie Finley. He inherited his team and his position, and he does not want baseball quickly or wildly altered. Indeed, it may well be that he wishes the game to be more as it was when he first came to it as a youth. He is shy, self-effacing, and apparently incapable of public attitudinizing. He attends every home game but is seldom recognized, even by the hoariest Giants fans. His decisions are arrived at after due consideration, and the most common criticism leveled at him is that he often sticks with a losing manager or an elder player long after his usefulness to the club has been exhausted. He relies on old friends for baseball counsel and for company; most of his advisers and colleagues—men like Tom Sheehan; Garry Schumacher; Rosy Ryan; Carl Hubbell, director of player development; and Jack Schwarz, farm director—have been with the Giants for thirty or forty years. Perhaps because Stoneham grew up in a time when baseball was the only game in town and thus seemed to succeed on its own merits, he has a limited interest in vivid public relations, commercial tie-ins, and other hypes. His relations with the press have been cordial (in the words of Wells Twombly, of the San Francisco *Examiner*, he treats reporters like "beloved guests"), and his dealings with his players are marked by generosity and mutual admiration. In 1972, when his dwindling financial resources forced him at last to trade away Willie Mays, perhaps the greatest Giant of them all, he arranged a deal that permitted Mays to move along to the Mets with a salary and a subsequent retirement plan that would guarantee his comfort for the rest of his life. Horace Stoneham is convivial with his friends but instinctively private, and it is possible to guess that the only quality he may share with Charlie Finley is loneliness. He has been losing, and now he has lost, and he is thus fair game for the glum attention of writers and the secret scorn of men who understand nothing but success.

Early this summer, I began compiling information and talking to West Coast ballplayers and baseball writers with the idea of trying to interview Charlie Finley, perhaps while watching a game with him. For some reason (for *several* reasons), I kept holding off on the story, however, and then, when I read that the San Francisco Giants were up for sale, it suddenly came to me that the baseball magnate I really wanted to spend an afternoon with was Horace Stoneham. I got on the telephone to some friends of mine and his (I had never met him), and explained that I did not want to discuss attendance figures or sales prices with him but just wanted to talk baseball. Stoneham called me back in less than an hour. "Come on out," he said in a cheerful, gravelly, Polo Grounds sort of voice. "Come out, and we'll go to the game together."

•

I DRESSED all wrong for it, of course. The game that Stoneham and I had fixed upon was a midweek afternoon meeting between the Giants and the San Diego Padres in late June—a brilliant, sunshiny day at Candlestick Park, it turned out, and almost the perfect temperature for a curling match. I had flown out from New York that morning, and I reported to Stoneham's office a few minutes before game time. He shook my hand and examined my airy East Coast midsummer getup and said, "Oh, no, this won't do." He went to a closet and produced a voluminous, ancient camel's-hair polo coat and helped me into it. He is a round, pink-faced man with close-cropped white hair, round horn-rimmed spectacles, and a hospitable Irish smile, and he looked much younger than I had expected. (He is seventy-two.) He was wearing tweeds, with an expensive-looking silk tie—a gambler's tie—but he, too, put on a topcoat and buttoned it up before we went out into the sunshine. Stoneham's box, on the press level, was capacious but utilitarian, with none of the Augustan appointments and Late Hefner upholsteries I have seen in some sports-owners' piazzas. There was a perfect view of the ballplayers arrayed below us on the AstroTurf, a few hundred scattered fans—most of whom seemed to be kids in variously emblazoned windbreakers—and thousands of empty orange-colored seats. The game matched up two good young right-handed fastballers—the Giants' John Montefusco and the Padres' Joe McIntosh. I kept track of things for a few minutes, but then I quickly gave it up, because an afternoon of Horace Stoneham's baseball cannot be fitted into a scorecard.

"I think the first Giants game I ever saw was the first half of a doubleheader on the Fourth of July in 1912," he told me. "The Giants' battery was Christy Mathewson and Chief Meyers. They opened with their stars in the first game, you see, because they charged separate admissions for the morning and afternoon games, and that way they got out the crowds early. I've forgotten who the other team was. I was nine years old. My father grew up in New Jersey, and his boyhood idol, his particular hero, was the great Giant left fielder Mike Tiernan, who came from Jersey City. Later, when my pop bought the club, he liked to say that he'd followed Tiernan over to the Giants.

"My father bought the team in 1919, and in 1921, as you may know, we played the first of three consecutive World Series against the Yankees, who shared the Polo Grounds with us in those days. That Series in '21 had a funny kind of ending. We were ahead by one run—I think it was 1–0—in the ninth, and Aaron Ward got on base for the Yanks. Frank Baker—Home Run Baker—came up and knocked a ball to right that looked like a sure hit, but our second baseman, Rawlings, made a great play on it, running it down almost in right field, and threw to Kelly to get him. Ward must have thought the ball had gone through, because he passed second and just kept on running. George Kelly—oh, he had the best arm in baseball—saw him, and he fired the ball across to

Frisch at third, and Frisch took the throw and tagged Ward just as he slid in. I can still see that, with Ward in the dirt and Frank Frisch making the tag and then landing on his fanny, with the ball still in his glove. It was a double play and it ended it all, but it happened so fast that everybody in the stands just sat there for a minute. They couldn't believe the Series was over."

Stoneham talked in an energetic, good-humored way. He reminded me of a good standup, middle-of-the-night bar conversationalist. "I was in the stands that day. I was still in school, at Loyola School. I was a mediocre second baseman on the team there. I went to a lot of Giants games, of course. Jimmy Walker was a state assemblyman then, and he used to come to the game every day. I got to know him very well—Hey, look at *this!*"

Von Joshua, the Giant center fielder—the 1975 Giant center fielder—had singled, and a run was coming across the plate. Within another minute or two, the Giants were ahead by 3–0, still in the first inning, and McIntosh had been knocked out of the game.

Stoneham resumed, but we were in 1939 now, at a famous Polo Grounds disaster that I had seen. "You were there?" Stoneham said. "Then, of course, you remember what happened. It was early in the summer, but that game cost us the pennant. We were playing the Cincinnati Reds head and head, and if we win we have a good shot at first place. Then somebody hit that ball for them—maybe it was Harry Craft—that hooked foul into the left-field upper deck, and the umpire called it fair and waved the runners around. Everybody could see it was foul, so there was a big squabble, and Billy Jurges, our shortstop, he spit right in George Magerkurth's face, and Magerkurth swung on him. Well, they were both suspended, of course—the player and the umpire both together. We called up Frank Scalzi to take Jurges's place, but a few days later Lou Chiozza and Joe Moore had a collision going after a fly ball and Chiozza got a broken leg, and we never did get going again."

I asked Stoneham about his first job with the Giants, and he told me that he had gone to work in the ticket department when he was in his early twenties. "We had a lady, Miss Wilson, who ran it all then," he said. "None of this computer business. Well, bit by bit I got into the running of the ball park, and then my father put me in charge of operations there. In those days, in the twenties, the Polo Grounds was open for events maybe two hundred days out of the year. The Coogan family owned the real estate, but the park belonged to the club. We had football—pro games and college games—we had the circus there, we had tennis and the midget automobiles. We had a skating rink in the outfield once, and even a week of outdoor opera. We had soccer—the Hakoah team came in after they won some international title, I think it was, and drew fifty-two thousand, so we knew it was a popular sport even then. We had visiting British soccer teams, and a team, I remember, that represented the Indiana Flooring Company. I think we had every sport at the Polo Grounds except polo. I did my best to arrange that, but we never could work it out.

"I came to know the ballplayers then, of course. I used to see them in the mornings. I got to be friends with some of them, like Ross Youngs, the great outfielder who died so young. Ross Youngs, from Shiner, Texas. When he first came along—before I knew him—he was signed by the Giants at a time when the team was on the road. Ross was in town and the Giants were away, and he went right over and got into a pickup baseball game over by the docks on Seventy-ninth Street, next to the railroad yards there. It's where they have the marina now. He had that intense desire to play ball.

"I was about twenty years old when Mr. McGraw asked my father to let me go to spring training. We trained in Sarasota back then. I remember that Mr. McGraw called me up to his room there and showed me a letter he had just written to my father about a young prospect named Hack Wilson, who'd been on a Class B team in Portsmouth, Virginia. He wore a red undershirt under his uniform. Mr. McGraw had written, 'If hustle counts, he's sure to make it.' Everybody called him 'Mr. McGraw'—everybody but my father, of course. Mr. McGraw, he called my father 'Charlie' or 'C.A.'—C.A. for Charles Abraham Stoneham, named after Abraham Lincoln."

We were in the third inning, and the Padres had a base runner on second. The next Padre batter, shortstop Enzo Hernandez, is an indifferent hitter, but now he singled to left and drove in the first San Diego run. "Oh, you sucker," Stoneham said, shaking his head sadly. "That's the history of the game. The pitcher lets up on the out man, and he hurts you."

The rally died, and Stoneham cheered up quickly. "We were talking about John McGraw," he said. "Well, another time in spring training he wrote a letter back to my father that said, 'There's a young fellow down here named Ott who is the best hitter on the farm level I've ever seen.' As you know, Mr. McGraw never did let Mel Ott go out to the minors. He brought him up to the Giants when he was just seventeen years old. He didn't want anybody spoiling that funny batting style—some manager telling him, 'You can't hit that way. You've got to put that front foot down.' When Ott started out, he was a switch-hitter. He never hit righty in a game, as far as I know. Ott didn't get to play much the first couple of years, and McGraw would sometimes let him go over to New Jersey on the weekends and pick up some extra cash by playing with a semipro team. He played with the Paterson Silk Sox. Later on, Ottie and Carl Hubbell were roommates. Oh, my, there were so many games that Carl won by 2–0, 1–0—something like that—where Ott knocked in the winning run. You couldn't count them all."

•

In the fourth inning, Stoneham took a telephone call at his seat, and I overheard him say, "We've sent flowers, and I wrote Mrs. Gordon this morning." I had read in the newspaper that morning that Sid Gordon, a Giant infielder-outfielder in the nineteen forties, had dropped dead while playing softball. Strangely enough, I had read a story about him and Horace Stoneham in a sports column only a few days earlier. Gordon had been a holdout in the spring of 1949, but he finally came to terms for twenty-five hundred dollars less than he had demanded. Horace Stoneham was always made uneasy by prolonged salary disputes with his players, and in December of 1949 he mailed Gordon a check for the twenty-five hundred dollars—a considerable gesture, since Gordon had been traded in the autumn and was by then a member of the Boston Braves.

Now Stoneham hung up the telephone, and I asked him about the business of trades. "Well," he said, "you always hate to see your players leave. Maybe I'm too much of a sentimentalist. You can make mistakes trading, of course, but if you never make a mistake, you're not really trying. We made that big trade with the Braves involving Sid Gordon and the others because Leo Durocher wanted his own kind of team. He always had great success with players that could maneuver the bat. With younger players he was—well, he could be a little impatient. Everything with Leo was . . . *spontaneous.*

"One of the times that really hurt was when it came time to trade Freddie Fitzsimmons, who went over to the Dodgers in the middle thirties there, after more than ten years with us. He was really upset when he left us. He cried. What a competitor he was! He had no friends when he was out there on the mound. He'd show the batter his back when he pitched—he had that big rotation—and he was a remarkable fielder, with great agility for somebody with such a bulky build. Sometimes there'd be a hard grounder or a line drive hit through the box there, and he'd stick out his *foot* at it to stop it going through. Anything to win. I can still see him sticking out that foot and knocking the ball down or maybe deflecting it to some infielder.

"All those games in the Polo Grounds—well, most of the time I watched them from a window in the clubhouse, way out beyond center field. You remember what it was like there?" I did indeed. I always used to wonder about the distant figures that one could sometimes see peering out of the little screened windows set into that green, faraway wall. "There was just a table and chairs there—the same place where my pop used to sit and watch. I was out there when Bobby Thomson hit the home run in 1951 that beat the Dodgers in the last playoff game. We were down three runs in the ninth, and I was commiserating with Sal Maglie, who'd been taken out of the game, and trying to tell him what a great year it had been. We saw Lockman's hit that brought in the first run, but the side of the bleachers blocked our view so we couldn't see if Bobby's hit was going to go in, but I knew it was up the wall, so I said to Sal, 'Well, at least we've tied it up.' Some tie! The same thing with Willie's catch off Vic Wertz in the 1954 Series. I watched him come all the way out after it, and then he went out of sight behind that big black screen we had there that formed a background for the hitters. But I heard the crowd, and I knew he'd made the catch. I knew it anyway, I think, because I'd seen him make all those other impossible catches. I liked that view of things in the Polo Grounds. The last day we played there, I couldn't go to the game. I just didn't want to see it come to an end."

•

WE WERE in the fourth inning and the Giants had a couple of runners on, and now the Giants' second baseman, Derrel Thomas, delivered them both with a sharp single up the middle. A thin scattering of cheers reached us, and Stoneham beamed. I ventured to ask him if he had a favorite among all the Giant clubs he watched down the years.

"Ah, I've seen so many of them," he said. "You'd have to break them down into periods. People are always asking me how the ballplayers compare now with the old-timers, and all you can say is they're at least the equal. The equipment is much better now, of course, but the competition for athletes [he gave it the old New York sound: "athaletes"] is greater, with the other sports getting so big. The best of them can play all sports, you know. We've lost some of our top draft choices to football. When I was a young fellow, all the colleges had good baseball programs, but now a lot of them have given up the game.

"You know, we have a good team right here, but we've had injuries. Gary Matthews and Von Joshua got hurt on the same day. Matthews is going to miss about a month, they say, with the broken knuckle on his left hand. But I think we're going to pick up and pull ourselves together. This is a young team, and I do like that. We have a lot of young arms."

He looked up at the scoreboard. "Those Cubbies are beating the Phils again, I see," he said. "They must have some kind of wind there—look at all those home runs. Yes, so many things can happen to a team in a year, you know. We had a lot of strange events in '33, when we ended up winning the Series. Johnny Vergez had an appendectomy, and Charlie Dressen came up and filled in—he'd been managing in the Southern Association. He told Adolfo Luque how to pitch to the final Washington batter in the Series—it was somebody he'd seen down there. Lefty O'Doul came back with us that year, too, and he got a big pinch hit in the Series, off of Alvin Crowder. I remember that Luque was limping around at the party after we'd won the last game, and when we asked him about it, it turned out he'd split his big toenail throwing those curves during the game. He bore down that hard, he broke his toe.

"When Sal Maglie was first with us, he was just an average pitcher. [Stoneham had moved along about fifteen years.] But when he jumped down to the Mexican League, in 1946, the team he played for there was managed by Dolf Luque, and when we got him back he'd mastered all those great curveballs, and nobody could touch him."

We were joined now by Garry Schumacher, the retired press director for the Giants, who was for many years a redoubtable Polo Grounds press-box sage.

"Garry, we've been talking about Luque and Sal and some of the other old-timers," Stoneham said.

"Hey, do you remember how Maglie used to have fun with Roy Campanella?" Schumacher said. "Every now and then, in a game when it didn't mean anything, he'd plunk Roy right in the belly with one of those curveballs. You know how Roy used to look when he stood up there and crowded the plate."

Stoneham laughed. "Sure, I remember now," he said. "Oh, Campy was a good man. He was a friend of ours."

"Did you get to the time Marichal and Spahn hooked up against each other for sixteen innings?" Schumacher asked.

Stoneham nodded several times, thinking about it, and it suddenly came to me that he and Garry Schumacher and his other friends had probably talked together hundreds of times about each of these famous games and vanished companions. Old afternoons were fresh and past players stayed young, and it was the talking that kept them that way.

Now, however, the Padres had two base runners aboard, and Stoneham leaned forward in his seat. "They've been getting some strange-looking hits here," he said. "It looks like they're slapping at the ball." He called to his pitcher. "Bear down, John!"

Montefusco struck out the next batter, and Stoneham said, "Boy, that fastball is the answer."

"Did you tell about that doubleheader against the Cards in '33?" Schumacher said. "The one where Hubbell won the first, 1–0, in eighteen, and Parmelee beat Dean, 1–0, in the nightcap, and we held on to first place?"

"That was a day," Stoneham said. "Hubbell sure won a lot of big ones in his time. You know, he first belonged to the Tiger organization, but he never played in the majors with them, because they thought that screwball of his would only ruin his arm. Then it happened that our scout, Dick Kinsella, was a delegate to the Democratic National Convention of 1928, down in Texas, and one day when he was there he went to a game and saw Hubbell, who was pitching for the Beaumont club. He signed him up. He saw what that pitch would do for him."

Schumacher, who was not wearing a coat, had been blowing on his hands, and now he said goodbye and went inside to warm up.

"In any list of our teams, you'd have to mention the '54 club," Stoneham went on. (The Giants met the Cleveland Indians in the World Series of 1954, and beat them in four straight games, although the Indians had been prohibitive favorites. It was the only Stoneham team to win a World Series.) "Willie and Don Mueller and Dusty Rhodes. It's funny, but the thing I remember about that club is all the double plays they got that year that ended up with a base runner caught out of position—being put out by a throw behind him, or something like that. A great heads-up team. Dusty Rhodes got all the publicity for those pinch-hit homers, but I think Henry Thompson was the key man for us in that Series. Dusty's first home run was nothing—real Chinese—but the one he hit the next day went nine miles. You know, Dusty Rhodes works on a tugboat in New York Harbor now. He belongs to the seafarers' union, or whatever they call it. I still hear from him. And Davey Williams is a deputy sheriff down in Dallas. I try to keep in touch. I got a letter from Burgess Whitehead just this week, from—let me see. From Windsor, North Carolina."

I asked Stoneham when he had first seen Willie Mays.

"Willie Mays first reported to us in New York carrying a toilet kit and three bats," Stoneham said. His face was lit up. "But the first time I saw him play was way before that. He was with Trenton, in a Class B league, and we'd just played a game in Philadelphia, and some of us rented a car and drove out to watch him play. They had a little press box, just about the size of this box. Bill McKechnie, Jr., was the general manager there, and Chick Genovese was manager, and Bill warned us that Mays might be a little tight because of our being there. Well, Willie got about two hits in the first few innings, and in the seventh he came up and hit a ball into a gas station that was across the street beyond the left-field fence. That's how tight he was.

"Henry Thompson had seen him play in exhibitions, and he told me how Willie sometimes ran after a ball in the outfield and caught it in his bare hand. I said, 'Oh, sure.' You know—I didn't believe it. And then, of course, he did it lots of times for us. I missed his greatest play, when he made an unbelievable catch like that in Brooklyn, just as he crashed into the outfield wall. And I remember after Willie had been with us a couple of years I was out watching our farm club at St. Cloud, Minnesota, and I saw all the young players—Willie Kirkland and Orlando Cepeda and Andre Rodgers—making those basket catches in the outfield, and I said 'Hey, who loused up all these kids?' It was Willie, of course—they'd seen him on the television and they were all trying to imitate him. Nobody else had those reflexes, though, and nobody else could get away with what he did."

•

STONEHAM LEFT his seat for a few minutes to talk to some visitors who had been brought up to the box to be introduced, and then he made a couple of telephone calls. When he sat down again, we were in the eighth inning and the Giants were ahead by 6–1.

"We were talking about Juan Marichal," he said. "Well, one of the remarkable things about him was that even when he first came up he knew everything there was to know about the game of baseball. He came from the Dominican Republic, and young General Trujillo—the big man's son, I mean—he'd put Juan into the Air Force there in order to have him play on his team. There must have been some great coach or manager in that Air Force who taught Juan, because he did everything right from the beginning.

"I think we were the first club that signed players from that whole area. They'd have their winter leagues in the fall, and after the World Series we'd take a couple of scouts and go down and see our friends. I think the first time I ever saw Jose Pagan play—he came in a game to pinch-hit—he was fourteen years old. Our scout down there was Alex Pompez, who was a Cuban. He saw Fidel Castro play ball when Castro was a young fellow, and sent us a report on him. Castro was a right-handed pitcher. When he came up—you know, came into power—we checked back in our files, and it was the same Castro. A good ballplayer. I think if he'd stayed in the game he'd have made it to the majors. You know what a fan he is."

Bobby Murcer, the Giants' right fielder, doubled in a run, and a minute or two later Chris Speier drove in another. It was a Giants afternoon.

"I just hope fellows like Chris and Bobby get a break in the All-Star Game balloting," Stoneham said. "Bobby's done everything we expected when we got him from the Yankees —everything and more. He's a fine man. But the fans tend to overlook this year's play on their ballots, you know. They vote on reputation. Well, I'm not going to the All-Star Game this year anyway. They're having business meetings all day, before the game. Who wants *that*? That used to be a holiday. You'd go to the game and then you'd see your friends in the evening. It's the same way at our board meetings. When I first came on our board, all the conversation was about baseball. We'd sit and talk about the game. Now the lawyers outnumber the baseball people. In the old days, it was nothing but baseball people on the ball clubs—it was a personal thing. Even with somebody like Mr. Wrigley, it was him that owned the team, not the company."

The Padres came up in the ninth, trailing by 8–1, and Stoneham clapped his hands.

"Who would you pick on an All-Time Giants team?" he said. Then he answered his own question. "I'd have Travis Jackson at short," he said. "Travis never got in the Hall of Fame, but he came up with us and took Dave Bancroft's job away from him. Terry's the best first baseman. Can I play Frisch at second *and* at third? Mays and Ott and Ross Youngs in the outfield. But Monte Irvin's got to be out there somewhere, too. If Monte had come up from the Negro leagues a few years sooner, he'd be known now as one of the great ballplayers of all time. And we can't leave off Irish Meusel, either. Frank Snyder is catching. But Gus Mancuso was a great defensive catcher, and so was Wes Westrum."

Montefusco, who looked tired, walked his second Padre batter of the inning, and then threw a pitch past his catcher. "He's trying to aim the ball," Stoneham said. He stood up. "Come on, John!" he pleaded. Then he turned and said, "Oh, I almost forgot Willie McCovey. Where do we play him? Or Joe Moore, our best leadoff man. You'd try to bat him third and he'd hit .250. Put him back up top there and he'd hit .330."

His all-time roster was growing by the minute, but now there was a swift double play on the field, and the game ended. "All *right*," Stoneham said. The Giants had won.

We went back to Stoneham's office. I took off the polo coat, and Stoneham hung it up in the closet again. I suddenly wondered how many Giants games it had seen. Stoneham signed a couple of letters that were waiting on his desk, and buzzed his secretary on the intercom. "I'm getting a haircut in the morning," he told her, "so I'll be a little late getting in. Good night, Florence."

We went outside and walked down a ramp in the sunshine. The wind had dropped, and the low hills around the Bay were all alight. It was one of those afternoons when you felt that summer might never end. I started to say something to Stoneham about his parting with the Giants and how I felt about it, but he smiled and cut me off.

"You can't get discouraged over a few bad breaks," he said. "In this game, you're always losing sometimes. You can't let yourself complain or feel sorry for yourself."

He walked me to my car in the parking lot, and we shook hands and said goodbye.

13 Agincourt and After

October 1975

Tarry, delight, so seldom met. . . . The games have ended, the heroes are dispersed, and another summer has died late in Boston, but still one yearns for them and wishes them back, so great was their pleasure. The adventures and discoveries and reversals of last month's World Series, which was ultimately won by the Cincinnati Reds in the final inning of the seventh and final game, were of such brilliance and unlikelihood that, even as they happened, those of us who were there in the stands and those who were there on the field were driven again and again not just to cries of excitement but to exclamations of wonder about what we were watching and sharing. Pete Rose, coming up to bat for the Reds in the tenth inning of the tied and retied sixth game, turned to Carlton Fisk, the Red Sox catcher, and said, "Say, this is some kind of game, isn't it?" And when that evening ended at last, after further abrupt and remarkable events, everyone—winners and losers and watchers —left the Fens in exaltation and disarray. "I went home," the

Reds' manager, Sparky Anderson, said later, "and I was stunned."

The next day, during the last batting practice of the year, there was extended debate among the writers and players on the Fenway sidelines as to whether game six had been the greatest in Series history and whether we were not, in fact, in on the best Series of them all. Grizzled coaches and senior scribes recalled other famous Octobers—1929, when the Athletics, trailing the Cubs by eight runs in the fourth game, scored ten runs in the seventh inning and won; 1947, when Cookie Lavagetto's double with two out in the ninth ended Yankee pitcher Bill Bevens' bid for a no-hitter and won the fourth game for the Dodgers; 1960, when Bill Mazeroski's ninth-inning homer for the Pirates threw down the lordly Yankees. There is no answer to these barroom syllogisms, of course, but any recapitulation and reexamination of the 1975 Series suggests that at the very least we may conclude that there has never been a better one. Much is expected of the World Series, and in recent years much has been received. In the past decade, we have had the memorable and abrading seven-game struggles between the Red Sox and the Cardinals in 1967, the Cardinals and the Tigers in 1968, and the Orioles and the Pirates in 1971, and the astounding five-game upset of the Orioles by the Mets in 1969. Until this year, my own solid favorite—because of the Pirates' comeback and the effulgent play of Roberto Clemente—was the 1971 classic, but now I am no longer certain. Comebacks and late rallies are actually extremely scarce in baseball, and an excellent guaranteed cash-producing long-term investment is to wager that the winning team in any game will score more runs in a single inning than the losing team scores in nine. In this Series, however, the line scores alone reveal the rarity of what we saw:

In six of the seven games, the winning team came from behind.

In one of the games, the winning team came from behind twice.

In five games, the winning margin was one run.

There were two extra-inning games, and two games were settled in the ninth inning.

Overall, the games were retied or saw the lead reversed thirteen times.

No other Series—not even the celebrated Giants–Red Sox thriller of 1912—can match these figures.

It is best, however, not to press this search for the greatest Series any farther. There is something sterile and diminishing about our need for these superlatives, and the game of baseball, of course, is so rich and various that it cannot begin to be encompassed in any set of seven games. This Series, for example, produced not one low-hit, low-score pitching duel—the classic and agonizing parade of double zeros that strains teams and managers and true fans to their limits as the inevitable crack in the porcelain is searched out and the game at last broken open. This year, too, the Reds batted poorly through most of the early play and offered indifferent front-line pitching, while the Red Sox made too many mistakes on the base paths, were unable to defend against Cincinnati's team speed, and committed some significant (and in the end fatal) errors in the infield. One of the games was seriously marred by a highly debatable umpire's decision, which may have altered its outcome. It was not a perfect Series. Let us conclude then—before we take a swift look at the season and the playoffs; before we return to Morgan leading away and stealing, to Yaz catching and whirling and throwing, to Eastwick blazing a fastball and Tiant turning his back and offering up a fluttering outside curve, to Evans' catch and Lynn's leap and fall, to Perez's bombs and Pete Rose's defiant, exuberant glare—and say only that this year the splendid autumn affair rose to our utmost expectations and then surpassed them, attaining at last such a level of excellence and emotional reward that it seems likely that the participants—the members of the deservedly winning, champion Reds and of the sorely disappointed, almost-champion Red Sox—will in time remember this Series not for its outcome but for the honor of having played in it, for having made it happen.

•

ALTHOUGH THE four divisions produced between them only one semblance of a close pennant race—the Red Sox and Orioles in the American League East—the baseball summer never languished. I traveled about this year more than is my custom, and wherever I went strangers and friends (many of them minimal fans) talked avidly about baseball and the pleasures that the game was bringing this year. Various reasons for this suggest themselves—a post-Watergate unseriousness, the economy (a baseball ticket, by comparison with tickets to most other entertainments, is easily available and relatively cheap), the overexposure via television of so many inferior rival sports—but it seems to me that the most noticeable new assets of baseball are the wide distribution of its true stars among so many different teams, and the sudden and heartening emergence of so many remarkable young ballplayers. Rod Carew and Bill Madlock, the 1975 batting champions, play, respectively, for the noncontending Twins and Cubs; the best pitcher in the National League, Randy Jones, performed for the Padres, and the best in the American League, Jim Palmer, for the Orioles. The Phillies had the NL's home-run champion (Mike Schmidt) and RBI leader (Greg Luzinski); their counterparts in the AL were Reggie Jackson, of the Oakland A's, and the delightful George Scott, of the Milwaukee Brewers. Al Hrabosky, an utterly commanding relief pitcher, ran off a won-lost mark of 13-3 and an earned-run average of 1.67 for the Cardinals; Mickey Rivers stole seventy bases for the California Angels; Dave Kingman bopped thirty-six homers for the Mets. And so on. Carew's batting title, by the way, was his fourth in succession, and he led his nearest pursuer in the averages, Fred Lynn, by .359 to .331. Last year, he hit .364, as against .316 for the next man, and the year before that the margin was .350 to .306. No previous hitter except Rogers

Hornsby has ever dominated his league in this fashion. The refreshing and sometimes startling youngsters—rookies, most of them—included pitchers John Montefusco and Ed Halicki (Giants), Rawly Eastwick (Reds), John Candelaria (Pirates), Dennis Eckersley (Indians), and Frank Tanana (Angels), and hitters Mike Vail (Mets), George Brett (Royals), Mike Hargrove (Rangers), Claudell Washington (A's), and Fred Lynn and Jim Rice (Red Sox).

Baseball among the have-nots was often riveting. The most entertaining games I saw prior to the World Series were part of a set that I happened to catch in Anaheim in June between the Angels and the Rangers, neither of which was going anywhere in the American League West. In the opener, the Angels fell behind by 6–0, rallied to lead by 8–7, were tied at 8–8, gave up three runs to the visitors in the top of the eleventh, and won it with four runs in the *bottom* of the eleventh. There were thirty-seven hits, including innumerable singles chopped by speedy young Angels—Jerry Remy, Mickey Rivers, Dave Collins—off their cementlike infield. The pitching left something to be desired, but the next afternoon, in the opener of a twi-night doubleheader, Frank Tanana struck out seventeen Texas batters, thereby establishing a new American League one-game mark for left-handers. (Tanana, a curveballer, went on to win the AL's strikeout crown with 269 whiffs, thus succeeding his teammate, Nolan Ryan, who fell victim to injuries this year and went through a bone-chip operation on his right arm. Before going into drydock, Ryan pitched a no-hit game against the Orioles—his fourth no-hitter in four seasons, which ties the record held by Sandy Koufax and approached by no other pitcher in the history of the game.) In the nightcap, the Angels led, then trailed, then tied, and then lost, 6–5, on a homer in the ninth. The next two days, after my ill-advised departure, the Angels won, 1–0, on a two-hitter by Ed Figueroa, and lost, 1–0, in thirteen innings, after the two starters, Steve Hargan for the Rangers and Bill Singer for the Angels, threw shutout ball for eleven innings. The Angels hit 55 homers this year—I mean 55 as a team, or six fewer than Roger Maris in 1961—but they stole 220 bases, and while watching them in action I developed a new preference for the latter means of advancement. There is something *stately* about the home run.

Locally, the home clubs competed hotly against each other in out-disappointing their supporters. The Mets, offered almost innumerable late-summer chances to move up to the lead in their division, lost most of their crucial games, lost their good relief pitching, and lost at last their proud and famous defense. Amid the shambles, Rusty Staub batted in 105 runs, Eddie Kranepool batted .323, and Tom Seaver, finishing at 22-9 and 2.38, struck out more than two hundred batters for the eighth season running. He won eleven games more than in 1974, when he was suffering from a hip injury, and the Mets, by no coincidence, improved over their 1974 won-lost record by eleven games. The Yankees suffered from some damaging injuries (to Elliott Maddox, Ron Blomberg, and Bobby Bonds), and entirely proved the sagacity of everyone who had suspected the soundness of their infield. Thurman Munson hit .318 and batted in 102 runs. Catfish Hunter won 23 games and lost 14, with an ERA of 2.58, second best in the league, all without the semblance of a Rollie Fingers to help him in the late going. *With* such a semblance, he might have wound up around 27-8. He was, we may conclude, worth all that money.

Other events: The Tigers lost nineteen straight games. . . . On the night of June 10, before a Yanks-Angels game I attended at Shea Stadium, a U. S. Army unit, celebrating a gathering of the Sons of Italy and the two hundredth birthday of the Army, fired off a cannon during the playing of the national anthem and blew an enormous hole in a section of the center-field fence. Liveliest anthem you ever heard. . . . The Atlanta Braves staged a promotion in which twenty-five thousand dollars in one-dollar, five-dollar, and ten-dollar bills was scattered on the ball field. Six female fans were then selected, who were permitted to keep as much money as they could stuff into their blouses in ninety seconds. The Braves—one may hope not at all coincidentally—suffered a record loss of 446,413 at the gate this year.

A lot of managers, including both New York skippers, were unseated during the season or at its conclusion—a phenomenon that has caused some grumbling among friends of mine, who complain that they can no longer remember who is in charge of which club, or why. The second question is a cinch. Managers are changed whenever it becomes apparent to a slumping club's owners that *something must be done*, even though it is almost always plain that nothing can be done. The ideal qualification for a new manager is that he should have failed at the same post with another club (or sometimes with the same club). Come to think of it, "fired" and "hired" are probably the wrong words to use in the managers' game; it is more useful to envisage the whole process as a version of Going-to-Jerusalem, with about forty heavily tanned, wrinkle-necked skippers slowly circling twenty-four kindergarten chairs, into which they attempt to throw themselves from time to time. This year's roundabout was typical. It began, in a way, in 1973, when Whitey Herzog was fired as the manager of the Texas Rangers and replaced by Billy Martin (formerly manager of the Twins and Tigers). This summer, Martin was fired by the Rangers and then quickly replaced Bill Virdon (formerly of the Pirates, where he had replaced Danny Murtaugh, who also succeeded him), who had previously been fired as manager of the Yankees. Virdon was then engaged to replace Preston Gomez (former manager of the Padres) as manager of the Astros. (Going back to Murtaugh for a minute, we should all certainly remember that prior to preceding and succeeding Virdon as the Pirates' manager, he had also preceded and succeeded Larry Shepard at the same post.) Also fired this year were Yogi Berra (former manager of the Yankees), by the Mets; Gene Mauch (former manager of the Phillies), by the Expos; Clyde King (former manager of the Giants), by the Braves; Edward II (former king of

England and the son of Edward I and Eleanor of Castile . . . Aha! Now pay *attention*, class); Frank Quilici (no previous record), by the Twins; Del Crandall (no previous record), by the Brewers; Alvin Dark (former manager of the Giants, A's, and Indians), by the A's; and Jack McKeon (no previous record), by the Royals. McKeon was replaced by Whitey Herzog.

The irreplaceable departing manager was Casey Stengel, who died this summer at the age of eighty-five. His quirks and triumphs are so familiar to us all that they need no recapitulation here, but I think that a demurrer should be entered on the subject of Stengelese, which too many of his biographers seemed to consider as nothing but a comical difficulty with the English language. It always seemed to me that Casey's non-stop disquisitions—stuffed with subclauses, interruptions, rhetorical questions, addenda, historic examples, shifted tenses, and free-floating whiches—constituted a perfect representation of the mind of a first-class manager. Almost every managerial decision during a ball game—the lineup, who is to pitch, when to pinch-hit and with whom, when to yank a pitcher, who should pitch to the new pinch-hitter—is, or should be, the result of a dozen or two dozen pressing and often conflicting reflections, considerations, and ancient prior lessons. (Sparky Anderson, asked by the press why he had pinch-hit with a certain batter during the fourth game of this year's Series, responded with an explanation that went on for a good five minutes.) Stengelese had other uses. In April, 1962, when Casey held a press conference before the Mets' home opener in order to introduce the members of the newborn team, he went through his roster and his opening-day lineup extolling this has-been and that never-was and his ungainly rookies (he called them "the youth of America"), and when he came at last to his right fielder, Gus Bell, he explained that this was a man which has come to us from Cincinnati, where he hit a lot of home runs, and he would hit some more here because he was the prop and support of a family that included two children, and he mentioned Bell's other attributes and sterling qualities at greater and greater length, during which time it became apparent to everyone present that he had forgotten Bell's name. (He always had a terrible time with names.) He finally dropped the search and went on to other players and other promises, and concluded, reluctantly and at long, long last, with ". . . and so you can say this tremendous and amazin' new club is gonna be ready in every way tomorrow when the bell rings and that's the name of my right fielder, Bell."

Perhaps it is best to say goodbye with a garland of Stengelflowers:

To himself, in 1921, on entering the Polo Grounds after being purchased by the Giants from the Phillies: "Wake up, muscles—we're in New York now."

After winning still another pennant as manager of the Yankees: "I couldna done it without my players."

On being seventy-five: "Most people my age are dead, and you could look it up."

Concluding his acceptance speech at Cooperstown, when he was taken into the Baseball Hall of Fame: "And I want to thank the treemendous fans. We appreciate every boys' group, girls' group, poem, and song. And keep goin' to see the Mets play."

•

By September 16, the Pirates and the A's were enjoying comfortable leads in their divisions, the Reds had long since won their demi-pennant (they clinched on September 7—a new record), and the only serious baseball was to be found at Fenway Park, where the Orioles, down by four and a half games and running out of time, had at the Red Sox. The game was a pippin—a head-to-head encounter between Jim Palmer and Luis Tiant. Each of the great pitchers struck out eight batters, and the game was won by the Red Sox, 2–0, on two small mistakes by Palmer—fastballs to Rico Petrocelli and Carlton Fisk in successive innings, which were each lofted into the left-field screen. Tiant, who had suffered through almost a month of ineffectiveness brought on by a bad back, was in top form, wheeling and rotating on the mound like a figure in a Bavarian clock tower, and in the fourth he fanned Lee May with a super-curve that seemed to glance off some invisible obstruction in midflight. The hoarse, grateful late-inning cries of "Lu-is! Lu-is! Lu-is!" from 34,724 Beantowners suggested that the oppressive, Calvinist cloud of self-doubt that afflicts Red Sox fans in all weathers and seasons was beginning to lift at last. The fabulous Sox rookies, Jim Rice and Fred Lynn, did nothing much (in fact, they fanned five times between them), but Boston friends of mine encouraged my belief with some of the shiny new legends—the home run that Rice hammered past the Fenway Park center-field flagpole in July; the time Rice checked a full swing and snapped his bat in half just above his hands; Lynn's arm, Lynn's range, Lynn's game against the Tigers in June, when he hit three homers and batted in ten runs and the Sox began their pennant drive. The night before my visit, in fact, against the Brewers, Lynn and Rice had each accounted for his one hundredth run batted in *with the same ball*—a run-forcing walk to Lynn and then a sacrifice fly by Rice. I believed.

Baltimore came right back, winning the next game by 5–2, on some cool and useful hitting by Tommy Davis and Brooks Robinson, and the Sox' cushion was back to four and a half. The Orioles' move, we know now, came a little too late this year, but I think one should not forget what a loose and deadly and marvelously confident September team they have been over the last decade. Before this, their last game at Fenway Park this year, they were enjoying themselves in their dugout while the Sox took batting practice and while Clif Keane, the Boston *Globe*'s veteran baseball writer (who is also the league's senior and most admired insult artist), took them apart. Brooks Robinson hefted a bat, and Keane, sitting next to manager Earl Weaver, said, "Forget it, Brooksie. They pay you a hundred and twenty-four thousand for your glove, and a thousand for the bat. Put that back in your valise." He spotted Doug DeCinces, the rookie who will someday take over for Robinson in the Oriole infield, and said, "Hey, kid, I was just talkin' to Brooks, here. He says he'll be back again. You'll be a *hundred* before you get in there. Looks like 1981 for you." Tommy Davis picked out some bats and went slowly up the dugout steps; his Baltimore teammates sometimes call him "Uncle Tired." Keane leaned forward suddenly. "Look at that," he said. "Tom's wearin' *new shoes*—he's planning on being around another twenty years. Listen, with Brooks and Davis, Northrup, May, and Muser, you guys can play an Old Timers' Game every day." Davis wandered off, smiling, and Keane changed his tone for a moment. "Did you ever see him when he could play?" he said, nodding at Davis. "He got about two hundred and fifty hits that year with LA, and they were all line drives. He could *hit*." His eye fell on the first group of Oriole batters around the batting cage. "See them all lookin' over here?" he said to Weaver. "They're talking about you again. If you could only hear them—they're really fricasseein' you today, Earl. Now you know how Marie Antoinette felt. . . ." The laughter in the dugout was nice and easy. The men sat back, with their legs crossed and their arms stretched along the back of the bench, and watched the players on the ball field. The summer was running out.

The Sox just about wrapped it up the next week, when they beat the Yankees, 6–4, at Shea, in a game that was played in a steadily deepening downpour—the beginning of the tropical storm that washed away most of the last week of the season. By the ninth inning, the mound and the batters' boxes looked like trenches on the Somme, and the stadium was filled with a wild gray light made by millions of illuminated falling raindrops. The Yankees got the tying runs aboard in the ninth, with two out, and then Dick Drago struck out Bobby Bonds, swinging, on three successive pitches, and the Boston outfielders came leaping and splashing in through the rain like kids home from a picnic. The winning Boston margin, a few days later, was still four and a half games.

•

THE PLAYOFFS, it will be remembered, were brief. Over in the National League, the Reds embarrassed the Pittsburgh Pirates, winners of the Eastern Division title, by stealing ten bases in their first two games, which they won by 8–3 and 6–1. Young John Candelaria pitched stoutly for the Pirates when the teams moved on to Three Rivers Stadium, fanning fourteen Cincinnati batters, but Pete Rose broke his heart with a two-run homer in the eighth, and the Reds won the game, 5–3, and the pennant, 3–0, in the tenth inning. I had deliberated for perhaps seven seconds before choosing to follow the American League championship games—partly because the Red Sox were the only new faces available (the Reds, the Pirates, and the A's have among them qualified for the playoffs fourteen times in the past six years), but mostly because I know that the best place in the world to watch baseball is at Fenway Park. The unique dimensions and properties of the Palazzo Yawkey (the left-field wall is 37 feet high and begins a bare 315 feet down the foul line from home plate —or perhaps, according to a startling new computation made by the Boston *Globe* this fall, *304* feet) vivify ball games and excite the imagination. On the afternoon of the first A's-Sox set-to, the deep green of the grass and light green of the wall, the variously angled blocks and planes and triangles and wedges of the entirely occupied stands, and the multiple seams and nooks and corners of the outfield fences, which encompass eleven different angles off which a ball or a ballplayer can ricochet, suddenly showed me that I was inside the ultimate origami.

There were two significant absentees—Jim Rice, who had suffered a fractured hand late in the campaign and would not play again this year, and Catfish Hunter, the erstwhile Oakland meal ticket, whose brisk work had been so useful to the A's in recent Octobers. Boston manager Darrell Johnson solved his problem brilliantly, moving Carl Yastrzemski from first base to Rice's spot under the left-field wall—a land grant that Yaz had occupied and prospected for many years. Oakland manager Alvin Dark found no comparable answer to his dilemma, but the startling comparative levels of baseball that were now demonstrated by the defending three-time champion A's and the untested Red Sox soon indicated that perhaps not even the Cat would have made much difference. In the bottom of the very first inning, Yastrzemski singled off Ken Holtzman, and then Carlton Fisk hit a hopper down the third-base line that was butchered by Sal Bando and further mutilated by Claudell Washington, in left. Lynn then hit an undemanding ground ball to second baseman Phil Garner, who muffed it. Two runs were in, and in the seventh the Sox added five more, with help from Oakland center fielder Bill North, who dropped a fly, and Washington, who somehow played Lynn's fly to the base of the wall into a double. Tiant, meanwhile, was enjoying himself. The Oakland scouting report on him warned he had six pitches—fastball, slider, curve, change-up curve, palm ball, and knuckler—all of which he could serve up from the sidearm, three-quarter, or overhand sectors, and points in between, but on this particular afternoon his fastball was so lively that he eschewed the upper ranges of virtuosity. He did not give up his first hit until the fifth inning or, incredibly, his first ground ball until the eighth. The Sox won, 7–1. "Tiant," Reggie Jackson declared in the clubhouse, "is the Fred Astaire of baseball."

The second game, which Alvin Dark had singled out as the crucial one in any three-of-five series, was much better. Oakland jumped away to a 3–0 lead, after a first-inning homer by Jackson, and Sal Bando whacked four successive hits—*bong! whang! bing! thwong!*—off the left-field wall during the afternoon. The second of these, a single, was converted into a killing out by Yastrzemski, who seized the carom off the wall and whirled and threw to Petrocelli to erase the eagerly advancing Campaneris at third—a play that Yaz and Rico first perfected during the Garfield Administration. The same two elders subsequently hit home runs—Yaz off Vida Blue, Rico off Rollie Fingers—and Lynn contributed a run-scoring single and a terrific diving cutoff of a Joe Rudi double to center field that saved at least one run. The Sox won by 6–3. The A's complained after the game that two of Bando's shots would have been home runs in any other park, and that both Yastrzemski's and Petrocelli's homers probably would have been outs in any other park. Absolutely true: the Wall giveth and the Wall taketh away.

Not quite believing what was happening, I followed the two teams to Oakland, where I watched the Bosox wrap up their easy pennant with a 5–3 victory. Yastrzemski, who is thirty-six years old and who had suffered through a long summer of injuries and ineffectuality, continued to play like the Yaz of 1967, when he almost single-handedly carried the Red Sox to their last pennant and down to the seventh game of that World Series. This time, he came up with two hits, and twice astonished Jackson in the field—first with a whirling throw from the deep left-field corner that cleanly excised Reggie at second base, and then, in the eighth, with a sprinting, diving, skidding, flat-on-the-belly stop of Jackson's low line shot to left that was headed for the wall and a sure triple. The play came in the midst of the old champions' courageous two-run rally in the eighth, and it destroyed them. Even though it fell short, I was glad about that rally, for I did not want to see the splendid old green-and-yallers go down meekly or sadly in the end. The Oakland fans, who have not always been known for the depths of their constancy or appreciation, also distinguished themselves, sustaining an earsplitting cacophony of hope and encouragement to the utter end. I sensed they were saying goodbye to their proud and vivid and infinitely entertaining old lineup—to Sal Bando and Campy Campaneris, to Joe Rudi and Reggie Jackson and Gene Tenace and Rollie

Fingers and the rest, who will almost surely be broken up now and traded away, as great teams must be when they come to the end of their time in the sun.

•

THE FINALISTS, coming together for the Series opener at Fenway Park, were heavily motivated. The Reds had not won a World Series since 1940, the Sox since 1918. Cincinnati's Big Red Machine had stalled badly in its recent October outings, having failed in the World Series of 1970 and '72 and in the playoffs of 1973. The Red Sox had a record of shocking late-season collapses, the latest coming in 1974, when they fizzled away a seven-game lead in the last six weeks of the season. Both teams, however, were much stronger than in recent years —the Reds because of their much improved pitching (most of it relief pitching) and the maturing of a second generation of outstanding players (Ken Griffey, Dave Concepcion, George Foster) to join with the celebrated Rose, Morgan, Perez, and Bench. The Red Sox infield had at last found itself, with Rick Burleson at short and Denny Doyle (a midseason acquisition from the Angels) at second, and there was a new depth in hitting and defense—Beniquez, Cooper, Carbo, and the remarkable Dwight Evans. This was a far better Boston team than the 1967 miracle workers. The advantage, however, seemed to belong to Cincinnati, because of the Reds' combination of speed and power (168 stolen bases, 124 homers) and their implacable habit of winning ball games. Their total of 108 games won had been fashioned, in part, out of an early-season streak of 41 wins in 50 games, and a nearly unbelievable record of 64–17 in their home park. The Red Sox, on the other hand, had Lynn and Tiant. . . .

Conjecture thickened through most of the opening game, which was absolutely close for most of the distance, and then suddenly not close at all. Don Gullett, a powerful left-hander, kept the Red Sox in check for six innings, but was slightly outpitched and vastly outacted over the same distance by

Tiant. The venerable stopper (Tiant is listed as being thirty-four and rumored as being a little or a great deal older) did not have much of a fastball on this particular afternoon, so we were treated to the splendid full range of Tiantic mime. His repertoire begins with an exaggerated mid-windup pivot, during which he turns his back on the batter and seems to examine the infield directly behind the mound for signs of crabgrass. With men on bases, his stretch consists of a succession of minute downward waggles and pauses of the glove, and a menacing sidewise, slit-eyed, Valentino-like gaze over his shoulder at the base runner. The full flower of his art, however, comes during the actual delivery, which is executed with a perfect variety show of accompanying gestures and impersonations. I had begun to take notes during my recent observations of the Cuban Garrick, and now, as he set down the Reds with only minimal interruptions (including one balk call, in the fourth), I arrived at some tentative codifications. The basic Tiant repertoire seems to include:

(1) Call the Osteopath: In midpitch, the man suffers an agonizing seizure in the central cervical region, which he attempts to fight off with a sharp backward twist of the head.

(2) Out of the Woodshed: Just before releasing the ball, he steps over a raised sill and simultaneously ducks his head to avoid conking it on the low doorframe.

(3) The Runaway Taxi: Before the pivot, he sees a vehicle bearing down on him at top speed, and pulls back his entire upper body just in time to avoid a nasty accident.

(4) Falling Off the Fence: An attack of vertigo nearly causes him to topple over backward on the mound. Strongly suggests a careless dude on the top rung of the corral.

(5) The Slipper-Kick: In the midpitch, he surprisingly decides to get rid of his left shoe.

(6) The Low-Flying Plane (a subtle development and amalgam of 1, 3, and 4, above): While he is pivoting, an F-105 buzzes the ball park, passing over the infield from the third-

base to the first-base side at a height of eighty feet. He follows it all the way with his eyes.

All this, of course, was vastly appreciated by the Back Bay multitudes, including a nonpaying claque perched like seagulls atop three adjacent rooftop billboards (WHDH Radio, Windsor Canadian Whiskey, Buck Printing), who banged on the tin hoardings in accompaniment to the park's deepening chorus of "Lu-is! Lu-is! Lu-is!" The Reds, of course, were unmoved, and only three superior defensive plays by the Sox (including another diving, rolling catch by Yastrzemski) kept them from scoring in the top of the seventh. Defensive sparks often light an offensive flareup in close games, and Tiant now started the Sox off with a single. Evans bunted, and Gullett pounced on the ball and steamed a peg to second a hair too late to nail Tiant—the day's first mistake. Doyle singled, to load the bases, and Yaz singled for the first run. Fisk walked for another run, and then Petrocelli and Burleson singled, too. (Gullett had vanished.) Suddenly six runs were in, and the game—a five-hit shutout for Tiant—was safely put away very soon after.

The next afternoon, a gray and drizzly Sunday, began happily and ended agonizingly for the Sox, who put six men aboard in the first two innings and scored only one of them, thanks to some slovenly base running. In the fourth inning, the Reds finally registered their first run of the Series, but the Sox moved out ahead again, 2–1, and there the game stuck, a little too tight for anyone's comfort. There was a long delay for rain in the seventh. Matters inched along at last, with each club clinging to its best pitching: Boston with its starter, Bill Lee, and Cincinnati with its bullpen—Borbon and McEnaney and Eastwick, each one better, it seemed, than the last. Lee, a southpaw, had thrown a ragbag of pitches—slow curves, sliders, screwballs, and semi-fastballs—all to the very outside corners, and by the top of the ninth he had surrendered but four hits. Now, facing the heaviest part of the Reds' order, he started Bench off with a pretty good but perhaps predictable outside fastball, which Bench whacked on a low line to the right-field corner for a double. Right-hander Dick Drago came on and grimly retired Perez and then Foster. One more out was required, and the crowd cried for it on every pitch. Concepcion ran the count to one and one and then hit a high-bouncing, unplayable chop over second that tied things up. Now the steal was on, of course, and Concepcion flashed away to second and barely slipped under Fisk's waist-high peg; Griffey doubled to the wall, and the Reds, for the twenty-fifth time this year, had snatched back a victory in their last licks. Bench's leadoff double had been a parable of winning baseball. He has great power in every direction, but most of all, of course, to left, where the Fenway wall murmurs so alluringly to a right-handed slugger whose team is down a run. Hitting Lee's outside pitch to right—going with it—was the act of a disciplined man.

Bill Lee is a talkative and engaging fellow who will discourse in lively fashion on almost any subject, including zero population growth, Zen Buddhism, compulsory busing, urban planning, acupuncture, and baseball. During the formal postgame press interview, a reporter put up his hand and said, "Bill, how would you, uh, characterize the World Series so far?"

Two hundred pencils poised.

"Tied," Lee said.

•

THE ACTION now repaired to the cheerless, circular, Monsanto-toed close of Riverfront Stadium. The press box there is glassed-in and air-conditioned, utterly cut off from the sounds of baseball action and baseball cheering. After an inning or two of this, I began to feel as if I were suffering from the effects of a mild stroke, and so gave up my privileged niche and moved outdoors to a less favored spot in an auxiliary press section in the stands, where I was surrounded by the short-haired but vociferous multitudes of the Cincinnati. The game was a noisy one, for the Reds, back in their own yard, were sprinting around the AstroTurf and whanging out long hits. They stole three bases and hit three home runs (Bench, Concepcion, and Geronimo—the latter two back-to-back) in the course of moving to a 5–1 lead. Boston responded with a will. The second Red Sox homer of the evening (Fisk had hit the first) was a pinch-hit blow by Bernie Carbo, and the third, by Dwight Evans, came with one out and one on in the ninth and tied the score, astonishingly, at 5–5. The pattern of the game to this point, we can see in retrospect, bears a close resemblance to the classic sixth, and an extravagant dénouement now seemed certain. Instead, we were given the deadening business of the disputed, umpired play—the collision at home plate in the bottom of the tenth between Carlton Fisk and Cincinnati pinch-hitter Ed Armbrister, who, with a man on first, bounced a sacrifice bunt high in the air just in front of the plate and then somehow entangled himself with Fisk's left side as the catcher stepped forward to make his play. Fisk caught the ball, pushed free of Armbrister (without trying to tag him), and then, hurrying things, threw to second in an attempt to force the base runner, Geronimo, and, in all likelihood, begin a crucial double play. The throw, however, was a horrible sailer that glanced off Burleson's glove and went on into center field; Geronimo steamed down to third, from where he was scored, a few minutes later, by Joe Morgan for the winning run. Red Sox manager Darrell Johnson protested, but the complaint was swiftly dismissed by home-plate umpire Larry Barnett and, on an appeal, by first-base umpire Dick Stello.

The curious thing about the whole dismal tort is that there is no dispute whatever about the events (the play was perfectly visible, and was confirmed by a thousand subsequent replayings on television), just as there is no doubt but that the umpires, in disallowing an interference call, cited apparently nonexistent or inapplicable rules. Barnett said, "It was simply a collision," and he and Stello both ruled that only an intentional attempt by Armbrister to obstruct Fisk could have been called interference. There is no rule in baseball that exempts simple collisions, and no one on either team ever claimed that Armbrister's awkward brush-block on Fisk was anything but accidental. This leaves the rules, notably Rule 2.00 (a): "Offensive interference is an act . . . which interferes with, obstructs, impedes, hinders, or confuses any fielder attempting to make a play." Rule 6.06 (c) says much the same thing (the baseball rule book is almost as thick as Blackstone), and so does 7.09: "It is interference by a batter or a runner when (1) He fails to avoid a fielder who is attempting to field a batted ball. . . ." Armbrister failed to avoid. Fisk, it is true, did not make either of the crucial plays then open to him—the tag and the peg—although he seemed to have plenty of time and room for both, but this does not in any way alter the fact of the previous interference. Armbrister should have been called out, and Geronimo returned to first base—or, if a double play had in fact been turned, *both* runners could have been called out by the umps, according to a subclause of 6.06.*

There were curses and hot looks in the Red Sox clubhouse that night, along with an undercurrent of feeling that Manager Johnson had not complained with much vigor. "If it had been

* I have truncated this mind-calcifying detour into legal semantics, because time proved it to be both incomplete and misleading. Shortly after the publication of this account, the news filtered out of the league offices that the Series umpires had been operating under a prior "supplemental instruction" to the interference rules, which stated: "When a catcher and a batter-runner going to first have contact when the catcher is fielding the ball, there is generally no violation and nothing should be called." This clearly exonerates Larry Barnett and explains his mystifying "It was simply a collision." What has never been explained is why the existence of this codicil was not immediately divulged to the fans and to the writers covering the Series, thus relieving the umpires of a barrage of undeserved obloquy. We should also ask whether the blanket exculpation of the supplemental instructions really does fit the crucial details of *Armbrister v. Fisk*. Subsequent pondering of the landmark case and several viewings of the Series film have led me to conclude that fairness and good sense would have been best served if Armbrister had been called out and the base runner, Geronimo, returned to first. It is still plain, however, that Carlton Fisk had the best and quickest opportunity to clarify this passionate affair, with a good, everyday sort of peg down to second; irreversibly, he blew it.

me out there," Bill Lee said, "I'd have bitten Barnett's ear off. I'd have van Goghed him!"

•

UNTIDINESS CONTINUED the next night, in game four, but in more likely places. The Reds did themselves out of a run with some overambitious base running, and handed over a run to the Sox on an error by Tony Perez; Sparky Anderson was fatally slow in calling on his great relief corps in the midst of a five-run Red Sox rally; the Boston outfield allowed a short fly ball to drop untouched, and two Cincinnati runs instantly followed. The Sox led, 5–4, after four innings, and they won it, 5–4, after some excruciating adventures and anxieties. Tiant was again at center stage, but on this night, working on short rest, he did not have full command of his breaking stuff and was forced to underplay. The Reds' pitcher over the last three innings was Rawlins J. Eastwick III, the tall, pale, and utterly expressionless rookie fireballer, who was blowing down the Red Sox hitters and seemed perfectly likely to pick up his third straight win in relief. Tiant worked slowly and painfully, running up long counts, giving up line-drive outs, surrendering bases on balls and singles, but somehow struggling free. He was still in there by the ninth, hanging on by his toenails, but he now gave up a leadoff single to Geronimo. Armbrister sacrificed (this time without litigation), and Pete Rose, who had previously hit two ropes for unlucky outs, walked. Johnson came to the mound and, to my surprise, left Tiant in. Ken Griffey ran the count to three and one, fouled off the next pitch, and bombed an enormous drive to the wall in deepest center field, four hundred feet away, where Fred Lynn pulled it down after a long run. Two outs. Joe Morgan, perhaps the most dangerous hitter in baseball in such circumstances, took a ball (I was holding my breath; everyone in the vast stadium was holding his breath) and then popped straight up to Yastrzemski, to end it. Geronimo had broken for third base on the pitch, undoubtedly distracting Morgan for a fraction of a second—an infinitesimal and perhaps telling mistake by the Reds.

Tiant, it turned out, had thrown a total of 163 pitches, and Sparky Anderson selected Pitch No. 160 as the key to the game. This was not the delivery that Griffey whacked and Lynn caught but its immediate predecessor—the three-and-one pitch that Griffey had fouled off. Tiant had thrown a curve there—"turned it over," in baseball talk—which required the kind of courage that baseball men most respect. "Never mind his age," Joe Morgan said. "Being smart, having an idea—that's what makes a pitcher."

•

MORGAN HIMSELF has the conviction that he should affect the outcome of every game he plays in every time he comes up to bat and every time he gets on base. (He was bitterly self-critical for that game-ending out.) Like several of the other Cincinnati stars, he talks about his own capabilities with a dispassionate confidence that sounds immodest and almost arrogant—until one studies him in action and understands that this is only another form of the cold concentration he applies to ball games. This year, he batted .327, led the National League in bases on balls, and fielded his position in the manner that has won him a Gold Glove award in each of the past two years. In more than half of his trips to the plate, he ended up on first base, and once there he stole sixty-seven bases in seventy-seven attempts. A short (five foot seven), precise man, with strikingly carved features, he talks in quick, short bursts of words. "I think I can steal off any pitcher," he said to me. "A good base stealer should make the whole infield jumpy. Whether you steal or not, you're changing the rhythm of the game. If the pitcher is concerned about you, he isn't concentrating enough on the batter. You're doing something without doing anything. You're out there to make a difference."

With the Reds leading, 2–1, in the sixth inning of the fifth game, Morgan led off and drew a walk. (He had singled in the first inning and instantly stolen second.) The Boston pitcher, Reggie Cleveland, now threw over to first base seven times before delivering his first pitch to the next Cincinnati hitter, Johnny Bench—a strike. Apparently determining to fight it out along these lines if it took all winter, Cleveland went to first four more times, pitched a foul, threw to first five more times, and delivered a ball. Only one of the throws came close to picking off Morgan, who got up each time and quickly resumed his lead about eleven feet down the line. Each time Cleveland made a pitch, Morgan made a flurrying little bluff toward second. Now Cleveland pitched again and Bench hit a grounder to right—a single, it turned out, because second baseman Denny Doyle was in motion toward the base and the ball skipped through, untouched, behind him. Morgan flew around to third, and an instant later Tony Perez hit a three-run homer—his second homer of the day—and the game was gone, 6–2. Doyle said later that he had somehow lost sight of Bench's hit for an instant, and the box score said later that Perez had won the game with his hitting and that Don Gullett, who allowed only two Boston batters to reach first base between the first and the ninth innings, had won it with his pitching, but I think we all knew better. Morgan had made the difference.

•

GAME SIX, Game Six . . . what can we say of it without seeming to diminish it by recapitulation or dull it with detail? Those of us who were there will remember it, surely, as long as we have any baseball memory, and those who wanted to be there and were not will be sorry always. Crispin Crispian: for Red Sox fans, this was Agincourt. The game also went out to sixty-two million television viewers, a good many millions of whom missed their bedtime. Three days of heavy rains had postponed things; the outfield grass was a lush, Amazon green, but there was a clear sky at last and a welcoming moon—a giant autumn squash that rose above the right-field Fenway bleachers during batting practice.

In silhouette, the game suggests a well-packed but dangerously overloaded canoe—with the high bulge of the Red Sox' three first-inning runs in the bow, then the much bulkier hump of six Cincinnati runs amidships, then the counterbalancing three Boston runs astern, and then, *way* aft, one more shape. But this picture needs colors: Fred Lynn clapping his hands once, quickly and happily, as his three-run opening shot flies over the Boston bullpen and into the bleachers . . . Luis Tiant fanning Perez with a curve and the Low-Flying Plane, then dispatching Foster with a Fall Off the Fence. Luis does not have his fastball, however. . . .

Pete Rose singles in the third. Perez singles in the fourth—his first real contact off Tiant in three games. Rose, up again in the fifth, with a man on base, fights off Tiant for seven pitches, then singles hard to center. Ken Griffey triples off the wall, exactly at the seam of the left-field and center-field angles; Fred Lynn, leaping up for the ball and missing it, falls backward into the wall and comes down heavily. He lies there, inert, in a terrible, awkwardly twisted position, and for an instant all of us think that he has been killed. He is up at last, though, and even stays in the lineup, but the noise and joy are gone out of the crowd, and the game is turned around. Tiant, tired and old and, in the end, bereft even of mannerisms, is rocked again and again—eight hits in three innings—and Johnson removes him, far too late, after Geronimo's first-pitch home run in the eighth has run the score to 6–3 for the visitors.

By now, I had begun to think sadly of distant friends of mine—faithful lifelong Red Sox fans all over New England, all over the East, whom I could almost see sitting silently at home and slowly shaking their heads as winter began to fall on them out of their sets. I scarcely noticed when Lynn led off the eighth with a single and Petrocelli walked. Sparky Anderson, flicking levers like a master back-hoe operator, now called in

Eastwick, his sixth pitcher of the night, who fanned Evans and retired Burleson on a fly. Bernie Carbo, pinch-hitting, looked wholly overmatched against Eastwick, flailing at one inside fastball like someone fighting off a wasp with a croquet mallet. One more fastball arrived, high and over the middle of the plate, and Carbo smashed it in a gigantic, flattened parabola into the center-field bleachers, tying the game. Everyone out there—and everyone in the stands, too, I suppose—leaped to his feet and waved both arms exultantly, and the bleachers looked like the dark surface of a lake lashed with a sudden night squall.

The Sox, it will be recalled, nearly won it right away, when they loaded the bases in the ninth with none out, but an ill-advised dash home by Denny Doyle after a fly, and a cool, perfect peg to the plate by George Foster, snipped the chance. The balance of the game now swung back, as it so often does when opportunities are wasted. Drago pitched out of a jam in the tenth, but he flicked Pete Rose's uniform with a pitch to start the eleventh. Griffey bunted, and Fisk snatched up the ball and, risking all, fired to second for the force on Rose. Morgan was next, and I had very little hope left. He struck a drive on a quick, deadly rising line—you could still hear the loud *whock!* in the stands as the white blur went out over the infield—and for a moment I thought the ball would land ten or fifteen rows back in the right-field bleachers. But it wasn't hit quite that hard—it was traveling too fast, and there was no sail to it—and Dwight Evans, sprinting backward and watching the flight of it over his shoulder, made a last-second, half-staggering turn to his left, almost facing away from the plate at the end, and pulled the ball in over his head at the fence. The great catch made for two outs in the end, for Griffey had never stopped running and was easily doubled off first.

And so the swing of things was won back again. Carlton Fisk, leading off the bottom of the twelfth against Pat Darcy, the eighth Reds pitcher of the night—it was well into morning now, in fact—socked the second pitch up and out, farther and farther into the darkness above the lights, and when it came down at last, reilluminated, it struck the topmost, innermost edge of the screen inside the yellow left-field foul pole and glanced sharply down and bounced on the grass: a fair ball, fair all the way. I was watching the ball, of course, so I missed what everyone on television saw—Fisk waving wildly, weaving and writhing and gyrating along the first-base line, as he wished the ball fair, *forced* it fair with his entire body. He circled the bases in triumph, in sudden company with several hundred fans, and jumped on home plate with both feet, and John Kiley, the Fenway Park organist, played Handel's "Hallelujah Chorus," *fortissimo*, and then followed with other appropriately exuberant classical selections, and for the second time that evening I suddenly remembered all my old absent and distant Sox-afflicted friends (and all the other Red Sox fans, all over New England), and I thought of them—in Brookline, Mass., and Brooklin, Maine; in Beverly Farms and Mashpee and Presque Isle and North Conway and Damariscotta; in Pomfret, Connecticut, and Pomfret, Vermont; in Wayland and Providence and Revere and Nashua, and in both the Concords and all five Manchesters; and in Raymond, New Hampshire (where Carlton Fisk lives), and Bellows Falls, Vermont (where Carlton Fisk was *born*), and I saw all of them dancing and shouting and kissing and leaping about like the fans at Fenway—jumping up and down in their bedrooms and kitchens and living rooms, and in bars and trailers, and even in some boats here and there, I suppose, and on back-country roads (a lone driver getting the news over the radio and blowing his horn over and over, and finally pulling up and getting out and leaping up and down on the cold macadam, yelling into the night), and all of them, for once at least, utterly joyful and believing in that joy—alight with it.

It should be added, of course, that very much the same sort of celebration probably took place the following night in the midlands towns and vicinities of the Reds' supporters—in Otterbein and Scioto; in Frankfort, Sardinia, and Summer

Shade; in Zanesville and Louisville and Akron and French Lick and Loveland. I am not enough of a social geographer to know if the faith of the Red Sox fan is deeper or hardier than that of a Reds rooter (although I secretly believe that it may be, because of his longer and more bitter disappointments down the years). What I do know is that this belonging and caring is what our games are all about; this is what we come for. It is foolish and childish, on the face of it, to affiliate ourselves with anything so insignificant and patently contrived and commercially exploitative as a professional sports team, and the amused superiority and icy scorn that the non-fan directs at the sports nut (I know this look—I know it by heart) is understandable and almost unanswerable. Almost. What is left out of this calculation, it seems to me, is the business of caring—caring deeply and passionately, really *caring*—which is a capacity or an emotion that has almost gone out of our lives. And so it seems possible that we have come to a time when it no longer matters so much what the caring is about, how frail or foolish is the object of that concern, as long as the feeling itself can be saved. Naïveté—the infantile and ignoble joy that sends a grown man or woman to dancing and shouting with joy in the middle of the night over the haphazardous flight of a distant ball—seems a small price to pay for such a gift.

•

THE SEVENTH game, which settled the championship in the very last inning and was watched by a television audience of seventy-five million people, probably would have been a famous thriller in some other Series, but in 1975 it was outclassed. It was a good play that opened on the night after the opening night of *King Lear*. The Red Sox sprang away to an easy 3–0 lead in the third inning—easy because Don Gullett was overthrowing and walked in two runs in the course of striking out the side. By the fifth inning, the Sox had also left nine runners aboard, and a gnawing conviction settled on me that this was not going to be their day after all. It occurred to me simultaneously that this lack of confidence probably meant that I had finally qualified as a Red Sox fan, a lifelong doubter (I am *sort* of a Red Sox fan, which barely counts at all in the great company of afflicted true believers), but subsequent study of the pattern of this Series shows that my doubts were perfectly realistic. The Red Sox had led in all seven games, but in every game after the opener the Reds either tied or reversed the lead by the ninth inning or (once) put the tying and winning runs aboard in the ninth. This is called pressure baseball, and it is the absolute distinguishing mark of a championship team.

Here, working against Bill Lee, the Reds nudged and shouldered at the lead, putting their first batter aboard in the third, fourth, and fifth innings but never quite bringing him around. Rose led off with a single in the sixth. (He got on base eleven times in his last fifteen appearances in the Series.) With one out, Bench hit a sure double-play ball to Burleson, but Rose, barreling down toward second, slid high and hard into Doyle just as he was firing on to first, and the ball went wildly into the Boston dugout. Lee, now facing Perez, essayed a looping, quarter-speed, spinning curve, and Perez, timing his full swing exactly, hit the ball over the wall and over the screen and perhaps over the Massachusetts Turnpike. The Reds then tied the game in the seventh (when Lee was permitted to start his winter vacation), with Rose driving in the run.

The Cincinnati bullpen had matters in their charge by now, and almost the only sounds still to be heard were the continuous cries and clappings and shouts of hope from the Reds' dugout. Fenway Park was like a waiting accident ward early on a Saturday night. Ken Griffey led off the ninth and walked, and was sacrificed to second. Willoughby, who had pitched well in relief, had been lost for a pinch-hitter in the bottom of the eighth, and the new Boston pitcher was a thin, tall left-handed rookie named Jim Burton, who now retired a pinch-hitter, Dan Driessen, and then (showing superb intelligence,

I thought) walked Pete Rose. Joe Morgan was the next batter, and Burton—staring in intently for his sign, checking the runners, burning with concentration—gave it his best. He ran the count to one and two and then threw an excellent pitch—a slider down and away, off the outer sliver of the plate. Morgan, almost beaten by it, caught it with the outer nub of his bat and lofted a little lob out to very short center field that rose slightly and then lost its hold, dropping in well in front of the onrushing, despairing Lynn, as the last runner of the year came across the plate. That was all; Boston went down in order.

I left soon, walking through the trash and old beer cans and torn-up newspapers on Jersey Street in company with hundreds of murmuring and tired Boston fans. They did not look bitter, and perhaps they felt, as I did, that no team in our time had more distinguished itself in the World Series than the Red Sox—no team, that is, but the Cincinnati Reds.

• • •

THIS SERIES, of course, was replayed everywhere in memory and conversation through the ensuing winter, and even now its colors still light up the sky. In the middle of November that fall, a Boston friend of mine dropped into a tavern in Cambridge—in the workingman's, or non-Harvard, end of Cambridge—and found a place at the bar. "It was a Monday night," he told me later, "and everybody was watching the NFL game on the TV set up at the other end of the bar. There wasn't a sound in the place, and after I'd been there about ten minutes the old guy next to me put down his beer glass and sort of shook his head and whispered to himself, 'We never should have taken out Willoughby.' "

14 In the Counting House

April 1976

SPRING AFTERNOONS are warming, daylight lingers, and the news of baseball flowers about us once again. The news, that is, of games and scores and standings, of late rallies and shut-out pitching, of rejuvenated veterans and startling young rookies—the good old summertime news, and not the news of the other side of the sport, the economics of baseball, which so confused and wearied us during the off-season. The same chilling blight has recently overtaken most major professional team sports; this year's eruption of labor troubles and money squabbles represented only the newest stage in a long national struggle between athletes and entrepreneurs for the upper hand (or perhaps only an equal hand) in the regulation of their sports and the apportionment of profits. In baseball, however, the collisions of this past winter and early spring were notable for their bitterness and naked hostility, which suggests that a time of decision in these matters may be close at hand. The players' strike of 1972, which erased the first few days of that season, was an unpleasant but relatively insignificant affair, caused by the owners' refusal to arbitrate a minor pension issue—which was in fact eventually negotiated and quickly resolved. This year's difficulties were altogether serious—something close to open warfare. The preseason camps in Florida, Arizona, and California were shut down for seventeen days—almost half the normal spring term—by a lockout called and enforced by the club owners. This year, the disagreement reached such a level of acrimony that for a time the regular season itself seemed threatened: baseball might stop altogether.

The center of it all was a decision handed down last December by a three-man arbitration panel, which ruled that two players, Andy Messersmith and Dave McNally, were released from affiliation with their clubs—Messersmith from the Dodgers, McNally from the Montreal Expos—as a result of their having played out their existing contracts plus an additional year, and were now free agents, entitled to sign up with whatever club they wished, at any pay they could command. This affirmation of a seemingly minimal right was in fact a ruling of revolutionary significance—an athletes' *Miranda* decision—for it marked the long-expected end of the ancient "reserve clause," which had bound every player irrevocably to the club holding his contract, thus fixing his place of employment and insuring that his salary was always ultimately determined by the pleasure of the owner. The decision in the Messersmith case (Dave McNally, a pitcher, had actually retired from baseball, because of a sore arm, by the time the case was settled) may have appeared historically inevitable, but it unleashed a storm of passions and legal complexities. Through the cold-weather months, the baseball hot-stove news mostly concerned the owners' trips to court to have the arbitrators' decisions overturned (the pleas were denied); ill-tempered, staccato haggling over the free-agent issue; onerously complex proposals and counteroffers put forward by rival professional negotiators speaking for the owners' Player Relations Committee and for the Executive Board of the Players Association; lengthy statements of position that only confirmed the deepening division and stalemate; and, finally, the lockout. A fan searching the back pages for some word of Nolan Ryan's elbow or Billy Martin's pitching rotation could be forgiven if he sometimes threw down his newspaper in despair.

When the spring camps did at last suddenly open, on order of Commissioner Bowie Kuhn, the still unresolved dispute over the new Basic Agreement—the agreement on which every individual contract is founded, covering everything from meal money to transportation, trading procedures, schedules, and spring-training pay—receded a bit in urgency, only to be replaced by a succession of highly publicized, pugnacious salary negotiations and holdouts involving some of the topmost stars of the game (Messersmith, Tom Seaver, Reggie Jackson, and others), whose money demands soared and swooped in rumored multiples of millions of dollars. These flights, accelerated by the collapse of the reserve system, were watched with avidity by the players and with horrified anxiety by the owners—and with various emotions, as yet imperfectly understood, by the fans. At the same time, there were further commercial surprises, which, taken with the rest, caused the once elegant estate of baseball more and more to resemble a littered, slovenly Oz. The franchise of the San Francisco Giants was lost, then reprieved, then saved, then lost again, and then, at the last possible instant, won back for good. Bill Veeck, the cheerful showman, formed a partnership that purchased the Chicago White Sox, and instantly infuriated his fellow owners (just as they *knew* he would) with the pronouncement that his players would wear shorts on hot summer afternoons on the South Side. The American League announced its expansion to fourteen clubs in 1977; the National League announced its firm resolve to continue at the present twelve-club level, and refused also to consider the scandalous adventure, suggested by the AL, of interleague play.

I am a baseball fan in good standing, and my first reaction on regarding the enormous and unsavory dog's breakfast that was plunked down before me on the morning of this new season was simply to push back from the table and walk away. A lot of fans, I suspect, may be on the point of leaving the game. Even more of them will try to ignore the whole mess—the lockout, the free-agent issue, the gigantic new salaries, the franchise squabbles—and follow the sport as if it were unchanged, follow it as they did when they were children. This is tempting, I must admit, for it is the game itself—the game inside the lines, as the phrase now has it—that has always most absorbed me. Part of me, much of the fan in me, is attracted to baseball games exactly because they connect me on a long straight line to my own boyhood, and because they so often seem to be the perfect release from the daily world of money, strikes, strife, and complexity. And yet . . . Somehow, I sense that this can't work for long—that games considered as pure escape can't continue to hold us entirely, because we must keep our first and best connections with the world of today. Professional sports now form a noisy and substantial, if irrelevant and distracting, part of that world, and it seems as if baseball games taken entire—off the field as well as on it, in the courts and in the front offices as well as down on the diamonds—may now tell us more about ourselves than they ever did before. Perhaps we should stay here in the gloomy counting house a little longer, then, before we grab our shades and head for the park.

•

THE MOST radical alteration in the relations between baseball players and baseball owners may in the long run prove to have come not with the Messersmith decision but at the moment when Catfish Hunter signed a multiyear contract to pitch for the Yankees for a total (including various long-term retirement and insurance benefits) of three and a half million dollars. Hunter had been declared a free agent by Peter Seitz, the same arbitrator who later cast the deciding vote in the Messersmith case, but Hunter's liberation had nothing to do with the reserve clause; Seitz ruled that Catfish was his own man because his former club, the Oakland A's, had failed to make payments on an insurance policy that was an integral part of his contract. Hunter is one of the two or three best pitchers in baseball today, and the extended, scrambling, knockdown auction in late 1974 among several well-heeled clubs to sign him for almost any sum he cared to mention startled everyone, probably including Catfish himself. Suddenly there seemed to be no limit to the money that a baseball superstar could command—a realization that probably had much to do with the nastiness and anxiety of the negotiations over free-agency between owners and players this year.

Tom Seaver, the Mets' shining paladin, this spring demanded something in the neighborhood of $275,000 per year over a span of three years—a pay level that caused M. Donald Grant, the chairman of the Mets' board, to open immediate discussions with the Dodgers about the possibility of a Seaver trade. This move is believed to have been made either in sudden pure anger or as a considered corporate warning to Seaver and other high-priced stars. After a short, tense holdout, Seaver settled for a base of $225,000 a year (he had been getting $170,000), which could come to another $30,000 or $40,000, because of various bonus stipulations, if he sustains his normal high level of performance. Andy Messersmith, after nearly coming to terms with the Yankees, the Padres, and the Angels (he received other offers, too, but many of these were halfhearted publicity gestures), signed with the Atlanta Braves for a three-year, no-cut contract worth about a million dollars. Reggie Jackson, suddenly traded to the Orioles last month by Oakland (with whom he had not yet signed for the current year), has not reported to his new club; he will play in Baltimore, he is reported as saying, only for an extended contract of considerable proportions—say, five years for something like three million dollars. Dick Allen, who in 1973 became the first player to earn a quarter of a million dollars for a single season, has not come to any agreement with his current club, the Phillies. And so on. A decade ago, there were fewer than half a dozen players in the majors who earned over $100,000 per year. Last year, there were three stars (Catfish Hunter, Dick Allen, and Hank Aaron) who earned $200,000 or more per year, and forty-five who earned between $100,000 and $200,000; both groups have grown much larger this year. The world-champion Cincinnati Reds now have two stars, Johnny Bench and Joe Morgan, in the $200,000 class, and two others, Pete Rose and Tony Perez, who earn well over $100,000. (Pete Rose, whom many consider to be the team's main man, has always seemed to be somewhat slighted by the Reds at contract time.) On the other hand, the *average* pay for a major-league baseball player last year was $46,000. (Salaries for other professional team sports in 1975, according to a survey made by the *Washington Post*, averaged $42,000 for players in the National Football League, $75,000 for players in the National Hockey League, $95,000 for players in the American Basketball Association, and, up on top, $110,000 for players in the National Basketball Association.)

The size of the money game has changed, and a lot of other baseball values are changing as a result. The most interesting alteration may be among the fans. I know of no reliable or continuing system of fan-polling, and much of what I can conclude here is intuitive or based on conversations with and letters from friends who care about sports. There seems to be absolutely no doubt that large numbers of fans are disturbed about the level of some player salaries, and that they are angry about the curtailment of spring training this year. (Many of them referred to the lockout as a strike—a startling one-hundred-and-eighty-degree error that was also repeatedly made by some sportswriters.) The reader mail received by the *Sporting News*, the ancient, extremely conservative weekly sports paper published in St. Louis, ran very heavily against the players; one typical letter—typical except for the mildness of its tone—said, "Professional athletes are overestimating their value. Unless they begin to realize this, they are going to continue the already downhill relationship with the fans and ultimately destroy spectator sports." Fan-in-the-street interviews in many big-league-city newspapers turned up similar expressions of this view. The anti-money, anti-player feeling does not seem to carry over to the box office, however; early-season attendance this year has been unusually healthy.

It is significant, I think, that there was no major outcry from fans last year when Catfish Hunter signed for his epochal three and a half million. Nor do I recall many shouts of rage when Muhammad Ali and Joe Frazier each cleared more than two million dollars for their heavyweight-title fight in Manila last autumn, or when Jimmy Connors took down a quarter of a million for a one-sided three-set victory in a televised tennis match a couple of months ago. On almost any weekend, some golfer or other can be seen on our television sets in the act of winning $30,000 or $40,000, and one of them, Hubert Green, recently hit a hot streak and ran up winnings of $118,000 in three weeks. Money won on television, to be sure, has always seemed a trifle unreal, more like Monopoly dollars than the real thing, but what I think we can begin to understand is that there is an enormous difference between our attitude toward the individual great athlete—the superstar, the hero-entrepreneur, the nonpareil—and what we feel about the team player. We seem to derive excitement and deep pleasure from the accomplishments of a single performer. ("This putt—*sh-h-h*—may be worth *twenty-two-thousand* dollars. . . .") The multimillion-dollar heavyweight-title fight involves not just the biggest, toughest men anywhere but an almost unimaginable prize for the winner, and the two elements are somehow the same. When I was growing up, the fact that Babe Ruth was paid a salary of $80,000 was almost as awesome to me as his feat of hitting sixty home runs in a single season; I memorized both figures. But large payments to athletes are not enjoyed or approved of by us, the fans, if the payment is made broadly, to all the athletes engaged in a particular trade at the big-league level—all basketball players, all hockey players, and so on. "The players have gotten too greedy," "They're all paid too much"—these are current grandstand convictions, which I also hear from many other people, in and out of the sports world. As I pick up this complaint, however, it seems to apply more to a well-paid journeyman than to the superstar—more to Rusty Staub or Roy White, say, than to Johnny Bench or Jim Palmer. It would be extremely interesting to measure this, if we could. What it means, I think, is that high pay for athletes is resented if they are seen as *employees*. And when these employees behave like contemporary workmen, trying to extract the most money and the most favorable working conditions and retirement benefits from a typically reluctant and unsympathetic employer, and forming a union to press their demands—which is what the baseball and football and basketball players have all done in recent years—then they are resented even more deeply, almost to the point of hatred. This is an extraordinary turn of events in a labor-conscious, success-oriented society like ours.

I think that the view of the athlete as an employee and a card-carrying union man violates our fan vision of the athlete as a mythic figure, a lone hero. The athlete should live and perform by himself, in a place far removed from our own mundane concerns for good working hours and fair pay. What he does should be impossible, or nearly so, and it is quite acceptable that his reward for this great deed should be unbelievable, beyond our measuring. If, on the other hand, we see the athlete as a mere clock-puncher and then compare his pay scale with ours, we feel envy and rage. Our indignation is deepened when we realize that he is being paid all that bread for something that is probably much more pleasurable than whatever it is we do. Come to think of it, by God, he is being paid for having *fun!* This gnawing ill humor is at its worst, surely, when the athlete on view is a ballplayer, for baseball looks like the easiest of all professional sports—almost easy enough for us to have been hired to play it ourselves, except that . . . if only . . . The fact that the game is in reality extraordinarily difficult results in the very same rancor, for everybody, including the best-paid star, is bound to fall on his face if we only wait long enough. There—look at that! And we pay him two hundred grand for *that!* This is the way the old sour-mouthed Yankee fans used to sound, back when the Yankees won every year. All of us have become that sort of fan now, I think, and the kind of understanding affection we once had for the hopeless, losing Mets, who so resembled ourselves, has been lost, probably for good.

I should add, of course, that there are many people who despise high pay for athletes on principle—because such gigantic funds and such exorbitant passions are expended for such trivial ends, in a time when so many areas of our country and our social fabric are deteriorating or dying for lack of money and attention. For myself, I can say only that I think of this irony almost every day but that it no longer seems to have the capacity to shock me, or even surprise me. These polarities do not seem reversible—there is no way to siphon the purse for the Indianapolis 500 into Bedford-Stuyvesant—and it may even be that they are inevitable, locked into our society. Professional sports are an escape—probably our prime national escape just now. During the Depression, we happily paid the largest salaries in the country to Clark Gable and Mickey Rooney and Jean Harlow; today, we pay them to Kareem Jabbar and Richard Petty and Catfish Hunter. I see no difference.

•

THE MESSERSMITH case was the latest in a long series of tests challenging the courts' habitual protection of baseball's monopoly status. In 1972, Supreme Court Justice Harry Blackmun, delivering the 5–3 majority opinion that upheld the owners in a suit brought by Cardinal outfielder Curt Flood, wrote, "Professional baseball is a business and it is engaged in interstate commerce"—and thus normally subject to federal business law. But it is "in a very distinct sense an exception and an anomaly," and he added, "The aberration is an established one." This curious logic soon impelled other players to challenge the reserve clause by appealing to the arbitration panel—a body set up in the Basic Agreement of 1970 and reluctantly accepted by the owners. Separate tests were undertaken by Ted Simmons, Sparky Lyle, and Bobby Tolan, but dropped when each of the players ultimately signed a new contract. The Messersmith-McNally grievance, when it arrived last year, had accumulated a considerable momentum. The issue in the case was straightforward—whether the standard player contract should be taken literally (as Messersmith and McNally claimed) in its provisions that seemed to say a player completing the full term of his contract and then playing one additional season under the same terms was thus freed of all obligation to his club, or whether (as the owners claimed) the obligation and the contract were infinitely extensible under the precedents of the reserve clause. Suddenly aware of a very dark shadow on the road ahead, the owners hurried to court to request that the entire arbitration process be enjoined. The action was denied, but Peter Seitz, the neutral third arbitrator (along with the owners' labor adviser, John Gaherin, and Marvin Miller, the executive director of the Players Association), seized the occasion to urge all parties to take the immense issue out of his hands by negotiating their differences. Not a bit of it, the owners responded; mind your own business and press on to a decision. Seitz obliged, and, on December 23, cast the deciding vote that sustained Messersmith and McNally in their grievance. The reserve clause was dead. The owners reacted at once, firing Seitz from his job—an action within their rights under the rules of the arbitration panel. The bad news had come, and the messenger was put to the sword.

The group behavior of the owners—by turns stiff-necked, contradictory, apprehensive, and vengeful, and always accompanied by loud offstage trumpetings of defiance and rage from their small Tarquin minority—sometimes invites irreverence, but the truth remains that the Messersmith ruling violently disrupted their once somnolent nineteenth-century industry. Their worst ancient fear, the family nightmare, had come to pass, and other frights now seemed sure to follow. From the beginning, they had defended the reserve clause—in the courts and in the newspapers and at congressional hearings—by claiming that its removal would invite hundreds of ballplayers, including most of the great stars, to sell themselves each year to the highest bidder, thus assuring an automatic championship to the franchise holder who had the largest bankroll, and also making it certain that no club could hope to maintain the year-to-year personnel and identifying character that preserve fan loyalty. Although there is new evidence every day to suggest that this is not happening, and not about to happen, in either league, the fear of it is still very much alive among the owners, and does much to explain their recent behavior. Their second difficulty is much more concrete. Baseball, they point out, is such a demanding game that the average player must spend four years (far more than in any other sport) at the minor-league and rookie levels before he attains major-league competence and begins to pay off his owner's considerable investment in him. It would be unconscionable to allow the player to walk away at that moment and sell his services to a rival club.

The owners, having applied unsuccessfully to the United States District Court in Kansas City to have the Messersmith ruling overturned, and having also failed in the same plea in the Circuit Court of Appeals, now slowly tried to come to grips with the horrid new reality. Their Player Relations Committee had been negotiating with a committee of the Players Association in a foot-dragging sort of way since the previous August, and not until last February 11 did the owners come up with their first version of a new reserve clause—free-agent status for a player after nine years' service in the major leagues (where the average player's tenure is just over four and a half years). The players, who, of course, had no legal obligation to accept *any* modification of the basic contract-plus-one-year formula, nonetheless agreed in principle that some form of player continuity seemed essential, and suggested a six-year term, with a year's advance notice if a player then intended to cut loose from his club.

The distance separating the two sides was canyonlike, with an entirely different economic view of things from each rim, and now there came into the discussions a legal dispute of true complexity—the so-called liability issue. Marvin Miller, having asserted the Players Association's willingness to settle on a minimum tour of duty with a particular ball club, asked what he was expected to do about any player or players who would not agree to such a compromise—who, in fact, would be prepared to sue for damages if their basic contract-plus-one-year rights, achieved in the Messersmith decision, were bargained away. (One player, the notoriously prickly Mike Marshall, of the Dodgers, had already said that he was prepared to fight it out on just those lines.) Not our concern, replied John Gaherin for the owners. All these issues are of concern to *both* groups and have to be faced, said Miller. Then, even as the two sides seemed to be inching closer together, the owners announced the lockout, on the eve of spring training. The stated motive—to forestall another players' strike—was an empty one, since the Players Association had offered a four-year no-strike pledge while any new form of reserve clause was being tested. It must thus be assumed that the owners' purpose was simply to submit the negotiations to severe pressure, in hopes that public opinion would turn against the players—as it did, in fact—and that the players, for their part, would become anxious about the impasse and the onrushing season and press their union for a quick compromise. A public-relations firm, T. J. Ross & Associates, was engaged by the owners, and players and reporters were subjected to frequent news releases depicting management's plight and sweet reasonableness.

From the beginning, spokesmen for the owners, as well as

Commissioner Kuhn, had frequently mentioned the rising cost of all baseball operations, the shrinking farm systems, the chronically invalid franchises like San Francisco, Minnesota, Atlanta, and Baltimore, and the unfortunate effects of any large jump in ticket prices. These are problems of some urgency, of course, but the owners' habitual cries of poverty have always been slightly disingenuous. For one thing, player salaries and pensions still form a very modest portion—less than twenty percent—of the clubs' annual outlays. Attendance is excellent, totaling 29,790,000 last year, or a hair under the all-time mark of 30,109,000 set two seasons ago, and baseball has just renegotiated its basic television agreements with the networks for a record sum, amounting to ninety-three million dollars payable over the next four years. The clubs' total radio and TV income now amounts to one and a half times the total paid out for player salaries and retirement benefits. Some franchises lose money, but it is hard to say how many and how much, because most baseball clubs now represent only a special corner of a much larger commercial entity, and because tax write-offs and benefits can assist, or even turn around, an apparently weak performance in any given year. It is not generally known, for instance, that ballplayers can be depreciated, like oil wells or factory buildings, on the corporate ledgers. In any case, the owners have never formally pleaded inability to pay in the course of their negotiations with the Players Association—a plea that is perfectly within their rights but would require them, under the law, to open their books. Neither have the owners hesitated to pluck another favorite old, sweet chord—team loyalty. How will the fans continue to care about our teams, they ask, if players are free to deal for themselves and then heartlessly move along to any club that makes them a good offer? A strange refrain, surely, from the dealers who traded off more than a hundred players between the 1975 and 1976 seasons, who have moved or invented eighteen franchises since the Second World War, and who propose to draft away fifty players from existing clubs to stock the two utterly superfluous new franchises that they now envision.

•

THE LOCKOUT, an enormous predicament, lasted for more than two weeks, and its most startling moment—surely a scene like no other in the history of the game—came on March 11, when fifty-odd players stood or sat down behind a long table in a conference room of the Host International Hotel, in Tampa, and debated the structure of baseball with the owners' Player Relations Committee. The meeting had overtones that stretched far beyond the day and the place, for the owners' unspoken conviction had always been that six hundred ballplayers, taken as a group, would prove to be scattered, undisciplined, poorly informed, and probably insufficiently educated, and thus unable to stand together during a long, tough bargaining period. The players' group included not only members of their Executive Board (team representatives like Lou Brock, Tom Seaver, Rick Monday, Merv Rettenmund, and Carl Morton) but a sizable contingent of newly aroused participants—Johnny Bench, Ted Simmons, Rusty Staub, Willie Stargell, Jim Wynn, and others—who had recently assembled informally and made requests that an end be found to the impasse. The newcomers sat in on the next policy session of the Executive Board (any player may attend meetings) and, on hearing the logic and bargaining history behind the Players Association positions, were apparently convinced of their justice. Any secret hope the owners may have entertained that the new faces on the scene represented an unraveling of the Players Association ended abruptly when Johnny Bench, who had previously said in public that some simple solution to these issues must be easily discoverable, stood up at the hotel meeting and delivered an extended discourse on the players' stake in the liability issue. The champion Cincinnati Reds, taken from top to bottom, are the most conservative, old-line club in baseball, and players who were at the meeting that afternoon have told me that the expression on the face of Bob Howsam, the Reds' president, as he listened to this address by his famous star was a *picture*. (Since that day, it has been observed that Howsam, who had been one of the loudest opponents of any major concessions to the players, has been notably more reasonable in attitude. Change is sometimes possible, even in baseball.)

A few days later, in St. Petersburg, the owners delivered their "best and final" offer—a lengthy document that, among other things, conceded free-agent status for players who play out their options under current contracts (conceded the Messersmith decision, that is) but proposed various future restrictions that would limit the number of clubs that a free agent could dicker with and the number of free agents that any one club could sign. This new offer was rejected by Marvin Miller, who observed that it listed fourteen unresolved and largely undiscussed issues and concluded with a clause that could throw the entire Basic Agreement into a fresh round of negotiations in 1978. The next day, however, the players' Executive Board passed a resolution calling the owners' offer incomplete but admitting that it represented considerable progress. Some liability for obdurate players might be accepted by the Players Association, they said, and further negotiations should proceed at once. These joint whispers of concession were enough for Commissioner Kuhn, who ordered the spring camps to open forthwith. Baseball was back in business, to everybody's relief—with the exception, to be sure, of Gussie Busch, the president of the Cardinals, who said, "It would be insane to open the camps," a dissenting opinion supposedly endorsed by six other clubs. Change is sometimes impossible, especially in baseball.

•

THE TWO sides have continued to meet since the season got under way, but progress on the new Basic Agreement has been minimal: many divisive issues, including the limitation of free agents' rights and the size of the clubs' rosters after more expansion, remain entirely unresolved. No one knows if the agreement can be signed this summer, or what new crisis will arise if it is not. The owners remain very apprehensive about the number of players who have not signed contracts for the current year and will thus become free agents in October. At last count, that number was about sixty (there are six hundred players in the majors), and not all of them were regulars. The total is diminishing slowly as players come to terms, but the roster of the still unsigned includes not only stars like Reggie Jackson and Dick Allen but Carlton Fisk, Fred Lynn, Bert Blyleven, Ted Simmons, Don Gullett, and Willie McCovey. There is, moreover, a knot of celebrated Oakland players—Sal Bando, Joe Rudi, Gene Tenace, Rollie Fingers, Vida Blue, and Bert Campaneris: the Oakland team, in effect—who have not signed, because of their dissatisfaction with the contracts offered them by their boss, Charles O. Finley. He has responded by paying them for the current season at the minimum permissible level, which is twenty percent below their last contracts. What will happen to all these players—what offers will be made to them, how many of them will in fact sign up—will determine the condition of baseball for the next few years, and should be watched with at least the same attentiveness that we will be giving to the pennant races.

I am not optimistic. Bargaining with employees in an open market requires frankness and some perception of variations in human character and motivation. The owners, as a group, do not qualify on either count. It is perhaps unfair, by the way, to apply this pejorative tag, "the owners," to the strange agglomeration of old baseball lords, highly trained, tennis-playing young business executives, sudden millionaires, careful industrialists, and second- or third-generation baseball families who, in one form or another, control the twenty-four clubs, but the fact remains that the most vivid continuous characteristic they display is a rigid and violently cautious group mentality, which seems to bear little resemblance to the energy and imagination and business courage that most of them must have possessed at some time or another in order to amass their present fortunes. This is a unique phenomenon in American business, and it suggests to me that many team owners may have chosen to enter the sports world not for its surface attractions —excitement, publicity, camaraderie, front-row seats, and so forth—but because its fixed, ancient corporate privileges looked like such a safe harbor after their turbulent fiscal voyages. They found a home.

In group negotiations, as we have seen, the first attitude taken by the owners is the posture invariably struck by their most reactionary, intransigent members—the Finley-Busch-Howsam statuary group. In employee relationships, the owners' basic attitude is paternalistic, sentimental, and insensitive. In spite of the grinding struggles between the owners and the Players Association in recent years, most ball clubs pride themselves deeply on the good relationship between their front office and their players, and for some—the Pirates, the Dodgers, the Orioles, and perhaps the Red Sox—the claim seems valid. On almost every club, however, family feeling has not always prevented the sudden throwaway trade of a fading long-term star, the subtle browbeating of a rookie at contract time, or the winter deal that disposes of a clubhouse freethinker, an irreverent joker, a particularly vigorous player representative, or other "agitators." Last year, the Mets' M. Donald Grant forced a veteran outfielder, Cleon Jones, to abase himself by making a public apology, at a large press conference, for a minor sexual peccadillo. Many clubs, including the Yankees and the Reds, enforce smaller humiliations on their players in the form of dress codes—short haircuts, low stocking stirrups, ties and jackets on the road—in the name of "team pride." These leftovers from baseball's baronial past may be slowly drifting out of the game, but their persistence suggests that the owners do not trust their players or understand their motives. A general manager of the old days much preferred the ritual of calling a player into his office to talk contract terms rather than having to make an appointment with the tieless, mod-dressed lawyer or agent who now probably represents the same young pitcher or slugger in his money dealings. (One lawyer-agent, Jerry Kapstein, is employed by many of the notable current holdouts, including Lynn, Fisk, Holtzman, and Rudi.) Suspicions are deepening, and the owners, like the fans, are watching their players with ill-concealed misgivings. Owners *are* fans, of course; they are the ultimate in fandom. What's *happening*, they wonder. Doesn't anybody care about team loyalty anymore? All these kids are paid too damned much. All they think about now is money. . . .

I doubt it. The players' new privileges will surely produce a few high-priced freebooters, who will be perfectly eager to play for any team as long as the money is right (Andy Messersmith may have been the first of these), but most players of established worth on the field have also established themselves considerably in the city—or one of its suburbs, more likely—where their team plays. They are apt to be men around thirty years old, with children in school, good-sized houses (with good-sized mortgages), and long-term local business and social connections. All these, I suspect, are more significant and more stabilizing forces than "team loyalty." Thurman Munson, before eventually signing a four-year contract with the Yankees this spring (for a salary that will exceed $150,000 in its final year), said that he wanted to play only in New York or in Cleveland, which is near his hometown. Ken Holtzman, before Finley traded him off to the Baltimore Orioles, said to a *Times* reporter, "All he would have to do is negotiate with me in good faith, in a civil tone of voice, and I probably would sign. I like the Oakland area, I like the guys on the ball club. I don't want to leave." His former teammate Joe Rudi, who is also unsigned, said to me in Arizona last month, "I want to stay in Oakland. I have my home and my business and my friends there. Most of us want to stay, but we don't feel Charlie will pay us what we need." In Arizona, I also talked with Rick Monday, the splendid Cub outfielder, who had just signed a one-year contract. He said, "The owners have this terrible fear of the players' playing out their contracts en masse and jumping to other clubs, and I think it's wildly exaggerated. They don't seem to know what matters to a player, and how many factors there are that work to keep him where he is, as long as he's treated fairly."

•

WHEN THE lockout was unlocked, I scurried south and then west, anxious to rid myself of my pale, winter fan's face—a complexion brought on by the tedious diet of court cases and labor law. Never was spring training more delicious, and never were its rituals more reassuring. In Pompano Beach, on my first day, the visiting Orioles trotted out a very tall right-handed pitcher named Sam Stewart in the fourth inning of a game against the Texas Rangers. Stewart, a raw rookie, pitched for the Bluefield, West Virginia, Orioles in the Appalachian League last year, but he had "thrown like hell" in batting practice a few days earlier, thus earning this shot. Now he retired a batter, threw two very wide balls to the Rangers' Tom Grieve, and then hit him on the hip with a fastball. "Yahrr!" Grieve bellowed. Stewart then gave up a walk, a single, then another single, got an infield out, then surrendered a two-run double off the fence by Roy Howell, then a single, and then fanned Toby Harrah: four hits, five runs, one left on, one broken heart.

At Winter Haven, the Red Sox trotted out Ferguson Jenkins, the splendid veteran righty (191 lifetime wins) they picked up in a trade last winter. Throwing like running water, Jenkins zipped through three innings against the White Sox in about nine minutes, and came off the field in a lather of sweat and pleasure. All the Bosox looked remarkably cheerful, perhaps because they were just beginning to understand the extent of the celebrity that has come to them as a result of their performance against the Reds in last year's peerless World Series. Their bijou park, hard by the shores of Lake Lulu, was packed with grateful followers, and the warm afternoon air was alive with herons, gnats, and cries of optimism. The day before my visit, the Red Sox had played the Phillies in Clearwater, where the elderly resident fans tottered to their feet to greet the Boston starter, Luis Tiant, with chants of "Lu-is! Lu-is!" In the press box at Winter Haven, I was told that Jim Willoughby still had the ball that second baseman Denny Doyle had thrown wildly into the Red Sox dugout in an attempt at a double play during the final Series game—a crucial mistake that allowed the Reds to begin their comeback toward victory. That ball, however, was damaged: its cover had been badly torn by Johnny Bench's swing—an accident that must have affected Doyle's peg. Doyle has refused to confirm this or to answer questions about it. "I should have made the play," he says. Class.

In Bradenton, I approached Pirate manager Danny Murtaugh and asked him a useful, well-thought-out, mid-March-type scribe-query: "How many innings will your starting pitchers be able to go by opening day, Danny? Because of—you know—the late start this year?"

Murtaugh got rid of a little tobacco juice and murmured, "I've had pitchers who couldn't go more than one inning in July."

At Payne Park, in Sarasota, I spotted Bill Veeck sitting in the open grandstand behind first base, and climbed up to say hello. He was stripped to the waist, with his Ahab-like peg leg propped on the row in front of him. He was a light, dusty tan all over, and somehow suggested a garrulous holy man. Laughing, squinting in the sunlight, hunching against the warm wind to light innumerable cigarettes, he talked exuberantly about baseball—Veeck baseball. "We've just finished taking up the artificial surface on the infield at Comiskey Park and replacing it with grass," he said. "This is an outdoor game—people are trying to get away from steel and plastic. We got the turf down in five hours. Now it looks like a ball park. How important the old parks are! We all saw that in the World Series last fall. In Boston, you had beautiful Fenway Park and thirty-five thousand participants. Then, over in Cincinnati, you had fifty-five thousand spectators. I think the thirty-five thousand almost won the Series. It had a tremendous effect on the play—nobody who saw those games can doubt that.

"I opposed the lockout, I guess to nobody's surprise. I don't think you should fool around with the fans that way. And who loses in the end if the fans become disenchanted? Management, nobody else. How can you hope to bargain away the verdict in a lawsuit? And did you see about the two presidents' each announcing that his league was going to expand to Toronto? Nobody in charge, as usual! Nothing changes much in baseball, but *we're* trying to change. You heard about our new road uniforms? The lettering on the shirts is from the 1903 Sox, and the blue color we took from the nineteen twenties. And we'll have white socks. Isn't it ridiculous to have a team called the White Sox wearing red socks? How did *that* ever happen?

"We really needed the full training period. We have five center fielders and we don't know if any of them can hit, and we have a mess of young pitchers who all deserve our consideration. None of us here has the slightest idea of what is happening in this club. To say we are in a state of confusion is putting it mildly."

He laughed delightedly and lit another cigarette, and then autographed a program for a waiting white-haired gentleman, who was wearing a visor. "I've been a Chicago fan since 1916," the man said, shaking Veeck's hand. "Now we're going someplace again."

The game that afternoon was a windy, sleepy, languorous affair against a visiting half-squad of Red Sox. Cleon Jones, who had been dropped by the Mets last year, rapped out four solid hits for the White Sox, but neither team was able to move its base runners along. Several of those young Chicago pitchers came on and proved in turn why they were not yet ready for the majors, but the score remained stuck at 1–1 for many innings. Up in the sunstruck, cratelike press box, the writers yawned and stretched and made jokes, and then began to bait Harry Caray, who was broadcasting the game back to Station WMAQ, in Chicago, from the adjoining booth. "Oh, *Har-ry!*" one shouted over in a loud falsetto. "Yoo-hoo, Harry *Ca-ray!*" Another tried cat noises. "*Mee-ow!*" he called. "*Meee-iouww*, Harry! *Arf-arf!*" The writers doubled over laughing. In time—at last, *weeks* later—the two teams ran out of pitchers, and the thing was called at 1–1, after fifteen innings. The only flicker of excitement had come when one of Caray's broadcasting assistants burst into the press box and threw himself head first over the front row of typewriters—an apparent suicide. "Grab my legs!" he called back at the last instant, and we did. Finally he reappeared, smiling and red-faced, holding two pieces of paper he had retrieved from the foul screen below us. "Commercials," he explained.

On another day, the Mets and the visiting Yankees had at each other at Campbell Park, in St. Petersburg's black ghetto—a stylish little green bandbox that served the Mets and the Cardinals this year while their regular park, Al Lang Field, was being totally rebuilt. Tom Seaver, who had gone through a long but fruitless contract-bargaining session with Met general manager Joe McDonald that morning, was slightly cuffed about by the Yanks, but it was plain that he was not yet cutting loose with his fastball. In the fourth, though, with the Yankees' new, extremely quick center fielder, Mickey Rivers, on third base, Seaver speared a comeback grounder hit to the mound by Roy White, and whirled and ran directly at Rivers, who had stopped twenty feet down the line and now looked like a rabbit lost on a freeway. Tom made the tag and then spun and threw out White at second base—threw him out a mile. Tom Seaver *executes*. Later in the afternoon, Dave Kingman hit a two-run homer to tie up the game in the ninth, and then totally missed an attempted sliding catch in right field, in the tenth, to help untie it—a perfect preview, perhaps, of coming events at Shea Stadium this summer.

I was up very early the next morning to catch a plane to Phoenix, and as I left the cashier's counter at the St. Petersburg Hilton I spotted Jesus Alou standing alone on the other side of the lobby, with a suitcase beside him. Eddie Yost, a Met coach, stepped out of the elevator, saw Alou, and came over and shook his hand. "What do you think you'll do?" Yost said.

"Go home," Alou said. "Then I'll see."

He had been released the day before—the end of the Alou brothers in big-league ball. He looked in terrific shape.

•

I DIDN'T entirely forget about the other side of baseball during spring training—the lockout and the rest of it. It would have been impossible, in any case, because the players themselves, both in Florida and in the Arizona camps, seemed so anxious to talk about it. Listening to them, I became aware of a common theme—a word that they mentioned with equal frequency when they talked about their performance on the field and their relationship with their parent club and with the owners in general. Pride is the spur.

Joe Morgan, second baseman, Cincinnati Reds; National League's Most Valuable Player for 1975: "I don't think ballplayers are paid too much. The price of everything has gone up. The presidents of big corporations make more money than we do—we're just getting the going rate. If the highest-paid players got only thirty thousand, that would be OK with me. I played ball a long time for free and enjoyed it—maybe I enjoyed it even more then than now. Money puts more pressure on you. I'll play for free again in a few years and enjoy that. I'll go back to the sandlots and have a lot of fun. Nobody on our team plays just for the money—they play because they like it, and to *win*. That's the thing. I'd be just as happy to play in the World Series for no money at all, just for the chance to be the champions. The pride of being the champions—that's what matters. In time, the money for the Series will be gone, but I will be a world champion forever. Maybe it's gone already, but that don't matter. Years from now, people will read the *Baseball Encyclopedia* and see us in there—'Champions of the World, 1975'—and nobody will care how much money I made."

Dave Giusti, relief pitcher, Pittsburgh Pirates: "Money is always a motivating factor for a pro. I've heard players say they never think about money once their contract is signed, but I think about next year all the time. But pride comes first, of course. You don't want to embarrass yourself out there. Most players want to hold to a level, I think—play up to their own best. That's what it's all about."

Rick Monday, center fielder, Chicago Cubs: "I'm tickled to death to have signed my contract. They're back in business, I'm back in business. I don't enjoy haggling with a general manager—it makes me feel like a prize heifer. No player likes that part of it, because it almost seems to demean him. Once I put on my uniform, the last thing I think about is money. This game is hard enough as it is—trying to hit that little ball that's coming in on you faster every year. Every time I look up, there's some kid out there about five inches taller and throwing that thing at me, so I'm not out there thinking about *money*. It's the day-in-day-out challenge that keeps you out there. If you've played forty straight games—played with an injury half the time—you've got to have something in the well to keep you going. Money doesn't help at all."

Maury Wills, retired shortstop, six-time National League base-stealing leader, now base-running coach for the Cubs, the Padres, and other teams; forty-three years old: "I never dreamed we'd see the end of the reserve clause. It was always being discussed back when I was playing. That was the biggie on the list, and bit by bit we chipped away at it. At contract time, I only wanted to be rewarded for my hard work, but once it was signed I forgot about it. I think I was always underpaid a little, but it didn't bother me. Now you can get the figures and find out if you're being properly taken care of.

"Nowadays, you keep hearing that playing should be fun.

Enjoy yourself and all that. A lot of young players have that wrong—they think it should be fun, ha-ha, as if it's some kind of joke. My satisfaction all came from succeeding. I wasn't out there on the field being sociable. I never talked to anybody on the other team—the pitcher who was about to deck me, the catcher who was about to rack me up for making him look bad. The only man I ever talked to was Joe Torre. Once, he was playing first for the Cardinals and guarding the bag against me—trying to hold me off. I slid back in and cut him up, about eight stitches worth. He never complained, never said a word, because he knew I was only taking what was mine by rights. He was a professional, and I respected him. I talked to him after that, but not the others.

"I don't know why the owners have been doing all this complaining. Football has had the one-year play-out-your-option thing for a long time, and you don't see the big-city clubs grabbing off everybody. I think management should be grateful to have the money issues handled by negotiators and by the players' business agents. It doesn't help to have the GM butting heads with a player every year. It's distracting, and it leaves bitterness. I've always thought baseball was the victim of custom and tradition. Any change and they think the world is coming to an end. I remember when a new kind of spikes were being tried out, and there was a *panic* about it."

•

SCOTTSDALE, ARIZONA, is a rich next-door sister of Phoenix, and almost the only shabby part of it is Scottsdale Stadium, where the Cubs train. The dark-green outfield wall there is so rickety you can see daylight between the planks. The wood of the fence is aged to a pitch of low C, and Reggie Jackson, leading off for the visiting A's in the sixth inning of a game there, whacked a double off the wall that made it resound like a plucked cello. Like so many hard-hit balls I have seen Jackson smash over the years, this one struck the distant fence almost before I could pick it up in its flight. It *leaped* to the wall. It was the last line drive I was to see Jackson hit for the Oakland A's, and I remembered it a couple of days later, when I read in the papers about his trade. Then I tried to think if I had ever seen him do anything dull on the field—or, come to think of it, *off* the field. The day before the game in Scottsdale, Reggie had let it drop to an Oakland reporter that he had just signed with Finley—a five-year contract for a million and a quarter. The writer sprinted for his typewriter, wrote the story, and then, for no particular reason, checked back with Reggie just before filing his copy. Jackson laughed, and said well, no, it wasn't entirely true. It wasn't *exactly* the truth. In fact, none of it was. Most of all, perhaps, Reggie Jackson is an actor.

The trade that sent Jackson and Holtzman to the Orioles in return for Don Baylor, Mike Torrez, and an extremely promising young pitcher named Paul Mitchell is generally regarded as an act of retribution by Charlie Finley. Holtzman was deeply involved in the Players Association negotiations this year, and Jackson has always belonged only to himself. As usual, no one claims to understand what Charlie Finley is up to this year. The latest addition to the Oakland roster is a team astrologer.

•

BASEBALL-WATCHERS need spring training, too. During an insignificant game between the have-not Cubs and Padres at Scottsdale, I sat in the sun-drenched open grandstand behind first base and allowed my interior clock to begin slowing itself to the pace of summer, to baseball time. As I watched the movements and patterns on the field, my interest in the game merged imperceptibly with my pleasure in the place and the weather. The sunlight was dazing, almost a weight on my head and arms, and my shadow, thrown on the empty bench to my right, had edge and substance. After an infield play, I wrote "4–3" with my pencil in a box on the scorecard on my lap, and a drop of sweat fell from my wrist and made its own blurry entry on the same page. The Cub coaches sat together on a row of folding chairs outside the home-plate end of their dugout, leaning back against the foul screen with their arms folded and their caps tipped low over their foreheads, and the Padre brain trust, over on the first-base side, made an identical frieze. We were a scattered, inattentive crowd, at times nearly silent, and between pitches we stared off at the jagged, blue-tan silhouettes of low desert peaks set about the distant rim of our gaze.

I half-closed my eyes and became aware at once that the afternoon silence was not quite perfect but contained a running pattern of innocuous baseball sounds. I could hear the murmurous play-by-play of some radio announcer up in the press box—the words undistinguishable but their groups and phrases making a kind of sense just the same—and this was accompanied by the unending sea-sound of the crowd itself, which sometimes rose to shouts or broke apart into separate words and cries. "Hey, OK!" . . . *Clap, clap, clap, clap* . . . "Hot dogs here" . . . "Hey, peanuts and hot dogs!" . . . *Clap, clap, clap* . . . *Whoo-wheet!* (a whistle from some player in the infield). *Whoo-wheet!* . . . *Clap-clap, clap-clap, clap-clap* . . . "The next batter, Number One, is . . . Hosay *Carr*denal, right field!" (The p.a. announcer was giving it his best—the big, Vegas-style introduction—and the crowd tried to respond.) "OK, *Ho*-say!" . . . "Hey-hey!" . . . "Let's *go*, Ho-say!" . . . *Clapclapclapclap* . . . *Wheet!* There was a sudden short flat noise: *Whocck!*—the same sound you would hear if you let go of one end of a long one-by-eight plank, allowing it to fall back on top of a loose stack of boards. I leaned forward and watched Cardenal sprinting for first. He slowed as he took his turn and then speeded up again as he saw the ball still free in the outfield, pulling into second base with a standup double. Real cheering now, as the next batter stood in (". . . Number Eighteen, Bill *Mad*-lock, thirrd base!"), but soon the game wound down again and the afternoon sounds resumed. *Clap, clap, clap* . . . "Hey, Cokes! *Get* yer ice-cold Cokes here!"

. . . *Clap, clap, clap, clap* . . . A telephone rang and rang in the press box—*pring-pring, pring-pring, pring-pring:* a faraway, next-door-cottage sort of noise. *Clap, clap, clap* . . . "Hey, Tim! Hey, Tim!" (a girl's voice). "Hey, Tim, over *here!*" . . . *Clap, clap* . . . "Streeough!" . . . "Aw, come *on*, Ump!" . . . *Clap, clap, clapclapclap* . . . "Get yer Cokes! Ice-cold Cokes here" . . . *Whoo-wheet!* . . . *Clapclap* . . . "*Ice*-cold." Then there was another noise, a regular, smothered slapping sound, with intervals in between: *Whug!* . . . *Whup!* . . . *Whug!* . . . *Whup!*—a baseball thrown back and forth by two Padre infielders warming up in short-right-field foul territory, getting ready to come into the game. The sounds flowed over me—nothing really worth remembering, but impossible entirely to forget. They were the sounds I had missed all winter, without ever knowing it.

•

THE MOST exciting last-minute rally in baseball this season came on March 2, in San Francisco, when Robert A. Lurie, a local real-estate nabob, put through a telephone call to Arizona and talked to Arthur (Bud) Herseth, a Phoenix meat-packer, whose name he had first heard just a few minutes before. Lurie asked Herseth if by any chance he would like to put up four million dollars and become half owner of the San Francisco Giants. Herseth asked a few questions and then said sure, why not? The deal was made, in something like that fashion, less than three hours before the expiration of a National League deadline that would have sent the Giants to Toronto. Bob Lurie had been waiting to buy the Giants for several years, and when the longtime owner of the Giants, Horace C. Stoneham, finally put the club on the market last year, Lurie, who had four million dollars of his own to invest in the team, undertook an intensive search for a partner who could deliver the other half of the necessary capital. He tried to come to terms with a group of Japanese financiers, and then almost closed with the owners of the Pizza Hut fast-food chain. Nothing worked, and only a last-minute injunction obtained by the San Francisco mayor, George Moscone, in February, kept the team from being whisked away by the Toronto carpetbaggers. Lurie then formed a partnership with Bob Short, the erstwhile owner of the Texas Rangers (né Washington Senators), but this quickly fell through, because of a dispute over team control. All seemed lost, until, lo, a Herseth arose from out of the desert.

During a Giants-Indians game at Municipal Stadium in Phoenix, I slipped into a seat beside Bud Herseth in a box right behind the Giants' dugout. Herseth had been conversing in a loud and friendly way with most of the fans in the section where he was sitting, so it seemed all right to join him. He was wearing black shoes, black trousers, horn-rimmed spectacles, a Giants cap, and an eye-bending Hawaiian shirt. If I had had any remaining doubts about his identity, I could have consulted his wide, tooled-leather belt, which was cut in back so that it spelled "BUD HERSETH, PHOENIX, ARIZ." above his hip pockets. Although Herseth's understanding with his new partner is that the day-to-day baseball operations of the Giants will be Lurie's exclusive concern, I had heard that Herseth had awakened the new Giant manager, Bill Rigney, that day with a telephone call just before six o'clock in the morning to ask whom he was planning to pitch. ("Who *is* this?" Rigney cried, in disbelief.) Now I asked Herseth if he often made calls at that time of day.

"Six in the morning isn't a bit early for me," he said rapidly. "I'm down at my feedlot way before five every day, seven days a week, about fifty weeks in the year. Sundays and every other day. We kill two hundred and fifty head a day, and there's a lot to do—get out the sick cattle, turn on the lights, get the cooler going, clean out the irrigation ditches. I fill in if anybody gets drunk and don't show up. I'll do anything. Hell, I been doing this all my life, I'm fifty-five years old, and I figure it's time I had a little fun. That's why I bought me this team—half a team. Six o'clock—why, hell, I bought me a little Vega before *five* in the morning the other day. Needed it for a friend of mine. Paid seven hundred and fifty in cash. It runs real good."

He kept his eyes on the game while he talked, and I noticed that he was keeping score. I asked him how long he had been interested in baseball.

"All my life," he said. "I can remember coming down with my dad from Aberdeen—Aberdeen, South Dakota—in '32 and going to Chicago, where we saw the Series game where Charlie Root pitched against Babe Ruth, and the Babe pointed to the stands before he hit that home run. You've heard of that? I was there. I've been a Giants fan from a long time back. Even back when they had those pitchers like Grove and Earnshaw and Parmelee and—Schumacher, wasn't it?"

He looked at his program and clapped vigorously for the Giant hitter just coming up to bat. "This is Bobby Murcer," he said. "He's the highest-priced player we have." He frowned momentarily and then corrected himself. "It wasn't Grove and Earnshaw on those Giants," he said. "It was Hubbell and Fat Freddie Fitzsimmons. Carl Hubbell. I knew that all along, but I got it wrong the first time."

He had been consulting from time to time with an associate over the terms of a contract with some radio station that would form part of the network carrying the Giants' games this year, and now the man came back down the aisle and told him that the deal seemed to be off.

"I damn well don't understand that!" Herseth said loudly. "We make a deal, and now they go and change their mind. I'm glad I don't buy cattle that way. I buy three, four thousand head at a time, and nobody has to worry if I'm going to pay off. My word is my bond—just ask anybody. I pay off like a slot machine. I know what these radio people are. I won't say it, though, because there are ladies present. I'll just write it down here on my program." He wrote something and showed me his program. He had written "S.O.B."

There was action on the field, and Herseth cried, "Hit-and-run! Hit-and-run! Right through the hole! You know, these kids may not hit homers, but they sure look like they hit steady. I'd like to get back that big guy we had who hits all those home runs—that Dave Kingman. *He'd* help this club."

I said that Kingman also struck out a lot.

"Is that so?" Herseth said. "I didn't know that." He shook his head again. "I just can't understand those radio people," he said. "I don't go for that kind of stuff."

I asked him if he had ever played much baseball.

"Sure I did," he said. "I grew up in Houghton, South Dakota —my dad had five quarters there, about eight hundred acres— but I went to high school in Hecla, South Dakota, which was on down the line. I batted cleanup on the team there for two years. I hit .400-and-something my junior year, and .666 all year when I was a senior. I played in a regional tournament then, and I remember a fellow called Al Face struck me out four times in one game. That was when I knew I wasn't a real ballplayer. I still hear from Al Face. Once a year, he sells me a calf. He sent me a picture that somebody took of us back then, and I was wearing stripèd overalls. You know, by the time I was ten years old I could guess the weight of a steer right within a few pounds."

He stood up and called out to Bobby Winkles, the Giants' third-base coach, "Hey, Bobby, how come you're chewin' and spittin' out there? What kind of example is that for my young players, hey?" He laughed uproariously, and Winkles waved and smiled.

I was about to ask Bud Herseth what he thought about the reserve clause and player salaries and the lockout and Marvin Miller, but then I decided not to. He was having too much fun. Instead, I asked him how many of the Giants' games he hoped to see at Candlestick Park this year.

"The good Lord willing and the creek don't rise," he said, "all of them."

•

Two weeks later, with the season under way, I took a subway up to the Bronx for the Yankees' home opener. It was a big day, because it marked the reopening of Yankee Stadium—a homecoming for the famous team to the famous old park, which had been rebuilt by the City of New York over the past two years. The new place looked fine. The overhanging roof around the top deck was gone, and the old thick supporting columns and girders had disappeared, giving us a new, clean triple sweep of bright-blue seats from right field all the way around to left. The whole place was blue and white, and it sparkled. There were three new banks of escalators, and a new, tree-lined promenade outside the first-base side of the Stadium, where a street used to be. The playing field had been lowered and its outlines altered a little, but most of that enormous green pasture in left was there, so you knew it was still the Stadium, all right. There were some big new scoreboards out behind the bleachers, with a white scrim on top in the shape of the lacy coppery-green top-deck façade of the old park. The wall of scoreboards cut off our view of the elevated-station platform and the nearby apartment-house roofs, where in the old days you could always spot a few neighborhood fans watching from a great distance. The new Stadium is cut off from the city around it, and nobody can watch baseball casually there anymore.

There were 54,010 of us there for the opener. Three bands played, and the sun shone, and a lot of celebrities—Joe Louis, Joe DiMaggio, Mickey Mantle, and Mrs. Lou Gehrig and Mrs. Babe Ruth, and some others—were introduced, and then the Yankees played the Twins and beat them, 11–4, coming back from a four-run deficit. The Yankees have a sprightly, quick-running team this year, with a marvelous-looking new young second baseman named Willie Randolph, and they may be in the thick of things all summer long in their tough division. There was a lot of hopeful noise at the Stadium that first afternoon—a terrific amount of cheering—but the truth is I didn't have much fun. I don't know what to make of the new Yankee Stadium. It cost the city a hundred million dollars to rebuild and finance, and the city can't pay its bills, can't pay for new schools or hospitals, can't pay its teachers, can't keep its streets or its neighborhoods up; the South Bronx, where Yankee Stadium stands, is a disaster area. These are the realities and insolubles that we all know so well, and maybe they are the things that make us give so much attention to sports in the first place—why we need these long diversions at the ball park. I don't think we should use sports as a hiding place, but I have always been willing to try to carry the two conflicting realities in my head at the same time—poor cities and rich sports, a lot of unnoticed kids playing in burned-out playgrounds, and a few men playing before great crowds in a new sports palace. As the paradox deepens, however, it begins to seem as if we are trying to make the irony disappear—that we are hoping to rub out one side of the equation by vastly increasing the other. By spending more and more millions of dollars on sports, we may be trying to tell ourselves that sports matter almost more than anything else simply because we do spend so much money on them. The name for this is addiction. I'll probably get used to the Stadium in time, but on the first afternoon all I could think of was the quiet, slow afternoons I had just spent in Bradenton and Winter Haven and Scottsdale and Phoenix, and the games I had seen there. Those games seemed like elegies now. It was strange to be sitting in Yankee Stadium, where I had grown up watching baseball, and no longer feeling at home there. I don't know what to think, because it may be that the money and the size of sport have grown too big for me after all.

15 Scout

July 1976

Baseball has so altered in recent years that many of the classic prototypes of the game seem on the point of disappearing altogether. The rookie pitcher called up to the parent club in midseason does not arrive with cinders in his hair and a straw suitcase in his freckled paw but strolls into the carpeted, air-conditioned big-league clubhouse with a calfskin flight bag over his shoulder (and a Kurt Vonnegut paperback in the bag), where he is greeted by some teammates who played college ball with him or against him a year or two earlier in southern California. Over in the corner, the club's famous slugger, having just prolonged his slump by going 0 for 5 in a nationally televised game, now abandons his attempt to find surcease in transcendental meditation and suddenly seizes his hair-dryer and bashes it to smithereens against the wall. The manager, dressing in his office, asks a writer about the commotion, smiles and shakes his head, then slaps a little cologne on his ungrizzled cheeks and steps into his fawn leisure suit. His telephone rings: the general manager wants him to stop by upstairs for a minute to hear about the latest meeting with the personal agent of the angry (and still unsigned) famous slugger. If these contemporary patterns are startling, it is probably only because they contrast so vividly with the images of baseball's dramatis personae that most of us memorized in our youth. Over the years, sometimes reluctantly, sometimes willingly, I have gradually given up my boyhood impressions of baseball stars, and of baseball veterans and owners and writers, until only one old portrait remains. In this scene, a man sits alone on a splintery plank bleacher seat, with a foot cocked up on the row in front of him and his chin resting on one hand as he gazes intently at some young ballplayers in action on a bumpy, weed-strewn country ballfield. He sits motionless in the hot sunshine, with a shapeless canvas hat cocked over his eyes. At last, responding to something on the field not perceptible to the rest of us, he takes out a little notebook and writes a few words in it, and then replaces it in his windbreaker pocket. The players steal a glance at the lone stranger as they come in from the field at the end of a half inning; the managers pretend to ignore him. Nobody knows his name, but everybody recognizes him, for he is a figure of profound, almost occult knowledge, with a great power over the future. He is a baseball scout.

I have often noticed scouts at spring-training games, where they appear in numbers and always seem to roost together, and now and then I have spotted one at a big-league park, but I never tried to penetrate their arcane company. This spring, it occurred to me that these brooding, silent birds might constitute another threatened species, and I decided to attempt some field studies. Several baseball friends advised me to look up Ray Scarborough, who is a regional and special-assignment scout for the California Angels. Scarborough, I was told, was a veteran field man, with a high reputation for his baseball knowledge and his exceptional independence of judgment. He had been a member of the outstanding scouting staff put together by Harry Dalton, who was responsible in great part for assembling the formidable Baltimore teams that dominated the

American League in the late nineteen sixties and early seventies. Dalton had moved along to the Angels in 1971 to take the pivotal general manager's position, and soon thereafter he sent for Ray Scarborough and five other stalwarts of his Baltimore G-2. Early in May, I reached Scarborough by telephone at his home in Mount Olive, North Carolina, and proposed myself as a traveling companion on his next safari. Scarborough, who talks in an attractive Tarheel legato, responded with such alacrity and friendliness that it occurred to me for the first time that the life of a baseball scout might be a lonely one. He told me that I had caught him in a rare moment at home during the busiest part of his year—the weeks just prior to organized baseball's annual June talent draft—during which he was scouting free agents: high-school and college players who appeared promising and were about to graduate or otherwise surrender their amateur athletic status. He was leaving soon to look over a young pitching prospect in Kentucky and another in Michigan, and he invited me to come scouting with him.

Two days later, as I waited by the gate in the Louisville airport where Ray Scarborough's inbound morning flight had been announced, I began to wonder how I would recognize him. I remembered him as a big, hardworking, right-handed curveball pitcher with the Washington Senators—and later the Red Sox and the Yankees—but that had been a good twenty-five years back. I needn't have worried. Scarborough is a heavy, energetic, deep-chested man, with an exuberant nose (his baseball contemporaries called him Horn), curly black hair, and a sunburst smile, and the moment I spotted him among the arriving passengers my baseball unconscious offered up some instant corroboration: a younger Ray Scarborough, in baggy old-fashioned baseball pants, wheeling and firing on the mound; Scarborough in an old-style, low-crowned baseball cap emblazoned with a big "W," staring out at me in black-and-white from some ancient sports page. We greeted each other and retrieved his bags, and in a few minutes we were in our rented wheels, rolling south through some lovely, soft-green Kentucky hill country, and Scarborough had made me feel that we were already old friends. He told me that we were headed for Elizabethtown, some forty miles away, to see a young pitcher named Tim Brandenburg, a lefty who would be starting that afternoon for his Elizabethtown High School team in a state district tournament game. I asked Ray how he had heard about Brandenburg (I had in mind a whispered midnight telephone call from a back-country baseball sleuth, or a scribbled note from some old teammate of Scarborough's now buried in the boonies), and then I learned that scouting, like everything else in baseball, is undergoing some revolutionary changes.

The twenty-four big-league clubs are rivals in a narrow and intensely competitive business arena, and until very recently the proudest emblems of their independence were probably their enormous scouting staffs. The 1974 edition of the *Baseball Blue Book*, which is the business directory of the game, listed the names and clubs of 659 scouts—or 59 more than the total number of players carried on major-league rosters. A few of these were part-timers, or "bird dogs" (who are paid a fee only when a player they have spotted is signed to a contract), but each club was carrying somewhere between twenty and thirty full-time scouts, whose rather modest salaries and rather sizable travel expenses added up to a very considerable item on the corporate books. In 1965, Branch Rickey estimated that the scouting expenses of the twenty clubs of that time came to at least five million dollars, and if the figure is extended by a decade of inflation and the addition of four expansion teams, the bottom-line scouting figure must have reached at least seven and a half million dollars. This is a high price even for top-level corporate intelligence, and, reluctantly but inevitably, the owners voted in 1974 to establish a centralized scouting force. This body, the Major League Scouting Bureau, which is now in its second year of a three-year initial contract, deploys a total of sixty-nine scouts, who work under the direction of Jim Wilson, the former general manager of the

Milwaukee Brewers. Operating out of Newport Beach, California, it issues computerized scouting reports on every free-agent prospect in high-school and college ball; the reports, which are brought up to date at intervals as fresh scouting data come in, are sent to all the clubs that subscribe to the service. Conformity is not a distinguishing characteristic of baseball owners, and so far six clubs—the Dodgers, Mets, Phillies, Cardinals, Giants, and Padres—have stubbornly passed up the Bureau and are going along with their old costly but independent intelligence apparatuses. The world-champion Cincinnati Reds and the Boston Red Sox are subscribers but have so far also retained their full private rosters of scouts. Most of the other clubs have cut back extensively on their scouting staffs. (Charles Finley's pinchpenny Oakland A's got along with four non-Bureau scouts last year.) The Angels, who listed twenty-two scouts before the advent of the Bureau, now carry fifteen, of whom six (including Ray Scarborough) are full-timers. Most of his springtime travels, Ray told me, were for the purpose of "cross-checking"—that is, evaluating an apparently thorough but anonymous MLSB report on free-agent players, whose qualifications had also gone out to seventeen rival clubs. We were on our way to cross-check Tim Brandenburg.

"It's changed now, because I don't know who wrote the report we have on Brandenburg," Scarborough said. "The Bureau scouts came from the different clubs, and they're experienced men, but in the old days you always knew the man in your organization who had written a report, and you knew if he was conservative or the other way, so you could make a pretty good evaluation. There was an intimacy to it that made for group confidence and good decisions. It's different now, and cross-checking is more important than ever, especially with the high-rated prospects, so you try to get as many people as possible in your organization to see them. As you know, in the annual June draft of free agents the club that finished last the year before gets to pick first, and the club that finished next to last picks second. That's the way it goes until six or seven hundred names are disposed of—sometimes even more. We pick sixth next month. But the real talent in free agents never runs very deep—some baseball people think it drops way off after the first seven or eight names—and you just can't make a mistake in your two top choices, because then you have to wait till next year. Those first two or three draft picks we make next month have to be *right*, and that means that the scouts who have seen them need thorough judgment. If you see a good-looking high-school player who isn't throwing well or running well on the day you happen to be there, you have to find out why. You don't want a kid knocked out of your thinking for one bad day. But if there's something wrong, if you have some kind of doubt, you'd better go back and check that doubt.

"I think almost anybody can recognize the tools. You or me or the popcorn man can see if a boy is throwing hard or making pretty good contact at the plate. The hard part about free-agent scouting is being able to project. What will this pitcher be like in five years? Will he throw faster? Will he have a better curve? You check his build, and let's say you see narrow shoulders and heavy legs. Will he develop, or will that condition prevail? Jim Kaat was a frail, skinny kid, but he grew with his ability and became a huge man. In the end, I think, size is much less important with a pitcher than a good, loose arm and that good body action. You see a Nolan Ryan, and he's jumping at you off that mound. With a seventeen- or eighteen-year-old pitcher, you hope for a good fastball rather than a first-rate curve, because the curve can be taught but the fastball may never come. Even then you can't be sure. Tom Seaver had an indifferent fastball when he was young, and now look at him! Projecting a youngster isn't easy. What you really want to know about him is how much *stomach* does he have. If you could cut a boy open and look at his heart and guts, and then go home with him and see what kind of preparations he makes for a game, why then . . . then . . ." Scarborough laughed and shook his head. "Then my job would be a whole lot easier."

Scarborough, who was driving, was wearing a plaid sports jacket, a navy-blue polo shirt, yellow twill pants, and black alligator shoes. I had entertained some fears that considerations of security might make him cautious in talking to me about his profession, but for the most part he sounded like any good traveling man talking about the special demands of his territory and the splendors of his line.

I asked him to tell me about some of the top prospects he had scouted so far this year.

"Well, let's see," he said, sitting up a little straighter at the wheel. "There's a boy in Springfield, Ohio, named Glass—Timothy Glass, a catcher. He goes about two hundred and fifteen pounds. Runs real well—gets to first in about four-two. A good, strong arm and good hands. He hits with power, but he uppercuts and swings through a lot of pitches. He wears contact lenses, and there has to be some question about his eyesight. But he's almost a complete player. I think he'll be gone by the time it comes around to us, and we're only number six. Then, we've checked a pitcher named Richard Whaley, from Jackonsville, North Carolina. I've seen him four times already, and I like what I've seen. He's a left-hander, six-two, sort of lean and willowy, with an excellent rotation on his curve. And there's another pitcher down in Hialeah High School—Hialeah, Florida, that is. He's a big right-hander named Ben Grassbeck or Gribseck—something like that [the name is Grzybek]. He goes about six-six, and he can throw *hard*. He broke his foot a few weeks ago, and that might cost him a lot of money."

I said to Scarborough that it seemed to me he had already covered a good deal of ground in this young baseball season.

"Well, I have to see about fifty free agents in the spring," he said. "Fifty boys who can play a little. I'm flying more than I used to, so maybe it's a little less tiring. Up to a couple of years ago, I was doing about twenty-five or thirty thousand miles a year. Just the week before last I drove up to Baltimore, then to

Richmond and Norfolk, and then back up to Trenton, New Jersey. About seventeen hundred miles. It takes a lot out of you, and sometimes it can be sort of a lonesome job. Once in a while, I take my wife with me, if it's a local trip—to Tidewater or someplace like that. We get these Bureau scouting reports so late that you've got to jump if you want to catch a boy. If he's not in a tourney or a playoff or something, you might miss him altogether."

As Scarborough was saying this, it came to me that he had meant twenty-five or thirty thousand miles *by automobile*—miles he had put in at the wheel in search of one summer's young ballplayers. I looked out my window for a while at some Kentucky farms and silos and tried to imagine this. Then I asked Ray which players among the current major-leaguers he had scouted or signed.

"People always ask that," he said. "The truth is, what with the draft, almost nobody in scouting can take that kind of credit anymore."

"What about bird dogs?" I asked.

Ray laughed and said, "Well, it's supposed to be sort of crude to call them that now. A few years back, they suddenly all became 'commission scouts.' I guess there are still a few of them left. They're simply the most dedicated men—the best baseball fans—in the whole game. They do what they do out of love for the game. They don't make any money at it—probably they lose money, even after they've picked up that little commission for a boy who gets signed. They can be high-school coaches, newspaper reporters, schoolteachers—anybody. A friend of mine named Mack Arnette was just about your perfect commission scout. He was the sales manager at Station WWNC, in Asheville. He had good judgment, and I had complete confidence in him. We signed quite a few of his boys. I don't know how active he is now.

"The bird dogs were part of a whole network of contacts that each territorial scout put together, and the moment they sent him word about some good-looking boy, he'd hustle right out and take a look himself, and then tell his regional supervisor about him. The territorial scout is what this business is all about. If the club signed up somebody he'd seen, he could always think, 'That's *my* player.' A lot of them have gone out of business since the Bureau, and it's a real shame.

"Well, as I was saying, it's a group sort of thing now, and, of course, it's just luck if your club gets to draft a particular player you're after—even some kid you've been downright enthusiastic about. The only players in the majors right now who I've had anything to do with came up in the Baltimore organization, because there hasn't been time yet for the Angels' draft choices I've seen to make it up to the top. With Baltimore, I saw Paul Mitchell, that young pitcher who just went to Oakland in the Jackson trade. He's a real live one—a regular bulldog. And there's Don Hood, who's with the Indians now. And that big kid who's doing all that good work with the Orioles now—I think he's even leading the league in earned-run average. . . ." He paused and frowned. "Seems like I can't remember *anybody's* name some days," he murmured. "Garland! Wayne Garland, of course. Listen, I first saw him in Connie Mack ball, over in Jackson, Tennessee. He was just about to pitch, and he was drinking a Pepsi and eating the biggest hot dog you ever saw, but he pitched a good game that night. A big right-hander, and he could really hump up and throw that ball. Harry Dalton and Dee Phillips came and had a look at him, and when we got him in the draft we gave him what he wanted. I think he got about thirty thousand. You've got to sign those good ones when you can—there aren't enough good arms available.

"I'll tell you a funny thing. The finest left-handed pitcher I ever scouted in a high school is with the Angels right now—Frank Tanana. But I didn't have a single thing to do with his being with us, because I was scouting for Baltimore then, and we didn't get him. He was pitching in a high-school league in Detroit where they only gave you three balls and two strikes, and those batters were *mesmerized!* He had stuff and poise, and an outstanding change of pace, and his attitude was just about perfect. He really knew how to pitch."

Ray bent forward and peered up at the sky, which had become gray and threatening. "Now, don't tell me," he said. "Yes, it's going to rain, sure as the devil. Do you know, that's the number-one occupational hazard of this profession. You have to wait over a day, and that means you often miss another game and another prospect. It's a real problem."

Ray Scarborough is a cheerful man, and even the spattering of the first few raindrops on our windshield didn't make him gloomy for long. "At least it's easier to get to a boy than it sometimes was in the old days," he said. "Back in 1959 or 1960, when I was just starting, I found a pitcher named James Barrier, who lived way up on top of a mountain in Jonas Ridge, North Carolina. I had to walk the last couple of miles up. He lived in a little old house with his parents and a whole lot of brothers and sisters, and he walked I don't know how many miles to school every day. I saw him pitch a game on a field where it looked like they hadn't mowed the outfield for weeks, and they had a ground rule that a ball lost in the tall grass behind the outfielders was a double, but if you lost it in front of you it was a homer, because you should have kept your eye on it. That's the truth. We signed him and gave him a bonus so he could go to Appalachian State Teachers College, and he went on and won about fifteen games one year with Newton-Conover, in the Western Carolina League. He never made it into Class A ball, and he quit after about four years, but I imagine he was always a kind of an example to a lot of kids he played with. The last I heard of him, he'd got a Ph.D. from Clemson and was head of biology at Baptist College, down in Charleston, South Carolina. I always thought that was one of the best signings I ever made."

•

WE CAME to Elizabethtown and found the high school, but it was still raining lightly when we pulled into the parking lot next to the wet green ballfield, and it had begun to look like a wasted journey. There was nobody in sight but a little group of middle-aged men in golf caps and assorted rain gear who were standing together and glumly looking up at the sky—more baseball scouts, it turned out. They greeted Ray warmly, and he introduced them to me: Floyd Baker, of the Twins; Ray Holton, of the Scouting Bureau; Joe Bowen, the director of scouting for the Reds; and Nick Kamzic, who is one of the Angels' supervisors of scouting. All of them had come to see Tim Brandenburg. Kamzic and Scarborough moved a few steps away from the others and compared notes on their recent travels and discoveries (Kamzic was optimistic about Steve Trout, a young left-handed pitcher from South Holland, Illinois, who is the son of the old Tiger hurler Dizzy Trout), but soon the rain began to come down harder, and we all ran for shelter. Back in our car, Ray opened a briefcase and handed me his copy of the Bureau's scouting report on Brandenburg—a single mimeographed sheet, with Brandenburg's vital statistics printed out in drab computeresque capitals, and then two parallel columns of figures under the headings "PRES" and "FUT." On the left-hand side of the page, there was a rating key with figures ranging from eight ("OUTSTANDING") down to two ("POOR"), and then a column of categories marked "FASTBALL," "CURVE," "CONTROL," "CHANGE OF PACE," and (bracketed together) "SLIDER, KNUCKLEBALL, OTHER," followed by "POISE," "BB INSTINCTS," "AGGRESSIVENESS." Brandenburg's "PRES" ratings were all fours and fives, except for a zero in the bracketed entry; in the "FUT" column the ratings had all gone up to five, and his curveball had become a six ("ABOVE AVE."). Down at the bottom of the page I read: "AVE. MAJOR LEAGUE CURVEBALL AT THIS TIME & CAN THROW IT FOR A STRIKE WHEN HE WANTS TO. GOOD FIELDER. HAS FULL ARM ACTION. FOLLOWS THROUGH GOOD & USES BODY TO ITS FULLEST. ONLY WEAKNESS I CAN SEE IS BELOW-AVE. MAJOR LEAGUE FASTBALL. HOWEVER, I DO PROJECT A MAJOR LEAGUE FASTBALL IN FUTURE." Then, under "SUMMATION & SIGNABILITY," I saw

"HAS THE TOOLS TO BECOME A GOOD MAJOR LEAGUE PITCHER. . . . MUST ALSO COMBAT COLLEGE OFFERS." The report depressed me; I felt as if I had accidentally glanced into a brightly lit window across the street and then had secretly begun to watch the activities of a stranger there.

The rain was letting up, but a fresh wind was buffeting the trees beyond the outfield fence. Scarborough wiped the inside of our foggy windshield with his handkerchief. "Golly Pete," he said. "If I was young Mr. Brandenburg, I'd be a little nervous right now, waiting all this time. There's more pressure than you can hardly imagine on a young player in a situation like this. Usually, there aren't too many folks in the stands at a high-school game, and he can see those scouts all sitting there, with their little hats on. Come *on*, rain—just quit, now."

The rain did stop, and half an hour later we were sitting on some damp bright-yellow aluminum bleacher seats, and the stands had suddenly filled up with spectators: high-school kids, most of them, in jeans and overalls and emblazoned T-shirts and floppy far-out hats and shiny rain jackets and big boots—high-school kids anywhere. Everyone was clapping for the game to begin. Directly in front of me, an older man wearing a camouflage-spotted hunting cap turned around and said, "If Brandenburg wasn't pitching, I'd be off fishin' right now." Then the players for the visiting team—North Hardin High, from Radcliff, Kentucky—ran out on the wet field, wearing electric-blue shirts and white pants (the teams had drawn for the home-team last-up privilege, and the visitors had won), and the game began at last—not much of a game, at that, because the Elizabethtown Panthers (gold shirts with a gigantic purple ventral "E" and striped white pants) immediately batted around, scoring five runs, thanks in part to a bases-loaded single by Tim Brandenburg. Ray watched all this with considerable impatience, casting glances from time to time at the low, hurrying clouds just above us. The teams changed sides, and Brandenburg sauntered very slowly out to the mound. Some of the girls in the stands called "Tim! Tim!

Tim!" in unison. Brandenburg had curly hair and a Roman nose; he didn't look heavily muscled, but he had the sloping shoulders and long arms of a pitcher. I could not remember how long it had been since I had seen a ballplayer who looked so young. Throwing left-handed, and pitching, for some reason, with no windup at all, he ran up a full count on the first batter and then struck him out with a sharp-breaking curve.

"Look at that," Ray murmured in a puzzled way. "Why is he pitching like that, I wonder. Why doesn't he wind up? It's like he's playing catch out there. . . . Well, I see he's bowlegged —there aren't many real athletes who aren't, they tell me."

Brandenburg struck out the second batter and retired the third on an easy grounder.

"Yes, that's a pretty good curveball," Ray said to me. "It has a good, tight spin on it. I think if he'd push off the mound he'd get more action on it. But it's hard to see a guy with his build getting much faster. He can pitch in the minors, that's for sure."

Elizabethtown kept scoring runs, and Tim Brandenburg kept dismissing the enemy batters without effort, and after three innings the score had gone to 8–0. Nick Kamzic climbed up the stands and squeezed in next to Ray, and after Brandenburg surrendered a single—the first hit of the day for North Hardin—he said, "He seems to have more drive when he pitches off the stretch. He drops down and pushes off better."

"Yes, but he may have trouble holding men on," Ray said. "I mean, the way he rocks back instead of coming straight on down. But that's correctable."

Brandenburg gave up a foul and then rubbed up the new ball with great deliberation. He looked around at the crowd in rather imperious fashion.

"Hey, now!" Ray said, grinning. "He's a showman. He's a candidate for *New York*. I'll tell you, if I had an eight-run lead and it looked like rain, I'd be firin' that ball. But this kid has a pretty good arm. You want to make him throw harder, but you can't. His best stuff is up out of the strike zone. When he comes down with it, he loses velocity. If he could get some mustard on it, on top of his breaking stuff, he'd be in pretty good shape. I think it's that no windup. You want to teach a kid like this to drive that lead shoulder toward the catcher's mitt. That makes the ball come in low, and we have a low strike zone now."

All this was perfectly evident to me as soon as Ray pointed it out. I had the curious feeling that I was listening to a brilliant English instructor explicating some famous novel or play. I thought I had known some of the passages by heart—known them almost too well—but now I began to hear different rhythms and truths. An old text had become fresh and exciting again.

"This kid is pretty advanced in most areas," Ray went on, "but you always look for places where a boy can be improved." He paused, and then, almost to himself, he murmured, "You always want them to be better."

The game ended—it was a seven-inning affair—with Elizabethtown on top by 9–0, and some of the young people in the stands ran out on the field and stood around Tim Brandenburg in a happy circle. He had given up two hits and struck out seventeen batters. I had begun to play scout, of course, and had become hard to please, and it was not until Scarborough and I were in our car and on the way back to Louisville that it came to me that Tim Brandenburg was almost surely the best high-school pitcher I had ever seen.

I asked Ray what he thought, and he remained silent for some time. "I'm thinking what I'll write on my report," he said at last. "Overall, the boy has a chance to pitch. He's not an outstanding prospect, but he has a good opportunity. Off what I saw today, I'd say he might go in the fourth or fifth round of the draft. If you had to, you might take him in the third round. He looks sort of like the kind of pitcher that tops out at about the AA level, because of his lack of velocity. That curve is a good one, but he might have to develop another pitch—a slip pitch or something—if he's going to make it to the majors. In the end, it will probably depend on his intelligence and how much he wants to make it to the top."

I asked Scarborough what was meant by the word "signability," which I had seen on the Bureau's report, and he pointed out that although each club had exclusive rights to a player it acquired in the draft, it still had to negotiate financial terms with that player. If they couldn't agree, the player would once more become a free agent and might be drafted all over again—usually in a redraw that forms part of another draft each year, in January—by a different club, or even by the same club. "If you think a boy is worth fifteen thousand dollars and he and his parents and his coach think he's worth fifty, *that's* a signability problem," Scarborough said. "More players than you'd think don't get signed—especially the high-school kids, because they can always choose to go off to college instead. Sometimes, if you're lucky, you can sign half of them. Your main effort is always to sign your top five or six draft picks. It seems unusual, but a good college player is always more signable than a high-school boy, because he has no place else to go after he graduates. He's got to come to you. One real headache for us is the salary levels for these young players while they're beginning to work their way up through minor-league ball. Down in Class A or lower, they can get only five hundred a month in their first year, and up to seven hundred in Double A. And the per-diem is strictly hamburger money. I think we lose a lot of prospects right there.

"Of course, signing a player you want real bad is absolutely different from what it was back before the clubs pushed through the draft system, about ten or twelve years ago, after they'd all spent so much money on those bonus babies. If this was back then, and we wanted this boy, I'd have made it a point to get to know his parents on this trip, so that when the time came we might get in there ahead of the other clubs. That used to be about the liveliest part of it all, especially with a really and truly top prospect, and it was downright enjoyable sometimes what you had to do."

Scarborough grinned and slapped the steering wheel with one hand. "I'll never forget signing a fellow named Cotton Clayton, way back in the early sixties," he said. "He was an outfielder, and he could do it *all*. He was a valuable piece of property. Harry Dalton wanted him, and Lee MacPhail, who was our GM at Baltimore then—he wanted him. I made an appointment to see Clayton down in his hometown of Henderson, North Carolina, and I checked into the local motel. You had to make an appointment, because just about every other club was anxious to get him, too, but especially the Cardinals. I made damn sure to get him to come up to my motel room, and I swore to myself he'd never get out until I'd signed him. I also made sure that Harry and Lee, up in Baltimore, were ready on the other end of the phone. This was in the bonus days, you understand, and I had about fifty thousand dollars at my disposal, but when Clayton came in and sat down I just didn't know how to get around to the subject at hand."

Ray laughed delightedly. "Well, sir, we talked about rabbits and about farming and about basketball—everything but money. He was one tough bargainer. When we finally got to it, we began around twenty-five thousand, and every time he'd tilt the pot a little I'd shake my head and say, 'Well, let me talk to Harry,' and I'd go off and make a telephone call. We talked and talked, and we got awful tired in that room, and finally he said, 'Well, I can't take one penny less than fifty thousand.' I pulled back—sort of recoiled—and said, 'You just knocked me out of the box,' but I said that we needed a left-hand-hitting outfielder *so* bad that I'd make one last call to Lee MacPhail and see if I could talk him into it. I said, 'If I can somehow do that, will you sign for ten thousand a year for five years, with a starting salary of a thousand dollars a month, and will you sign *before you leave this room?*'

"Well, he squirmed and squirmed, because, of course, he'd

promised the Cardinals and some of the other scouts he'd never sign anything without talking to them first. But he finally said yes, and I called Lee, and Lee whispered 'Sign him!' and I pulled out the contract—which I'd had ready all along, of course—and he signed, and I shook his hand and checked out of the motel and went home. And do you know that the next man who checked into that exact room that day was Eddie Lyons, of the Cardinals? He wanted Clayton just as bad as we did, only he'd stopped off on the way to sign a third baseman down there he'd liked. He got my room, but I'd got his outfielder!"

I couldn't remember having heard of Cotton Clayton in big-league ball, and I asked Ray what had happened to him.

"Cotton Clayton ended up playing in the International League for about four or five years," he said. "He had some bad breaks along the way—that's the way it is sometimes—and he never did get to the majors. Now he has a tire business down in Henderson—along with the farm that I bought with that fifty thousand."

•

THE NEXT MORNING, Ray Scarborough and I caught an early flight to Detroit, where we would pick up another car and drive to Ypsilanti to scout a highly celebrated pitching prospect named Bob Owchinko, who played for Eastern Michigan University. During the flight, I asked Ray if he could remember when he himself had first been scouted. He told me he had grown up on a small farm in Mount Gilead, in central North Carolina. He was the fourth of six brothers (there was one sister), and all the Scarboroughs loved to play ball. Work on the farm was long and hard, but their father made a little diamond out behind the house, and there was time for some family baseball there in the evenings. Sometimes Ray and his next-older brother, Steve, would walk five miles in to town to play in a pickup game. Eventually, Ray was given an athletic scholarship to Rutherford Junior College, in the Carolina

Piedmont section, where another brother, Bill, was doing some coaching.

In the summer when Ray turned seventeen, a shiny black Cadillac rolled up to the Scarborough farm one day, and a man wearing a suit and tie stepped out. "It was a Cardinal scout named Pat Crawford," Ray said, "and he'd come to look me over. He was a real Dapper Dan, and I was *impressed.* 'Can you th'ow for me?' he asked, and I said yes, sir. But there wasn't anybody else at home right then, so we didn't know who I could throw *to.* I offered to throw to him, but he declined. Well, finally he pointed to a red clay bank off across the road and said, 'Son, how would you like to th'ow into that bank?' We paced off the distance and he took a white handkerchief out of his pocket and stuck it up in place on that bank with a little rock. Then he got some baseballs out of the trunk of the Cadillac, and I threw for about ten minutes at his old hanky. He must have liked what he saw, because he invited me to a Cardinals tryout camp in Charlotte. Mr. Rickey was there, and some others, and they picked three of us out of about a hundred or more, so I knew they thought I could play. But they only offered me sixty dollars a month, so I decided I wasn't ready to go into baseball yet."

Ray wanted to continue with college after his two years at Rutherford, but he knew he had to earn his way. He hoped to pick up some cash by playing in the semipro Coastal Plain League but was told that he was too small. "I only weighed about a hundred and twenty-eight, which wasn't big enough even for mumblety-peg," he said to me. "I finally hooked on with a town team in Aberdeen, North Carolina, in the Sand Hill League. We played ball two days and picked peaches the rest of the time. I got twelve dollars and fifty cents a week for playin' and pickin'. No bonus, no Social Security."

He stayed out of school that winter and worked as a carhop in a drive-in, but he had begun to grow, and the next spring—the spring of 1938—he was given a tryout with a team in Hickory, North Carolina, in the Carolina League.

"That was an outlaw league," Ray said. "You know—outside of regular organized baseball. It was just a string of teams from little cities like Concord and Gastonia and Kannapolis. Strictly semipro, but there were a lot of players I'd heard of—Art Shires and Packy Rogers and Prince Henry Oana—and we all got paid. Well, I won myself a job and, do you know, I actually pitched the opening game of the season for the Hickory Rebels, against Lenoir. I was just a squirt with a curve and a fastball, but I thought I was the biggest dog in town."

Ray's route to the big time was not quite arrowlike. Pitching with the Rebels won him an athletic scholarship to Wake Forest, and there he began to receive some attention from big-league scouts—famous men like Gene McCann, of the Yankees, and Paul Florence, of the Reds. He was treated to a special courtesy trip to Philadelphia, where he visited Shibe Park and shook hands with Connie Mack. Money and celebrity seemed to be in the offing, but Scarborough injured his arm while pitching in the fifth game of his senior year at Wake Forest, and the scouts suddenly disappeared. He took his degree and taught high school for a year, at Tabor City, North Carolina, while he waited for his arm to come around, and then signed on with Chattanooga, in the Class A Southern League, for a fifteen-hundred-dollar bonus—a fraction of the sum the scouts had been talking about before his injury. He was sent down to Selma, Alabama, in Class B, and there, at last, he began to win. He broke the league strikeout record there, came back to Chattanooga, and joined the Washington Senators in June 1942, just a month before his twenty-fifth birthday. "I'd finally made it off the farm," Ray said. He pitched in the majors until 1953.

•

EASTERN MICHIGAN is a rising power in college baseball, and the trim diamond and attractive little roofed grandstand that Ray Scarborough and I found in Ypsilanti that day were much more inviting than a lot of spring-training ball parks I could recall. We were there for a Mid-American Conference doubleheader between the Eastern Michigan Hurons and the Falcons, from Bowling Green State University, in Ohio. The home team was just finishing infield practice under a cloudy sky, and the Huron squad members, in white uniforms with green lettering, were ranged along the third-base line, where they gave some noisy cheers for each of their starting infielders as he whipped his last peg in to the catcher and trotted off the field. Football stuff. Ray Scarborough greeted some scouting friends and then sat down with a California colleague, Al Hollingsworth, who is also a special-assignment scout for the Angels, operating out of Texas. Hollingsworth has thick white hair, blue eyes, and a tanned, classic old-ballplayer's face, with crinkly lines around the eyes and mouth. If you were casting for the part of a veteran scout in a baseball movie, you would pick Al Hollingsworth.

"Hey, I hear we won last night!" he said to Ray. "Somebody told me. It was about 7–5."

Scarborough had been complaining that morning that it was often impossible on the road to pick up the results of Angels games from the West Coast, and he brightened at the news. (Angels victories had been rare in recent weeks; in fact, the club was dead last in the American League West.) "That's more like it," he said. "Who pitched?"

"All I heard was Alvarez hit a home run," Hollingsworth said. He told Ray he had just flown in from Denison, Texas, where he had seen a young pitcher named Darwin the day before. "He's about twenty years old, and he's comin' on," he said. "He threw about eighty-six, eighty-seven on the speed gun. He got ripped pretty good yesterday, though. He reminds you a little of a Granger or a Perzanowski. His arm's way over here, and his ball don't tail."

"I hear there's a catcher on this Bowling Green team," Ray said. "I don't recall his name, though."

"You got anything on a kid named Brown, in Indiana?"

Hollingsworth said. "All I have on him is a phone number."

And then the game began, and we all began to watch Bob Owchinko, who had brought us there. The Bureau scouting report on him had rated him a premium choice, with an above-average fastball, a curveball with a tight spin, a screwball, and a loose overhead arm action. He was a tall, solidly built left-hander, and he was using a full windup, with a high-kicking delivery and a long stride. He was hiding the ball well between pitches. He fanned the first two Bowling Green hitters, gave up a single to the catcher (whose name, it turned out, was Larry Owen), walked a batter, and then got the side out with another strikeout.

"A nice big boy," Ray murmured. "He's got heavy legs and sort of a big tail, but that never hurt Lolich, did it? Pitchers can get away with that better than others. I like the way this boy comes at the batter."

The stands were filling up, and Ray kept getting up to exchange greetings with more scouts as they took seats around us, in a companionable cluster directly behind home plate—Dick Teed and Brandy Davis, of the Phillies; Pat Gillick and Dave Yoakum, of the Yankees; Howie Haak (a famous name in scouting), of the Pirates; Syd Thrift, of the A's; Joe Bowen, of the Reds, who had been with us the day before in Elizabethtown. (If you were writing a baseball movie or a baseball novel, you would give your scouts names like these.) The scouts sat back quietly, some with their arms folded or a knee cocked up, and watched the field with motionless intensity. They looked like businessmen at a staff conference. Nobody seemed to be taking any notes.

I remarked that Owchinko appeared to be a good drawing card, and Ray said, "In the old days, you'd have had a *drove* of scouts at a game like this. They tell me the Bureau tries to discourage their men from being too close with any of the rest of us, because they're supposed to represent their clubs impartially, but I can't see how that's going to work. You just can't keep friendship out of scouting, because so many of these fellows have been buddies for years. A lot of us have played with each other or against each other, and we go back a long way together. It's a fraternity."

The teams changed sides, and the home-plate umpire—a short, dark-haired man, whose black suit was already stained with sweat and dust—walked back to the stands with his mask in one hand and chatted with the scouts. He poked a fore-finger through the wire of the foul screen and gravely shook fingers with Ray Scarborough.

"That's Tom Ravashiere," Ray said after the umpire had gone back to work. "He was a good ump in the International League for years and years. He's out of baseball now, but I guess he still does games like this. He lives around here some-place."

Both the teams on the field looked well trained and extremely combative, and the young players made up for their occasional mistakes with some eye-popping plays. At one point, Ow-chinko hustled off the mound, snatched up an attempted sac-rifice bunt, and whirled and threw the Falcon base runner out at second with a fiery peg. In the bottom of the same inning—the fourth—a Bowling Green outfielder made a div-ing, sliding catch on his belly in short center field, and then Owen, the catcher, threw out a base runner trying to steal second—threw him out a mile. The Falcon pitcher, whose name was Kip Young, was not quite in Owchinko's class, but he was putting up a battle, throwing a lot of low curves and showing good control. In the fifth, an Eastern Michigan threat was extinguished when the Bowling Green shortstop speared a line drive on his knees and converted it into a lightning double play at second, thus preserving the scoreless, eventful tie. Ray and the other scouts shook their heads and exchanged little smiles, enjoying it. The clouds had begun to break up, and the green of the outfield grass had turned light and glis-tening. Good game.

Owchinko had been striking out enemy batters in considerable numbers, but now, in the sixth, he seemed to lose his concentration, walking the first two men. Then there was an error behind him on an easy double-play grounder, and a moment later a Bowling Green outfielder named Jeff Groth whacked a long drive over the left-field fence for a grand-slam home run. Silence in the stands—a very brief silence, it turned out, for in the home half the Eastern Michigan hitters came alive, with a walk, a ground-rule double, and a two-run single, and then, after a couple of mistakes by the visitors, a culminating three-run homer to center by the Eastern Michigan right fielder, Thom Boutin. The whole Huron team came out to the third-base foul line to welcome him home, and the student fans around us screeched ecstatically. Owchinko walked the leadoff man in the top of the seventh and seemed to be struggling ("Come *on*, Chink!" the fans pleaded), but the tying run died at second, and the Hurons had won it, 5–4.

"I don't know if he got tired, or what, but his velocity wasn't good at the end," Ray said. "I'd like to have seen if he could get two strikes on a man and then break off the curveball. When he gave up that homer, he'd got in the position of trying to throw strikes past the batter, instead of trying to get the man out. He threw that pitch sort of easy—a mistake pitch. But that's normal. I try never to notice if a pitcher gives up a hit. It's his motion I'm watching. Same thing with a hitter—I don't care if he hits, as long as he's making contact and swings well. But this was a good performance by Owchinko. You could make a few mechanical changes with his delivery. Being sort of big-assed, he stops his right leg sometimes, so his body can't open up, and he has to throw from over *here*. But he's got a chance to make a pretty good pitcher. I think this boy might go in the first round. I'd love for us to get him along about the second round, but he won't be around that long."

Most of the scouts had disappeared, but we waited for the second game of the doubleheader, because Ray wanted to have a look at the next Eastern Michigan pitcher—a junior named Bob Welch. During the interval, I wandered out beyond the left-field stands and found Bob Owchinko lying on his stomach on the grass, with a towel around his neck. His face was red and he was streaming perspiration. I asked him if he had noticed the scouts behind home during the game.

"Yeah, I saw them there, staring me in the face," he said. "They don't bother me—I know what they're here for."

"Do you care about which club will draft you next month?" I said.

"I've been waiting for a career in major-league ball since I was eleven, and now it's here," he said. "It's about time. I don't care where I go, but I do like hot weather."

The second game began, and after Bob Welch had thrown about six pitches Ray Scarborough exclaimed, "There's a good-looking body! He's almost got these boys overmatched already."

Welch, a right-hander, looked even taller and stronger than Bob Owchinko, and he threw with a kind of explosive elegance. There was something commanding about him.

"See out there?" Ray said. "See him cocking his wrist like that behind his back? That can strain your elbow. It could hurt him. He's cutting the ball a little—turning his hand—which takes off some velocity. If he did it a little more, it would be a slider. I wish he'd turn loose—he's got a real good arm."

Welch fired two fastballs, fanning the batter.

"*There!*" Ray said. "I like that! He comes off that mound like he means business." He stood up, smiling with pleasure. "I believe I'll be making a trip back here a year from now. Maybe we better go quick, before I get dissatisfied with the whole 1976 draft."

•

RAY SCARBOROUGH and I parted in Detroit that evening. I went home to New York, and he flew to Madison, Wisconsin, where he planned to watch a prospect from the University of Michigan in a game the next day. What he met there, however, was rain. Early in June, Ray went out to Anaheim and, in company with Harry Dalton and Walter Shannon (the Angels' director of scouting) and Nick Kamzic and Al Hollingsworth and nine other Angel scouts and executives, participated in four days of intensive discussions and appraisals of all the high-school and college free agents that they had scouted and cross-checked and talked about. The draft, which came on June 8, was conducted in the baseball commissioner's office, in New York, over an open telephone hookup to all twenty-four clubs. The Houston Astros, with first pick, chose a much admired left-handed pitching star from Arizona State University named Floyd Bannister. The Angels' first choice, on the sixth pick, was a power-hitting outfielder named Kenny Landreaux, also from Arizona State. Tim Brandenburg went to the Kansas City Royals in the second round —the forty-second player in the country to be drafted. The Angels did not bid on him. As for Bob Owchinko, he went to the San Diego Padres on the fifth pick in the first round. A little later in June, at the National Collegiate Athletic Association championships in Omaha, the Eastern Michigan ball team went all the way into the finals before losing to the University of Arizona. On the way, they upset the favorites, Arizona State, thanks to a seven-hitter thrown by Owchinko.

I thought about Ray Scarborough while the draft was going on, and later I looked up the names of some of the players he had scouted. Timothy Glass, the catcher from Springfield, Ohio, went to the Indians in the first round. Ben Grzybek, the pitcher from Hialeah, was the first-round choice of the Royals —thus becoming a potential future teammate of Brandenburg's. Richard Whaley, the willowy left-hander from Jacksonville, North Carolina, had developed a sore arm late in the spring, which probably dropped him in the draft; he was picked by the Phillies in the third round—No. 65 nationally. None of the free agents Ray had talked to me about with such enthusiasm went to the Angels. Larry Owen, the Bowling

Green catcher we had seen in Ypsilanti, was chosen by the Angels in the eighteenth round. Seven hundred and eighty-six players were drafted in all, most of whom would perform only briefly in professional ball, if at all.

•

I CAUGHT up with Ray Scarborough again on the evening of July 5, in another baseball setting: we were part of a crowd of 60,942 spectators at a holiday game between the Phillies and the Dodgers, in Philadelphia's Veterans Stadium. Scarborough was there in a different scouting capacity—evaluating players on both clubs (but especially the Phillies) as potential material for postseason trades with the Angels. This process, which is known as professional scouting, goes on through the middle and latter stages of the regular season and eventually produces scouting reports for Harry Dalton on all major-league players and a considerable number of Class AAA minor-league players as well. (Another kind of scouting—team scouting—collects tactical information about enemy hitters and pitchers to help a club prepare for an upcoming season or series; team scouting before the autumn playoffs and the World Series produces the crucial "book" on the opposition.) Ray looked younger and more rested than he had during our trip in May, and he told me that he had been taking it easy since the draft, putting in a lot of time working in his vegetable garden at home in Mount Olive. He had also caught up on his own business interests, which include real estate, a small tobacco farm, a bank directorship, and a share in a musical-instrument-and-records business.

I asked him how he felt about the Angels' draft, and he said, "Well, you always want to be associated with your club's top man, of course. I did see Bob Ferris, who we picked in the second round, and a fellow named Porter we took a little farther down, but otherwise we didn't get any of the boys I'd checked. The only fruits of your work are the boys who end up with your own organization, and the luck of the draft can sure knock you down. You work like hell all year, and then . . . Sure, I felt bad—I felt *punctured*—but on the other hand, when I listened to what our people had to say about Ken Landreaux at our meeting in Anaheim, I had confidence that he was a better first choice for us than Glass or Owchinko or the others I'd seen. Next year, it might be the other way around. You know, a scout can go for years and years and never get in on a top pick. You take Mace Brown, of the Red Sox. Mace is a real fine scout, and he went for I don't know how many years without much luck, and I remember once he said, 'All this work for nothing,' or something like that. But he hung on, and then he came up with Jim Rice, who was a first-round pick, and then he had a great kid named Otis Foster last year."

I said that this sounded like more patience and optimism than most men could be expected to bring to their work, and Ray nodded. We were sitting behind home plate at Veterans Stadium, and he looked slowly around at the glittering, brightly lit field and the noisy throng filling every seat in the circular, triple-decked park. "I think it has to be a private thing," he said at last. "You don't go around saying it, but I'm *devoted* to the club I work for. It was downright satisfying being connected with that winning Baltimore outfit, and I do like working for a man like Harry Dalton. I'm interested in being with him and Walter Shannon and the rest, trying to make California the same kind of organization. But first of all it's the baseball. Those airports and motels and cars are pretty taxing on a man, and I keep thinking I'm going to ease off one of these years, but I never quite do it. It's love of the game of baseball that keeps me at it. I still feel there's no greater reward a young man can achieve than attaining the major leagues as a player. I truly mean that. I don't care what the price is, I think it's worth it. Nothing can beat it."

The Philadelphia fans had turned out in cheerful expectation of another slugging spree by their powerful young team, which had already opened up a nine-game lead in the National

League East, but as happens so often in baseball, things turned out quite the other way, with the Dodgers moving off smartly to a three-run lead and the Phillies going down in rather helpless fashion before the pitching of the Dodger starter, Burt Hooton. Ray occasionally made a brief note on his program, but I had the impression that he was watching the proceedings with less intensity than he had displayed at the earlier games I shared with him. He told me that he would stay with the Phillies for four or five games—until he had seen their full pitching rotation and, with any luck, most of their bench as well. He said that in professional scouting he operated on the premise that any player, including a team's top stars, might become available for a trade but that in practice, of course, the second-liners or players having a bad year were the ones he paid the most attention to.

"Evaluating the physical attributes of a major-leaguer isn't very hard," he said. "It's when he begins to change that you have a tougher time of it. Is he washed up? Is he not on good terms with the manager? Is he getting a divorce? Does he have an injury we don't know about? You stay until you find out, and in that time you may hardly ever see him in a game. A man who's showing a big change for the better is sometimes just as mysterious. Can you tell me why this Bob Boone is having such a great year with the Phillies? He's batting thirty or forty points over his best, and he's doing everything right. Maybe it's their other catcher, Johnny Oates, coming on the club last year and playing so well—maybe Boone needed that push. Maybe it's just being on a winning club, or maybe he's suddenly grown up, found himself. Now, over on the Dodgers you see this catcher Yeager, who's never been much of a hitter. The club has just traded away Joe Ferguson, who did a lot of the catching, and you wonder what kind of effect it will have on Yeager. Will he begin to hit better? Will he pick up because he feels less threatened? All the time, you keep thinking, 'What about this man? Can this man help the Angels? Does he fit our plans?' I'm here to improve the club I'm working for. Right now, our prime needs are catching, a topnotch center fielder, and a home-run-hitting first baseman. I may not find anybody in those positions who's available for a trade, but you don't always have to have a perfect fit. Sometimes one trade can set up another. You keep watching and listening."

In the third inning, Ray made admiring noises about a fine play and peg to first by Mike Schmidt, the Phillies' third baseman. "In Elizabethtown, Kentucky, that would have been a double," he said. "You have to remember, baseball in the big leagues always looks a lot easier." A few minutes later, Greg Luzinski, the big Philadelphia left fielder, was a bit sluggish going after a drive to left by Reggie Smith, and because the center fielder, Garry Maddox, failed to back up the play, Smith wound up with a triple. "There's no excuse in the world for that," Ray said.

The Phillies' starter, the veteran Jim Lonborg, appeared to be struggling. "His arm looks a little slow tonight," Ray said. "He's not using his fastball at all—just sliders and that fork-ball, or whatever it is. That's what you have to do, but it's awful hard to win with just two pitches."

The game wore on, and the great crowd, with nothing at all to cheer about, fell into an irritable silence. Bobby Tolan, the Philadelphia right fielder, grounded weakly out to first, and Ray said, "He didn't have a chance on that pitch, up on his hands like that. He's got a big hitch in his swing, and you've got to be awful strong to come back up again with the bat and hit the ball with any kind of power. Reggie Jackson can do it, or maybe Lee May, but it certainly isn't advisable. But that was some kind of pitch Hooton made."

Hooton, in fact, threw a two-hit shutout, winning by 6–0, and Ray Scarborough was overcome with admiration for what we had seen. "That's as good a night's work as you ever want to see in the major leagues," he said later that evening. "Hooton was throwing more overhand than I'd ever seen him. Maybe you saw sometimes he even had to lean his head over to the side to make room for his arm comin' over. He had more stuff, velocity-wise, than I'd ever seen, and he used that overhand curve just enough to make the fastball work. He was just eatin' up that outside corner. He sold that pitch to the ump"—it was Bruce Froemming—"in the very first inning. He showed him right then that he could hit that front corner. That *alerts* the umpire—puts him on his toes—and if he sees you can do it he'll give it to you all night long. If you're sort of wild—throwing up here, then down there, then way inside or someplace—he'll sort of lose interest, and he won't give you that little corner even if you do hit it. Control is *so* important. It makes the catchers look better, as well as the umpire, and the infielders do a lot better, too. They will anticipate the play. Hell, even the fans are better!"

I pointed out to Ray that he and I had seen several remarkable pitching exhibitions.

"Well, there's no doubt that pitching is much better now than it was when I was playing," he said. "There aren't any better arms, but pitchers are much better coached, and they have amazing poise, even when they're just breaking in. The biggest difference now is the slider, which was just coming in when I was pitching. A few pitchers had it naturally back then—Bob Muncrief, he was one of them. We called it the short curve. I was a curveball pitcher, but mine was a real old-fashioned curve, and that took a lot more effort to throw."

He groaned and rolled his eyes comically. "When I first came up to the Senators, I was one of the wildest goats in the AL," he said. "I used to throw that big four-foot curve, and if they didn't swing at it it was a ball. I pitched a long time in the majors when every game was a struggle, and I guess it was five years before I got control and knew how to *pitch*—knew how to get a man out. I finally learned that with a good hitter you never threw him the same pitch twice. Never put it in the same place or at the same speed. That's how I got them to hit my pitch—the one I wanted them to swing at, whatever it was. I never threw a change of pace in my life that I didn't want the batter to swing at.

"I always had a lot of luck against Ted Williams, because I knew he was a great one for timing a pitch. He was always thinking, and I could think along with him. But Hank Majeski, who wasn't a great batter—he could always hit anything I threw. A lot of baseball is just confidence, of course. I finally got to feeling that if I threw a pitch behind Hank Majeski, he'd hit it somehow. I think he sometimes froze in the batter's box on a curveball, and that always made me afraid I'd hurt him someday. George Kell was the same way."

I asked if he'd been known as a knockdown pitcher.

"Well, we didn't have the slider then, but what we did have was that good, hard inside pitch." He said this with considerable relish. "The umpires have taken that away now, but I always felt I deserved to have that pitch. I needed to keep that batter honest—let him know that I was out there earning my living against him. What I used to hate to see was a batter stepping in and holding up his hand for time while he scratched around in the back of that batter's box with his spikes and dug himself a toehold for his back foot. I remember a game once when Luke Appling came up against me and started that. He kicked and dug and scraped around in the box and finally got all set, and I walked halfway in and said, 'You sure you got that all fixed up just the way you like it, Luke?' He looked at me sort of puzzled, and I could see Cal Hubbard, the plate umpire, beginning to shake his shoulders laughing. Luke said, 'Sure, Horn. It's fine.' I said, 'You don't think you ought to improve that some and dig it a lot deeper back there, Luke?' He said, 'What for?' And I said, ' 'Cause I'm going to *bury* you!' Well, sir, I popped him on that first pitch as pretty as you please! Got him right on the hip. He went down like a sack, but he jumped up and went on down to first, and then he called over, 'Say, you really meant that, didn't you?' I said, 'Don't you *ever* dig in against me.' "

I had already looked up Ray Scarborough's pitching record, which came out to eighty wins and eighty-five defeats in ten years of campaigning, mostly with terrible teams. (He missed the seasons of 1944 and 1945, when he served in the Navy.) Later, I went back and checked his fifth year in the majors, 1948—the year when he had finally learned how to pitch. That summer, he had an earned-run average of 2.82 and won fifteen games and lost eight for the Senators, a seventh-place club that hit thirty-one home runs for the season and finished forty games out of first.

•

RAY AND I went to one more game together—the meeting between the Phillies and the Dodgers on the following night, which the Dodgers took by 5–1, scoring all their runs in the third inning. There was a much smaller crowd. Doug Rau pitched well for the visitors, though not as spectacularly as Hooton. Ray Scarborough took only a few notes. He told me that he had had a call that afternoon from Harry Dalton, who had asked him to curtail his report on the Phillies for the moment and come out and help the Angels with a full-scale evaluation of their own minor-league players—a preparation for the coming American League expansion in the fall, when all the AL clubs will have to contribute some of their players to an expansion draft to man the new teams in Seattle and Toronto. Ray was leaving the next day, and would go first to El Paso, to look over the Diablos, the Angels' team in the Class AA Texas League, and then move along to Salt Lake City to study the Gulls, their Class AAA team in the Pacific Coast League.

Scarborough looked a bit worn, and he told me he had already spent a lot of time scouting that day—scouting by telephone. He had been talking about various players on the Philadelphia club with local baseball people—people he declined to name. "This is confidential information," he said. "It's absolutely essential, and it comes from your friendships and contacts all around the league. You have to have facts about a player that you can't pick up just by watching him play or seeing him throw in infield practice. What is his club not telling you about this man? Does he have a physical drawback they're keeping quiet? How good a man is he in the clubhouse? How much does he care? Will he fight for his team, or is he a troublemaker, a complainer? Does he drink? Does he use drugs? I could tell you the names of some bad customers in the major leagues who have absolutely torn some clubs apart. If we're going to spend half a million dollars on an article, we have to know what we're getting. His club isn't going to tell you, but there are ways of finding out. You have to be careful and avoid a suggestion of tampering, so you learn how to listen and how to get the facts in an informal way. Everybody does this. It's what a lot of the friendships in baseball are for. I'm loyal to the Angels, but I wouldn't hesitate to tell a good friend of mine about one of our players who was less than he seemed."

Ray looked unhappy as he said this, and I wondered if it was because he disliked this aspect of his job. "We have something in baseball that we call 'the lower half,' " he went on. "It means the personal makeup of the individual player—what he's like inside, how he lives, what he believes in. I think finding that out is the biggest thing in scouting today. Individuals are changing, and I don't just know how to evaluate the changes. I don't know for sure how many of the kids today have the dedication you need in order to play this game. All these players who haven't signed their contracts, because they want to move along to some other club for a lot of easy money —I never dreamed we'd see something like that. Why, I know some young players who are just starting out their careers—barely been up a whole season in the majors yet—and *they're* playing out their options. They've got some agent who's telling them to hold back and get on one of those expansion teams for a lot of money. I just—I don't know how to comprehend that."

He shook his big head two or three times and stared out at the field. His face had become clouded and heavy. A few minutes later, he gestured with his scorecard at the Phillies' first baseman, out on the field. "Now, there's a man, Dick Allen, who once walked out on a two-hundred-thousand-dollar contract in the middle of September," he said. "Just walked away. Now his bat looks as if it's begun to slow down a lot, and I wonder if he isn't kicking his tail for the time he's missed. We never had anybody in our day who would have done anything like that."

I tried to think of something to say. Ray and I had talked several times about the Messersmith decision, which last year suddenly ended baseball's reserve clause, and about the turbulent labor relations and enormously inflated contracts and million-dollar deals that had marked this baseball summer, and I had found him profoundly unsympathetic to the Players Association and to the players' side of things. This should not have surprised me; I had deliberately sought out Scarborough, after all, because he represented a part of baseball that seemed fixed and unalterable. Now I had run headlong into a paradox: I badly wanted Ray to feel better about the real shift in style that has recently come to the sport—a shift which may be the result of the new beliefs that many young players and black players hold about personal independence and corporate loyalty and other considerable issues. I hoped that Ray might become less unhappy about this change than he seemed to be, because I liked him so much and so admired his spirited and generous nature. On the other hand, I also wanted him obdurate and preserved, because I had begun to sense that he still embodied the classic attitudes of baseball—the sunlit verities of the game that had first moved and attracted so many of us when we were young. At times, he almost seemed to encompass the entire history of the sport. His own country beginnings in the game sounded exactly like the boyhood memoirs of famous early-twentieth-century baseball stars that I had read in Lawrence S. Ritter's splendid book *The Glory of Their Times*, and yet Ray had survived in baseball into the superjet age—into a time when his own hard-won professional judgments were in competition with computerized data, and his long hours and months of work could be nullified in an instant by the cold economics and deadly luck of the business draw. If this game, in achieving its inevitable contemporary alterations of form and attitude, could not continue to reward a man like Ray Scarborough, it would have lost something precious and probably irretrievable.

I stole a look at Ray and said, "What will it be like down in El Paso?"

"Hot!" he said instantly. "You watch a game and then you jump back to your motel—back into that air-conditioning. But at least they have grass down there—not this carpet. Baseball is an outdoor game. And we have some good boys down there. Our second baseman, Fred Frazier, is leading the whole league in hitting, and we have a kid at first base named Willie Mays Aikens, who's already hit about twenty home runs. Willie Mays Aikens! With young players like that, you only want to be sure not to bring them along too fast. I'm certainly looking forward to seeing them."

16 Cast a Cold Eye

October 1976

THE LAST OUT of the year was an uninteresting fly ball struck by the Yankees' Roy White, which ascended briefly through the frigid South Bronx darkness and then fell into the glove of George Foster, the Cincinnati left fielder. Foster and his teammates, who had at this instant captured an utterly one-sided and almost passionless World Series and thus reconfirmed their title to the championship of the world, cavorted briefly in time-honored postures of jubilation and then departed from the arena, leaving behind them a silenced half-frozen audience and the filth-strewn vacant turf of Yankee Stadium—a panorama that inescapably suggested the condition of another, larger game: the state of baseball itself. I visited the clubhouses and entered in my notebook the expected antipodal quotes from variously disappointed, triumphant, heartbroken, generous, bitter, and overmodest athletes and coaches and officials, and then headed for the subway and home, with the old, late-October tang of sprayed champagne on my sleeve and an unfamiliar gloom in my heart. For a while, I ascribed this weight to a childish, partisan disappointment over the double outcome of that last game—Reds 7, Yankees 2; Reds 4 games, Yankees 0 games—but I am not, in truth, much of a Yankee fan, and I have watched enough baseball to know that four-game sweeps are not such a rarity as to strike a grownup aghast. My discontent lay elsewhere, and when it persisted I mentioned it to friends and colleagues and new acquaintances, and found that all of them—every fan among them, that is—was suffering from a similar sense of dissatisfaction and emptiness over this baseball season and its ending. The 1976 World Series, in spite of its brevity and skimped drama, was a significant one. It profoundly enhanced and deepened the reputation of the Cincinnati Reds, who must now be compared seriously with the two or three paramount clubs of the last half-century, and it was equally notable, I think, for the harsh music of complaint that preceded and accompanied and trailed after its brief October passage—sounds of cynicism and anger and sadness from so many people and places that they almost drowned out the thump and tootlings of our favorite old parade.

The causes of this widespread unhappiness are hardly new. They include, in no particular order, night baseball, Sunday-night baseball, the extension of the season far beyond its appropriate weather, the extension and promotion of the controversial designated-hitter device by permitting its introduction into World Series play, artificial turf and its effects on players and strategies, the televising of baseball and television's enormous influence on scheduling and on almost every other aspect of the game, and, most of all, the irresolute, insensitive, and hypocritical leadership of the executives of the sport, who permitted most of these vulgarities and dumb ideas to creep into their sport in the first place and to flourish until they now almost strangle it. Further uneasy and unresolved elements that afflict the game are the arrival of the free-agent status for players and its accompanying inflation of salaries and trade prices, the violence and anarchy of ballpark crowds, the suspicions and tensions that separate players and owners as a result of the dissolution of the reserve clause, and the utterly unneeded forthcoming expansion of the American League, with the resultant dilution of talent in the league that, as the Reds horribly proved, is already much the inferior one. These grievances, as I have said, are not exactly new—only the scheduling of two important post-season games (one playoff, one Series) in Sunday-night prime time and the entrance of Howard Cosell into the quiet chambers of the game came as true startlers this fall—but the list is so long and depressing that one's fervent wish is simply to throw it away and to think only about the distractions and pleasures of baseball itself, to watch the games. This has been easy to do in recent years, when several riveting pennant races and a remarkable succession of World Series matchups, culminating in the epochal Reds vs. Red Sox collision last fall, have encouraged this kind of distraction; six of the last ten World Series have gone the full seven games, and only the one-sided five-game victory of the Orioles over the Reds in 1970 ranked close to this year's affair as unnews. And here, no doubt, is the real reason for my unhappiness. This fall, the baseball games could not distract us from the truth about baseball, which is that it may well be on the point of altering itself, if not out of existence, then out of any special or serious place in the American imagination.

•

THE SEASON's news was not *all* dismal. The summer provided a basket of surprises, including the discovery that the clubs could prosper without a vestige of a pennant race in any of the divisions. By the first week of June, the four eventual winners—the Reds and Phillies in the National League, and the Yankees and Kansas City Royals in the American—had all moved into first place for good, and by the time of the All-Star Game break in mid-July the nearest second-place team, the Dodgers, was six full games to the rear. The Phillies and Royals, it will be recalled, suffered late-season comas that brought them almost within touching distance of their pursuers, but then steadied at the end. In spite of these torpid campaigns, baseball attendance for 1976 reached an all-time high of 31,320,535—a leap of a million and a half over the previous year. Most of the new or renewed fans turned up in the American League, which improved its gate by 1,470,583, to draw within two million of the perennially more robust NL. The real causes of the surprising turnouts (aside from a numbing surfeit of Bat Days, Helmet Days, Jacket Days, Camera Days, Family Days, Bronzed-Baby-Shoe Days, and other promotions) were probably the memory of that great World Series last fall and the fact that three of the four summer leaders were new to such eminence and thus a reason for local fervor. Among them, the champion Reds and the upstart Yankees, Phillies, and Royals picked up more than two million new fans.

The only races in either league turned out to be for the batting titles, which were settled in both cases by the last couple of swings of a bat. In the National League, the Reds' Ken Griffey held an average of .337 on the final day of the regular season, and received permission from his manager, Sparky Anderson, to sit out the Reds' meaningless closing game against the Braves, and thus protect his lead over the Cubs' Bill Madlock, whose average stood at .333. (An inescapable memory here is the last day of the 1941 season, when Ted Williams was told by his manager, Joe Cronin, of the Red Sox, that it would be perfectly all right if he chose to skip that afternoon's closing doubleheader in order to protect his batting average, which was tremblingly balanced at .3996—officially .400, that is. Williams chose to play, went six-for-eight for the day, and finished at .406—the only over-.400 average of the past forty-six years.) Halfway through the Reds-Braves game, word came over the sports wire that Madlock was enjoying a terrific afternoon at the plate against the Expos; Griffey hurriedly entered the lineup, but went hitless in two at-bats and lost the title to Madlock, who had gone four-for-four and raised his average to .339. Madlock's batting title was his second in succession. In the American League, the matter ended even more improbably, in a Twins-Royals game in which *three* participants—Hal McRae (.330784) and George Brett (.330733), of the Royals, and Rod Carew (.329), of the Twins—all began play with a shot at the championship. McRae and Carew each went two-for-four, thus losing to Brett, whose crucial hit, bringing him to three-for-four for the day and .333 for the year, was a short fly that landed in front of the Minnesota left fielder and bounced over his head for an inside-the-park homer. McRae, who is black, later claimed that the outfielder, Steve Brye, who is white, played the ball into a hit intentionally, thus handing the title to Brett, who is also white, and that he did so with the connivance of the Twins' manager, Gene Mauch. This sad matter will never be entirely resolved, but it must be pointed out that to *plan* such a malfeasance seems utterly unlikely.

Other numbers were less disputable. Hank Aaron retired, after twenty-three years and seven hundred and fifty-five homers. Walter Alston retired, after twenty-three years at the Dodger helm—a technically impeccable but (according to many of his players) distant and impersonal leader; he won seven pennants and four world championships. Lou Brock, now thirty-seven years old, batted .301 and stole fifty-six bases—his twelfth straight summer of more than fifty swipes. Twenty-eight more stolen bases will put him past Ty Cobb's lifetime mark of eight hundred and ninety-two, a record that has been considered one of the game's holy minarets. The Oakland A's, short of power thanks to the trading away of Reggie Jackson, stole three hundred and forty-one bases—only six short of the all-time record set by the 1911 Giants. Nolan Ryan led both leagues in strikeouts (327) and losses (18), thus proving something or other, and failed, for the first time since 1972, to pitch a no-hitter. The Tigers, in a game in May against the Yankees, committed three errors on one play. This horror show began when, with two Yankee runners on base, center fielder Ron LeFlore dropped a fly hit by Roy White, but picked up the ball in time to throw out the second runner at the plate; catcher John Wockenfuss, under the mistaken impression that this was the third out, lightheartedly rolled the ball out toward the mound, where it was seized by pitcher Bill Laxton, who then flung it wildly past third base, allowing White to chug home with the winning run.

The Tigers, a young and improving team, enjoyed some much happier days than this one, and raised their home attendance by more than four hundred thousand fans—a great many of whom came trooping in whenever the phenomenal young Tiger pitcher Mark Fidrych was slated to work. Fidrych finished his first season with a won-lost mark of 19–9 and an earned-run average of 2.34; the latter figure was the best among all starters in the league, which meant that Fidrych had a better summer than Vida Blue, Frank Tanana, Jim Palmer, and Luis Tiant, among others. This is notable work by any standard, but positively electrifying for a twenty-two-year-old rookie who performed for most of last season at the Class-A level of the minors and was not even on the Tigers' roster in spring training this year. I caught The Bird's act late in the season, in the first game of a September Sunday doubleheader at Yankee Stadium, when he gave up nine scattered, harmless hits and defeated the league leaders by 6–0. It was only the second shutout thrown against them by a right-hander all year. On the mound, Fidrych presented the classic profile and demeanor of a very young hurler—long legs and a skinny, pleasing gawkiness (he is six-three); a pre-delivery flurry of overexcited twitches, glances, and arm-loosening wiggles; and a burning anxiety to get rid of the ball, to see what would happen next, to get *on* with this, man! The results were something altogether different. His pitching was wholly cool and intelligent, built around some middling-good fastballs and down-slanting sliders, all delivered with excellent control just above or below the hemline of the strike zone, with an ensuing five strikeouts, one walk, and innumerable harmless fly balls. Fidrych also showed us some of his celebrated eccentricities—sprinting to the mound to start each inning, kneeling to pat down the dirt in front of the mound, applauding plays by his teammates, and shaking hands with some of his infielders after an important out—but his pitching outweighed his oddities. After the game, The Bird performed again with grace and flakiness, this time for the Gotham scribes. One reporter had noticed that he always tossed the ball back to the umpire after an enemy base hit, and asked why. "Well, that ball had a hit in it, so I want it to get back in the ball bag and goof around with the other balls there," Fidrych said. "Maybe it'll learn some sense and come out as a pop-up next time." Another writer, thinking ahead to the enormous salaries and lucrative commercial endorsements that now instantly reward young sporting pheenoms, asked, "What's come your way so far, Mark?"

Fidrych thought for an instant and then smiled almost shyly. "Happiness," he said.

Another happy pitcher was the Mets' Jerry Koosman, who won twenty-one games and lost ten—his first twenty-game season ever. He was 12–4 after the All-Star break, and finished just behind Randy Jones, the Padres' sinkerball artist, in the Cy Young Award balloting. (Koosman is on everybody's All-Good-Guy first team.) The only other twenty-game man in the Mets' annals, Tom Seaver, wound up this time at 14–11, in spite of a league-leading 235 strikeouts and an ERA of 2.59. No runs was the reason. During a typical outing of his in late July, I watched him shut out the Pirates for ten innings, fanning ten and allowing no one to reach third base—all literally for naught, since the Mets went scoreless, too, and eventually lost in the thirteenth. They played so badly in the first two-thirds of the season that their fans fell into the habit of booing them in the middle innings—booing quietly and resignedly, more out of principle than out of passion. But the Mets came on like an express train in the late going, winning twenty-five of their last forty games, taking third place, and playing a small but deadly part in the NL East pennant race.

The Phillies, who led their division by fifteen games on August 27, quickly lost eight straight games, and an eventual sixteen of twenty-one, thus permitting Pittsburgh to close to within three games on September 17. The next day, however, the Mets beat the Pirates 6–2 (Seaver pitched); the day after that, they beat the Pirates 7–6 (Dave Kingman hit two home runs); and the day after *that* they beat the Pirates 5–4 (rookie outfielder Lee Mazzilli hit a two-run homer with two out in the ninth). The Pirates never recovered.

•

THE TRUE feat of this past baseball summer—a development far more startling than a World Series sweep or a sudden batting title or any other miracle afield—was the drafting and acceptance of a revolutionary four-year pact between the owners and the players, which was drawn up, in memorandum form, on July 12 and subsequently affirmed by the Players Association, by the owners' Player Relations Committee, and, eventually, by a binding majority of seventeen of the twenty-four major-league clubs. Very little public attention was given to the significance of this event at the time, because the headlines and news accounts concentrated on the most unusual and most immediately interesting of the document's subclauses, which was a system establishing the drafting and readmission to the game of free agents—players who would sever their connection with their existing clubs at the end of this season. Such a system, to be sure, was urgently necessary, since the pool of coming free agents—there were twenty-five of them in the end—included a number of the game's most expensive stars and prime talents, such as Reggie Jackson, Bobby Grich, Don Gullett, Joe Rudi, Rollie Fingers, and Dave Cash. The "reëntry draft" (a terrific space-age locution) that took place just after the World Series at the Plaza Hotel in New York, thus began the most interesting redistribution of talent in the history of the game.

The reëntry draft, however, was only one part of the pact,

which was in fact a four-year renewal of the Basic Agreement governing every aspect of player-owner relations, including salary minimums, salary arbitration, retirement benefits, and so on—and, most significantly, free agency and trading rights. The new provisions in the last two areas call for immediate free agency, on request, for any player who has completed six years with a major-league club, and establish his right to demand a trade after five years' service with one club. "Repeater rights" also establish a player's privilege to proceed from trade demand to free agency, from free agency to free agency, and so forth, in various spans of five years or three years. The system appears straightforward and almost unarguably fair to all parties, and yet these are precisely the issues that profoundly divided the owners and the Players Association last winter and spring, and ultimately led to the bitter, owner-enforced lockout that delayed the opening of the spring-training camps by about three weeks last March. The signing of this agreement is a cause for rejoicing.

The accord was reached because the rival negotiators—Marvin Miller, who is the executive director of the Players Association, and John J. Gaherin, a professional labor negotiator retained by the clubs' Player Relations Committee—had begun to sense that after months of almost continuous desultory or impassioned bargaining, with frequent intervening consultations with their larger bodies, they were on the very brink of a formal impasse, an eventuality that ultimately would force the parties into court, with unforeseeable but chaotic results. Unwilling to face such risks, the two men, accompanied only by the league presidents—the National League's Charles S. Feeney and the American League's Lee MacPhail—met on July 6 in a small conference room at the Hotel Biltmore, in New York, to begin a series of informal but highly intensive negotiating sessions. These Biltmore Talks, as they are now referred to, more or less in the style of the Diet of Worms or the Treaty of Ghent, at last broke through the accumulated barnacle crust of suspicions and postures, and led to hard, precisely detailed, but non-acrimonious bargaining. At the end of four days, the basic memorandum had been hammered out, with the central agreement coming after Mr. Gaherin, for the Player Relations Committee, accepted free agency for the players after six years' service (the owners had been holding out for nine), in return for a five-year span before a player could again achieve free agency, instead of the three years that the Players Association had wanted.

Described in these terms, the accord sounds like a simple and civilized accommodation of differences, but the truth is that both sides had to travel an enormous distance over extremely bumpy terrain to arrive at a meeting place. Marvin Miller, for the P.A., had retreated from the basic "one-and-one" rights (free agency at the end of a player's current contract plus one year's additional service) that he appeared to have secured for the players after the Messersmith decision of last winter, which upset the reserve clause. He did so, one may surmise, in part because unlimited free agency seemed likely to destroy any form of player development or long-range team planning by the owners, and also because the cessation of the reserve clause (which had forbidden free agency) had been determined by an arbitrator's ruling but never tested all the way up to the Supreme Court level—a long, costly fight for both sides, with an impossible final verdict for one litigant or the other.

Mr. Gaherin, for his part, had perhaps an even more horrendous task, which was to persuade first the six-man Player Relations Committee and eventually most of the twenty-four club owners or presidents that the agreement was an essential document, and that it represented what so many of those owners had, in varying degrees and to various excruciating lengths, squirmed and shuddered and shouted to avoid: a fair accommodation. It was, by any measurement, a triumph for him and his employers. Faced with the real possibility of total free agency, he had come up with a solution to the slippery problem of readmitting free agents to the ordered hierarchy of the clubs, and had also arranged matters so that in all likelihood each long-term major-league player would achieve free agency only once in his career. Mr. Gaherin—a slim, pale, precise man of sixty-two, who has an unsettling resemblance to James Joyce—has worked for the Player Relations Committee for nine years, and is thus fully accustomed to the burdens of multi-employer labor work, but his treatment at the hands of the owners on this occasion must have startled him a little. Early in August, he and the National League president, Feeney, were vilified in an unbridled statement to the press issued by Gussie Busch, the owner of the Cardinals, who said that the clubs had been "kicked in the teeth in the labor matter," and demanded that the two men be dismissed. Since then, the owners in both leagues have held private ballotings that resulted in an expression of no confidence in Mr. Gaherin—a movement toward his dismissal that was only halted by Edmund B. Fitzgerald, who is chairman of the board of the Milwaukee Brewers and also the chairman of the Player Relations Committee.

The work of translating the memorandum of agreement into the full language of a formal Basic Agreement is not yet near completion, mostly because of the owners' attempts to redraft it or alter it unilaterally, but the memorandum itself was signed, and is thus a binding document. Since it came as the result of extensive bargaining, it is expected to be a strong instrument that will withstand any future court tests. It is true that Mr. Gaherin (along with Mr. Fitzgerald) was the planner and promulgator of the player lockout last spring, but it is also true that he and Marvin Miller, who somehow kept his youthful, scattered six-hundred-man union informed and unified through two years of unrelenting hostility and pressure from their employers, came out at the end with an agreement that looks like a Gibraltar in the churning seas of big-time American sport.

A somewhat more lighthearted view may be taken of the summer's other great off-diamond dustup, which was Commissioner Bowie Kuhn's abrupt action in June to stop a multi-million-dollar sale of three of Charles O. Finley's celebrated chattels. The deal, it will be recalled, would have delivered Joe Rudi and Rollie Fingers to the Boston Red Sox for one million dollars each, and sent Vida Blue to the Yankees for one and a half million. After a meeting with Mr. Finley, Commissioner Kuhn announced that he was ordering the players back to the Oakland roster under powers entitling him to "preserve the honor of the game," and said that "public confidence in the integrity of club operations and in baseball would be gravely undermined should such assignments not be restrained." Mr. Finley stated that "Kuhn sounds like the village idiot," and filed a ten-million-dollar lawsuit against him for restraint of trade. He also refused to allow the returned merchandise to go on playing for his team—a ban that lasted for two weeks and was lifted by him only in the face of a strike by the other members of the A's.

Two interpretations of Mr. Kuhn's motives may be postulated:

(1) He was truly concerned about maintaining the competitive balance of the leagues, and felt that the sale of such famous stars to well-heeled contending clubs would breed cynicism and despair in the heart of American fandom. (Footnote: The chart of Mr. Kuhn's concern may be plotted with some precision, since he had offered no let or hindrance to a just previous deal involving the sale of Minnesota pitcher Bert Blyleven to the Texas Rangers for three hundred thousand dollars.)

(2) He and his employers, the owners, were truly concerned about a sale that would establish such a high price tag for free agents on the open market—a market in which most of the clubs would have to deal at the end of the season. (Footnote: The major-league clubs, by a vote of twenty-two to two, pledged to make good any financial buffeting the Commissioner's office may undergo as the result of a judgment in

the Finley suit. The nay votes were Baltimore and, of course, Oakland.)

•

THE RED Sox never thrived after the opening of their season, but the vivid symbol of their fall from grace this year came in the bottom of the sixth inning in a game at Yankee Stadium on May 20, when Boston catcher Carlton Fisk took a marvelous peg from right fielder Dwight Evans and tagged out the Yankees' Lou Piniella at the plate. Piniella arrived at full speed and banged into Fisk's chest with his upraised knees in an effort to jar the ball loose; Fisk held on, but the crash—the most violent plate collision I have ever seen—knocked both players sprawling, and instantly set off a prolonged and extremely ugly fight on the field, from which Bill Lee, Boston's only left-handed starting pitcher, emerged with a severe injury to his pitching shoulder. The Red Sox responded at once in the game, burying the Yankees with eight runs in the next three innings, including two home runs by Carl Yastrzemski, but the loss of Lee for many weeks was irreparable. The Sox—the mettlesome and exciting runners-up of last year's bright October—fell into torpor and dissension, and eventually even into disfavor at home, finishing third in their division and never mounting even a minimal run at the dominant Yankees. The team lost its manager, Darrell Johnson, who was fired in midseason, and its modest and much admired longtime owner, Tom Yawkey, who died in July. Many of the Fenway Park fans blamed the club's apparent loss of pride on the fact that three of the Sox stars—Fisk, Fred Lynn, and Rick Burleson—did not sign contracts until late in the summer and were obviously prepared to become free agents if their demands were not satisfied. More dispassionate watchers, however, came to the conclusion that the Bosox were beaten by weak pitching and by the whetted competitiveness that rival clubs bring to bear against a defending pennant winner. The Sox played all summer as if they expected at any moment to regain their edge and brilliance of 1975, but that never happened. Doing it over again is the hardest task in professional sport. What was most missed at Fenway Park this year was the deep, startled pleasure of the Red Sox' winning campaign and that extraordinary Series. Even the Cincinnati Reds mourned it. After the Reds had swept the Yankees last month, Joe Morgan said, "I'm glad we won, but last year was a lot more fun."

Similar joys came this summer to the refurbished blue-and-white expanses of Yankee Stadium, where, right from the first week of the campaign, fans could collect the images and patterns of a team coming together, doing all the small things right, no longer being surprised by its own abilities, expecting always to win. My own summer album is full of these pictures: Mickey Rivers approaching the plate like an old man—like Walter Brennan limping up to a horse stall. Rivers batting, shifting his feet and tilting back his head and twitching his bat, and then tapping a little bunt down toward third and flying up the line—not just beating the throw but making a throw useless. . . . Graig Nettles taking a pitch in an odd, slightly bowlegged stance, with his hands low and back. Nettles waiting unhappily but silently through his implacable early-season slump, and then, in July at last and in August, beginning to crash the ball. Nettles expunging a bases-loaded rally in a September game against the Red Sox by scooping up a hard grounder behind third and racing to the bag and then throwing ahead, past the runner's ear, to engineer a startling double play at the plate. . . . Willie Randolph, the very image of an infielder, restoring a sense of confidence and youthful expectation to the right side of the Yankee infield which had not been there since the departure of Bobby Richardson. Randolph diving over second base to snaffle a low drive by the Indians' Larvell Blanks, and then diving the other way to tag the bag and double up the base runner. . . . Thurman Munson hitting all summer long. Munson driving in five runs against the A's one night, with a homer and three singles. Munson talking in a clubhouse near the end of his great season, permitting himself to smile a little, and perhaps at last overcoming part of his chronic self-doubt. . . . And Billy Martin, the manager, standing in the front of the dugout with his hands in his jacket pockets and staring out from under his long-billed cap with a cold and ferrety edginess—a glare of suspicion and barely contained hostility directed at umpires and enemy batters and pitchers, and at all the hovering, invisible accidents and waiting disasters of the game that stand in the way of each day's essential win.

These men and many others—Ed Figueroa, Fred Stanley, Dick Tidrow, Chris Chambliss, Catfish Hunter, Dock Ellis, and the rest—made it a cheerful and noisy summer up in the Bronx, but perhaps the one irreplaceable Yankee was the man who invented this team, who saw it in his mind's eye before it ever existed on the field—the club's president, Gabe Paul. A plump, energetic man of sixty-six, Paul came to the Yankees in 1973 and immediately undertook a series of purchases and deep-level trades that entirely altered the club. Only two members of this year's squad—Roy White and Thurman Munson—came up from the Yankee's minor-league system. Paul's best-known transaction was the acquisition of Catfish Hunter, in 1975, in a bidding war against several other clubs after Hunter had been declared a free agent. Accusations began to be heard then that the Yankees intended to dominate their league with cash, but this easy bad-mouthing does not alter the fact that most championship clubs now are built on trades and purchases, and that "buying a pennant" is far more difficult than it sounds. Gabe Paul, to be sure, enjoys a marvelous working relationship with the seemingly bottomless wallet of his general partner, George M. Steinbrenner III, but his success has been much more due to imagination and trading courage and a profound judgment of baseball talent. Two deals that he made last winter started the club toward its pennant. In 1974, he had given up a longtime Yankee favorite, Bobby Murcer, in order to acquire Bobby Bonds, a potential superstar outfielder, from the Giants, but when the chance came, a year later, he did not hesitate to give up Bonds to the California Angels in return for the little-known Mickey Rivers and Ed Figueroa. This summer, Bonds was injured and played very little; Rivers led off for the Yankees all year, batted .312, and stole forty-three bases, and Figueroa won nineteen games. In the other trade, he sent Doc Medich, an established Yankee pitcher (and a medical student), to the Pirates for Dock Ellis, Willie Randolph, and Ken Brett, a subsequently retraded pitcher. Randolph, a brilliant prospect, had had virtually no major-league testing, while Ellis, a talented but moody pitcher, had fallen out with his manager and had enjoyed little success in the past three seasons. It was known, however, that Ellis's best pitch, a sinkerball, was ill-suited to the Pirates' artificial home turf, and word had also come that Ellis was anxious to play for a manager like Billy Martin. This summer, Dock Ellis, relishing the innumerable enemy outs attributable to grounders hammered along the slower Stadium grass, finished with seventeen wins and eight losses, while Randolph established himself as one of the premier infielders in the league. Doc Medich did not fare quite as well, winding up with an 8–11 record for the Pirates. My favorite comment about Gabe Paul's trading abilities was made one night this summer in the press box at Shea Stadium, when a veteran Pittsburgh baseball writer who had watched Medich struggle on the mound for several unimpressive innings finally tossed his pencil in the air and cried, "Ellis is a better *doctor* than this guy!"

•

FAMISHED FOR a pennant race, I packed a bag on the last Monday of the regular season and impulsively flew to Oakland, where the young Kansas City Royals were opening a three-game set against the veteran, campaign-hardened A's, who now suddenly trailed them by only four and a half games. The Royals, who had fallen into an epochal batting slump, had scored a total of five runs in their last five games. My trip almost made up for the whole bland summer. In the first game, a rain-delayed affair played before an enormous and cacophonous Famly Night (i.e., half-price) audience, the A's had to abandon their customary go-go, base-stealing offense because of the slow track, but by the fourth inning they had begun to whack some long line shots off the Royals' starter, Dennis Leonard, including a homer by a newly acquired late-season helper, Ron Fairly. The Royals evened things up at 3–3, with pokes off Vida Blue by their marvelous hitting duo of George Brett and Hal McRae, but Fairly, in his next at-bat, in the fifth, hit a double off the wall, eventually coming around to score, and Sal Bando led off the sixth with another screamer, which disappeared over the center-field fence. This was clearly more than enough for Leonard, whose next pitch, by no mischance, caught Don Baylor on the right shoulder, thus emptying both benches and bullpens. The lengthy ensuing scrimmage around the mound was eventually dispersed, but it resumed almost immediately, with different topography and tactics, out at the visitors' bullpen in short right field, where some hometown fans had been showering the K.C. pitchers with beer—not a trifling insult, since some of the Oakland Coliseum beer containers are half-gallon jobs. Six of the malt-dampened relief men eventually got into the game, to little avail, as the A's won by 8–3.

The next evening, after another rainstorm, we were given a perfect counterpiece to these rowdy doings—a thrilling pitching duel between Oakland's Mike Torrez and the Royals' Marty Pattin, who is a slider specialist. Pattin limited the on-rushing A's to four hits, but lost, 1–0, to Torrez's two-hitter. The game distilled itself into two splendid moments. In the third, with Fred Patek on second base for the visitors, Tom Poquette smashed a Torrez fastball on a lofty arc toward the left-center-field wall; Joe Rudi, running at full tilt from the moment the ball was struck, slithered and splashed through the mud of the warning track and made a sailing, last-second grab at the base of the wall, saving a sure triple and a run, and then easily doubled up Patek, who was well around third by the time the great catch was made. Then Sal Bando, leading off in the seventh, duelled with Pattin for several minutes, fouling off pitches repeatedly until he found the one he wanted, a fastball, and drove it into the left-field seats for the only run of the day.

This was my farewell taste of such famous Oakland specialties. I could not stay for the next game, in which the Royals' Larry Gura at last closed the door on the Oakland hopes, winning by 4–0; the A's were eliminated two nights later, when they lost to the Angels in twelve innings. I also missed the champagne party in the A's clubhouse after the last game of the season, when six of the newborn Oakland free agents—Joe Rudi, Sal Bando, Gene Tenace, Rollie Fingers, Campy Campaneris, and Don Baylor—celebrated a moment more exquisite than a mere championship: liberation from Charles O. Finley.

•

ANY OBSERVATIONS here about the Phillies, whom I watched in their home park as they dropped their first two playoff games to the Cincinnati Reds, will strike Philadelphia fans as being typically insufficient and unfair. (Lifelong Phillies fans closely resemble the victims of a chronic sinus condition; they sometimes feel better, but never for long.) Their team, of course, will now be remembered mostly for having almost collapsed in the later stages of the pennant race and then playing miserably in the championship playoffs, but such is the heartless way of the world. The Phillies did in fact finish strongly, winning thirteen of their last sixteen after their late-summer catalepsy, and ended with 101 victories in the regular season. Their lineup offered three .300 hitters (Jay Johnstone, Garry Maddox, and Greg Luzinski), three genuine slugging threats (Luzinski, Mike Schmidt—who led the majors with thirty-eight homers—and Dick Allen); a splendid double-play combination in shortstop Larry Bowa and second baseman Dave Cash; and three tough, experienced front-line pitchers

(Steve Carlton, Jim Lonborg, and Jim Kaat). On paper, the club looked almost a match for the Reds. Those first games, however, were played on the faded green Tartan Turf carpet of Veterans Stadium—where the Phillies, strangely enough, seemed not at all at home. They lost the opener by 6–3, largely because of some frightful defense—right fielder Ollie Brown played two singles into triples, and Larry Bowa allowed two routine grounders to skid under his glove untouched—and because the home-team pitchers, Carlton and Tug McGraw, permitted the speedy Cincinnati base runners to take enormous leads off first base, thus encouraging four stolen bases and the infliction of a debilitating nervousness on the Philadelphia defense. Anxiety, of course, is the Reds' prime weapon; their speed and power and opportunism and experience breed the conviction in the opposing team that it must play an almost superhuman level of baseball to have any kind of a chance. This is the same brain fever that used to afflict opponents of the old, all-conquering Yankees. The state of mind became perfectly visible the next afternoon, when the Phillies started off in much better fashion, and actually led by 2–0 after five innings. Jim Lonborg had not permitted any Cincinnati hits at all in this span, but he began the sixth by walking Dave Concepcion—an apparently insignificant lapse that seemed utterly to destroy his concentration and control. His elbow began to drop down and his pitches came up; singles by Pete Rose and Ken Griffey swiftly produced a run, center fielder Garry Maddox threw to a wrong base, and within a bare few minutes Lonborg and the Phillies' lead were gone together, and the Reds won again, this time by 6–2.

It is not suggested here that this Reds Fever is purely psychosomatic or easily resistible. The next—and, this time, fatal—onset of the disease came in the bottom of the ninth inning of the third game, which was played in Cincinnati and watched by me on television. The Reds at this point were behind in the game by 4–6—a deficit and a setting that suddenly caused me to recall a leadoff home run under almost identical circumstances, hit by Johnny Bench against the Pirates in 1972, and *two* catch-up homers, by Pete Rose and Johnny Bench, that ruined Tom Seaver and the Mets in a 1973 playoff game. The same frightful visions undoubtedly came shimmering into the mind of Ron Reed, the Phillies' pitcher, who worked too carefully on the Reds' leadoff hitter, George Foster, ran up a 1–2 count, and came in, unnecessarily, with a fastball, which Foster hit for a homer. Reed repeated the process exactly with the next batter, Bench, with exactly the same inexorable, incredible result. The game was tied, and Reed's jittery, doom-stricken successors then swiftly gave up the single (by Concepcion), walk, sacrifice, intentional walk, and infield chopper (by Griffey) that meant the game and the pennant.

I also tried to take in the first two games of the Royals-Yankees playoffs, in Kansas City, by television, but the medium just about wiped out the message. In the first game, the Yankees left the post swiftly, scoring two runs in the very first inning on a pair of singles and a pair of throwing errors by the Royals' third baseman, George Brett—a winning margin right there, since Catfish Hunter, who started for the visitors, was in impeccable form, giving up five hits (three of them by Brett) and a lone run, for a 4–1 win. In the second game, played on Sunday evening, the Yanks rapped out twelve hits but played egregiously afield, committing five errors, while losing, 7–3; Paul Splittorf, coming on for K.C. in relief in the third inning, was the winning pitcher. These minimal messages would seem well within the capabilities of a major television network, but ABC almost buried them under a mind-bending barrage of statistics, color, bad jokes, personality struggles, distracting intercut interviews with players and other people (this often while the game was actually in progress), useless information, misinformation—and rivers, estuaries, tidal basins, oceans of talk. (I will not bother to complain about the commercials, except to mention a series of repellent house ads touting baseball as an institution or a way of life, and a super-schlock promotion, evidently approved by the Commissioner, in which a man from the Rolaids company was permitted to give an award to somebody as the Relief Pitcher of the Year.) ABC took up baseball for the first time this summer, and, by general critical consensus, had formidable difficulties with the old pastime. The telecasting team that the network dispatched to Kansas City did not, for some reason, include either of its two best baseball reporters—Al Michaels (who was doing the Phillies-Reds games) and Bob Gibson. This three-man crew was captained by Howard Cosell, and included Bob Uecker and a visiting celebrity-expert, Reggie Jackson. Mr. Cosell has been a long-term disparager of baseball, which he considers to be old-fashioned and draggy, but it became clear within the first inning or two of the first game that his handicap was not prejudice but lack of knowledge. In the second inning, John Mayberry, a left-handed Royals slugger, flied out to the left fielder, causing Cosell to state that he had been attempting to hit the ball to left field. Mayberry, in truth, suffered acutely last summer from the fact that he could not, or would not, hit the ball to the opposite field—a widely known weakness that was mostly responsible for his miserable .232 average and mere thirteen homers this year—and it had also been clear on my screen that Hunter had simply jammed him for the out. Reggie Jackson corrected Howard Cosell gently, but Cosell does not take contradiction lightly, and he now evidently set out to prove that he knew more baseball than Reggie Jackson. Through the last few innings, he predicted insistently that Catfish Hunter was tiring, or was about to tire and be driven to cover, when it was plain that the Cat, who had to face only thirty batters over the full nine innings, was breezing. Again Jackson tried to enlighten him: when Catfish Hunter gets knocked out, it usually happens in the *early* innings.

The next day, the third man in the crew (replacing Bob Uecker) was Keith Jackson, a football specialist, whose excited, rapid-fire delivery makes a routine double play sound like a goal-line stand. Three-man broadcasting crews, by the way, probably make sense covering football, where a great many things happen at the same time, but baseball has no such problem, and three hyperglottal observers usually succeed only in shattering the process of waiting that is such a crucial part of the game. People who don't know or don't like baseball make poor announcers, for they are too impatient to sense the special pace of each game, and thus habitually overdramatize. Since they suggest that almost every play we see is memorable, we become distracted and then dulled, so that we are unlikely to remember the actual incidents in a game—sometimes very small ones indeed—on which the outcome truly depended. In the third inning of the second game, the Yankees scored two runs, to take a 3–2 lead, and had Chris Chambliss on first base, with one out. The next batter, Carlos May, hit a bounder to the right side that took a high hop off the artificial carpet and over first baseman Mayberry's head. It went for a single, but Chambliss progressed only as far as second base, thanks to a bit of mime by the Royals' shortstop, Fred Patek, who put out his glove for the imaginary incoming peg with such verisimilitude that Chambliss actually slid into the bag. The fake deprived the Yankees of a run when the next batter flied out; it may even have cost them the game. Yet the telecast buried this pivotal moment in its customary over-reporting, and it was soon forgotten. Network television makes every baseball game sound just about like every other. But this is perhaps an inescapable handicap of an instantaneous and unreflective medium. What I cannot forgive is the networks' implacable habit—and NBC, which handles the World Series, is almost as much at fault here as the ABC people—of dismantling the game of baseball and putting it back together on our screens in a form that they find more manageable. That form, of course, is "entertainment," and thus centers on personalities rather than events. Reggie Jackson is a perceptive young man, and by the middle of the second game from Kansas City it had become plain that he was no longer just describing a ball game; he was engaged in an open duel with his more-celebrated colleague for dominance in the proceedings. He had already come to understand a first principle of television—that while we at home may think we are simply watching a game, what we are in fact attending is Howard Cosell.

•

THIS PLAYOFF now moved east, permitting me to take in the action at Yankee Stadium, unfiltered. In Game No. 3, it will be recalled, the Yankee starter, Dock Ellis, was on the verge of extinction in the first inning, when he gave up three runs, but then got his down-breaking stuff together and shut out the visitors the rest of the way, allowing only three fly balls during his eight-inning stint. The Yankees started back with a two-run homer by Chris Chambliss and then batted around in the sixth against five K.C. pitchers, to win by 5–3. The next afternoon—a startling time of day by now for postseason baseball, which permitted the action to be peculiarly illuminated by a single large overhead light—the visitors treated Catfish Hunter with extreme disrespect and went on to an easy 7–4 win, rapping out an awesome assortment of triples and tweener doubles to the distant reaches of the Stadium lawns.

I had by this time developed a considerable attachment to the spirited visiting nine, in their powder-blue double-knits, who had now twice come back to tie up this interesting series. Their veteran shortstop, Patek—who, at five feet four inches, is the smallest man in the major leagues—was having a splendid time of it afield and at the plate, and the whole lineup, although clearly short on power (their main muscle man, Amos Otis, had been lost with an injury in the first inning of the first game), seemed to be crowded with youngsters who attacked the ball with great confidence and relish. Foremost among these, of course, was George Brett, who had begun to look like the hardest out I had seen since my first glimpse of Al Kaline. (Brett batted .444 for the playoffs.) He is a lefty swinger who stands deep in the box and begins his action with a sweeping forward stride, his bat flattening and his hands held well back. He goes with the pitch, hitting the ball to all fields but most often to center or left—a classic inside-out, high-average swing. I had heard that Brett and a number of his young teammates, including Hal McRae and Tom Poquette, were pupils and fervent admirers of the Royals' batting coach, Charley Lau, who had profoundly altered their physical and mental approach to batting. Lau avoids interviews (and is known, of course, as the Mysterious Dr. Lau), but George Brett is not at all reticent about Lau's influence and teaching powers. "He's made hitting seem like the easiest thing in the world," he told me. "I used to be embarrassed against some pitchers. I was getting jammed a lot and sort of stepping out even before I'd take a swing. No more. I can hardly wait to get up there, even when I'm in a slump. He changed my whole style, and I went from being a Carl Yastrzemski hitter to a Joe Rudi hitter almost overnight." Brett said that he first asked Lau for tutelage about midway through the 1974 season, when he was batting in the neighborhood of .225. Lau told him that he could have the option of being a .330 hitter with about ten home runs per season or a .280 hitter with twenty homers. Brett, who did not take either prediction seriously, chose the former. He finished that season at .282, batted .308 last year, and wound up, as we all know, at .333 this summer.

I also asked Hal McRae what Charley Lau meant to a hitter. "Charley Lau means one hundred grand," he said.

The fifth game, a night affair played before 56,821 frigid, roaring watchers, was a marvel. It began with a double flurry of hits and runs in the first inning—a two-run homer by John Mayberry; a countering triple by Mickey Rivers, followed by two singles and a sac., to tie it. The Yankees relentlessly chewed away at the Kansas City pitching, getting rid of Leonard, Splittorf, and Pattin within four innings, and led after six innings by 6–3, with Ed Figueroa comfortably in charge of things. The top four hitters in the Yankee lineup—

Rivers, White, Munson, and the red-hot Chambliss—had truly outdone themselves in their first four times around: sixteen trips to the plate, good for six runs, ten hits, two walks, two sacrifices, two stolen bases, and a bare two outs. Figueroa gave up a leadoff single to Cowens in the eighth and was taken out, to a screeching ovation ("Ed-*die!* Ed-*die!* Ed-*die!*"). Jim Wohlford singled off Grant Jackson; and George Brett, on the count of 0–1, socked a middling-deep, medium-high fly ball that landed just within the second or third row of the short-right-field seats, for a tying three-run homer. The silence of the Stadium was so sudden and startling that one had the impression that somebody had kicked a plug out of a wall socket. Brett had confirmed himself as a great hitter, for if ever a home run was intentional it was this one. It was the first pitch I had ever seen him try to pull.

The ending was a sudden multiple tableau—almost a series of movie stop-frames—now fixed in the New York sporting memory. Frame 1: Chris Chambliss has just swung at Mark Littell's very first pitch of the ninth inning, a fastball. He has swung from the heels, and the ball is now suspended somewhere out in the darkness above the right-center-field fence. Chambliss stands motionless at the plate, with his feet together and the bat still in his right hand and his head tipped back as he watches the ball—watching not in admiration (as Reggie Jackson has been known to do) but in true astonishment and anxiety. Frame 2: Al Cowens and Hal McRae, the Kansas City center fielder and right fielder, stand together at the base of the wall, waiting and looking straight up in the air, like a pair of bird-watchers anxious to confirm a rare species. Frame 3: McRae leaps, twisting his whole body into a single upward plane, with the left arm extended and the open, straining glove at its apex. Frame 4: McRae descends empty-handed, and falls back against the fence in despair, slumping there like a discarded marionette. A whole season is gone. Frame 5: Now it is Chambliss's turn to leap—a great bound of joy, with both hands raised high in triumph. He begins his ritual tour of the bases, running slowly at first and then (Frame 6, Frame 7) with increasing attention and urgency, as he sees surging, converging waves of out-scattering, frantically leaping spectators pouring onto the field from the left-field and right-field grandstands. These people sprint through descending streamers of toilet paper and torn-up newspaper and other debris, and through the reverberating, doubly and triply reëchoed explosions of shouting. They all meet near second base—Chambliss, the thickening and tumbling crowds, the waves of noise, and the waves of people (multiple frames here, faster and faster, all blurring together)—and now it is plain that he is almost running for his life. He is knocked down between second and third, and springs up again, holding on to his batting helmet and running now like a fullback, twisting and dodging through the appalling scene. It is a new game—one for which we have no name yet, and no rules. Chambliss makes it at last to the dugout, without touching third or home (third base has disappeared), and vanishes under the lip of the dugout, with his uniform shirt half torn away and the look on his face now is not one of joy or fear or relief but just the closed, expressionless, neutral subway look that we all see and all wear when abroad in the enormous and inexplicable city. Later, Chris Chambliss comes back onto the ripped-up, debris-strewn field with two cops, and after a few minutes' search they find home plate and he steps on it.

•

THE WORLD SERIES, as we know, brought us no such games or passions, and can thus be dealt with here in brief summary. The Yankees, undoubtedly flat after their long and late play-off exertions, played languidly in the opener at Riverfront Stadium, losing, 5–1, to Don Gullett before a full house of confident and captivated hometown rooters, who—to judge by a good many smug comments I overheard—were fully as proud of their litter-free, un-Bronxlike playing field as they were of their team's brisk performance. A pattern of these games began to suggest itself in the sixth inning, when the Yanks messed up an attempted sacrifice bunt and also had their whippet, Mickey Rivers, cut down while stealing; the Reds, given about the same chances, broke up an attempted double play, pulled off a steal, and scored a run. Joe Morgan had hit a homer earlier, and Tony Perez wound up with three hits off the Yankee starter, Doyle Alexander. Game No. 2 was the only absorbing or truly close contest of the four—thanks not at all to the Baseball Commissioner or to the National Broadcasting Company, who, having together scheduled the thing for eight-thirty on a Sunday night in the middle of October, were then together forced to pretend that the evening's miserable, bone-chilling weather was a trifling surprise, hardly worth anyone's notice. In the game, Catfish Hunter threw high and wild during most of the second inning (he was having trouble with his footing on the mound), and was lucky to escape with no more damage than three runs. He loaded the bases again in the third but wriggled free, and then, almost startlingly, became very nearly untouchable. No other pitcher in baseball settles into stride with quite this sort of nearly audible click, or, once there, throws such elegant, thoughtful, and flowing patterns—up and out, up and in, down on the hands, out and away, with each part and pitch connected, in psychology and tactics, to its predecessor and its quickly following next variant. The Yankees now caught up, with a run in the fourth and two more in the seventh, and the game stuck there, frozen fast at 3–3. The wretched, blanket-wrapped, huddled masses in the stands flumped their mittened paws together in feeble supplication, pleading now for almost any result that would send them home. Hunter sailed through the first two outs of the ninth, and then threw a slider that Ken Griffey bounced weakly to the middle of the infield. Yankee shortstop Fred Stanley galloped in, taking the ball on the dead run and coming down on his right foot—the wrong foot, that is, for a proper throw. He had to fling the ball to first off-balance and across his body, and threw it instead into the Reds' dugout. Griffey, who is the fastest of all the Cincinnati fliers—he had thirty-eight infield hits this year—had very nearly beaten the play in any case, but the error automatically moved him along to second, from where he scored, after an intentional pass to Morgan, on Tony Perez's first-pitch single. Speed kills.

Now a World Series came back to Yankee Stadium for the first time in twelve years, and even the wrong weather and the wrong time of day (it was another shivery, after-dark affair) and the altered details and colors of the park could not dim for me its evocative visions—the unique, flattened declination and cavelike depths of the sweeping, entirely filled lower stands, and the steep, tilted topmost deck stuffed with spectators to its highest, farthest reaches: a great beach of faces, a surf of sounds. Only the baseball failed us. Again the Reds ran away with the game, notching three quick runs off Dock Ellis in the second inning, on four hits and a pair of stolen bases—all helped no end by some sudden uncertainty in the Yankee infield. Matters stood at 4–1 in the fifth inning—still anybody's game, really—when Mickey Rivers led off with a single, and Roy White walked. Munson, who was having a terrific Series, whacked a bulletlike drive to the right side but almost directly at first baseman Tony Perez, who jumped and gloved the ball, pivoted, and threw instantly to Concepcion, covering second, to double Rivers off the bag. It was a moment when one suddenly sensed how the game of baseball should be played. The other base runner, White, had been only a couple of yards in front of Perez when he caught the liner, and four out of five—or perhaps nineteen out of twenty—first basemen would have made a dive at him, or tried to beat him back to that base. But Perez, without an instant's pause, knew the right play, the deadly play, and made it. Rivers, it must be added, did not. Any low line drive is a red light for a well-trained base runner—a signal for a sudden full stop until the ball has gone through. Mickey was caught in flagrante delicto. The two parts of the play, commission and omission, summed up these two teams like an epigram. The Reds went on to win, 6–2.

The final game, which was played after a rainout, was closer for most of its distance, and was not actually resolved until the second of Johnny Bench's two home runs put the issue beyond reach in the ninth inning. The Yankees, although behind by only 3–2 up to that point, had struggled glumly from the beginning against the impossible burden of the Reds' three-game lead. They scored first, but the visitors' catchup began when Ed Figueroa, the Yankee pitcher, allowed Morgan such an enormous jump off first base that he stole second without drawing a peg. Thurman Munson had four straight singles, but the Yankees stranded nine base runners. Billy Martin, unstrung by despair, was ejected from the game in the ninth. The Reds won, 7–2, and the arctic night and the premises were no longer embarrassed by these leftover summer doings.

•

IT WOULD be an injustice if this one-sided and undramatic World Series should somehow cause us to overlook the breadth and versatility and effulgent skills of the Cincinnati Reds. The first evidence is the simple fact that they have now won the world championship two years running—a feat too difficult for any other National League team since 1921. Another indication of their quality—a double hallmark—is the manner in which they seemed to strip bare their opponents, leaving the Yankees almost without hope or resource (and, incidentally, exposing serious deficiencies in their outfield defense and their right-handed hitting), while they themselves did not even have to call on some of their own best abilities. They did not, for instance, often show us their marvelous and habitually impeccable ways of getting a base runner from first to third or from second to third by having the batter hit the ball to the proper side of the infield—"give himself up," in the parlance. All the Reds, it seems, know how to use the bat both ways—with power, and with punch and intent. This is the very stuff of inside, winning baseball, and it is far more exciting, when it is understood, than any mere slugging. It seems to me that not enough of us have recognized the fact that this is probably the first great team that has been specifically designed to take advantage of AstroTurf, which puts such a premium on team quickness and superior throwing, and that it is thus as much of a revolutionary innovation as the Yankees' first "Murderers' Row" club, in the mid-twenties, which was built around Babe Ruth, the home run, and the jackrabbit ball. The Reds' team speed puts enormous psychological pressure on every part of their opponents' defenses, but on AstroTurf it also forces the opposing shortstop and second baseman to "cheat"—to play much closer to second base, that is, in order to be able to make the force play—which, in turn, opens the field for more base hits. There is almost no way to win against this parlay.

Another tip-off to a truly fine club is that a fan constantly finds himself discovering fresh stars in the lineup. Most of us know all about Pete Rose and Joe Morgan and Tony Perez and Johnny Bench by now. The other four Cincinnati regulars are Dave Concepcion, who is the best defensive shortstop in the National League; Ken Griffey, whose speed and .336 batting have been mentioned here; George Foster, who hit twenty-nine home runs this year and batted .306; and Cesar Geronimo, who has the best center-field arm in the business, and who, hitting in the seventh and eighth positions this year, batted .307. All are between twenty-six and twenty-eight years old, which means that they are just arriving at their peak seasons. For me, the discovery of the Series was Concepcion, who seemed to be forever coming up with the essential play at some vital turn of events. During a Yankee uprising in the fourth inning of the first game, he stopped a wild throw behind second base—stopped it by sticking out his leg—and then made a heartbreaking, inning-ending grab and throw of an apparent hit by Willie Randolph: two runs saved. In the first inning of the last game, he went yards behind second base to seize a shot by Carlos May and throw him out, again snuffing out what looked like a big inning. Concepcion also batted

.357 in the Series—but this, it must be said, was not exactly a feat. The Yankee pitching corps contained the first two men in the Reds' batting order—Rose and Griffey—holding them to .188 and .059, respectively, but was a little less fortunate after that. The next seven Cincinnati regulars batted .333, .313, .357, .429, .533 (Bench, who was voted the best player of the Series), .308, and .357 (Concepcion). Further comment, I somehow sense, is superfluous.

•

THESE FEATS and colors are dimmed by the fact that the championship games and the World Series were played this year—as they will almost surely be played for years to come—in the wrong season and at the wrong time of day, with twisted rules and abnormal playing conditions, and, for the most part, in frightful weather. The players and the customers suffered doubly—from the discomfort and the loss of pleasure of having the chief festival of their sport held in depressing and inappropriate circumstances, and from the unmeasurable but inexorable loss in the quality of the baseball. I heard players in both dugouts cursing the cold. Billy Martin said, "When are we going to stop letting TV tell us when we are going to play? This is asinine, playing night games in October. It's damn near freezing out there." Before the Sunday-night game, in Cincinnati, Bob Howsam, the Reds' president, said, "The football people must be laughing at us"—a reference to the fact that NBC, for the price of seven hundred thousand dollars, bought the right to move the Sunday game to prime evening time and was thus able also to present its pro football games in the afternoon.

All this happened with the enthusiastic approval of the Baseball Commissioner. Responding to heavy criticism in the sporting press, Bowie Kuhn said that baseball had made these scheduling decisions independently of the networks, and then pointed to the game's need for increased revenues and to the much larger television audiences for the World Series produced by night games. But no one had suggested that the Commissioner had been bought off by television interests. That was never necessary, for Mr. Kuhn has shown that he shares the television producers' sense of priorities and state of mind. His prime concern is for audiences and profits, and he has proved willing to go along with almost any alteration of the game that will enhance or protect "the numbers." In addition to Arctic night ball, this has so far resulted in the designated hitter (a barbarism that was first conceived of to stimulate slumping attendance in the American League, and that found its way into the World Series this year), artificial turf (far cheaper for owners to maintain, of course, than real grass), and the extension of the already swollen season to make room for the playoffs (an instant television special that has automatically pushed the World Series ten days closer to winter).

The fans' deepening feeling of cynicism and hopelessness about the plight of baseball comes, I think, from their slow realization that apparently nothing can be done to alter this state of things. The profits of the game have become the preëminent consideration, and no one in the inner councils of the game seems much concerned about the quality of the product —the needs of the players, the claims of lifelong fans, the depth of attachment of the paying customer, in contrast to that of the television watcher, and so forth. The issue of artificial turf is a case in point. Almost without exception, the players detest the chemical carpet, which causes unusual injuries and imposes such wear and tear on their legs that it may prove to shorten outfielders' careers by as much as two years, and which is, in addition, miserably hot to play on in sunny weather. Now some of the fake surfaces are beginning to wear out (the infield at Veterans Stadium, in Philadelphia, for instance, is almost rocklike, because of the decay of the protective cushion beneath the green coverlet), but no owner (except Bill Veeck, a known maverick) has admitted that a mistake was made or has offered to give up the cheaper spread. Any change would go against the numbers, so nothing can be done.

An even darker view of baseball must now be set forth. It is my own pure, horrified guess that if the complaints about the weather and about the playing conditions of the autumn games persist or grow wider, the Commissioner and the owners will present us with a plan that will seem to solve everything: Mr. Kuhn will propose that the site of the World Series be moved permanently to some friendly metropolis in the Sunbelt, perhaps one that has a large, domed enclosure waiting to be filled—New Orleans, say, or Houston—or rotated each year, in the style of the Super Bowl, among two or three such cities. The World Series will thus be instantly transformed into Superweek—the Super Bowl multiplied by seven, the ultimate Sportsfest USA. It will become an obligatory status trip and expense-account holiday for business executives, prime corporate accounts, network people, politicians, and show-business celebrities. It will also be an unbeatable television property—the first all-American sports show truly worthy of a Howard Cosell. A few objections may be expected, of course, including some carping from hometown baseball fans, who will suddenly realize that, with the exception of a wealthy few among them, they have been done out of the chance ever to cheer for their team at a World Series game. But this will seem a trifling consideration when it is understood that, in addition to solving the weather difficulty, the plan will do away with the present expense and annoyance to the clubs involved in printing tickets and preparing concessions and finding hotel space for a World Series that often ends up at the last instant in another city. And, perhaps best of all, the unruly and passionate hooligan fans that make up part of some big-city sports crowds can at last be kept away from the game.

Superweek will be an enormous initial success. It will instantly surpass the Super Bowl, and its immense profits will lead to further promotion of the event and ever-increasing television revenues. And if it should happen (it *will* happen, of course) that at some future point there come two or three World Series in succession that are as one-sided and dull as the one we have just seen, and if the public, as a result, begins to sense that the sport has not measured up to the Event—that the games have been hyped out of all meaning, and that the World Series has become just another inflated and vulgarized TV show, another stop on the "Wide World of Sports"—well, then, the game of baseball can be changed, of course, like anything else on television: changed in some terrific new way that will take care of the numbers.

This nightmare vision will not affect or deter Mr. Kuhn or his employers. Their attitude toward those of us who share such fears is perhaps epitomized by the Commissioner's patronizing gesture during the three icy night games of the Series, which he attended wearing a business suit and no topcoat: You're wrong, folks—it *isn't* cold here. It has not occurred to these men (nor would it matter to them if it did) that we are entirely in earnest, that we are trying to conserve something that seems as intricate and lovely to us as any river valley. A thousand small relationships, patterns, histories, attachments, pleasures, and moments are what we draw from this game, and that is why we truly worry about it, grieve for it now, and are filled with apprehension and despair at the thought of its transformation into another bland and deathlike pause on the evening ribbon of dog food and gunfights and deodorants and crashing cars. Not everyone feels this way, of course, but who among us feels none of this?

•

BUT IT is wrong to leave baseball in such a dark corner for the winter, for the game rewards and surprises us still, and may outlast even its proprietors. (It never has belonged to the "owners," of course.) While I was watching batting practice at Yankee Stadium just before the third game of the World Series, I noticed that the thin, long-faced man standing directly to my right, wearing a tan raincoat, was Lefty Gomez, a great pitching star for the Yankees in the nineteen-thirties. I got up my nerve and introduced myself to him, and we shook hands.

"I saw you pitch your very first game in Yankee Stadium," I told him at once. "I still remember it. I was about nine years old."

Old ballplayers hear this sort of thing every day, of course, but Gomez was gracious about it. "Is that right?" he said. "I remember it, too. It was in May of 1930, against the White Sox. I beat Red Faber, 4–1." He pointed up at the great triple-decked stands and said, "I remember walking out here just before that game and looking around, and there were so many people in the stands that—well, there weren't just more people here than in my home town but in my home *county!*"

We laughed, and then Gomez looked down at the ground and shook his head a little. "Nineteen thirty," he said. "My God, do you realize that's forty-six years ago? I can't believe it."

"Neither can I," I said.

I think we both sensed the same thing. Time had destroyed the once-immeasurable difference between us, between a small boy and a hero. Now we were the same—two gents in winter raincoats watching the young men getting ready to play another game.

That Series game, it turned out, wasn't much. It wasn't nearly as interesting, for instance, as a Mets-Cubs game I went to on a Sunday back in the middle of September, with my wife and my son John Henry. It was the boy's first big-league game—he is six years old—so I had arranged to get good seats at Shea Stadium, right behind home plate. The only trouble was that it came up rain that morning. John Henry kept watch at the windows, however, and about one o'clock in the afternoon he discovered an almost invisible lightening in the clouds, and we decided to give it a try. By the time we arrived at Shea, it was raining again, but I parked the car, and we ran through the downpour and went into the park. There was a surprising crowd there, milling about in the dank passageways under the stands, and we all looked at each other in a self-congratulatory way. The Mets against the Cubs, in the *rain?* We were crazy, but we were fans, all right. John Henry announced that the three of us should sit down in our seats and get ready for the game to start, and we did. We found our places—an island of three people in the surrounding sea of slatted yellow seats—and huddled there cheerfully enough in our foul-weather gear, unsuccessfully trying to share a single umbrella. I watched my son as he inspected the lights and the scoreboard and the empty stands around and above us and the soaking tarpaulins and—now and then, glimpsed in the dugout—a player.

"Where's home plate?" he asked.

"Out there someplace," I said, gesturing.

Then, unexpectedly and after several false alarms, it stopped raining. The grounds crew came out and rolled up the tarps and put down the white bases, and the waiting crowds filled up a few hundred of the wet seats. The pitchers warmed, and the umps and players came out on the field, and we stood for the anthem, and sat down and clapped. Rick Monday came up to lead it off for the Cubs, and Jerry Koosman struck him out, swinging, and we yelled—and then it *really* began to rain.

We stuck it out there for another forty minutes or so, observing the unrolling of tarps and studying rain patterns and watching the out-of-town scores beginning to go up on the scoreboard. John Henry kept occupied somehow (1 Coke, ⅓ box popcorn, 1 ice cream, 1 Mets cap), and I kept looking up at the sky, hoping against hope. But at last we said the hell with it and went home, and by the time we got back to our part of the city the rain had stopped, of course, and the streets were almost dry. When we got home, I flipped on the TV set, and, sure enough, there were the Mets and the Cubs.

"I'm sorry, John Henry," I said. "I didn't think they were going to play today."

"Oh, that's all right," he said at once. "I liked it there. That was cool."

So it was all right, after all, and maybe one batter is plenty to see, the first time. It was a beginning.